COMPLETE
ITALIAN GRAMMAR
REVIEW

Marcel Danesi, Ph.D.

University of Toronto

BARRON'S

All inquiries should be addressed to:
Barron's Educational Series, Inc.
250 Wireless Boulevard
Hauppauge, NY 11788
www.barronseduc.com

Library of Congress Catalog Card Number 2005058868

ISBN-13: 978-0-7641-3462-3
ISBN-10: 0-7641-3462-0

Library of Congress Cataloging-in-Publication Data
Danesi, Marcel, 1946–
    Complete Italian grammar review / by Marcel Danesi.
        p. cm.
    ISBN 0-7641-3462-0 (alk. paper)
    1. Italian language—Textbooks for foreign speakers—English.
    2. Italian language—Grammar. I. Title.

PC1129.E5D356 2006
458.2′421—dc22   2005058868

Printed in the United States of America
9 8 7 6 5

Contents

Introduction

Studying the grammar of a foreign language is often perceived as "torture" by many. Alas, there is no way to avoid grammar! To become adept in any language one must know how its component parts work together. Imagine a pianist who cannot name notes by their technical names. You would hardly consider such a person to be a proficient pianist. Grammatical terms, like technical terms in music, put you in a better position to think about the Italian language in a coherent and precise way. They allow you, in other words, to become truly proficient in the language. This handbook is intended to take the torture of studying grammar away, so to speak, by providing a user-friendly practice and review manual. As an Italian teacher, I have come to realize that it is important to flesh out those features that cause the greatest degree of difficulty to a large number of students and identify them precisely and in clear terms. This book is the result of many years of preparing materials designed to do exactly that. It is intended for "grammar phobics" of any age, defined as students who are put off by grammatical explanations that take too much background knowledge for granted.

Needless to say, there are many good review grammars of Italian on the market. But they are rarely written in a "conversational style," as this one has been conceived. For this reason, it can be used as a tool for self-study, especially since most of the exercises are written to produce precise answers (true and false, multiple choice, fill-in-the-blanks, etc.). In this way, readers can check their answers right away at the back. However, there are also "open-ended" exercises that make this book usable in many classroom situations. These two types of exercises are identified as such in each chapter.

Complete Italian Grammar Review is one of a series of handy grammar review guides published by Barron's Educational Series. It is titled "complete" because it presents as complete a grammatical overview of Italian as possible, extending far beyond the norm followed by most review manuals. An overview tool is an important one in the process of learning another language because it gives you the opportunity to reflect upon what you know, to reinforce your skills, to fill in gaps, to clarify difficult points—in sum, to build a firm knowledge of the formal aspects of a language. But a handbook cannot do it all for you. It is not an encyclopedic volume of all there is to know about the Italian language. Like the other handbooks in the series, it will give you the most important facts, thus keeping the practice and review of the language within manageable proportions.

There are twenty chapters covering everything from the structure of simple sentences to the writing of e-mails. Each chapter is designed to cover a topic of grammar as completely as possible. Therefore, some chapters will be longer than others. This is due to the varying number of features that are included under the rubric of a specific grammatical topic. For example, the chapter on nouns is longer than the one on articles and partitives. Nevertheless, you will never find a chapter to be of an unwieldy length.

The chapters are organized into four main parts:

- Part I contains two chapters dealing with the basics of Italian pronunciation, spelling, and sentence structure.
- Part II contains five chapters covering all the verb tenses, moods, and forms of Italian, from the indicative tenses to all the subjunctive forms.
- Part III contains five chapters covering the other parts of speech, from nouns to prepositions and adverbs.
- Part IV contains eight chapters dealing with special topics, ranging from the pesky verb **piacere** (to like) to basic conversation and writing techniques.

At the end of each part there is a culture capsule, written in Italian with a glossary, which is designed to give information on a major component of Italian culture or civilization—information of which no intermediate or advanced learner of Italian should be unaware. As its name implies it is a "capsule"—no more, no less. The reader should consider it to be useful reading material.

This handbook can also be used as a textbook in intermediate courses of Italian, since it contains the same kinds of information and exercises that are normally found in such courses. The difference is that it takes nothing for granted. It contains many helpful charts and sidebars throughout to clarify, supplement, or complement a topic. The sidebars also provide tips on how to use a particular part of speech, notes on aspects of vocabulary or usage that are relevant to the chapter, and the like. This feature will allow you to stay within the confines of this single book. You will not need to resort to other materials. As mentioned, nothing has been taken for granted!

At the back of the book, you will find a list of the most frequently used words in the Italian language (nearly 800 of them), verb charts, and the answers to all the exercises.

PART I:
Reviewing and Practicing the Basics

1

Italian Sounds and Spelling

Quanto Sai Già? — How Much Do You Know Already?

Choose the correct spelling.

1. *who*
   a. chi
   b. qui

2. *why*
   a. perché
   b. perqué

3. *people*
   a. jente
   b. gente

4. *bye*
   a. chao
   b. ciao

5. *July*
   a. luglio
   b. lulio

6. *beautiful*
   a. bello
   b. belo

7. *when*
   a. quando
   b. cuando

8. *June*
   a. giunio
   b. giugno

9. *yes*
   a. sì
   b. si

Vowels
Le vocali

There are two basic kinds of sound in any language: *vowels* and *consonants*. The letters that represent the Italian vowels are **a**, **e**, **i**, **o**, **u**. Generally, Italian vowels are pronounced in a pure fashion: that is to say, there is no "gliding" of the vowels as in English *sale*, *send*, *sift*, *soft*, *sure*, which are pronounced, more or less, as "sayl" "sehynd," and so on.

Impara le vocali!
Vowels are produced by expelling the air through the mouth without blockage. Vowels are the main components of syllables.

Meet *il professor Pasqualucci, who will become your mentor throughout this book. Every time he appears, he will emphasize what it is that you must learn. Heed his advice!*

ALPHABET LETTERS	PRONUNCIATION	EXAMPLES
a	Similar to the **a** sound in *father*, or to the exclamation *ah*!	casa / *house* amica / *friend*
e	Similar to the **e** sound in *bet*, or to the exclamation *eh*!	bene / *well* esame / *exam*
i	Similar to the **i** sound in *machine*, or to the exclamation *eeh*!	vini / *wines* indirizzi / *addresses*
o	Similar to the **o** sound in *sorry*, or to the exclamation *oh*!	otto / *eight* oro / *gold*
u	Similar to the **oo** sound in *boot*, or to the exclamation *ooh*!	uva / *grapes* gusto / *taste*

Speakers in different regions of Italy might tend to pronounce **e** and **o** slightly differently. In some regions, they are pronounced with the mouth relatively more open; in others, they are pronounced with the mouth relatively more closed. In many areas of Italy today, however, both pronunciations are used.

To get an idea of what this means, consider how the **a** in *tomato* is pronounced in North America. In some areas, it is pronounced like the **a** in *father*; in other areas, it is pronounced like the **a** in *pay*. However, whether it is pronounced one way or the other, the word is still understood to be *tomato*. This is exactly what happens in the case of Italian **e** and **o** when they are pronounced as open or closed.

The letter **i** can also stand for semivowel sounds similar to those represented by the *y* in *yes* and *say*. The letter **u** can also stand for semivowel sounds similar to those represented by the *w* in *way* and *how*.

i = **y** (as in **yes**), **u** = **w** (as in **way**)	**i** = **y** (as in **say**), **u** = **w** (as in **how**)
ieri / *yesterday*	mai / *ever, never*
piatto / *plate*	poi / *then*
uomo / *man*	causa / *cause*
buono / *good*	laurea / *degree (university)*

This pronunciation feature occurs when the **i** or the **u** is next to another vowel and both vowels are pronounced rapidly together. The syllable is called a *diphthong*. If there is a slight pause between the two vowels, then **i** and **u** are pronounced in the normal way, as in the words **zio** /uncle and **suo** / his, her.

QUICK
PRACTICE 1

*Indicate if the letter stands for the vowel sounds **i** and **u**, or the semivowel sounds **y** and **w**. Pronounce each word as you go along.*

Modello:	io	pieno
	io = i	**pieno = y**

1. zia ɔ i
2. tua y
3. chiamare i
4. quando w
5. mai i

6. pausa w
7. dire i
8. diede y
9. sugo u
10. suonare w

Single Consonants
Le consonanti

The remaining sounds in a language are called consonants. With minor adjustments in pronunciation with respect to corresponding English consonants, the consonants represented by the letters **b, d, f, l, m, n, p, q, r, t, v** always represent the same sounds in Italian. Differences between English and Italian are discussed in the chart below. These might seem to be matters of detail, but they are important; otherwise you will speak Italian with a perceivable accent.

b, d, f, l, m, n, p, q, r, t, v =
always make the same sound

ALPHABET LETTERS	PRONUNCIATION	EXAMPLES
b	Identical to the b sound in *boy*.	bello / *beautiful* bravo / *good*
d	Like the d sound in *day*, but with the tongue touching the upper teeth. This is true even when followed by r; in English, the tongue is raised a bit more, as in *drop*.	dopo / *after* ladro / *thief*
f	Identical to the f sound in *fun*.	forte / *strong* frutta / *fruit*
l	Identical to the l sound in *love*. In English, the back of the tongue is raised when the l is at the end of a syllable or of a word, as in *bill*. This feature is not found in Italian pronunciation.	latte / *milk* alto / *tall*
m	Identical to the m sound in *more*.	matita / *pencil* mondo / *world*
n	Identical to the n sound in *nose*.	naso / *nose* nono / *ninth*
p	Identical to the p sound in *price*.	porta / *door* prezzo / *price*
q	Identical to the q sound in *quick*. It is always followed by u.	quanto / *how much* quinto / *fifth*
r	Similar to the rolled r sound in some Scottish dialects. It is pronounced by flapping the tongue against the upper gums.	rosso / *red* raro / *rare*
t	Pronounced like the t sound in *fat*, but with the tongue against the upper teeth. This is true even when followed by r; in English, the tongue is raised a bit more, as in *train*.	tardi / *late* treno / *train*
v	Identical to the v sound in *vine*.	vino / *wine* vero / *true*

The remaining consonant sounds in Italian are not that much different from English ones. However, various letters or combination of letters are used to represent them, and this can be a source of confusion.

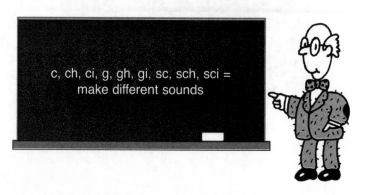

c, ch, ci, g, gh, gi, sc, sch, sci = make different sounds

Alphabet Letters	Pronunciation	Examples
c	Similar to the English **k** sound in *kit* and *cat*. Used in front of **a**, **o**, **u**, and any consonant.	**cane** / *dog* **come** / *how* **cuore** / *heart* **classe** / *class* **cravatta** / *tie*
ch	Represents the same **k** sound. Used in front of **e** and **i**.	**che** / *what* **chi** / *who* **chiesa** / *church*
c	Similar to the English **ch** sound in *church*. Used in front of **e** and **i**.	**cena** / *dinner* **cinema** / *movies*
ci	Represents the same **ch** sound in front of **a**, **o**, **u**.	**ciao** / *hi, bye* **cioccolata** / *chocolate*
g	Similar to the English **g** sound in *good*. Used in front of **a**, **o**, **u**, and any consonant.	**gatto** / *cat* **gola** / *throat* **guanto** / *glove* **gloria** / *glory* **grande** / *big, large*
gh	Represents the same **g** sound. Used in front of **e** and **i**.	**spaghetti** / *spaghetti* **ghiaccio** / *ice*
g	Similar to the English **j** sound in *just*. Used in front of **e** and **i**.	**gente** / *people* **giro** / *turn, tour*
gi	Represents the same **j** sound. Used in front of **a**, **o**, **u**.	**giacca** / *jacket* **giorno** / *day* **giugno** / *June*
sc	Represents the sound sequence **sk** in front of **a**, **o**, **u**, or any consonant.	**scala** / *staircase* **scopa** / *broom* **scuola** / *school* **scrivere** / *to write*
sch	Represents the same **sk** sequence in front of **e** and **i**.	**scherzo** / *prank* **schifo** / *disgust*
sc	Represents the **sh** sound in front of **e** and **i**.	**scena** / *scene* **sciocco** / *unsalted*
sci	Represents the same **sh** sound in front of **a**, **o**, **u**.	**sciopero** / *labor strike* **sciupare** / *to waste*

The sound represented by **gli** is similar to the *lli* in *million*; and the sound represented by **gn** is similar to the *ny* of *canyon*:

figlio / *son*
luglio / *July*
sogno / *dream*
giugno / *June*

The letter **s** is similar to either the "voiceless" *s* sound in *sip* or the "voiced" *z* sound in *zip*. The voiced sound is used before **b, d, g, l, m, n, r, v** and between vowels; otherwise, the voiceless one is used.

VOICELESS S-SOUND	VOICED Z-SOUND	VOICED Z-SOUND (BETWEEN VOWELS)
sapone / *soap*	sbaglio / *mistake*	casa / *house*
sete / *thirst*	svegliarsi / *to wake up*	peso / *weight*
specchio / *mirror*	slittare / *to slide*	rosa / *rose*
studente / *student*	smettere / *to stop*	cosa / *thing*

The letter **z** is, instead, similar to the *ts* sound in *cats* or the *ds* sound in *lads*:

zio / *uncle*
zero / *zero*
zuppa / *thick soup*
zaino / *knapsack, backpack*

The letter **h** does not represent any sound. It is analogous to the silent *h* of *hour*:

ho (pronounced "oh!") / *I have*

QUICK PRACTICE 2

Each of the following words is misspelled. Correct each one, pronouncing each word as you go along.

1. zmettere   *smettere*
2. coza   *cosa*
3. suppa   *zuppa*
4. sonio   *sogno*
5. filio   *figlio*
6. schopero   *sciopero*
7. skerzo   *scherzo*
8. schuola   *scuola*
9. jacca   *giacca*
10. cuanto   *quanto*

Double Consonants
Le consonanti doppie

Any single consonant can have a corresponding double articulation. The pronunciation of double consonants lasts twice as long as that of the corresponding single consonant and is slightly reinforced:

SINGLE CONSONANTS	DOUBLE CONSONANTS
fato / *fate*	fatto / *fact*
caro / *dear*	carro / *cart*
pala / *shovel*	palla / *ball*
sono / *I am*	sonno / *sleep*
casa / *house*	cassa / *case, crate*
zio / *uncle*	pizza / *pizza*
via / *road*	ovvio / *obvious*
oca / *goose*	occhio / *eye*
forte / *strong*	baffi / *mustache*

The sounds represented by **gli** and **gn** are already double in articulation and, thus, no doubling of the letters is required: **figlio, giugno**.

*Q*UICK
*P*RACTICE **3**

Indicate the meaning of each word. These are fairly simple words. However, if you have forgotten what they mean, you might have to use a dictionary. Pronounce each word as you go along.

1. fato *fate* vs. fatto *fact*
2. tipo *kind* vs. troppo *too much*
3. arte *gift* vs. arrivare *arrive*
4. vino *wine* vs. venne *they went*
5. filo *thread* vs. figlio *son*
6. poco *little* vs. pacco *package*
7. cosa *thing* vs. chissà *maybe*

Stress
L'accento

Knowing where to put the stress, or main accent, on an Italian word is not always easy, but you can always look up a word you are unsure of in a dictionary that indicates stress. Here are some general guidelines.

In most words, the stress falls on the next-to-last syllable. You can identify most syllables easily because they contain a vowel:

> amico / *friend* = **amíco**
> italiano / *Italian* = **italiáno**
> orecchio / *ear* = **orécchio**
> mattina / *morning* = **mattína**

Assume, in general, that the accent falls on the second-to-last syllable. Statistically speaking, this is the best strategy, since most Italian words are accented in this way. But, to be absolutely sure, always check a good dictionary.

Some words show an accent mark on the final vowel. This is, of course, where the stress occurs:

> città / *city*
> gioventù / *youth*
> perché (or perchè) / *why, because*
> benché (or benchè) / *although*
> virtù / *virtue*
> sé / *oneself*

ATTENZIONE!
The accent mark in Italian can always be made to slant to the left (città). However, in words ending in –ché, and in a few other cases, it normally slants to the right (perché).

QUICK PRACTICE 4

A word in each sentence is missing an accent. Correct the words accordingly.

1. Maria, perche dici questo?
2. Dov'e il tuo amico?
3. Ci hai messo lo zucchero nel caffe?
4. Lui abita nel centro della città.
5. A quale universita studi?
6. Lui fa sempre tutto da se.
7. Claudia non c'e.

The Alphabet and Spelling Conventions
L'alfabeto e l'ortografia

The Italian alphabet does not have the letters **j, k, w, x, y**, unless they occur in words that Italian has borrowed from other languages, primarily English. The Italian alphabet contains the following characters (the foreign characters are noted with (*)).

ALPHABET LETTERS	NAME	EXAMPLE	MEANING
a, A	a	amico	*friend*
b, B	bi	bene	*well*
c, C	ci	casa ciao che cena	*house* *hi/bye* *what* *dinner*
d, D	di	dopo	*after*
e, E	e	età	*age*
f, F	effe	figlia	*daughter*
g, G	gi	gatto gelo ghetto giorno	*cat* *frost* *ghetto* *day*
h, H	acca (always silent)	ho	*I have*
i, I	i	italiano	*Italian*
j, J (*)	i lunga	jazz	*jazz*
k, K (*)	cappa	karatè	*karate*
l, L	elle	lira	*lira*
m, M	emme	mano	*hand*
n, N	enne	nonno	*grandfather*
o, O	o	ora	*now*
p, P	pi	pane	*bread*
q, Q	cu	quando	*when*
r, R	erre	rosso	*red*
s, S	esse	sempre	*always*
t, T	ti	tanto	*a lot*
u, U	u	uva	*grapes*
v, V	vu/vi	vero	*true*
w, W (*)	doppia vu	weekend	*weekend*
x, X (*)	ics	xenofobia	*xenophobia*
y, Y (*)	ipsilon, i greca	yogurt	*yogurt*
z, Z	zeta	zucchero	*sugar*

Generally speaking, Italian orthography is highly phonetic: that is, each one of its letters stands generally for one sound. There are, however, some exceptions to this rule as you have already seen in this chapter.

Italian also uses the same punctuation marks as English (period, comma, semicolon, interrogative mark, exclamation point, etc.). And, as in English, capital letters are used at the beginning of sentences and to write proper nouns (**Maria**, **Italia**, etc.). However, there are a few different conventions worth noting.

- The pronoun **io** (*I*) is not capitalized (unless it is the first word of a sentence):

    Vengo anche io. / *I'm coming too.*

- Titles are not usually capitalized.

    il professor (or **Professor**) **Verdi** / *Professor Verdi*
    la dottoressa (or **Dottoressa**) **Martini** / *Dr. Martini*

- Adjectives and nouns referring to languages and nationality are not capitalized.

    Lui è italiano. / *He is Italian.*
    La lingua spagnola è interessante. / *The Spanish language is interesting.*

- Names of the seasons, months of the year, and days of the week are not capitalized.

    mercoledì / *Tuesday*
    maggio / *May*

- The pronoun **Lei** / *you (polite, singular)* is generally capitalized, in order to distinguish it from **lei** / *she.*

QUICK PRACTICE 5

There are spelling errors in each sentence. Correct them accordingly.

1. vedrò la mia famiglia a Maggio.
2. anch'Io studio l'Italiano.
3. ti piace il giazz?
4. coma si chiama, lei?
5. anche Tu pratichi il caratè?

PUTTING IT ALL TOGETHER

A. *Fill in the chart with the missing letters representing sounds as indicated. This is also a chance to review vocabulary you may have forgotten.*

MISSING VOWELS	MISSING SEMIVOWELS	MISSING SINGLE CONSONANTS	MISSING DOUBLE CONSONANTS
pane / bread	buono / good	cibo / food	tutto / everything
zia / aunt	cuore / heart	bacio / kiss	anno / year
bene / well	pieno / full	lasciare / to leave	freddo / cold
come / how	piano / slow	rosa / rose	formaggio / cheese
luna / moon	questo / this	vero / true	oggi / today
zuppa / thick soup	guerra / war	mano / hand	prezzo / price
molto / much	nuovo / new	madre / mother	nonno / grandfather
cane / dog	piatto / plate	dove / where	ghiaccio / ice
gente / people	dieci / ten	caldo / hot	occhio / eye
tipo / type	mai / never	forte / strong	palla / ball

B. *The following sentences have errors in them. Rewrite each sentence with the correct spelling of all the words.*

1. Domani è il tre Maggio, non e vero? *Domani e il tre maggio. Non e vero*
2. Anch'Io voglio parlare Italiano molto bene. *anch'io voglio parlar italiano molto bene*
3. Si, e vero. C'e solo un teatro in quella città.
4. Tuti gli studenti sono Americani.
5. Come si chiama cuella ragazza? E Italiana, vero?

C. *There are 15 words in the following word search puzzle. Each word starts with a letter or group of letters standing for the sounds "k" (as in "kiss"), "ch" (as in "church"), "j" (as in "just"), or "g" (as in "gift"). The words can be read from left to right or from the top down.*

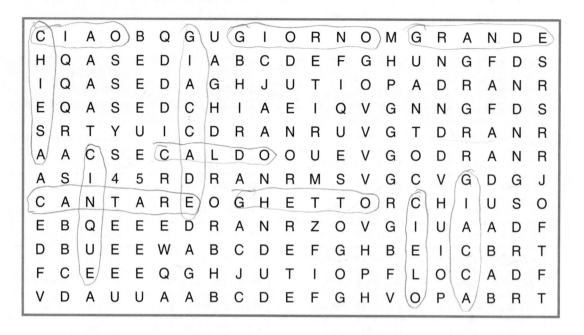

D. *Can you change each word into another one by changing just one sound?*

Modello: piano
            pieno

1. raro
2. pacco   *Rocco*
3. velo   *nero*
4. tanto   *tutto*
5. uomo

2

The Italian Sentence

Quanto Sai Già? — How Much Do You Know Already?

Each sentence is incorrect in some way. Can you correct each one?

1. La mela ha mangiato dal ragazzo.
2. Guardi perché sempre la televisione?
3. Marco aspetta per Maria ogni giorno.
4. Ieri sera ho telefonato la mia amica.
5. Sì, non mi piace affatto!
6. La ragazza chi sta leggendo il giornale è sua sorella.
7. Italiani sono simpatici.
8. Quanto costa quel cellulare?
9. Maria è già arrivato.

The Italian Sentence
La frase italiana

A *sentence* is an organized sequence of words that make up a statement, a question, etc. In writing, a sentence is easily identified because it starts with a capitalized word and ends with either a period, a question mark, or an exclamation mark:

Lui è italiano. / *He is Italian.*	→	affirmative sentence
Chi è quell'uomo? / *Who is that man?*	→	interrogative sentence
Vengo anch'io! / *I'm coming too!*	→	emphatic sentence

Sentences have two basic parts: a *subject* (**il soggetto**) and a *predicate* (**il predicato**). A subject is "who" or "what" the sentence is about. It is often the first element in a simple sentence:

Maria parla italiano. / *Mary speaks Italian.*
Lei è italiana. / *She is Italian.*

But be careful! The subject is not necessarily always the first word:

Sì, anche Maria parla italiano. / *Yes, Mary also speaks Italian.*
No, forse Lei non è italiana. / *No, maybe she is not Italian.*

A *predicate* is the remaining part of the sentence. It provides information about the subject. Its main part is the *verb* (**il verbo**), which represents the action or state either perpetrated by, or connected with, the subject. In many simple sentences, you will find it after the subject.

Alessandro parla italiano. / *Alexander speaks Italian.*
Lui è italiano. / *He is Italian.*

A sentence can have more than one subject or predicate, known as the *main clause*. The added parts are called *subordinate clauses*:

Maria	dice che	la sua amica	è italiana.
Mary	*says that*	*her friend*	*is Italian.*
↑	↑	↑	↑
main subject	main predicate	subordinate subject	subordinate predicate

A subject must contain a noun, substantive (anything that can stand for a noun), noun phrase, or pronoun. There is no equivalent to the English pronoun subject *it* (plural *they*) in ordinary Italian. In this case the subject slot is left empty.

È mio. / *It is mine.*
Sono miei. / *They are mine.*
Costa molto. / *It costs a lot.*
Costano molto. / *They cost a lot.*

In very formal style, the pronoun **esso** can be used. It agrees with the gender of its referent:

Esso è mio. / *It is mine.*   →   esso = il libro
Essi sono miei. / *They are mine.*   →   essi = i libri
Essa costa molto. / *It costs a lot.*   →   essa = la macchina
Esse costano molto. / *They cost a lot.* →   esse = le macchine

The equivalent of *there is/here is* is **c'è**; the equivalent of *there are/here are* is **ci sono**:

C'è Maria? / *Is Maria there?*
Ci sono i suoi amici? / *Are her friends here?*
C'è ancora tanto tempo. / *There is still a lot of time (left).*
Quanti giocatori ci sono in quella squadra? / *How many players are there on that team?*

Note that these are really present indicative forms of the verb **esserci**, which can, of course, be used in any tense and mood:

Ci sarà Maria alla festa? / *Will Mary be at the party?*
C'era molta gente allo stadio. / *There were a lot of people at the stadium.*

The form **ecco** is used instead when pointing out someone or something:

Ecco Maria! / *Here's Maria!*
Ecco i miei amici! / *There are my friends!*

Ecco un sommario!

IT IS	THEY ARE	HERE/THERE IS/ARE ...	HERE/THERE IS!
È nuovo. / *It is new.*	Sono nuovi. / *They are new.*	C'è Maria? / *Is Mary here?*	Ecco Maria! / *There's Mary (pointing her out)!*
È semplice. / *It is simple.*	Sono semplici. / *They are simple.*	Qui ci sono tanti italiani. / *There are many Italians here.*	Ecco 20 euro! / *Here are 20 euros (giving them to someone)!*
È un cellulare. / *It's a cell phone.*	Sono dei cellulari. / *They are cell phones.*	Che problema c'è? / *What problem is there?*	Ecco tutto! / *Here's everything!*

Match the parts in the two columns to make up sentences.

1. Come …	a. vengono alla festa.
2. Forse lui …	b. il mio libro; è il suo.
3. Sì, anche i miei amici …	c. si chiama tua sorella?
4. Mio fratello dice …	d. molto tempo.
5. Non è …	e. le amiche di Paola alla festa.
6. C'è ancora …	f. nuovi programmi televisivi.
7. Essi sono …	g. mia sorella!
8. C'erano anche …	h. che ci sono molti italiani nella nostra città.
9. Ecco …	i. è il professore d'italiano.

Affirmative and Negative Sentences
La frase dichiarativa e la frase negativa

Sentences have specific functions. They allow you to make statements, ask questions, express moods, and so on.

An *affirmative* sentence allows you to state or affirm something in a straightforward way.

> **Giovanni è italiano.** / *John is Italian.*
> **Quella bambina suona il violino.** / *That girl plays the violin.*
> **Tutti i nostri parenti vivono in Italia.** / *All our relatives live in Italy.*

The predicate of affirmative sentences may or may not have an object. An *object* (**l'oggetto/il complemento**) is the noun, substantive, or noun phrase that receives the action. It normally follows a verb. A pronoun can also function as an object.

There are two types of objects: *direct* (**diretto**) and *indirect* (**di termine/indiretto**). These can be identified very easily as follows:

- A noun, substantive, or noun phrase, that directly follows the verb is a direct object:

  > **Quella bambina suona il violino.** / *That girl is playing the violin.*

- A noun, substantive, or noun phrase that follows the verb but is introduced by the preposition **a** / *to, at* is an indirect object:

  > **Il professore telefona a tutti i suoi studenti.** / *The professor phones all his students.*

Whether the object of a sentence is direct or indirect depends on the verb. Some verbs must be followed only by one type of object or the other. Fortunately, most verbs in Italian match their English equivalents when it comes to whether or not a direct or indirect object should follow:

Lui ha mangiato la pizza. / *He ate the pizza.*
Lui è andato al negozio. / *He went to the store.*

However, there are differences! Here are the most important ones:

Impara queste differenze!

Verbs Requiring a Direct Object	Verbs Requiring an Indirect Object
ascoltare / *to listen (to)* **Mia madre ascolta la radio ogni sera.** / *My mother listens to the radio every evening.*	chiedere / domandare (a) / *to ask (someone)* **Gino chiede al professore di venire.** / *Gino asks the professor to come.*
aspettare / *to wait (for)* **Maria aspetta l'autobus.** / *Mary is waiting for the bus.*	telefonare (a) / *to phone* **Gina sta telefonando a sua madre.** / *Gina is phoning her mother.*
cercare / *to search, look (for)* **Tina cerca la sua borsa.** / *Tina is looking for her purse.*	rispondere (a) / *to answer* **La studentessa risponde alla domanda.** / *The student answers the question.*

Some verbs can take both types of objects:

Maria ha dato i soldi alla sua amica. / *Mary gave the money to her friend.*

Needless to say, an object is not always needed to make a complete sentence.

Il bambino dorme. / *The child is sleeping.*
Loro partono domani. / *They are leaving tomorrow.*

The opposite of an affirmative sentence is a negative sentence (**la frase negativa**). To make any sentence negative in Italian, just put **non** before the predicate:

TIPS
- sì / *yes*
- no / *no*
- non / *not*

FRASE DICHIARATIVA (AFFERMATIVA)	FRASE NEGATIVA
Maria aspetta l'autobus. / *Mary is waiting for the bus.*	Maria non aspetta l'autobus. / *Mary is not waiting for the bus.*
Il bambino dorme. / *The child is sleeping.*	Il bambino non dorme. / *The child is not sleeping.*
Maria mi ha dato il suo indirizzo. / *Maria gave me her address.*	Maria non mi ha dato il suo indirizzo. / *Maria did not give me her address.*

QUICK PRACTICE 2

Each sentence contains an error. Correct it.

1. Quel ragazzo suona al violoncello.
2. Io telefonò mio fratello ogni sera.
3. Maria è andata casa presto ieri.
4. Lui chiama tutti i suoi amici ogni giorno.
5. Claudia sta aspettando per suo fidanzato.
6. Perché non hai chiesto Alessandro di venire alla festa?
7. Chi ha risposto quella domanda?
8. Lui non ascolta mai alla professoressa d'italiano.
9. Nora sta cercando per le sue chiavi (*keys*).
10. Sì, Maria non mangia la pizza.

Interrogative and Emphatic Sentences
La frase interrogativa e la frase enfatica

An interrogative sentence (**la frase interrogativa**) is a type of sentence that allows you to ask a question. In writing, it always has a question mark at the end.

A common type of interrogative sentence is one that is designed to elicit a *yes/no* response. The two most common methods of turning an affirmative sentence into an interrogative one of this type are:

- Simply put a question mark at the end. In speaking, raise your voice slightly at the end of the sentence, as in English.

FRASE DICHIARATIVA (AFFERMATIVA)	FRASE INTERROGATIVA	RISPOSTA
Anna cerca il suo gatto. / *Anna is looking for her cat.*	Anna cerca il suo gatto? / *Is Anna looking for her cat?*	Sì, Anna lo sta cercando. / *Yes, Anna is looking for it.* No, Anna non lo sta cercando. / *No, Anna is not looking for it.*
Il bambino non dorme. / *The child is not sleeping.*	Il bambino dorme? / *Isn't the child sleeping?*	Sì, il bambino dorme. / *Yes, the child is sleeping.* No, il bambino non dorme. / *No, the child isn't sleeping.*

- Put the subject at the end of the sentence, adding a question mark:

FRASE DICHIARATIVA (AFFERMATIVA)	FRASE INTERROGATIVA
Anna cerca il suo gatto. / *Anna is looking for her cat.*	Cerca il suo gatto, Anna? / *Is Anna looking for her cat?*
Il bambino dorme. / *The child is sleeping.*	Dorme, il bambino ? / *Is the child sleeping?*

A second main type of interrogative sentence is the one that allows you to seek specific information. It allows you to ask "what?" "when?" "where?" etc. This is formed simply by putting a question word (**Quale? Perché?** etc.) in front of the subject. The relevant question words will be taken up in Chapter 10:

DOMANDA	RISPOSTA
Quale macchina preferisci? / *Which car do you prefer?*	Preferisco quella. / *I prefer that one.*
Come va? / *How's it going?*	Molto bene, grazie. / *Very well, thank you.*

Some questions allow you to seek approval, consent, agreement, etc. These are known as *tag questions* because they are formed by "tagging on" the expressions **no? non è vero?** or **vero?** at the end:

Giovanni è italiano, no? / *John is Italian, isn't he?*
Tua madre guida bene, vero? / *Your mother drives well, doesn't she?*
Lei parla molto bene, non è vero? / *She speaks very well, doesn't she?*

To put emphasis on the subject of a sentence, all you have to do is put the subject at the end. In writing add an exclamation mark to show the emphasis.

Frase normale	Frase enfatica
Io ho pagato il conto. / *I paid the bill.*	Ho pagato il conto io! / *I paid the bill!*
Il dottore l'ha detto. / *The doctor said it.*	L'ha detto il dottore! / *The doctor said it!*

QUICK PRACTICE 3

Form a question for each of the following responses.

Modello: Sì, lui è italiano.
     È italiano? / È italiano, lui?

     Sto bene, grazie.
     Come stai?

1. Sì, Alessandro cerca il suo cane. *È Alessandro cerca il suo cane?*
2. No, Sara non ha ancora un gatto. *Sara ha ancora un gatto?*
3. Voglio mangiare quella pizza, grazie.
4. Non c'è male.
5. No, il conto l'ho pagato io, non lui!

Other Types of Sentences
Altri tipi di frase

> **Clauses**
> A clause is a group of related words that contains a subject and a predicate and is part of a sentence.

  Sentences can have a simple or complex structure. A simple sentence has only one (main) subject and one (main) predicate. This is called a *main* or *principal clause*:

  Alessandro è intelligente. / *Alessandro is intelligent.*
  Sara è molto brava. / *Sarah is very good.*

A complex sentence has at least one other clause, known as a *subordinate* or *dependent clause*.

La ragazza	che legge il giornale	è italiana.
The girl	*who is reading the newspaper*	*is Italian.*
↑	↑	↑
main subject	subordinate clause	main predicate

There are two main types of subordinate or dependent clauses. A *relative clause* is a dependent clause introduced by a relative pronoun (see Chapter 11):

Main clause
La ragazza è italiana. / *The girl is Italian.*

Relative clause
(La stessa ragazza) legge il giornale. / *(The same girl) is reading the news-paper.*

Relative pronoun
che (= *who, that, which*)

Complex sentence
La ragazza che legge il giornale è italiana. / *The girl who is reading the newspaper is Italian.*

A *temporal clause* is a dependent clause introduced by subordinating conjunctions referring to time relations. A *conjunction* is a word that connects words, phrases, and clauses:

Quando Giacomo arriva, andremo al negozio. / *When Giacomo arrives, we will go to the store.*
Se viene Maria, vengo anch'io. / *If Maria comes, I'll come too.*
Dopo che sei andato via, è arrivata Sandra. / *After you left, Sandra arrived.*
La famiglia è arrivata appena sei andato via. / *The family arrived as soon as you left.*
Mentre tu dormivi, io leggevo il giornale. / *While you were sleeping, I read the newspaper.*

Other kinds of conjunctions can also introduce clauses into sentences. A number of these require the *subjunctive* form of the verb, and thus will be discussed in the sections dealing with the subjunctive.

SOME CONJUNCTIONS
- appena / *as soon as*
- quando / *when*
- dopo che / *after*
- se / *if*
- mentre / *while*

To join two sentences, two clauses, two words, etc., simply use the conjunctions **e** / *and*, **o** / *or*, or **ma** / *but*. These are called *compound forms* (compound subjects, compound phrases, etc.):

> **Maria studia e suo fratello guarda la TV.** / *Mary is studying and her brother is watching TV.*
> **La ragazza che ha i capelli biondi e che parla italiano molto bene è americana.** / *The girl with the blonde hair and who speaks Italian quite well is American.*
> **Gino e Gina parlano italiano.** / *Gino and Gina speak Italian.*
> **Vengo con la macchina o a piedi.** / *I'm coming by car or on foot.*

When we speak, we don't always use complete sentences—that is, sentences with a stated subject and predicate. Parts of a sentence may be left out when they are clearly implied.

> **Come stai?** / *How are you?*
> **Sto bene, grazie.** / *I am well, thanks.*
> **Bene, grazie.** / *Well, thanks.*

> **Quando è arrivato tuo padre?** / *When did your father arrive?*
> **Mio padre è arrivato alle tre.** / *My father arrived at three o'clock.*
> **È arrivato alle tre.** / *He arrived at three o'clock.*

> **Quando sei andato al teatro?** / *When did you go to the theater?*
> **Sono andato al teatro ieri.** / *I went to the theater yesterday.*
> **Ieri.** / *Yesterday.*

All the sentences illustrated so far have been *active* sentences. The verb in such sentences expresses the action performed by the subject. But for many active sentences there are corresponding *passive* ones in which the action is performed *on* the subject. The passive will be taken up in Chapter 7. For now, just observe how it corresponds to the English passive:

FRASE ATTIVA	FRASE PASSIVA
Maria mangia la torta. / *Mary is eating the cake.*	**La torta è mangiata da Maria.** / *The cake is eaten by Maria.*
Io ho comprato quella FIAT. / *I have bought that FIAT.*	**Quella FIAT è stata comprata da me.** / *That FIAT has been bought by me.*

Match the left-hand and right-hand columns to make complete sentences.

1. Quel libro… *i*
2. Quel libro appartiene *(belongs)* a …*h*
3. Chi vuole mangiare quella torta? Lui …*g*
4. Noi guardavamo la TV … *a*
5. Io vado alla festa … *a*
6. Lei è la studentessa …
7. Quello è un libro …
8. Alessandro è bravo in …*e*
9. Ecco gli amici …

a. mentre tu studiavi.
b. che studia più di tutti.
c. che ho letto molte volte.
d. se ci vai anche tu.
e. matematica e in chimica.
f. che vivono in Italia.
g. o lei?
h. Mario e a Maria.
i. è stato scritto da mio padre.

Home work

PUTTING IT
ALL TOGETHER

A. *Classify each sentence in the chart as belonging to one of the following categories.*
Each category must be assigned to one sentence.

Affirmative
Negative
Interrogative
Incomplete
Passive
Compound

1. Marco va spesso in Italia, ma quest'anno vuole andare in Francia. *compound*
2. Come si chiama tua cugina? *interrogat*
3. Bene, grazie. *affirmativ incomplete*
4. Quell'e-mail è stata scritta dalla mia amica. *incomplete passive*
5. Ci sono molti studenti in questa classe. *passiv affirm*
6. Non c'è nessuno qui. *negativ*

B. *How do you say the following in Italian?*

1. Uh, huh, you are right (**avere ragione** / *to be right*). *Ecco, ecco, hai ragione*
2. Yup, sure, she is also right. *Sca, già lei ha ragione anche*
3. There are many people at the party. *Qui ci sono tanti gentili a la*
festa

4. Where's Sara? There's Sara! *Dove Sara? Ecco Sara,*
5. Is there any more coffee? *c'è cafe?*
6. I never phone my friends. *mai telefono mi amici*
7. Did you ask the professor to come? *Chiedi professore venire?*
8. Who are you waiting for, Maria?
9. No, she is not coming to the party. *no, Lei non viene alla festa*

C. *Scrambled Words! Unscramble the words to make complete sentences.*

1. partita / noi / la / alla / radio / ascoltiamo
2. stai / Maria / la / ancora / tua / borsa / cercando
3. piace / la / non / mi / pizza
4. chi / persona / quella / è
5. detto / lui / l'ha
6. è / la / che / ha / Marco / detto / persona / quello
7. arriveranno / quando / cinema / andremo / al
8. torta / mangiata / è / quella / stata / lui / tutta / da
9. Marco / Maria / Fellini / amano / i / e / film / di

Culture Capsule 1

Greeting and Being Polite
Il saluto e la cortesia

Quando gli italiani si incontrano, di solito si danno la mano. In Italia i titoli—dottore, avvocato, ecc.—si usano molto di più che in Nord America. Il titolo di dottore/dottoressa si usa non solo per salutare un medico, ma anche per chiunque abbia una laurea universitaria. Quando due amici si incontrano, non solo si danno la mano, ma, specialmente se non si vedono da parecchio tempo, si abbracciano o si baciano sulle guance.

Agli amici, membri della famiglia, bambini, e, in generale, con chi si è in grande familiarità si dà del **tu** (*one uses the "tu" form of address*). Agli altri—alle persone con cui non si è in grande familiarità—si dà del **Lei**.

Se si parla a più di una persona, si usa il **voi** o il **Loro**. Il **voi** si può dare sia a persone con cui si è in familiarità che a persone che non conosciamo bene o a cui dobbiamo rispetto. Il **Loro** è molto formale. Si usa con più di una persona.

Infine, per indicare cortesia e per attenuare una richiesta, gli italiani in luogo del presente indicativo usano il condizionale o l'imperfetto indicativo: **Potrebbe aiutarmi? Saprebbe dirmi?** ecc.

CONTENT QUESTIONS

Vero o falso? *Indicate whether each statement is true or false.*

____ 1. Quando gli italiani si incontrano di solito si danno la mano.

____ 2. In Italia si usano raramente i titoli.

____ 3. Il titolo di **dottore/dottoressa** si usa non solo per salutare un medico, ma anche per chiunque abbia una laurea universitaria.

____ 4. Agli amici e ai membri della famiglia si dà del **Lei**.

____ 5. All'insegnante d'italiano si dà del **tu**.

____ 6. Si usa solo il **Loro** se si parla a più di una persona.

____ 7. Quando due amici non si vedono da parecchio tempo si abbracciano o si baciano sulle guance.

PART II:
Reviewing and Practicing the Verbs

3

The Present Indicative

Quanto Sai Già? — How Much Do You Know Already? (?)
True or False?

___T___ 1. **Finiscono** can mean *they are finishing*.
___T___ 2. **Ando** is the first person singular of the verb **andare**.
___F___ 3. Subject pronouns are always required with the present indicative.
___T___ 4. If the form of the verb is **capisco** the infinitive is **capire**.
___F___ 5. The second person singular of **leggere** in the present indicative is **legghi**.
___F___ 6. If the form of the verb is **esco** the infinitive is **escere**.
___T___ 7. The present indicative can be used to express immediate future actions.
___T___ 8. The third person plural of **avere** in the present indicative is **hanno**.
___F___ 9. The first person plural of **finire** in the present indicative is **finisciamo**.

Conjugating Regular Verbs in the Present Indicative
Verbi regolari al presente dell'indicativo

    Verbs are words that indicate the action performed by the subject of a sentence. For this reason, they agree with the subject in *person* (**la persona**) (first, second, third) and *number* (**il numero**) (singular or plural). In many cases this means simply matching the ending (**la desinenza**) of the verb to the subject.

> **Tu parli molto bene.** / *You speak very well.*
> **Loro arrivano domani.** / *They are arriving tomorrow.*

    Italian verbs are classified in terms of three main conjugations, which can be identified by their endings.

First Conjugation	Second Conjugation	Third Conjugation
parlare / *to speak*	**mettere** / *to put*	**dormire** / *to sleep*

A *regular verb* (**un verbo regolare**) is one whose conjugation is made up of a recurring pattern of endings. A verb that is not made up in this way is known as *irregular*.

The *indicative mood* (**il modo indicativo**) allows you to express facts or convey information. It is used for ordinary statements and questions (*I speak Italian; Where are you from?* etc.).

Subject Pronouns	
(Pronomi in funzione di soggetto)	
io	*I*
tu	*you (fam., sing.)*
lui	*he*
lei	*she*
Lei	*you (pol., sing.)*
noi	*we*
voi	*you (fam., pl.)*
loro	*they*
Loro	*you (pol., plural)*

To form the present indicative (**il presente dell'indicativo**) of regular verbs, do the following.

• Drop the infinitive ending. This produces the "verb stem," as it is called. Note that there are two types of third-conjugation verbs (as will soon be discussed).

parlare / *to speak*	→	**parl-**
mettere / *to put*	→	**mett-**
dormire / *to sleep*	→	**dorm-**
finire / *to finish*	→	**fin-**

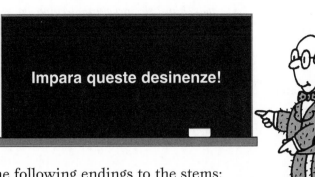

Impara queste desinenze!

- Add the following endings to the stems:

	First		Second		Third (1)		Third (2)	
(io)	*parlo*	-o	*mett*	-o	*dormo*	-o	*fin*	-isco
(tu)	*parli*	-i	*metti*	-i	*dormi*	-i	*fin*	-isci
(lui/lei/Lei)	*parla*	-a	*mette*	-e	*dorme*	-e	*fin*	-isce
(noi)	*parl*	-iamo	*mett*	-iamo	*dorm*	-iamo	*fin*	-iamo
(voi)	*parl*	-ate	*mett*	-ete	*dorm*	-ite	*fin*	-ite
(loro)	*parl*	-ano	*mett*	-ono	*dorm*	-ono	*fin*	-iscono

- Here's the result (*fam.* = *familiar, pol.* = *polite*):

First Conjugation (Prima coniugazione)

(io)	parlo	*I speak, I am speaking, I do speak*
(tu)	parli	*you (fam.) speak, you are speaking, you do speak*
(lui/lei)	parla	*he/she speaks, he/she is speaking, he/she does speak*
(Lei)	parla	*you (pol.) speak, you are speaking, you do speak*
(noi)	parliamo	*we speak, we are speaking, we do speak*
(voi)	parlate	*you speak, you are speaking, you do speak*
(loro)	parlano	*they speak, they are speaking, they do speak*

Second Conjugation (Seconda coniugazione)

(io)	metto	*I put, I am putting, I do put*
(tu)	metti	*you (fam.) put, you are putting, you do put*
(lui/lei)	mette	*He/she puts, he/she is putting, he/she does put*
(Lei)	mette	*you (pol.) put, you are putting, you do put*
(noi)	mettiamo	*we put, we are putting, we do put*
(voi)	mettete	*you put, you are putting, you do put*
(loro)	mettono	*they put, they are putting, they do put*

Third Conjugation (1) (Terza coniugazione)

(io)	dormo	*I sleep, I am sleeping, I do sleep*
(tu)	dormi	*you (fam.) sleep, you are sleeping, you do sleep*
(lui/lei)	dorme	*he/she sleeps, he/she is sleeping, he/she does sleep*
(Lei)	dorme	*you (pol.) sleep, you are sleeping, you do sleep*
(noi)	dormiamo	*we sleep, we are sleeping, we do sleep*
(voi)	dormite	*you sleep, you are sleeping, you do sleep*
(loro)	dormono	*they sleep, they are sleeping, they do sleep*

Third Conjugation (2) (Terza coniugazione)

(io)	finisco	*I finish, I am finishing, I do finish*
(tu)	finisci	*you (fam.) finish, you are finishing, you do finish*
(lui/lei)	finisce	*he/she finishes, he/she is finishing, he/she does finish*
(Lei)	finisce	*you (pol.) finish, you are finishing, you do finish*
(noi)	finiamo	*we finish, we are finishing, we do finish*
(voi)	finite	*you finish, you are finishing, you do finish*
(loro)	finiscono	*they finish, they are finishing, they do finish*

Examples:

Lui parla molto bene. / *He speaks very well.*
Marco dorme ancora? / *Is Mark still sleeping?*
Finisco di lavorare alle sei. / *I finish
  working at six.*
Loro dormono troppo. / *They sleep too much.*
Dove metti l'auto, di solito? / *Where do you
  usually put your car?*

The subject pronouns are optional with the present indicative. The reason for this is that the endings make it clear who the subject is.

To make any verb negative (**un verbo negativo**) in Italian, simply put **non** before it, as discussed in Chapter 2:

Lui non parla molto bene. / *He doesn't speak very well.*
Io non dormo mai più di sei ore. / *I never sleep more than six hours.*

The third person forms of the verb are also used, of course, with subjects that are not pronouns.

> **TIPS**
> Be careful when you pronounce the third person plural forms! The accent is *not* placed on the ending, but before it.
>
> párlano / *they speak*
> méttono / *they put*
> dórmono / *they sleep*
> finíscono / *they finish*

Quella ragazza studia molto. / *That girl studies a lot.*
La madre di Paolo finisce di lavorare alle sei. / *Paolo's mother finishes working at six.*

Also note that the "indefinite" subject pronoun *it* (plural *they*) is not normally expressed in Italian as it is in English (also as discussed in Chapter 2):

Apre a mezzogiorno. / *It opens at noon.*
Chiudono alle sei. / *They close at six.*

Polite forms of address require third person endings. These are used, essentially, to address anyone with whom you are not on a first-name basis. Familiar forms are used instead to address friends, family members, children, and anyone with whom you are not on a first-name basis:

FAMILIAR ADDRESS	POLITE ADDRESS
Tu parli molto bene. / *You speak very well.*	**Lei parla molto bene.** / *You speak very well.*
Tina, parli francese? / *Tina, do you speak French?*	**Signora, parla francese?** / *Madam, do you speak French?*

Homework

QUICK PRACTICE 1

Put each infinitive into its appropriate present indicative form according to sense.

Modello: Tina (parlare) italiano molto bene.
   Tina parla italiano molto bene.

1. Anch'io (parlare) italiano molto bene.   *parlo*
2. Io non (scrivere) l'italiano molto bene.   *scrivo*
3. Sì, io (capire) tutto.   *capisco*
4. No, io non (dormire) molto la notte.   *dormo*
5. Anche tu (parlare) italiano molto bene, non è vero?   *parli*
6. È vero che tu (scrivere) l'italiano molto bene?   *scrivi*
7. Maria, tu (capire) quello che ho detto?   *capisci*
8. Perché tu (dormire) così poco?   *dormi*
9. Anche Lei (parlare) italiano molto bene, non è vero?   *parla*
10. È vero che Lei (scrivere) l'italiano molto bene?   *scrivono*
11. Signorina, Lei (capire) quello che ho detto?   *capiscono*
12. Perché Lei (dormire) così poco?   *dorme*
13. Quel negozio (aprire) alle sette e mezzo.
14. Mio fratello (arrivare) dall'Italia domani.   *arriva*

15. A che ora (finire) di lavorare, la tua amica? *finisci*
16. Che cosa (vedere / *to see*) il tuo amico? *vede*
17. Noi non (parlare) italiano. *parliamo*
18. Anche voi non (parlare) italiano, vero? *parlate*
19. Noi non (vedere) niente. *vedono*
20. Anche voi non (vedere) niente, vero? *vedete*
21. Noi (dormire) fino a tardi il sabato. *dormiamo*
22. Anche voi (dormire) fino a tardi il sabato, no? *dormite*
23. Noi (finire) di lavorare alle sette. *finiamo*
24. Anche voi (finire) di lavorare alle sette, non è vero? *finite*
25. A che ora (arrivare) i tuoi amici? *arrive*
26. Chi (vedere) loro? *vede*
27. A che ora (chiudere) i negozi? *chiudomo*
28. A che ora (finire) di lavorare i tuoi amici? *finisco*

Common Regular Verbs
Verbi regolari comuni

Below are common regular verbs that will come in handy for expressing your-self in the present indicative. Some are used in the quick practice exercise below, and the others in the putting it all together section at the end of the chapter.

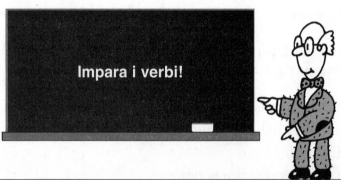

COMMON FIRST CONJUGATION VERBS			
abitare	*to live*	entrare	*to enter*
amare	*to love*	guardare	*to look at, to watch*
arrivare	*to arrive*	lavorare	*to work*
ascoltare	*to listen to*	parlare	*to speak*
aspettare	*to wait for*	portare	*to wear, to carry*
ballare	*to dance*	preparare	*to prepare*
cantare	*to sing*	sperare	*to hope*
comprare	*to buy*	suonare	*to play an instrument*

COMMON SECOND CONJUGATION VERBS			
chiudere	to close	ridere	to laugh
comprendere	to comprehend	rompere	to break
correre	to run	scrivere	to write
credere	to believe	temere	to fear
godere	to enjoy	vedere	to see
leggere	to read	vendere	to sell
mettere	to put	vivere	to live
prendere	to take		

Common Third Conjugation Verbs

There is no way to predict to which type of conjugation (1 or 2) an -ire verb belongs. A good dictionary will provide this kind of information. However, as a rule of thumb, if you see two consonants before the -ire ending (aprire, partire) the conjugation is usually Type 1; if there is a vowel (capire, pulire), the conjugation is usually Type 2. This is only a rule of thumb, but it works very often.

TYPE 1			
aprire	to open	mentire	to lie
coprire	to cover	offrire	to offer
dormire	to sleep	partire	to leave, to depart
fuggire	to escape, to flee	sentire	to hear, to feel

TYPE 2			
capire	to understand	pulire	to clean
finire	to finish	punire	to punish
garantire	to guarantee	spedire	to send, to mail
preferire	to prefer	unire	to unite

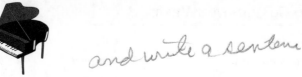

QUICK PRACTICE 2

and write a sentence

Conjugate the following verbs in the present indicative as indicated.

Modello: io...
            aprire
            chiudere
            etc.

            io apro
            io chiudo
            etc.

1. io...
   a. abitare   *abito*   *Abito a casa.*
   b. prendere   *prendo*   *Prendo vino, per favore*
   c. aprire   *apro*   *apro Roberto*
   d. capire   *capisco*   *Capisco niente*

2. tu...
   a. amare   *ami*   *Amai tuo marito*
   b. leggere   *leggi*   *Leggi l'italiano, un po*
   c. offrire   *offri*   *offri un avvertimento*
   d. spedire   *spedisci*   *spedisci un lettera.*

3. lui/lei...
   a. entrare   *entra*   *Entra ed concorso*
   b. vedere   *vede*   *Lui vede un spetta*
   c. aprire   *apre*   *lui apre la birra*
   d. preferire   *prefisce*   *Lei guidare rapido prefice*

4. Lei *(pol., sing.)*...
   a. guardare   *guarda*   *Lei guarda l'uomo bello*
   b. ridere   *ride*   *Lei ride il cane*
   c. offrire   *offre*   *Lei offre un cappuccino*
   d. unire   *unisce*   *Lei unisce in canzone* *the same old story*

5. noi...
   a. comprare   *compriamo*   *Compriamo un Casa in Italia*
   b. godere   *godiamo*   *Godiamo professore Giambi.*
   c. sentire   *sentiamo*   *Sentiamo felici*
   d. spedire   *spediamo*   *Spediamo molto amore.*

check these

6. voi...
   a. ascoltare *ascoltate*   *Ascoltate la musica*
   b. vivere *vivete*   *vivete la dolce vita.*
   c. fuggire *fuggite*   *Fuggite dai carabinieri*
   d. garantire *garantite*   *garantitemi una "A" in l'italiano.*

7. loro...
   a. portare *portano*   *Portano molto verdure*
   b. credere *credono*   *credono alla mia bugia (lie.)*
   c. partire *partono*   *Partino en il treno.*
   d. pulire *puliscono*   *Puliscono il bagno*

Spelling Peculiarities
Peculiarità ortografiche

If the first-conjugation infinitive ending is **-ciare** or **-giare**, then drop the **-are** and retain the **-i** of the ending to indicate a soft sound for "**c**" and "**g**", but do not write a "double **-i**" when adding on the endings **-i** and **-iamo**:

cominciare / *to begin* → cominci-		
(io)	comincio	*I begin, I am beginning, I do begin*
(tu)	cominci	*you (fam.) begin, you are beginning, you do begin*
(lui/lei)	comincia	*he/she begins, he/she is beginning, he/she does begin*
(Lei)	comincia	*you (pol.) begin, you are beginning, you do begin*
(noi)	cominciamo	*we begin, we are beginning, we do begin*
(voi)	cominciate	*you begin, you are beginning, you do begin*
(loro)	cominciano	*they begin, they are beginning, they do begin*

mangiare / *to eat* → mangi-		
(io)	mangio	*I eat, I am eating, I do eat*
(tu)	mangi	*you (fam.) eat, you are eating, you do eat*
(lui/lei)	mangia	*he/she eats, he/she is eating, he/she does eat*
(Lei)	mangia	*you (pol.) eat, you are eating, you do eat*
(noi)	mangiamo	*we eat, we are eating, we do eat*
(voi)	mangiate	*you eat, you are eating, you do eat*
(loro)	mangiano	*they eat, they are eating, they do eat*

Here are a few useful verbs ending in **-ciare** and **-giare**:

abbracciare	*to hug*
allacciare	*to fasten*
annunciare	*to announce*
assaggiare	*to taste*
baciare	*to kiss*
lanciare	*to throw*
lasciare	*to let, to leave (behind)*
noleggiare	*to rent (car, movie, etc.)*
parcheggiare	*to park*
pronunciare	*to pronounce*
viaggiare	*to travel*

If the infinitive ends in **-iare**, the same rule of "not doubling the vowel **-i**" applies, unless the **-i** is stressed during the conjugation, in which case it is retained before the **-i** ending only:

UNSTRESSED	STRESSED
cambiare / *to change*	deviare / *to deviate*
copiare / *to copy*	inviare / *to send*
studiare / *to study*	sciare / *to ski*

> **TIP**
> In the case of most verbs ending in -iare, the -i is unstressed unless otherwise indicated by a dictionary. Therefore, the most common conjugation pattern is the one exemplified by cambiare.

Examples:

cambiare / *to change* → cambi-		
(io)	cambio	*I change, I am changing, I do change*
(tu)	cambi	*you (fam.) change, you are changing, you do change*
(lui/lei)	cambia	*he/she changes, he/she is changing, he/she does change*
(Lei)	cambia	*you (pol.) change, you are changing, you do change*
(noi)	cambiamo	*we change, we are changing, we do change*
(voi)	cambiate	*you change, you are changing, you do change*
(loro)	cambiano	*they change, they are changing, they do change*

sciare / *to ski* → sci-		
(io)	scio	*I ski, I am skiing, I do ski*
(tu)	scii	*you (fam.) ski, you are skiing, you do ski*
(lui/lei)	scia	*he/she skies, he/she is skiing, he/she does ski*
(Lei)	scia	*you (pol.) ski, you are skiing, you do ski*
(noi)	sciamo	*we ski, we are skiing, we do ski*
(voi)	sciate	*you ski, you are skiing, you do ski*
(loro)	sciano	*they ski, they are skiing, they do ski*

If the infinitive ending is **-care** or **-gare**, drop the **-are** but add an "**h**" before the present indicative endings **-i** and **-iamo**. This indicates that the hard "**c**" and "**g**" are to be retained:

cercare / *to look for, to search for* → cerc-		
(io)	cerco	*I search, I am searching, I do search*
(tu)	cerchi	*you (fam.) search, you are searching, you do search*
(lui/lei)	cerca	*he/she searches, he/she is searching, he/she does search*
(Lei)	cerca	*you (pol.) search, you are searching, you do search*
(noi)	cerchiamo	*we search, we are searching, we do search*
(voi)	cercate	*you search, you are searching, you do search*
(loro)	cercano	*they search, they are searching, they do search*

pagare / *to pay (for)* → pag-		
(io)	pago	*I pay, I am paying, I do pay*
(tu)	paghi	*you (fam.) pay, you are paying, you do pay*
(lui/lei)	paga	*he/she pays, he/she is paying, he/she, does pay*
(Lei)	paga	*you (pol.) pay, you are paying, you do pay*
(noi)	paghiamo	*we pay, we are paying, we do pay*
(voi)	pagate	*you pay, you are paying, you do pay*
(loro)	pagano	*they pay, they are paying, they do pay*

Here are a few useful verbs ending in **-care** and **-gare**:

comunicare	*to communicate*
criticare	*to criticize*
giocare	*to play (a game)*
indicare	*to indicate*
legare	*to tie*
negare	*to deny*
pregare	*to pray, to beg*
spiegare	*to explain*

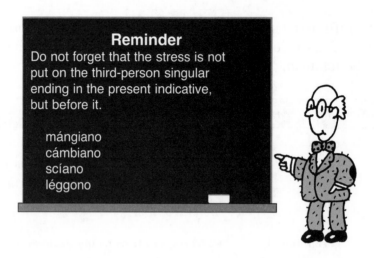

Reminder
Do not forget that the stress is not put on the third-person singular ending in the present indicative, but before it.

mángiano
cámbiano
scíano
léggono

Note that **giocare** means *to play* a game, sports, and so on, whereas **suonare** means *to play* an instrument:

Lui gioca a calcio molto bene. / *He plays soccer very well.*
Lei suona il pianoforte molto bene. / *She plays the piano very well.*

The spelling and pronunciation peculiarities described above apply only to the first conjugation. A second-conjugation verb such as **conoscere** or **leggere**, for instance, is conjugated in the usual way and the consonant is pronounced as hard or soft as the case may be. Here is an example:

(io) leggo / *I read*	→	pronounce the "g" as hard
(tu) leggi / *you (fam.) read*	→	pronounce the "g" as soft
(lui/lei) legge / *he/she reads*	→	pronounce the "g" as soft
(Lei) legge / *you (pol.) read*	→	pronounce the "g" as soft
(noi) leggiamo / *we read*	→	pronounce the "g" as soft
(voi) leggete / *you (pl.) read*	→	pronounce the "g" as soft
(loro) leggono / *they read*	→	pronounce the "g" as hard

QUICK PRACTICE 3

As in Quick Practice 2 before, conjugate the following verbs in the present indicative as indicated.

1. io...
   a. lanciare — *lancio* (throw)
   b. viaggiare — *viaggio*
   c. copiare — *copio* (copy)
   d. comunicare — *comunico*

2. tu...
   a. allacciare — *allacci*
   b. parcheggiare — *parcheggi*
   c. studiare — *studi*
   d. giocare — *giochi*

3. lui/lei...
   a. annunciare — *annuncia*
   b. viaggiare — *viaggia*
   c. deviare — *devia*
   d. indicare — *indica*

4. Lei *(pol., sing.)*...
   a. abbracciare — *abbraccia* (embrace)
   b. assaggiare — *assaggia* (taste)
   c. sciare — *scia*
   d. comunicare — *comunica*

5. noi...
   a. baciare — *baciamo*
   b. noleggiare — *noleggiamo* (rent)
   c. inviare — *inviamo* (send-mail)
   d. negare — *neghiamo* (negate)

6. voi...
   a. pronunciare — *pronunciate*
   b. vigiare — *vigiate*
   c. cambiare — *cambiate*
   d. pregare — *pregate*

7. loro...
   a. lasciare — *lasciano* (left)
   b. mangiare — *mangiano*
   c. sciare — *sciano*
   d. spiegare — *spiegano* (explain)

Main Uses

Usi principali

The **presente dell'indicativo** is used in everyday conversation to refer to actions, events, and ideas that imply the present situation or some permanent or habitual action, activity, event, or situation. Specifically, it is used:

- To indicate an action or a state of being that is taking place at the present time:

  Parlo a Claudia in questo momento. /*I am speaking to Claudia at this moment.*
  Guardo la TV adesso. /*I am watching TV now.*

- To indicate an action or a state of being that is permanent or continuous:

  Parlo italiano anch'io. / *I too speak Italian.*
  Lei capisce sempre tutto. / *She always understands everything.*

> **TIP**
> The present indicative is often used with words and expressions such as:
>
> **a quest'ora**
> *at this hour*
>
> **adesso/ora**
> *now*
>
> **in questo momento**
> *in/at this moment*
>
> **oggi come oggi**
> *nowadays, these days*
>
> **ogni giorno**
> *every day*

- To emphasize something at the present time:

  Sì, capisco! / *Yes, I do understand!*
  No, non sento niente! / *No, I do not hear anything!*

- To indicate an habitual action:

  Suono la chitarra ogni giorno. / *I play the guitar every day.*
  Il lunedì puliamo la casa. / *On Mondays we clean the house.*

- To convey a general truth:

  I negozi aprono alle sette e mezzo. / *Stores open at 7.30 A.M.*
  Gli italiani lavorano molto. / *Italians work a lot.*

- To express an action that may occur in the near future:

  Lui arriva domani. / *He's arriving tomorrow.*
  Tra poco scrivo un'e-mail. / *In a little while I'm going to write an e-mail.*

The **presente dell'indicativo** is generally equivalent to three English verb forms:

(io) parlo	=	*I speak, I am speaking, I do speak*
(tu) mangi	=	*you (fam.) eat, you are eating, you do eat*
(lui/lei) finisce	=	*he/she finishes, he/she is finishing, he/she does finish*
(Lei) aspetta	=	*you (pol.) wait, you are waiting, you do wait*
(noi) lavoriamo	=	*we work, we are working, we do work*
(voi) cominciate	=	*you (pl.) begin, you are beginning, you do begin*
(loro) leggono	=	*they read, they are reading, they do read*

With the preposition **da** (which in this case means both *since* and *for*) it can be used to render the English present progressive tense:

Vivo qui dal 1999. / *I have been living here since 1999.*
Studio l'italiano da nove anni. / *I have been studying Italian for nine years.*

The present indicative is also used in Italian to express immediate future actions, that is, actions that will occur in the near future:

Domani andiamo al teatro. / *Tomorrow we are going to the theater.*
Domani parlo al professore. / *Tomorrow I will speak to the professor.*

Note that in the singular, the **tu** forms are used for familiar address and the **Lei** forms for polite address:

Cosa preferisci, tu? / *What do you (fam.) prefer?*
Cosa preferisce, Lei? / *What do you (pol.) prefer?*

Second person plural forms are commonly used to address anyone in general:

Cosa mangiate, voi? / *What are you (in general) eating?*
Cosa preferite, voi? / *What do you (in general) prefer?*

Third person plural forms are used to address people politely in very formal situations:

Cosa scrivono, Loro? / *What are you (very formal) writing?*
Cosa preferiscono, Loro? / *What do you (very formal) prefer?*

The predicate of sentences in the present indicative may or may not have an object (see Chapter 2). An *object* (**il complemento oggetto**) is the noun, substantive, or noun phrase that receives the action (again, see Chapter 2). It normally follows the verb. There are two types of object: *direct* and *indirect*. Each one can be identified very easily with the following two rules of thumb:

- A noun, substantive, or noun phrase that directly follows the verb is a direct object.

  Lui suona il violino. / *He plays the violin.*
  Loro mangiano sempre gli spaghetti. / *They always eat spaghetti.*

- A noun, substantive, or noun phrase that follows the verb but is introduced by a preposition such as **a** (*to, at*) is an indirect object.

  Lei va al negozio più tardi. / *She is going to the store later.*
  A che ora vai a scuola? / *At what time do you go to school?*

Some verbs must be followed only by one type of object or the other. Verbs that take a direct object are known as *transitive* (**verbi transitivi**); those that do not take a direct object are known as *intransitive* (**verbi intransitivi**). Most verbs in Italian match their English equivalents when it comes to whether or not a direct or indirect object should follow. However, there are differences, as you saw in Chapter 2. Here are the most important ones.

Verbs Requiring a Direct Object in Italian (But Not in English)
ascoltare / *to listen (to)*
aspettare / *to wait for*
cercare / *to look for, to search for*

Examples:

Mia madre ascolta la radio ogni sera. / *My mother listens to the radio every evening.*
Giorgio aspetta Maria. / *Giorgio is waiting for Mary.*
Tina cerca la sua penna. / *Tina is looking for her pen.*

Verbs Requiring a Direct Object in English (But Not in Italian)
chiedere (a) / *to ask*
telefonare (a) / *to phone*
rispondere (a) / *to answer*

Examples:

Gino chiede al professore di venire. / *Gino asks the professor to come.*
Claudia telefona a sua madre ogni sera. / *Claudia phones her mother every evening.*
Perché non rispondi alla mia domanda? / *Why aren't you answering my question?*

Maybe this one

QUICK PRACTICE 4

Say the following things in Italian.

1. I am watching TV now. *Guardo adesso.*
2. I too do speak Italian. *Parlo italiano anch'io*
3. No, I do not hear anything! *No, non sento niente.*
4. On Saturdays we always clean the house. *el sabato puliamo la casa*
5. Italians work too much. *Gli italiani lavorano troppo*
6. They're arriving tomorrow. *arrivano domani*
7. I have been studying since this morning. *Studio italiano da mattina.*
8. I have been studying Italian for five years. *Studio italiano da cinque anni*
9. What do you (*fam., sing.*) prefer? *Cosa preferisci, tu*
10. What do you (*pol., sing.*) prefer? *Cosa preferisce, lei*
11. What do you (*fam., pl.*) prefer? *Cosa preferite, voi*
12. What do you (*pol., pl.*) prefer? *Cosa preferiscono, loro*
13. She plays the piano very well. *Lei suona pianoforte molto bene*
14. He is always waiting for the bus when I run into (**incontrare** / *to run into*) him. *Lo aspetta l'autobus quando incontro lui*
15. She always answers the questions correctly. *Le risponde les domande giusta correttamente*

Essere and *avere*
To Be and to Have

The verb **essere** / *to be* is an irregular verb. Unlike the verbs that you have learned to conjugate previously, you cannot predict its forms. You will simply have to memorize them:

essere / *to be*		
(io)	sono	*I am*
(tu)	sei	*you (fam.) are*
(lui/lei)	è	*he/she is*
(Lei)	è	*you (pol.) are*
(noi)	siamo	*we are*
(voi)	siete	*you are*
(loro)	sono	*they are*

Among the many uses of **essere**, here are some of the more common ones.

* To tell time

> **È l'una.** / *It's one o'clock* (= the only singular form).
> **Sono le due.** / *It's two o'clock.*
> **Sono le sedici e cinquanta.** / *It's 4:50 P.M.*
> **Sono le ventidue e cinque.** / *It's 10:05 P.M.*

* To indicate and refer to dates

> **È il quindici settembre.** / *It's September 15.*
> **È il ventun settembre.** / *It's September 21.*
> **È sabato.** / *It's Saturday.*

* To indicate origin or nationality

> **Di dove è Lei?** / *Where are you from?*
> **Sono di Milano.** / *I am from Milan.*
> **Noi siamo italiani.** / *We are Italian.*

- To describe something or someone

  > **Mio fratello è alto.** / *My brother is tall.*
  > **Mia sorella è intelligente.** / *My sister is intelligent.*

- To indicate a job or a profession

  > **Io sono un avvocato.** / *I am a lawyer.*
  > **Tu sei un medico, vero?** / *You're a doctor, aren't you?*

As we saw in the second chapter, also common in everyday conversation is the verb form **esserci** / *to be there*. It is used to acknowledge that something or someone is somewhere. It thus has only two forms:

> **C'è l'insegnante?** / *Is the teacher here/there?*
> **Ci sono gli insegnanti?** / *Are the teachers here/there?*

The form **ecco** is used instead to actually point out something or someone:

> **Ecco l'insegnante!** / *Here/there is the teacher!*
> **Ecco gli insegnanti!** / *Here/there are the teachers!*

Like **essere**, **avere** / *to have* is an important irregular verb. Following is its present indicative conjugation:

Impara il verbo avere!

avere / *to have*		
(io)	ho	*I have*
(tu)	hai	*you (fam.) have*
(lui/lei)	ha	*he/she has*
(Lei)	ha	*you (pol.) have*
(noi)	abbiamo	*we have*
(voi)	avete	*you have*
(loro)	hanno	*they have*

Note that the "**h**" is not pronounced. It is only written and can be compared to the "silent *h*" of English *hour*.

Avere is used in many idiomatic expressions. Here are the most common ones:

avere bisogno (di)	*to need*
avere caldo	*to be hot*
avere fame	*to be hungry*
avere freddo	*to be cold*
avere fretta	*to be in a hurry*
avere paura	*to be afraid*
avere pazienza	*to be patient, to have patience*
avere ragione	*to be right*
avere sete	*to be thirsty*
avere sonno	*to be sleepy*
avere torto	*to be wrong*
avere vergogna	*to be ashamed*
avere voglia (di)	*to feel like*

When using **molto** / *much, a lot* or **poco** / *little* with such expressions make sure you treat them as adjectives. They must agree with the gender of the noun:

Ho molta fame. / *I am very hungry* (**la fame** = feminine).
Ha molto sonno. / *He/she is very sleepy* (**il sonno** = masculine).
Abbiamo poca voglia di uscire. / *We have little desire to go out* (**la voglia** = feminine).

Two other common uses of **avere** are as follows:

- To indicate age

    Quanti anni hai? / *How old are you?* (literally: *How many years do you have?*)
    Ho trentasei anni. / *I am 36 years old.* (literally: *I have 36 years.*)

- To indicate possession

    Ho molti amici. / *I have many friends.*
    Anche tu hai una nuova FIAT, vero? / *You also have a new FIAT, don't you?*

QUICK PRACTICE 5

Say the following sentences in Italian.

1. It's two thirty.   *Sono le due e trenta*
2. It's Saturday, October the twelfth.   *È Sabato . settembre*
3. I am from New York.   *Sono da New York*

4. Are you *(fam., sing.)* intelligent? *È intelligente?*
5. Are you *(pol., sing.)* a lawyer? *Lei è un avocato?*
6. They are always late (**in ritardo**). *Sono sempre in ritardo.*
7. Are you *(fam., pl.)* intelligent? *Siete intelligente?*
8. Are you *(pol., pl.)* intelligent? *c'è l'insegnante?*
9. Is the teacher here? *Ci sono*
10. Are they also here? *Ho bisogno di l'aute nuovo*
11. I need a new car.
12. Are you *(fam., sing.)* hot? *Hai freddo?*
13. Are you *(pol., sing.)* very hungry? *Hai molto fame?*
14. Are you *(fam., pl.)* in a hurry? *hai fretta?*
15. Are you *(fam., sing.)* very sleepy? *hai molta sonno*
16. How old are they? *Quanti anni hai?*

Sapere **and** *conoscere*
To Know

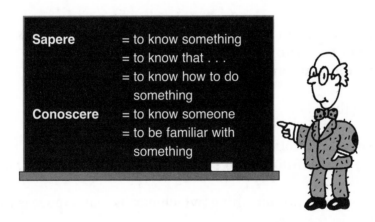

The verb **sapere** / *to know* is an important and often-used irregular verb in the present indicative. It is conjugated as follows:

sapere / *to know*		
(io)	so	*I know, I do know*
(tu)	sai	*you (fam.) know, you do know*
(lui/lei)	sa	*he/she knows, he/she does know*
(Lei)	sa	*you (pol.) know, you do know*
(noi)	sappiamo	*we know, we do know*
(voi)	sapete	*you know, you do know*
(loro)	sanno	*they know, they do know*

There is another verb in Italian meaning *to know*: **conoscere**. It is a regular second-conjugation verb.

conoscere / *to know*		
(io)	conosco	*I know, I do know, I am familiar with*
(tu)	conosci	*you (fam.) know, you do know, you are familiar with*
(lui/lei)	conosce	*he/she knows, he/she does know, he/she is familiar with*
(Lei)	conosce	*you (pol.) know, you do know, you are familiar with*
(noi)	conosciamo	*we know, we do know, we are familiar with*
(voi)	conoscete	*you know, you do know, you are familiar with*
(loro)	conoscono	*they know, they do know, they are familiar with*

The main uses and features of the verbs **sapere** and **conoscere** can be summarized as follows.

Sapere is used to indicate:

- knowing something

    Marco sa il tuo indirizzo. / *Marco knows your address.*
    Io non so il tuo nome. / *I don't know your name.*
    Noi non sappiamo chi è. / *We don't know who he is.*

- knowing that…

    So che lui è felice. / *I know that he is happy.*
    Loro non sanno che io sono qui. / *They do not know that I am here.*

- knowing how to do something (which means that **sapere** is followed by the infinitive in this case)

    Alessandro sa suonare il pianoforte. / *Alexander knows how to play the piano.*
    Io non so scrivere in italiano. / *I do not know how to write in Italian.*

Conoscere is used instead to indicate:

- knowing someone

    Claudia, conosci un buon medico? / *Claudia, do you know a good doctor?*
    Noi non conosciamo questa persona. / *We do not know this person.*

• being familiar with something (such as a place)

Conosci Roma? / *Are you familiar with Rome?*
Conosco un ristorante qui vicino. / *I know a restaurant near here.*

5-23

QUICK
PRACTICE 6

How do you say the following in Italian?

1. I do not know...   *Non so il tuo nome..*
   a. your name.
   b. your parents.   *non conosco tui genitori.*

2. You *(fam., sing.)* know...   *(suonare)*
   a. how to play the violin very well.   *Conosce molto bene il violino*
   b. that restaurant, don't you?   *Conosci quella ristorante, vero?*

3. You *(pol., sing.)* know...   *conosci*
   a. how to speak Italian very well.   *Parle molto bene l'italiano*
   b. that city, don't you?   *Conosci quella città, no?*

4. You *(fam., pl.)* know...
   a. how to play the violin very well.   *Sai suonare molto bene*
   b. that restaurant, don't you?   *Conosci quella ristorante, no?*

5. You *(pol., pl.)* know...
   a. how to play the piano very well.   *Sapete suonare il pianoforte molto bene.*
   b. that restaurant, don't you?   *conoscete la ristorante vero?*

6. We do not know...
   a. your name.   *Sappiamo tu nome.*
   b. your friends.   *conosciamo tu amici.*

Other Irregular Verbs
Altri verbi irregolari

The verbs **bere**, **dare**, **dire**, and **fare** are common irregular verbs. They will come in handy for everyday conversation. So, here are their forms in the present indicative:

bere / *to drink*		
(io)	bevo	*I drink, I am drinking, I do drink*
(tu)	bevi	*you (fam.) drink, you are drinking, you do drink*
(lui/lei)	beve	*he/she drinks, he/she is drinking, he/she does drink*
(Lei)	beve	*you (pol.) drink, you are drinking, you do drink*
(noi)	beviamo	*we drink, we are drinking, we do drink*
(voi)	bevete	*you drink, you are drinking, you do drink*
(loro)	bevono	*they drink, they are drinking, they do drink*

dare / *to give*		
(io)	do	*I give, I am giving, I do give*
(tu)	dai	*you (fam.) give, you are giving, you do give*
(lui/lei)	dà	*he/she gives, he/she is giving, he/she does give*
(Lei)	dà	*you (pol.) give, you are giving, you do give*
(noi)	diamo	*we give, we are giving, we do give*
(voi)	date	*you give, you are giving, you do give*
(loro)	danno	*they give, they are giving, they do give*

dire / *to say, to tell, to speak*		
(io)	dico	*I say, I am saying, I do say*
(tu)	dici	*you (fam.) say, you are saying, you do say*
(lui/lei)	dice	*he/she says, he/she is saying, he/she does say*
(Lei)	dice	*you (pol.) say, you are saying, you do say*
(noi)	diciamo	*we say, we are saying, we do say*
(voi)	dite	*you say, you are saying, you do say*
(loro)	dicono	*they say, they are saying, they do say*

fare / *to do, to make*		
(io)	faccio	*I make, I am making, I do make*
(tu)	fai	*you (fam.) make, you are making, you do make*
(lui/lei)	fa	*he/she makes, he/she is making, he/she does make*
(Lei)	fa	*you (pol.) make, you are making, you do make*
(noi)	facciamo	*we make, we are making, we do make*
(voi)	fate	*you make, you are making, you do make*
(loro)	fanno	*they make, they are making, they do make*

Here are some common expressions in which these verbs are used:

bere alla salute	*to drink to health*
bere forte	*to drink heavily*
dare del Lei	*to be on polite terms*
dare del tu	*to be on familiar terms*
dare la mano	*to shake hands*
dare un film	*to show a movie*
dire di no	*to say no*
dire di sì	*to say yes*
dire la verità	*to tell the truth*
dire una bugia/la bugia	*to tell a lie, to lie*
fare del bene	*to do good (things)*
fare del male	*to do bad (things)*
fare il medico/l'avvocato/…	*to be a doctor/a lawyer/…*

(handwritten annotation: diamoci dello tu)

Note that the verb **fare** is also used to indicate weather conditions:

Che tempo fa? / *How's the weather?*
Oggi fa freddo. / *It is cold today.*
Fa molto caldo. / *It is very hot.*
Fa un po' fresco. / *It's a little cool.*

The verbs **dovere**, **potere**, and **volere** are known as *modal verbs* (**verbi servili**, **verbi modali**). They are irregular in the present indicative. Here are their forms:

dovere / *to have to ("to must")*		
(io)	devo	*I have to, I must*
(tu)	devi	*you (fam.) have to, you must*
(lui/lei)	deve	*he/she has to, he/she must*
(Lei)	deve	*you (pol.) have to, you must*
(noi)	dobbiamo	*we have to, we must*
(voi)	dovete	*you have to, you must*
(loro)	devono	*they have to, they must*

potere / *to be able to*		
(io)	posso	*I am able to, I can*
(tu)	puoi	*you (fam.) are able to, you can*
(lui/lei)	può	*he/she is able to, he/she can*
(Lei)	può	*you (pol.) are able to, you can*
(noi)	possiamo	*we are able to, we can*
(voi)	potete	*you are able to, you can*
(loro)	possono	*they are able to, they can*

volere / *to want to*		
(io)	voglio	*I want to*
(tu)	vuoi	*you (fam.) want to*
(lui/lei)	vuole	*he/she wants to*
(Lei)	vuole	*you (pol.) want to*
(noi)	vogliamo	*we want to*
(voi)	volete	*you want to*
(loro)	vogliono	*they want to*

These verbs allow you to express permission, desire, necessity, and other similar kinds of states. They are, thus, normally followed by an infinitive:

Posso venire anch'io? / *Can I come too?*
Non devi andare in Italia oggi? / *Don't you have to go to Italy today?*
Voglio comprare un nuovo computer. / *I want to buy a new computer.*

Here are a few other useful irregular verbs. Their present indicative forms are given below:

andare / *to go*		
(io)	vado	*I go, I am going, I do go*
(tu)	vai	*you (fam.) go, you are going, you do go*
(lui/lei)	va	*he/she goes, he/she is going, he/she does go*
(Lei)	va	*you (pol.) go, you are going, you do go*
(noi)	andiamo	*we go, we are going, we do go*
(voi)	andate	*you go, you are going, you do go*
(loro)	vanno	*they go, they are going, they do go*

salire / *to climb, to go up*		
(io)	salgo	*I climb, I am climbing*
(tu)	sali	*you (fam.) climb, you are climbing*
(lui/lei)	sale	*he/she climbs, he/she is climbing*
(Lei)	sale	*you (pol.) climb, you are climbing*
(noi)	saliamo	*we climb, we are climbing*
(voi)	salite	*you climb, you are climbing*
(loro)	salgono	*they climb, they are climbing*

scegliere / *to choose, to select*		
(io)	scelgo	*I choose, I am choosing, I do choose*
(tu)	scegli	*you (fam.) choose, you are choosing, you do choose*
(lui/lei)	sceglie	*he/she chooses, he/she is choosing, he/she does choose*
(Lei)	sceglie	*you (pol.) choose, you are choosing, you do choose*
(noi)	scegliamo	*we choose, we are choosing, we do choose*
(voi)	scegliete	*you choose, you are choosing, you do choose*
(loro)	scelgono	*they choose, they are choosing, they do choose*

tenere / to keep, to hold

(io)	tengo	*I keep, I am keeping, I do keep*
(tu)	tieni	*you (fam.) keep, you are keeping, you do keep*
(lui/lei)	tiene	*he/she keeps, he/she is keeping, he/she does keep*
(Lei)	tiene	*you (pol.) keep, you are keeping, you do keep*
(noi)	teniamo	*we keep, we are keeping, we do keep*
(voi)	tenete	*you keep, you are keeping, you do keep*
(loro)	tengono	*they keep, they are keeping, they do keep*

uscire / to go out

(io)	esco	*I go out, I am going out, I do go out*
(tu)	esci	*you (fam.) go out, you are going out, you do go out*
(lui/lei)	esce	*he/she goes out, he/she is going out, he/she does go out*
(Lei)	esce	*you (pol.) go out, you are going out, you do go out*
(noi)	usciamo	*we go out, we are going out, we do go out*
(voi)	uscite	*you go out, you are going out, you do go out*
(loro)	escono	*they go out, they are going out, they do go out*

venire / to come

(io)	vengo	*I come, I am coming, I do come*
(tu)	vieni	*you (fam.) come, you are coming, you do come*
(lui/lei)	viene	*he/she comes, he/she is coming, he/she does come*
(Lei)	viene	*you (pol.) come, you are coming, you do come*
(noi)	veniamo	*we come, we are coming, we do come*
(voi)	venite	*you come, you are coming, you do come*
(loro)	vengono	*they come, they are coming, they do come*

5-23

How do you say the following?

1. I...
   a. am coming to the party. *vengo alla festa*
   b. am going out tonight. *esco ce sera* *vado*
   c. go to Italy every year. *esco a italia tutti anni* *quest anno*
   d. want to go to Italy this year. *Voglio andare italia di anni*
   e. have to study Italian. *Devo studiare l'italiana*
   f. can come with you (**te**). *Posso venire conte*
   g. am a doctor. *Sono Posso un medico*
   h. always tell the truth. *Sempre disco la verità*
   i. always give money to my children. *Sempre do lire a mia bambini*
   j. always drink white wine. *Sempre Bevo vino bianca*

2. You (*fam., sing.*)...
   vieni
   a. are coming to the party. *Ceci a la festa*
   b. are going out tonight. *Ceci ce sera*
   c. go to Italy every year. *vai italia tutti anni*
   d. want to go to Italy this year. *Vivi andare italia que anni*
   e. have to study Italian. *Devi studiare l'italiano*
   f. can come with me (**me**). *Puoi venire con me*
   g. do many things, don't you? *Fai molti cosi nero?*
   h. always tell the truth. *Sempre disi la verità*
   i. always give money to your children. *Sempre dai lire a sua bambini*
   j. always drink white wine. *Sempre beri il vino bianca*

3. They...
   a. are coming to the party. *vengona a la festa*
   b. are going out tonight. *Escono ce sera*
   c. go to Italy every year. *vanno all italia tutti anni*
   d. want to go to Italy this year. *vogliona andare all'italia le anni*
   e. have to study Italian. *Possono studiare l'italiano*
   f. can come with me (**me**). *Possono con me*
   g. do many things, don't they? *fanno molti cosi nero?*
   h. always tell the truth. *Sempre dicono la verità*
   i. always give money to their children. *Sempre danno lire a loro bambini*
   j. always drink white wine. *Sempre Bevono vino bianca*

PUTTING IT ALL TOGETHER

A. *Conjugate the following regular verbs in the present indicative by filling in the chart with their appropriate forms:*

	lavorare	baciare	giocare	viaggiare	negare	studiare	inviare	leggere	offrire	finire
io										
tu										
lui										
lei										
Lei										
noi										
voi										
loro										

B. *Which of the following two options, **a** or **b**, is the correct one?*

1. Buongiorno, Lei _B_ l'italiano?
   a. capisci
   b. capisce

2. A che ora _B_ gli amici di Alessandro?
   a. finisce
   b. finiscono

3. Anche tu _B_ sempre la casa?
   a. pulisce
   b. pulisci

4. Molti americani _B_ la lingua italiana.
   a. preferite
   b. preferiscono

5. Le mie amiche americane _A_ per l'Italia domani.
   a. partono
   b. partiamo

6. I miei amici italiani non _A_ la lingua inglese.
   a. capiscono
   b. capisce

7. Anche Lei pulisce sempre la casa?
   a. Sì, anch'io pulisco sempre la casa.
   b. Sì, anche lei pulisce sempre la casa.

8. Mio cugino ... parlare spagnolo molto bene.
   a. sa
   b. conosce

9. Io non ... tanta gente in questa città.
   a. so
   b. conosco

10. Signor Marchi, Lei ... dov'è via Nazionale.
   a. sa
   b. conosce

11. Noi ... un buon ristorante in via Nazionale.
   a. sappiamo
   b. conosciamo

12. Tu ... mio fratello?
   a. sai
   b. conosci

13. Chi ... la città di Firenze?
   a. sa
   b. conosce

14. Che fa la sorella di Maria?
   a. Fa il medico.
   b. Faccio l'avvocato.

15. Che tempo fa oggi?
   a. Facciamo caldo.
   b. Fa caldo.

C. *Now, choose the appropriate verb form, **a**, **b**, or **c**, according to sense.*

1. Ogni estate io … in Italia per le vacanze.
   a. vado
   b. esco
   c. vengo

2. Anche tu oggi non ~~B~~ con gli amici per andare al bar perché fa cattivo tempo, vero?
   a. vai
   b. esci
   c. vieni

3. Quando ~~D~~ il tuo amico? Sono già le otto e mezzo. È tardi!
   a. va
   b. esce
   c. viene

4. Noi … sempre al mare per le vacanze.
   a. andiamo
   b. usciamo
   c. veniamo

5. Con chi ~~B~~ per andare al cinema stasera?
   a. andate
   b. uscite
   c. venite

6. A che ora … qui?
   a. vanno
   b. escono
   c. vengono

7. Di solito, io … ~~B~~ i film italiani quando voglio andare al cinema.
   a. salgo
   b. scelgo
   c. tengo

8. Il suo amico ~~A~~ le scale in modo rapido.
   a. sale
   b. sceglie
   c. tiene

9. Noi ~~C~~ sempre le mani in tasca quando fa freddo.
   a. saliamo
   b. scegliamo
   c. teniamo

10. Marco e Maria, perché ~~B~~ sempre gli stessi film?
    a. salite
    b. scegliete
    c. tenete

D. *Missing from each of the following sentences are the verbs. These are given to you in their infinitive forms. Put each one, in its correct present indicative form, in each sentence according to the sense. Some of the verbs might be needed more than once.*

guardare, amare, ascoltare, pulire, capire, chiudere, vivere, arrivare, suonare, bere, dare, dire, fare

1. Mia sorella _suona_ il pianoforte molto bene.
2. I miei amici _amano_ l'Italia.
3. Adesso noi _viviamo_ in Italia perché desideriamo parlare la lingua italiana bene.
4. In questo momento loro _guardano_ la TV.
5. A che ora _arrivano_ gli amici di Paolo?
6. Ogni giorno io e mia moglie _puliamo_ la casa.
7. Anch'io _capisco_ un po' di francese.
8. Quando _____ quel negozio? _chiude_
9. A quest'ora mio fratello _ascolta_ sempre la radio.
10. I loro amici _bevono_ sempre alla salute di tutti.
11. Oggi tira vento e _fa_ molto freddo.
12. Le loro amiche _dicono_ sempre la verità.
13. Purtroppo, tuo cugino _dice_ sempre le bugie.
14. Voi, invece, _dite_ sempre la verità.
15. Dove _guardano_ quel film nuovo? _Danno_
16. Che tempo _fa_ oggi?
17. Loro _fanno_ sempre una passeggiata la domenica.
18. Franco, è vero che tu _fai_ il meccanico?

E. *Missing from each of the following sentences are the verbs **essere, esserci, avere, sapere,** and **conoscere.** Put each verb, in its correct present indicative form, in each sentence according to sense. Any one of these verbs might be needed more than once.*

1. Mio zio _ha_ molti anni.
2. Mio zio _è_ molto simpatico.
3. _C'è_ anche mio zio a casa tua, vero?
4. _Sono_ le nove e mezzo.
5. Noi _siamo_ di Firenze.
6. Anche voi _sapete_ molto alti. _siete_
7. Ma voi non _avete_ molta pazienza. _patience_
8. Mia zia _è_ un medico.
9. _C'è_ un medico qui?
10. Domani _è_ il quindici settembre, vero?

11. Signor Marchi, perché _ha_ paura?
12. Marco e Maria, quanti amici _hanno_? _avette_
13. Io non _conosco_ la città di Pisa.
14. Anche voi _sapete_ suonare la chitarra, non è vero?
15. È vero che tu _sai_ Paolo? _conosce_

F. *Answer each question with the appropriate form of* **essere, esserci,** *or* **ecco**.

Modello: Dov'è Paolo?
Ecco Paolo!

1. C'è Paolo? _Sì c'è Paolo_
2. Siete italiani, vero? _Sì, sono italiano_
3. Ci sono Marco e Mario? _Ecco Mario e Maria_ _Alessandro e Roberto._
4. Dove sono Marco e Maria? _Non so._
5. È martedì oggi? _Sì,_
6. Dov'è Maria? _Maria a Torino_
7. C'è Maria? _Sì, c'è Maria_

G. *Each question is given to you in a familiar form (singular or plural). Change each one to its corresponding polite form.*

Modello: Tu sai di dove sono io?
Lei sa di dove sono io?

1. Tu sai il nome di quella persona? _Lei sa il nome di quella persona_
2. Voi conoscete un buon ristorante in questa città? _same_
3. Anche tu sai suonare il pianoforte, vero? _Lei sa suonare_
4. Conoscete i genitori di quella persona? _conosce_
5. Sai il mio indirizzo? _Sapete il mio indirizzo?_
6. Conosci l'insegnante d'italiano? _Conosce_
7. Sapete chi sono io? _Sanno_
8. Cosa preferisci? _Cosa preferisce_
9. Dove abiti? _same_
10. Cosa leggete? _leggono_

H. *Write an e-mail in Italian! Here's what to say in it.*

Dear Maria,

How's it going? How old are you now? And how old are your brother and your sister? I am now a doctor. What car do you now have? Are you still very nice? You are certainly intelligent! I feel like phoning. Unfortunately, I always have little time. I am always very busy. Maybe you are right. I am too ambitious and I have little time for my friends.

Bye!

Francesca

Come stai? Adesso quanti anni hai? E Quanti anni ha il tuo fratello? Io sono una medico adesso. Adesso hai qualche macchina? Sei molto carina adesso. Sei intelligenti, certamente. Voglio telefonate. Forse sfortunamente. Sempre ho tempo pochi. Sempre sono occupato. Forse hai giusto. (ha ragione) Ho troppo ambiziosa e ho poca tempo per mie amici! Cia

I. **Cruciverba!**

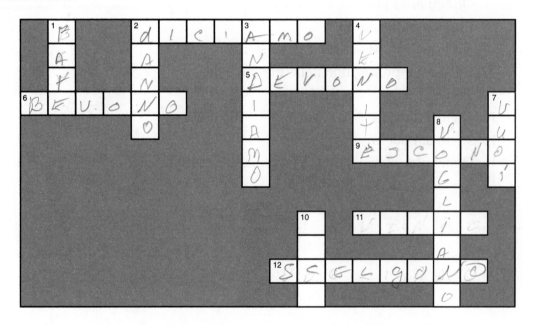

Orizzontali

2. Noi … sempre la verità
5. Loro … studiare di più.
6. Loro … sempre alla nostra salute.
9. Loro … ogni sabato sera.
11. Io … dalla voglia di andare al cinema.
12. I suoi amici … sempre i film italiani.

Verticali

1. Che cosa … voi stasera?
2. Loro si … del tu.
3. Noi … in Italia ogni estate.
4. … anche voi alla nostra festa?
7. Tu … uscire stasera con me?
8. Anche loro … comprare una macchina nuova.
10. Anche Sara … di solito il sabato, vero?

J. *If you are using this book in a classroom situation, answer the following questions in an appropriate manner from your personal perspective. Use complete sentences. If you are not using this book in a classroom situation, answer the best you can.*

Modello: Che cosa mangi generalmente per colazione?
    Per colazione, generalmente mangio un panino/una pasta/...

1. Che cosa mangi di solito per colazione?
2. Che cosa mangi di solito per pranzo?
3. Che cosa mangi di solito per cena?
4. Noleggi spesso i film? Quale tipo di film noleggi generalmente?
5. Quando esci con gli amici, chi paga generalmente?
6. Giochi a qualche sport? Se sì, quale?
7. Quanti anni hai?
8. Che macchina hai?
9. Tu hai molta pazienza? Perché sì/no?
10. Chi ha sempre ragione nella tua famiglia?
11. Tu dici sempre la verità?
12. A chi dai del Lei?
13. A chi dai del tu?
14. Quale film nuovo danno al cinema in questo momento?
15. Quando dici le bugie?
16. A chi dai la mano generalmente?

[handwritten answers]

Per colazione solito mangio cappuccino e farina d'avena
Per pranzo solito mangio una pasta.
Per cena solito pollo.
Generalmente noleggio un film italiano.
5. Quando esci con mi amici, ciascuno paga per se.
6. no gioco non sport, solo trovo, trovo, trovo.
7. Ho molto anni.
8. Ho una Corvette.
9. Ma no. Ho piccola pazienza.
10. Mamma ha sempre ragione, e noi non scommettitorela.
11. Forse, forse non, dico sempre la verità.
12. no sto.
13. ma non, non me.
14. nuovo film danno al cinema è "Dolce Vita".
15. Dico le bugie fare qualcuno sente meglio.
16. Generalmente, do mi mano a qualcuno. au bisogna.

4

The Past Indicative

Quanto Sai Già? — How Much Do You Know Already?

Can you fill in each blank with the correct past indicative tense form of the infinitive given to you in parentheses?

1. Ieri loro (**andare**) *sono andati* al cinema.
2. Il grande poeta Dante Alighieri (**scrivere**) *scrisse* La Divina Commedia nella prima parte del quattordicesimo secolo.
3. Mentre tu (**mangiare**) *mangiavi* ieri, io guardavo la partita alla televisione.
4. Io (**nascere**) *nacqui* in Italia.
5. I miei genitori (**venire**) *vennero* in America moltissimi anni fa.
6. Loro (**arrivare**) _____ già quando hai chiamato.
7. Chi (**dire**) _____ questo?
8. Che tempo (**fare**) _____ ieri?
9. Quante volte (**essere**) _____ in Italia tu?

The Past Participle
Il participio passato

Past indicative tenses such as the *present perfect* and the *pluperfect* are compound tenses, formed with an auxiliary verb plus the *past participle* of the verb, in that order:

(io) **ho mangiato** / *I have eaten, I ate, I did eat*

ho = auxiliary verb
mangiato = past participle

(lui) **è andato** / *he has gone, he went, he did go*

è = auxiliary verb
andato = past participle

To form the past participle of regular verbs, do the following.

- Drop the infinitive ending:

> parlare / *to speak* → parl-
> vendere / *to sell* → vend-
> finire / *to finish* → fin-

- Add the endings -ato, -uto, -ito, respectively:

> parlato / *spoken*
> venduto / *sold*
> finito / *finished*

The "i" of verbs such as **cominciare** and **mangiare** (Chapter 3) is retained in the formation of the past participle:

> cominciare / *to begin* → cominci- → cominciato / *begun*
> mangiare / *to eat* → mangi- → mangiato / *eaten*

In the case of the past participles of second conjugation verbs like **conoscere** an "i" must be added to indicate retention of the soft "c" sound:

> conoscere / *to know* → conosciuto / *known*

The following verbs have irregular past participles:

> accendere / *to turn on* → acceso / *turned on*
> apparire / *to appear* → apparso / *appeared*
> aprire / *to open* → aperto / *opened*
> bere / *to drink* → bevuto / *drunk*
> chiedere / *to ask for* → chiesto / *asked for*
> chiudere / *to close* → chiuso / *closed*
> coprire / *to cover* → coperto / *covered*
> correre / *to run* → corso / *run*
> dare / *to give* → dato / *given*
> dire / *to tell, to say* → detto / *told, said*
> essere / *to be* → stato / *been*

fare / *to do, to make*	➜	**fatto** / *done, made*
leggere / *to read*	➜	**letto** / *read*
mettere / *to put*	➜	**messo** / *put*
morire / *to die*	➜	**morto** / *died*
nascere / *to be born*	➜	**nato** / *born*
prendere / *to take*	➜	**preso** / *taken*
ridere / *to laugh*	➜	**riso** / *laughed*
rimanere / *to remain*	➜	**rimasto** / *remained*
rispondere / *to answer*	➜	**risposto** / *answered*
rompere / *to break*	➜	**rotto** / *broken*
scegliere / *to choose*	➜	**scelto** / *chosen*
scoprire / *to discover*	➜	**scoperto** / *discovered*
scrivere / *to write*	➜	**scritto** / *written*
soffrire / *to suffer*	➜	**sofferto** / *suffered*
vedere / *to see*	➜	**visto** / *seen*
venire / *to come*	➜	**venuto** / *come*
vivere / *to live*	➜	**vissuto** / *lived*

QUICK PRACTICE 1

Give the past participles of the following verbs.

1. noleggiare — *noleggiato*
2. arrivare — *arrivato*
3. conoscere — *conosciuto*
4. dormire — *dormito*
5. accendere — *acceso*
6. ridere — *riso*
7. rimanere — *rimasto*
8. nascere — *nato*
9. apparire — *apparso*
10. aprire — *aperto*
11. morire — *morto*
12. bere — *bevuto*
13. mettere — *messo*
14. chiedere — *chiesto*
15. chiudere — *chiuso*
16. coprire — *coperto*
17. leggere — *letto*
18. fare — *fatto*
19. essere — *stato*
20. dire — *detto*
21. dare — *dato*
22. correre — *corso*
23. rispondere — *risposto*
24. rompere — *rotto*
25. vivere — *vissuto*
26. venire — *venuto*
27. scegliere — *scelto*
28. scoprire — *scoperto*
29. soffrire — *sofferto*
30. scrivere — *scritto*

The Present Perfect
Il passato prossimo

The *present perfect tense* allows you to express simple actions completed at the present time. There are two auxiliary verbs: **avere** / *to have* and **essere** / *to be*. In the present perfect, these verbs are conjugated in the present indicative (see Chapter 3).

Verbs Conjugated with avere			
First Conjugation: parlare / *to speak*			
(io)	ho	parlato	*I have spoken, I spoke*
(tu)	hai	parlato	*you (fam.) have spoken, you spoke*
(lui/lei/Lei)	ha	parlato	*he, she, you (pol.) has/have spoken, he, she, you spoke*
(noi)	abbiamo	parlato	*we have spoken, we spoke*
(voi)	avete	parlato	*you have spoken, you spoke*
(loro)	hanno	parlato	*they have spoken, they spoke*
Second Conjugation: vendere / *to sell*			
(io)	ho	venduto	*I have sold, I sold*
(tu)	hai	venduto	*you (fam.) have sold, you sold*
(lui/lei/Lei)	ha	venduto	*he, she, you (pol.) has/have sold, he, she, you sold*
(noi)	abbiamo	venduto	*we have sold, we sold*
(voi)	avete	venduto	*you have sold, you sold*
(loro)	hanno	venduto	*they have sold, they sold*
Third Conjugation: finire / *to finish*			
(io)	ho	finito	*I have finished, I finished*
(tu)	hai	finito	*you (fam.) have finished, you finished*
(lui/lei/Lei)	ha	finito	*he, she, you (pol.) has/have finished, he, she, you finished*
(noi)	abbiamo	finito	*we have finished, we finished*
(voi)	avete	finito	*you have finished, you finished*
(loro)	hanno	finito	*they have finished, they finished*

Examples:

Maria ha venduto la sua macchina. / *Mary sold her car.*
Ieri ho parlato al signor Verdi. / *Yesterday I spoke to Mr. Verdi.*
Loro hanno dormito troppo ieri. / *They slept too much yesterday.*
Ho già mangiato. / *I have already eaten.*

The past participle of verbs conjugated with **essere** agrees in number and gender with the subject

Alessandro è partito stamani. / *Alexander left this morning.*
Anche Sara è partita stamani. / *Sara also left this morning.*

Verbs Conjugated with essere			
First Conjugation: arrivare / *to arrive*			
(io)	sono	arrivato/a	*I have arrived, I arrived*
(tu)	sei	arrivato/a	*you (fam.) have arrived, you arrived*
(lui)	è	arrivato	
(lei)	è	arrivata	*he, she, you (pol.) has/have arrived, he, she, you arrived*
(Lei)	è	arrivato/a	
(noi)	siamo	arrivati/e	*we have arrived, we arrived*
(voi)	siete	arrivati/e	*you have arrived, you arrived*
(loro)	sono	arrivati/e	*they have arrived, they arrived*
Second Conjugation: cadere / *to fall*			
(io)	sono	caduto/a	*I have fallen, I fell*
(tu)	sei	caduto/a	*you (fam.) have fallen, you fell*
(lui)	è	caduto	
(lei)	è	caduta	*he, she, you (pol.) has/have fallen, he, she, you fell*
(Lei)	è	caduto/a	
(noi)	siamo	caduti/e	*we have fallen, we fell*
(voi)	siete	caduti/e	*you have fallen, you fell*
(loro)	sono	caduti/e	*they have fallen, they fell*
Third Conjugation: uscire / *to go out*			
(io)	sono	uscito/a	*I have gone out, I went out*
(tu)	sei	uscito/a	*you (fam.) have gone out, you went out*
(lui)	è	uscito	
(lei)	è	uscita	*he, she, you (pol.) has/have gone out, he, she, you went out*
(Lei)	è	uscito/a	
(noi)	siamo	usciti/e	*we have gone out, we went out*
(voi)	siete	usciti/e	*you have gone out, you went out*
(loro)	sono	usciti/e	*they have gone out, they went out*

Examples:

Il nostro amico è arrivato ieri. / *Our friend arrived yesterday.*
Tua cugina è arrivata la settimana scorsa. / *Your cousin (f.) arrived last week.*
Quando siete caduti? / *When did you (pl.) fall down?*
Quando è partita, signora Verdi? / *When did you leave Mrs. Verdi?*

Recall the verb form **esserci** / *to be there* (Chapter 2). This is used in the past to acknowledge that something or someone has been or was somewhere. It has the following two forms in the present perfect:

Singular
C'è stato l'insegnante?
Has the teacher been here/there?

Plural
Ci sono stati gli insegnanti?
Have the teachers been here/there?

When do you use **avere** or **essere**? The best strategy is to assume that most verbs are conjugated with **avere** (which is true!), and then memorize the verbs that are conjugated with **essere**. A rule of thumb is as follows: If the verb answers the question *what*, it requires **avere**, while if it answers the question *where* or *when*, it requires **essere**.

The most common verbs conjugated with **essere** are as follows:

andare	*to go*
apparire (apparso)	*to appear*
arrivare	*to arrive*
cadere	*to fall*
correre (corso)	*to run*
diventare	*to become*
entrare	*to enter*
essere (stato)	*to be*
morire (morto)	*to die*
nascere (nato)	*to be born*
partire	*to leave*
salire	*to climb, to go up*
sembrare	*to seem*
stare (stato)	*to stay*
tornare	*to go back, to return*
uscire	*to go out*
venire (venuto)	*to come*
vivere (vissuto)	*to live*

With a modal verb (**potere, dovere, volere**), the general rule is to select the auxiliary of the following infinitive:

Verb Conjugated with avere	Verb Conjugated with essere
ho voluto chiamare / *I wanted to call*	sono voluto/a andare / *I wanted to go*
hanno potuto chiamare / *they were able to call*	sono potuti/e andare / *they were able to go*
hai dovuto chiamare / *you had to call*	sei dovuto/a andare / *you had to go*

However, in contemporary conversational usage, the tendency is to use only **avere** with modal verbs:

ho voluto andare   *rather than*   **sono voluto / a andare**

In the case of the verbs **correre** and **vivere** the auxiliary is **essere**, unless they are used as transitive verbs, in which case they are conjugated with **avere**:

Ho corso tutto il giorno. / *I ran the whole day.*
Sono corso per aiutare. / *I ran to help.*

Ho vissuto una vita intera in Italia. / *I lived an entire life in Italy.*
Sono vissuto in America. / *I lived in America.*

With the verbs **nevicare** / *to snow* and **piovere** / *to rain* either auxiliary can be used:

Ieri ha/è nevicato. / *It snowed yesterday.*

Finally, "impersonal" verbs are all conjugated with **essere**. These are verbs that have only third person forms.

durare / *to last*
Quel film è durato tre ore. / *That movie lasted three hours.*

costare / *to cost*
Quanto sono costate le mele? / *How much did the apples cost?*

succedere / *to happen*
Quando è successo? / *When did it happen?*

Remember that third person forms also apply to the polite address. Choose the ending of the past participle according to the sex of the person you are addressing.

Signor Verdi, è caduto Lei? / *Mr. Verdi, did you fall?*
Signora Verdi, è caduta Lei? / *Mrs. Verdi, did you fall?*

Basically, the present perfect allows you to express the equivalent of English forms such as *I have spoken, you have seen, he has studied,* etc. It is also translated as *I spoke, you saw, he studied,* etc. Simply assume that any immediate past tense is rendered by the **passato prossimo**, and most of the time you will be correct.

> **TIP**
> The present perfect is often used with words and expressions such as:
>
> appena / *just*
> fa / *ago*
> ieri / *yesterday*
> scorso/a / *last (week, etc.)*

A few verbs change their meaning when used in this tense. The two most common ones are:

	Present	Past
conoscere	*to know (a person/place)*	*to meet (for the first time)*
	Io conosco Maria molto bene. / *I know Mary very well.*	**Io ho conosciuto Maria ieri per la prima volta.** / *I met Mary yesterday for the first time.*
sapere	*to know*	*to find out/learn*
	Io so che vieni alla festa. / *I know that you are coming to the party.*	**Io ho saputo che vieni alla festa.** / *I found out that you are coming to the party.*

Finally, adverbs such as **già** / *already*, **appena** / *just*, and **ancora** / *yet* are placed generally between the auxiliary and the past participle:

Lei è già uscita. / *She has already gone out.*
Noi non abbiamo ancora finito di lavorare. / *We haven't finished working yet.*

6-6

QUICK PRACTICE 2

Say the following in Italian.

1. **io** *(I)*...
   a. ate all the pizza yesterday. *Ho mangiato tutta pizza ieri*
   b. saw Maria last month. *Ho visto Maria mese scorso*
   c. have not yet finished. *non ho finito anche*
   d. went out last night. *Sono uscita ieri sera, e due*
   e. have already gone to see that movie. *Sono ~~to~~ già uscito quella film* *Sono*

2. **tu** *(you)*...
   a. met Maria yesterday for the first time. *Tu hai conosciuto Maria ieri la prima volta*
   b. saw Paola. *Tu hai avisto Paola.*
   c. had to study yesterday. *Tu hai veduto studiare ieri*
   d. lived in Italy two years ago. *Tu (hai) vissuto in Italia due anni fa.*
   e. went downtown last week. *Tu sei andato/a settimana scorsa.*

3. **lui** *(he)*…
   a. wanted to go two years ago. *Lui ha voluto andato due anni scorsa.*
   b. ran to help. *Lui è corso per aiutare.*
   c. found out that you are coming to the party. *Lui ha scoperto a la festa.*
   d. arrived a few minutes ago. *Lui è arrivato pochi minuti.*
   e. has already finished. *Lui già ha finito*

4. **lei** *(she)*…
   a. wanted to go two years ago. *Lei ha voluto andato due anni scorsa.*
   b. ran to help. *Lei è corso per aiutare.* *what gender?*
   c. found out that you are coming to the party.
   d. arrived a few minutes ago. *arrivata*
   e. has already finished.

5. **noi** *(we)*…
   a. have done that already. *noi già*
   b. said that yesterday. *noi abbiamo*
   c. have given all our money to Maria. *noi abbiamo dato nostri tutti saldi a Maria*
   d. have not been to Italy yet. *noi non ci siamo andato a Italia non ancora.*
   e. went out last night. *noi siamo uscita la sera scorsa.*

6. **voi** *(you)*…
   a. have done that already. *voi siete fato già*
   b. said that yesterday. *voi siete detto ieri*
   c. have given all your money to Maria. *voi siete dato tutti soldi a Maria*
   d. have not been to Italy yet. *voi non siete andate a Italia ancora.*
   e. went out last night. *voi siete uscite scorsa sera.*

7. **i miei amici** *(my friends)*…
   a. wanted to go two years ago. *Loro hanno voluto andare due anni fa.*
   b. ran to help. *Sono corsi per aiutare*
   c. found out that you are coming to the party. *Loro hanno saputo che vieni alla festa*
   d. arrived a few minutes ago. *Sono arrivati poci minuti*
   e. have already finished. *Loro hanno finito già* *m. pl.*

8. **le mie amiche** *(my friends)*…
   a. wanted to go two years ago.
   b. ran to help. *Sono corse per aiutare*
   c. found out that you are coming to the party. *Loro hanno saputo che vieni alla festa,*
   d. arrived a few minutes ago. *Sono arrivati poci minuti*
   e. have already finished. *Hanno*

Stop 6-6

The Imperfect
L'imperfetto

As we have just seen, the present perfect allows you, in essence, to refer to a finished past action. This is an action that has started and ended.

Ieri ho dormito solo due ore. / *Yesterday I slept only two hours.*

If, however, it is necessary to refer to an action that continued for an indefinite period of time, then the *imperfect* tense is called for.

Ieri, mentre io dormivo, tu guardavi la TV. / *Yesterday, while I was sleeping, you watched TV.*

The imperfect is also used to refer to habitual or repeated actions in the past, and to describe the characteristics of people and things as they used to be.

Quando ero giovane, suonavo il pianoforte. / *When I was young, I used to play the piano.*
Da giovane, Sara aveva i capelli biondi. / *As a young woman, Sarah had (used to have) blonde hair.*

- Drop the **-re** from the infinitive endings **-are, -ere, -ire**:

parlare / *to speak*	➔	**parla-**
scrivere / *to write*	➔	**scrive-**
finire / *to finish*	➔	**fini-**

- Add the following endings according to person and number:

(io)	-vo
(tu)	-vi
(lui/lei/Lei)	-va
(noi)	-vamo
(voi)	-vate
(loro)	-vano

Here's the result:

First Conjugation: parlare / to speak

(io)	parlavo	*I was speaking, I used to speak*
(tu)	parlavi	*you (fam.) were speaking, you used to speak*
(lui/lei/Lei)	parlava	*he, she, you (pol.) was/were speaking, he, she, you used to speak*
(noi)	parlavamo	*we were speaking, we used to speak*
(voi)	parlavate	*you were speaking, you used to speak*
(loro)	parlavano	*they were speaking, they used to speak*

Second Conjugation: scrivere / to write

(io)	scrivevo	*I was writing, I used to write*
(tu)	scrivevi	*you (fam.) were writing, you used to write*
(lui/lei/Lei)	scriveva	*he, she, you (pol.) was/were writing, he, she, you used to write*
(noi)	scrivevamo	*we were writing, we used to write*
(voi)	scrivevate	*you were writing, you used to write*
(loro)	scrivevano	*they were writing, they used to write*

Third Conjugation: finire / to finish

(io)	finivo	*I was finishing, I used to finish*
(tu)	finivi	*you (fam.) were finishing, you used to finish*
(lui/lei/Lei)	finiva	*he, she, you (pol.) was/were finishing, he, she, you used to finish*
(noi)	finivamo	*we were finishing, we used to finish*
(voi)	finivate	*you were finishing, you used to finish*
(loro)	finivano	*they were finishing, they used to finish*

Examples:

Mentre tu studiavi, tuo fratello suonava il violoncello. / *While you were studying, your brother was playing the cello.*

Da giovane, mio cugino scriveva ogni mese. / *As a youth, my cousin used to write every month.*

Quando andava a scuola, Maria studiava molto. / *When she was going to school, Mary used to study a lot.*

> **TIP**
> Be careful when you pronounce the third person plural forms! The accent is placed on the first vowel of the ending:
>
> parlávano
> scrivévano
> finívano

You might get confused when comparing English and Italian past tense usage. This is because sometimes English uses a perfect tense that is normally covered by the imperfect in Italian.

You must therefore always look for clues among the other words in a sentence to determine whether the imperfect should or should not be used. Words such as **mentre** / *while*, **sempre** / *always*, **di solito** / *usually*, etc. generally require the use of the imperfect:

Mentre dormivo, tu guardavi la TV. / *While I slept or was sleeping, you watched/ were watching TV.*

In the case of verbs such as **cominciare** and **mangiare** (Chapter 3) the "i" is retained in the formation of the stem:

cominciare / *to begin* → **comincia-**		
(io)	cominciavo	*I was beginning, I used to begin*
(tu)	cominciavi	*you (fam.) were beginning, you used to begin*
(lui/lei/Lei)	cominciava	*he, she, you (pol.) was/were beginning, he, she, you used to begin*
(noi)	cominciavamo	*we were beginning, we used to begin*
(voi)	cominciavate	*you were beginning, you used to begin*
(loro)	cominciavano	*they were beginning, they used to begin*

mangiare / *to eat* → **mangia-**		
(io)	mangiavo	*I was eating, I used to eat*
(tu)	mangiavi	*you (fam.) were eating, you used to eat*
(lui/lei/Lei)	mangiava	*he, she, you (pol.) was/were eating, he, she, you used to eat*
(noi)	mangiavamo	*we were eating, we used to eat*
(voi)	mangiavate	*you were eating, you used to eat*
(loro)	mangiavano	*they were eating, they used to eat*

The verb form **esserci** / *to be there* has again only two forms, which are used in the imperfect to acknowledge that something or someone *was* somewhere:

Anche Maria, c'era alla festa. / *Mary, too, was at the party.*
Ma loro non c'erano. / *But they were not there.*

Good news!
Very few Italian verbs are irregular in the imperfect indicative. Here are the most common ones:

bere / to drink

(io)	bevevo	I was drinking, I used to drink
(tu)	bevevi	you (fam.) were drinking, you used to drink
(lui/lei/Lei)	beveva	he, she, you (pol.) was/were drinking, he, she, you used to drink
(noi)	bevevamo	we were drinking, we used to drink
(voi)	bevevate	you were drinking, you used to drink
(loro)	bevevano	they were drinking, they used to drink

dare / to give

(io)	davo	I was giving, I used to give
(tu)	davi	you (fam.) were giving, you used to give
(lui/lei/Lei)	dava	he, she, you (pol.) was/were giving, he, she, you used to give
(noi)	davamo	we were giving, we used to give
(voi)	davate	you were giving, you used to give
(loro)	davano	they were giving, they used to give

dire / to tell, to say

(io)	dicevo	I was saying, I used to say
(tu)	dicevi	you (fam.) were saying, you used to say
(lui/lei/Lei)	diceva	he, she, you (pol.) was/were saying, he, she, you used to say
(noi)	dicevamo	we were saying, we used to say
(voi)	dicevate	you were saying, you used to say
(loro)	dicevano	they were saying, they used to say

essere / to be

(io)	ero	I was, I used to be
(tu)	eri	you (fam.) were, you used to be
(lui/lei/Lei)	era	he, she, you (pol.) was/were, he, she, you used to be
(noi)	eravamo	we were, we used to be
(voi)	eravate	you were, you used to be
(loro)	erano	they were, they used to be

fare / to do, to make

(io)	facevo	I was making, I used to make
(tu)	facevi	you (fam.) were making, you used to make
(lui/lei/Lei)	faceva	he, she, you (pol.) was/were making, he, she, you used to make
(noi)	facevamo	we were making, we used to make
(voi)	facevate	you were making, you used to make
(loro)	facevano	they were making, they used to make

stare / to stay, to be

(io)	stavo	I was staying, I used to stay
(tu)	stavi	you (fam.) were staying, you used to stay
(lui/lei/Lei)	stava	he, she, you (pol.) was/were staying, he, she, you used to stay
(noi)	stavamo	we were staying, we used to stay
(voi)	stavate	you were staying, you used to stay
(loro)	stavano	they were staying, they used to stay

6-13
Spesso also
means "thick"

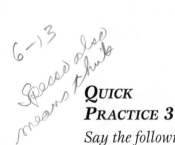

QUICK PRACTICE 3

Say the following in Italian.

Da bambino/a *(As a child)* / **Da bambini/e** *(As children)*…

1. I used to play the piano. *Da bambino Suonavo la pianoforte*
2. you (*fam., sing.*) used to sing very well. *Da bambino cantavi benissimo*
3. my brother used to go the movies often. *mi fratello andava la cinema*
4. you (*fam., pl.*) used to watch TV a lot. *Da bambini guardavate spesso. molto.*
5. his friends (*m.*) used to play soccer. *Da bambini suo amici suonavano il calcio*

6. I used to eat pasta often. *Da bambina mangiavo spesso.* 6-13

7. Mr. Tommasi used to go to the beach. *Da bambino Signore Tommasi andava ala spiaggia*

8. there was always a lot to do (**da fare**). *Da bambina faceva sempre da fare*

9. there were many things to do. *Da Bambina*

Now, give the imperfect indicative forms of the verbs as indicated.

10. **io...**
    a. stare *stavo*
    b. fare *facevo*
    c. essere *ero*
    d. dire *dicevo*
    e. dare *davo*
    f. bere *bevevo*
    g. mangiare *mangiavo*
    h. cominciare *cominciavo*

11. **tu...** *4 sentences from below (the rest)*
    a. stare *Tu stavi mentre andavo.*
    b. fare
    c. essere
    d. dire
    e. dare
    f. bere
    g. mangiare
    h. cominciare

12. **quell'uomo...**
    a. stare
    b. fare
    c. essere
    d. dire
    e. dare
    f. bere
    g. mangiare
    h. cominciare *Quell'uomo cominciava ad innamorarsi di bella signorina*

13. **quelle donne...**
    a. stare
    b. fare
    c. essere
    d. dire
    e. dare
    f. bere *quelle donne bevevano molto troppo essere bella*
    g. mangiare
    h. cominciare

14. noi...
    a. stare
    b. fare
    c. essere
    d. dire
    e. dare
    f. bere
    g. mangiare *noi mangiavamo come un lupo*
    h. cominciare

15. voi...
    a. stare
    b. fare
    c. essere
    d. dire
    e. dare *voi lavate soldi mentre davo tempo.*
    f. bere
    g. mangiare *Roberto d'Angelo non mangiavate molti, come alessandro,*
    h. cominciare

The Past Absolute
Il passato remoto

The *past absolute* has many of the same uses as the present perfect. Specifically, it allows you to talk about finished actions that occurred in the distant past.

First conjugation:

- Drop the infinitive ending -are:

    parlare / *to speak*   →   **parl-**

- Add the following endings to the stem according to person and number:

(io)	-ai
(tu)	-asti
(lui/lei/Lei)	-ò
(noi)	-ammo
(voi)	-aste
(loro)	-arono

- Here's the result:

First Conjugation: parlare / *to speak*		
(io)	parlai	*I spoke*
(tu)	parlasti	*you (fam.) spoke*
(lui/lei/Lei)	parlò	*he, she, you (pol.) spoke*
(noi)	parlammo	*we spoke*
(voi)	parlaste	*you spoke*
(loro)	parlarono	*they spoke*

Second conjugation:

- Drop the infinitive ending -ere:

  vendere / *to sell* ➔ vend-

- Add the following endings to the stem according to person and number:

(io)	-ei/-etti
(tu)	-esti
(lui/lei/Lei)	-é/-ette
(noi)	-emmo
(voi)	-este
(loro)	-erono/-ettero

- Here's the result:

Second Conjugation: vendere / *to sell*		
(io)	vendei/vendetti	*I sold*
(tu)	vendesti	*you (fam.) sold*
(lui/lei/Lei)	vendé/vendette	*he, she, you (pol.) sold*
(noi)	vendemmo	*we sold*
(voi)	vendeste	*you sold*
(loro)	venderono/vendettero	*they sold*

Third conjugation:

- Drop the infinitive ending -ire:

  finire / *to finish* ➔ fin-

- Add the following endings to the stem according to person and number:

(io)	-ii
(tu)	-isti
(lui/lei/Lei)	-ì
(noi)	-immo
(voi)	-iste
(loro)	-irono

- Here's the result:

Third Conjugation: finire / *to finish*		
(io)	finii	*I finished*
(tu)	finisti	*you (fam.) finished*
(lui/lei/Lei)	finì	*he, she, you (pol.) finished*
(noi)	finimmo	*we finished*
(voi)	finiste	*you finished*
(loro)	finirono	*they finished*

In the case of verbs such as **cominciare** and **mangiare** the "i" is retained in the formation of the stem:

cominciare / *to begin* → cominci-		
(io)	cominciai	*I began*
(tu)	cominciasti	*you (fam.) began*
(lui/lei/Lei)	cominciò	*he, she, you (pol.) began*
(noi)	cominciammo	*we began*
(voi)	cominciaste	*you began*
(loro)	cominciarono	*they began*

mangiare / *to eat* → mangi-		
(io)	mangiai	*I ate*
(tu)	mangiasti	*you (fam.) ate*
(lui/lei/Lei)	mangiò	*he, she, you (pol.) ate*
(noi)	mangiammo	*we ate*
(voi)	mangiaste	*you ate*
(loro)	mangiarono	*they ate*

Examples:

I miei genitori tornarono in Italia nel 1989. / *My parents returned to Italy in 1989.*
Marco Polo portò tanti tesori indietro con sé. / *Marco Polo brought back many treasures.*
Dopo che vendé (vendette) la macchina, lui comprò una motocicletta. / *After he sold the car, he bought a motorcycle.*
Finirono quel lavoro tanto tempo fa. / *They finished that job a long time ago.*

The past absolute cannot be used with temporal adverbs such as **già** / *already*, **poco fa** / *a little while ago*, etc., which limit the action to the immediate past (occurring within less than twenty-four hours). Only the present perfect can be used in such cases.

> **Alessandro è arrivato poco tempo fa.** / *Alexander arrived a little while ago.*
> **Ho già telefonato a lei.** / *I have already phoned her.*

Outside of this restriction, the past absolute can be used (in most situations) as an alternative to the present perfect.

> **TIPS**
> Again, be careful when you pronounce third person plural forms! The accent is placed on the first vowel of the ending:
>
> parlárono
> vendérono
> finírono

Present Perfect	Past Absolute
Maria è andata in Italia nel 1994. / *Mary went to Italy in 1994.*	**Maria andò in Italia nel 1994.**
Ieri ti ho telefonato alle due. / *Yesterday I phoned you at two.*	**Ieri ti telefonai alle due.**

The past absolute is, however, the only true "literary" past tense. It is used in particular in the narration of historical events.

> **Colombo arrivò nel Nuovo Mondo nel 1492.** / *Columbus arrived in the New World in 1492.*
> **Mozart morì molto giovane.** / *Mozart died very young.*

There are quite a number of irregular verbs in the past absolute. For many of these the general pattern goes as follows. Take, for example, **avere** / *to have*.

- The first person singular is irregular and provides the form for constructing the irregular stem:

> **ebbi** / *I had*   ➜   *stem =* **ebb-**

- This stem applies to the third person singular and plural forms:

ebbe / *he, she, you (pol.) had*
ebbero / *they had*

- The other forms are regular. Here's the complete conjugation:

(io)	ebbi	*I had*
(tu)	avesti (regular)	*you (fam.) had*
(lui/lei/Lei)	ebbe	*he, she, you (pol.) had*
(noi)	avemmo (regular)	*we had*
(voi)	aveste (regular)	*you had*
(loro)	ebbero	*they had*

Here are other common verbs conjugated according to this pattern:

conoscere / *to know, to be familiar with, to meet (for the first time)*		
(io)	conobbi	*I knew*
(tu)	conoscesti (regular)	*you (fam.) knew*
(lui/lei/Lei)	conobbe	*he, she, you (pol.) knew*
(noi)	conoscemmo (regular)	*we knew*
(voi)	conosceste (regular)	*you knew*
(loro)	conobbero	*they knew*

leggere / *to read*		
(io)	lessi	*I read*
(tu)	leggesti (regular)	*you (fam.) read*
(lui/lei/Lei)	lesse	*he, she, you (pol.) read*
(noi)	leggemmo (regular)	*we read*
(voi)	leggeste (regular)	*you read*
(loro)	lessero	*they read*

sapere / *to know*		
(io)	seppi	*I knew*
(tu)	sapesti (regular)	*you (fam.) knew*
(lui/lei/Lei)	seppe	*he, she, you (pol.) knew*
(noi)	sapemmo (regular)	*we knew*
(voi)	sapeste (regular)	*you knew*
(loro)	seppero	*they knew*

scrivere / *to write*

(io)	scrissi	*I wrote*
(tu)	scrivesti (regular)	*you (fam.) wrote*
(lui/lei/Lei)	scrisse	*he, she, you (pol.) wrote*
(noi)	scrivemmo (regular)	*we wrote*
(voi)	scriveste (regular)	*you wrote*
(loro)	scrissero	*they wrote*

venire / *to come*

(io)	venni	*I came*
(tu)	venisti (regular)	*you (fam.) came*
(lui/lei/Lei)	venne	*he, she, you (pol.) came*
(noi)	venimmo (regular)	*we came*
(voi)	veniste (regular)	*you came*
(loro)	vennero	*they came*

volere / *to want*

(io)	volli	*I wanted*
(tu)	volesti (regular)	*you (fam.) wanted*
(lui/lei/Lei)	volle	*he, she, you (pol.) wanted*
(noi)	volemmo (regular)	*we wanted*
(voi)	voleste (regular)	*you wanted*
(loro)	vollero	*they wanted*

Other common verbs following this pattern are the following. Only their first person singular forms are given here, since you can now figure out the remaining forms on your own:

apparire / *to appear*	→	apparvi (apparii) / *I appeared*
aprire / *to open*	→	apersi (aprii) / *I opened*
chiudere / *to close*	→	chiusi / *I closed*
comprendere / *to comprehend*	→	compresi / *I comprehended*
coprire / *to cover*	→	copersi (coprii) / *I covered*
correre / *to run*	→	corsi / *I ran*
dipingere / *to paint*	→	dipinsi / *I painted*
dolere / *to ache*	→	dolsi / *I ached*
decidere / *to decide*	→	decisi / *I decided*
mettere / *to put*	→	misi / *I put*
nascere / *to be born*	→	nacqui / *I was born*
prendere / *to take*	→	presi / *I took*

ridere / *to laugh*	→	**risi** / *I laughed*	
rimanere / *to remain*	→	**rimasi** / *I remained*	
rompere / *to break*	→	**ruppi** / *I broke*	
scegliere / *to choose*	→	**scelsi** / *I chose*	
scoprire / *to discover*	→	**scopersi (scoprii)** / *I discovered*	
soffrire / *to suffer*	→	**soffersi (soffrii)** / *I suffered*	
tenere / *to keep, to hold*	→	**tenni** / *I kept, I held*	
valere / *to be worthwhile*	→	**valsi** / *I was worth (something)*	
vedere / *to see*	→	**vidi** / *I saw*	
vincere / *to win*	→	**vinsi** / *I won*	
vivere / *to live*	→	**vissi** / *I lived*	

The following verbs are completely irregular:

bere / *to drink*			
(io)	**bevvi (bevetti)**	*I drank*	
(tu)	**bevesti**	*you (fam.) drank*	
(lui/lei/Lei)	**bevve (bevette)**	*he, she, you (pol.) drank*	
(noi)	**bevemmo**	*we drank*	
(voi)	**beveste**	*you drank*	
(loro)	**bevvero (bevettero)**	*they drank*	

dare / *to give*			
(io)	**diedi**	*I gave*	
(tu)	**desti**	*you (fam.) gave*	
(lui/lei/Lei)	**diede**	*he, she, you (pol.) gave*	
(noi)	**demmo**	*we gave*	
(voi)	**deste**	*you gave*	
(loro)	**diedero**	*they gave*	

dire / *to tell, to say*			
(io)	**dissi**	*I said*	
(tu)	**dicesti**	*you (fam.) said*	
(lui/lei/Lei)	**disse**	*he, she, you (pol.) said*	
(noi)	**dicemmo**	*we said*	
(voi)	**diceste**	*you said*	
(loro)	**dissero**	*they said*	

essere / to be

(io)	**fui**	*I was*
(tu)	**fosti**	*you (fam.) were*
(lui/lei/Lei)	**fu**	*he, she, you (pol.) was/were*
(noi)	**fummo**	*we were*
(voi)	**foste**	*you were*
(loro)	**furono**	*they were*

fare / to do, to make

(io)	**feci**	*I made*
(tu)	**facesti**	*you (fam.) made*
(lui/lei/Lei)	**fece**	*he, she, you (pol.) made*
(noi)	**facemmo**	*we made*
(voi)	**faceste**	*you made*
(loro)	**fecero**	*they made*

stare / to stay

(io)	**stetti**	*I stayed*
(tu)	**stesti**	*you (fam.) stayed*
(lui/lei/Lei)	**stette**	*he, she, you (pol.) stayed*
(noi)	**stemmo**	*we stayed*
(voi)	**steste**	*you stayed*
(loro)	**stettero**	*they stayed*

6-20

Quick Practice 4

Say the following in Italian using the past absolute tense.

Molti anni fa ...

1. my parents arrived from Italy.
2. I spent (**passare**) a year in Rome.
3. you (*fam., pl.*) went to Italy.
4. her son became an engineer (**un ingegnere**).
5. his daughter finished studying medicine (**medicina**).

The Past Indicative **89**

6. we discovered Italy. *Scoprimmo d'Italia*

7. our friends worked for that company (**quella ditta**). *(lavoravano)*
   noi amici lavorano per quella ditta.

Give the equivalent past absolute form of each present perfect form.

Modello: io ho bevuto
             io bevvi

sentence for each one

8. io...
   a. ho bevuto   *bevvi Io bevvi del vino di locale.*
   b. sono stato *Io fui felice essere qui.*
   c. ho fatto   *Feci la decisione stare in Italia*
   d. ho detto   *Dissi direzioni due*
   e. sono vissuto *Vissi a Cincinnati quando fui giovane.*

9. tu...
   a. hai vinto   *Vincesti la lotteria una volta.*
   b. hai visto   *vedesti tua nonna.*
   c. hai tenuto *Tenesti il cerchio de la nonna.*
   d. hai messo   *mettesti il deposito per la casa.*
   e. sei nato   *nacesti un secolo fa.*

10. lui/lei...
    a. ha cominciato *Comincio il litigio, non me.*
    b. ha avuto   *Ebbe un formaggiare buono.*
    c. ha conosciuto *Conobbe sua marito a Venezia.*
    d. ha letto   *Lesse racconto a la bambina.*
    e. ha saputo   *Seppe guidare la machina.*

11. noi...
    a. abbiamo deciso   *decidemmo di fare noi compiti.*
    b. abbiamo finito   *finimmo noi compiti.*
    c. siamo andati   *Andammo a modeno tempo fa.*
    d. abbiamo venduto *vendemmo noi biglietto*
    e. abbiamo mangiato *mangiammo male a McDonalds*

12. voi...
    you drank red water and thought it was wine.
    a. avete bevuto *Beveste aqua rosso e pensaste fode vino*
    b. avete dato   *Deste una bella festa.*
    c. avete detto   *Diceste sbagliato parole.*
    d. siete stati   *faste (steste) molte lontano da casa.*
    e. avete fatto   *Faceste la torta.*

13. loro...
    a. hanno scritto *Scrissero un canto per l'orchestra.*
    b. sono venuti   *vennero dopo noi mangiammo*
    c. hanno voluto   *Vollero comprare noi casa.*
    d. hanno aperto   *aprirono Apersero il vino quando arrivarono* OK
    e. hanno chiuso   *Chiusero la porta perche fece freddo.*

The Pluperfect
Il trapassato prossimo

The pluperfect is a compound tense. As such, it is conjugated with an auxiliary verb, either **avere** or **essere**, in the imperfect tense and the past participle of the verb. So, you know everything you need to know to conjugate verbs in the pluperfect.

Examples:

Verbs Conjugated with avere			
First Conjugation: parlare / *to speak*			
(io)	avevo	parlato	*I had spoken*
(tu)	avevi	parlato	*you (fam.) had spoken*
(lui/lei/Lei)	aveva	parlato	*he, she, you (pol.) had spoken*
(noi)	avevamo	parlato	*we had spoken*
(voi)	avevate	parlato	*you had spoken*
(loro)	avevano	parlato	*they had spoken*
Second Conjugation: vendere / *to sell*			
(io)	avevo	venduto	*I had sold*
(tu)	avevi	venduto	*you (fam.) had sold*
(lui/lei/Lei)	aveva	venduto	*he, she, you (pol.) had sold*
(noi)	avevamo	venduto	*we had sold*
(voi)	avevate	venduto	*you had sold*
(loro)	avevano	venduto	*they had sold*
Third Conjugation: finire / *to finish*			
(io)	avevo	finito	*I had finished*
(tu)	avevi	finito	*you (fam.) had finished*
(lui/lei/Lei)	aveva	finito	*he, she, you (pol.) had finished*
(noi)	avevamo	finito	*we had finished*
(voi)	avevate	finito	*you had finished*
(loro)	avevano	finito	*they had finished*

Verbs Conjugated with essere

First Conjugation: arrivare / to arrive

(io)	ero	arrivato/a	I had arrived
(tu)	eri	arrivato/a	you (fam.) had arrived
(lui)	era	arrivato	} he, she, you (pol.) had arrived
(lei)	era	arrivata	
(Lei)	era	arrivato/a	
(noi)	eravamo	arrivati/e	we had arrived
(voi)	eravate	arrivati/e	you had arrived
(loro)	erano	arrivati/e	they had arrived

Second Conjugation: cadere / to fall

(io)	ero	caduto/a	I had fallen
(tu)	eri	caduto/a	you (fam.) had fallen
(lui)	era	caduto	} he, she, you (pol.) had fallen
(lei)	era	caduta	
(Lei)	era	caduto/a	
(noi)	eravamo	caduti/e	we had fallen
(voi)	eravate	caduti/e	you had fallen
(loro)	erano	caduti/e	they had fallen

Third Conjugation: uscire / to go out

(io)	ero	uscito/a	I had gone out
(tu)	eri	uscito/a	you (fam.) had gone out
(lui)	era	uscito	} he, she, you (pol.) had gone out
(lei)	era	uscita	
(Lei)	era	uscito/a	
(noi)	eravamo	usciti/e	we had gone out
(voi)	eravate	usciti/e	you had gone out
(loro)	erano	usciti/e	they had gone out

The pluperfect tense (literally, "more than perfect" or "more than past") allows you to express an action that occurred *before* a simple past action (as expressed by the present perfect, the imperfect, or the past absolute):

> **Dopo che era arrivata, mi ha telefonato.** / *After she had arrived, she phoned me.*
> **Lui mi ha detto che le aveva già parlato.** / *He told me that he had already talked to her.*

> **TIP**
> Essentially, the trapassato prossimo is rendered by the English pluperfect: *I had spoken, you had written,* etc.

Incidentally, there is a second pluperfect tense, called the **trapassato remoto** in Italian, that is used to express an action that occurred before a past absolute action. It can be used in place of the **trapassato prossimo**:

Dopo che fu arrivata, mi telefonò. / *After she had arrived, she phoned me.*

This tense is used rarely, being limited mainly to literary and historical usage. It is formed with the past absolute of the auxiliary verb (which you know). Here are two verbs fully conjugated in this tense:

parlare / *to speak*			
(io)	ebbi	parlato	*I had spoken*
(tu)	avesti	parlato	*you (fam.) had spoken*
(lui/lei/Lei)	ebbe	parlato	*he, she, you (pol.) had spoken*
(noi)	avemmo	parlato	*we had spoken*
(voi)	aveste	parlato	*you had spoken*
(loro)	ebbero	parlato	*they had spoken*

arrivare / *to arrive*			
(io)	fui	arrivato/a	*I had arrived*
(tu)	fosti	arrivato/a	*you (fam.) had arrived*
(lui)	fu	arrivato	
(lei)	fu	arrivata	*he, she, you (pol.) had arrived*
(Lei)	fu	arrivato/a	
(noi)	fummo	arrivati/e	*we had arrived*
(voi)	foste	arrivati/e	*you had arrived*
(loro)	furono	arrivati/e	*they had arrived*

6-27

QUICK
PRACTICE 5

Say the following things in Italian.

1. They had already eaten when she arrived.
2. I had already finished when you called me.
3. As a child she could (was able to) watch TV only after she had studied.
4. After you (*fam., pl.*) had gone out, he finally arrived.
5. I was sure that you (*fam., sing.*) had already done it (**lo**).

The Past Indicative **93**

6. Bruno said that he had already seen those movies. And, it's true. He had seen them.

7. Nora wanted to go out only after she had finished (**di**) watching her favorite program.

8. Mrs. Santini indicated that she had already read that novel.

9. Everyone was happy that you (*fam., pl.*) had decided (**di**) to come to the party.

10. After they had gone shopping, the two friends (*f.*) went to the movies.

11. After they left America many years ago, they decided to go back. (*Use the* **trapassato remoto**.)

PUTTING IT ALL TOGETHER

A. *Given the following past participles, (1) reconstruct their infinitives, and (2) give the first person singular of the past absolute of each verb.*

Modello: messo
            mettere (infinitive)
            misi (past absolute)

1. acceso
2. letto
3. fatto
4. stato
5. detto
6. dato
7. corso
8. coperto
9. risposto
10. morto
11. rotto
12. riso
13. rimasto
14. preso
15. scoperto
16. sofferto

B. *Say the following phrases in Italian.*

VOCABOLARIO UTILE
insieme / *together*
il racconto / *story*
noleggiare / *to rent*
il conto / *bill*
accendere / *to turn on*
il mare / *the sea*

1. Maria and I have never watched that television program together.

2. They didn't understand the story that you (*fam., sing.*) read to them.

3. Paolo asked Carla to go out with him, but she only laughed.

4. Mr. Dini rented a new movie, but he didn't watch it.

5. We paid the bill yesterday, since we drank almost all the coffee.

6. Marco, who gave you that book?

7. Yesterday it rained. It was bad weather all day long.

8. I have already written that e-mail. Carla saw the e-mail.

9. Franca, did you turn on the television (set)? Yesterday I saw a new program.

10. What did they say? I didn't understand anything.

11. I met my Italian teacher last year.

12. They left for Italy this morning.

13. Your friend (*f.*) called this afternoon.

14. They went to the movies last night.

15. I have already done that.

16. My brother has just arrived.

17. My parents came to America many years ago.

18. While your brother was playing the cello, I slept (was sleeping).

19. When they were in Italy, they wanted always to go to the sea.

20. As a youth, I knew how to speak Spanish.

21. They always preferred going to the movies years ago, but I never wanted to go.

22. Sarah never said that she wanted to come to the party.

22. Sara non aveva detto aveva voluto venire ala festa

C. *Choose the verb form, **a** or **b**, that best completes each sentence according to sense.*

1. Quando sono arrivato, loro … già.
   a. avevano mangiato
   b. hanno mangiato

2. Quando lei ha chiamato, noi … già di andare al cinema.
   a. avevamo deciso
   b. abbiamo deciso

3. È proprio vero che tu … di lavorare alle sei ieri sera?
   a. avevi finito
   b. hai finito

18. Mentre tuo fratello era suonava il violoncello, io dormiva, era dormendo
19. Quando erano in Italia, sempre valevano erano andati a lu mare.
20. Quando ero giovane, ho conosciuto parlare spagnolo
21. Sempre faxino preferite erano andati la cinema, mas non avevo voluto andare. donna

The Past Indicative **95**

4. Dopo che mia sorella ... dall'Italia, ha deciso di studiare la lingua italiana.
   a. era tornata
   b. è tornata

5. Che tempo ... ieri?
   a. aveva fatto
   b. ha fatto

6. Maria, ... quella pasta?
   a. avevi mangiato
   b. hai mangiato

7. Hanno detto che ... già quel film.
   a. avevano visto
   b. hanno visto

D. **Cruciverba!**

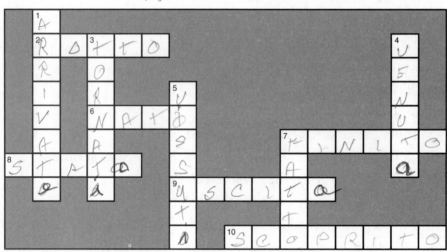

Orizzontali
2. Chi ha ... (**rompere**) quello?
6. Quando sono ... (**nascere**) i tuoi fratelli?
7. A che ora hai ... (**finire**) di lavorare?
8. Maria, sei mai ... (**essere**) a Roma?
9. Claudia, a che ora sei ... (**uscire**) ieri sera?
10. Ho ... (**scoprire**) la verità.

Verticali
1. Le ragazze sono ... (**arrivare**) ieri.
3. Loro sono ... (**tornare**) in italia.
4. Quando è ... (**venire**) tua sorella?
5. Loro sono ... (**vivere**) in Italia.
7. Che tempo ha ... (**fare**) ieri?

E. Quiz! *Do you know your history? Answer each question and then look up the answer at the back. Use complete sentences. Have fun!*

Modello: Chi inventò il telescopio? *(Who invented the telescope?)*
           Galileo Galilei inventò il telescopio.

1. Chi compose *(composed)* l'opera *Il Barbiere di Siviglia*?
2. Chi inventò la radio? *Marconi inventò la radio*
3. Chi scoprì il "Nuovo Mondo"? *Christofo Colombo scoprì il nuovo morde*
4. Quando scoprì il "Nuovo Mondo"? *Se nuova morde scoprì in mille quattordice novanta due.*
5. Chi compose l'opera *La Traviata*?

F. **Vero o falso?** *Indicate whether or not the following statements applied to you as a child.*

Da bambino/a...

____ 1. io ero molto felice.
____ 2. tutti nella mia famiglia erano felici.
____ 3. io ero molto vivace.
____ 4. ero molto studioso/a.
____ 5. io stavo a casa spesso. *meno che avevo visitato mia nonna.*
____ 6. io dicevo sempre la verità. *perche avevo punito si dicevo bugia*
____ 7. io bevevo sempre il latte. *perche avevamo avuto mucca.*
____ 8. io davo spesso via i miei giocattoli *(toys). Avevo tenute miei giocattoli*
____ 9. io ero molto ingenuo/a *(naive). ma non - Avevo vissuto un fattoria.*

5

The Future and Conditional

Quanto Sai Già? — How Much Do You Know Already?

Match the items in the two columns correctly.

1. Giovanni … in Italia tra un anno. _E_   a. sarà finita
2. Io … quella macchina, ma non ho i soldi. _f_   b. comincerai
3. Quando … i tuoi amici? _g_   c. sarebbe
4. Andremo appena … loro. _H_   d. ci saranno
5. Anch'io … quella casa, ma non avevo i soldi. _i_   e. andrà
6. Quante persone … alla festa? _d_   f. comprerei
7. Chi … quella persona? _C_   g. verranno
8. Quando … a lavorare per quella ditta? _B_   h. saranno arrivati
9. Andrò a dormire appena dopo che … _a_   i. avrei comprato
   quella partita.

The Simple Future
Il futuro semplice

The _simple future_, as its name implies, allows you to express an action that will occur in the future. To form the simple future, do the following:

First conjugation:

- Change the **-are** ending of the infinitive to **-er**:

    parlare / _to speak_ ➔ **parler-**

- Add the following endings to the stem according to person and number:

(io)	-ò
(tu)	-ai
(lui/lei/Lei)	-à
(noi)	-emo
(voi)	-ete
(loro)	-anno

- Here's the result:

First Conjugation: parlare / *to speak*		
(io)	parlerò	*I will speak*
(tu)	parlerai	*you (fam.) will speak*
(lui/lei/Lei)	parlerà	*he, she, you (pol.) will speak*
(noi)	parleremo	*we will speak*
(voi)	parlerete	*you will speak*
(loro)	parleranno	*they will speak*

- If the infinitive ending is **-ciare** or **-giare** change it to **-er**:

cominciare / *to begin*	➜	comincer-
mangiare / *to eat*	➜	manger-

- Add the same endings to the resulting stem:

First Conjugation: cominciare / *to begin* mangiare / *to eat*		
(io)	comincerò	*I will begin*
	mangerò	*I will eat*
(tu)	comincerai	*you (fam.) will begin*
	mangerai	*you (fam.) will eat*
(lui/lei/Lei)	comincerà	*he, she, you (pol.) will begin*
	mangerà	*he, she, you (pol.) will eat*
(noi)	cominceremo	*we will begin*
	mangeremo	*we will eat*
(voi)	comincerete	*you will begin*
	mangerete	*you will eat*
(loro)	cominceranno	*they will begin*
	mangeranno	*they will eat*

- If the infinitive ending is **-care** or **-gare** change it to **-er**, but add an "**h**" to the resulting stem to indicate that the hard sounds are to be retained:

    cercare / *to search for*   →   cercher-
    pagare / *to pay*   →   pagher-

- Add the same endings to the resulting stem:

First Conjugation: cercare / *to search for* pagare / *to pay*		
(io)	cercherò pagherò	*I will search for* *I will pay*
(tu)	cercherai pagherai	*you (fam.) will search for* *you (fam.) will pay*
(lui/lei/Lei)	cercherà pagherà	*he, she, you (pol.) will search for* *he, she, you (pol.) will pay*
(noi)	cercheremo pagheremo	*we will search for* *we will pay*
(voi)	cercherete pagherete	*you will search for* *you will pay*
(loro)	cercheranno pagheranno	*they will search for* *they will pay*

Second and third conjugations:

Drop the **-e** of the infinitive ending:

    scrivere / *to write*   →   scriver-
    finire / *to finish*   →   finir-

- Add the following endings to both stems according to person and number:

(io)	-ò
(tu)	-ai
(lui/lei/Lei)	-à
(noi)	-emo
(voi)	-ete
(loro)	-anno

- Here's the result:

Second and Third Conjugations: scrivere / to write finire / to finish		
(io)	scriverò	*I will write*
(tu)	scriverai	*you (fam.) will write*
(lui/lei/Lei)	scriverà	*he, she, you (pol.) will write*
(noi)	scriveremo	*we will write*
(voi)	scriverete	*you will write*
(loro)	scriveranno	*they will write*
(io)	finirò	*I will finish*
(tu)	finirai	*you (fam.) will finish*
(lui/lei/Lei)	finirà	*he, she, you (pol.) will finish*
(noi)	finiremo	*we will finish*
(voi)	finirete	*you will finish*
(loro)	finiranno	*they will finish*

Recall the verb form **esserci** / *to be there*, which is used in the future to acknowledge that something or someone will be somewhere. It has the following two forms:

Ci sarà l'insegnante? / *Will the teacher be here/there?*
Ci saranno gli insegnanti? / *Will the teachers be here/there?*

The future is used:

- to express an action or state of being that will take place at some time in the future.

   Domani andremo al cinema. / *Tomorrow we will be going to the movies.*
   Lo farò quando ho tempo. / *I will do it when I have time.*

- to express probability.

   Quanto costerà quell'automobile? / *How much does that car (probably) cost?*
   Saranno le cinque. / *It's (probably) five o'clock.*

- to express conjecture (wondering, guessing).

   Chi sarà che chiama a quest'ora? / *(I wonder) who is calling at this hour?*

Most irregular verbs in the future are formed by dropping the first and last vowels of the infinitive ending. Take, for example, andare / *to go*:

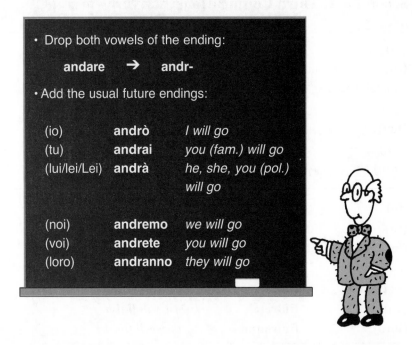

- Drop both vowels of the ending:

  andare → **andr-**

- Add the usual future endings:

(io)	**andrò**	*I will go*
(tu)	**andrai**	*you (fam.) will go*
(lui/lei/Lei)	**andrà**	*he, she, you (pol.) will go*
(noi)	**andremo**	*we will go*
(voi)	**andrete**	*you will go*
(loro)	**andranno**	*they will go*

Other common verbs conjugated in this way are as follows:

avere / *to have*		
(io)	avrò	*I will have*
(tu)	avrai	*you (fam.) will have*
(lui/lei/Lei)	avrà	*he, she, you (pol.) will have*
(noi)	avremo	*we will have*
(voi)	avrete	*you will have*
(loro)	avranno	*they will have*

cadere / *to fall*		
(io)	cadrò	*I will fall*
(tu)	cadrai	*you (fam.) will fall*
(lui/lei/Lei)	cadrà	*he, she, you (pol.) will fall*
(noi)	cadremo	*we will fall*
(voi)	cadrete	*you will fall*
(loro)	cadranno	*they will fall*

dovere / *to have to*

(io)	dovrò	*I will have to*
(tu)	dovrai	*you (fam.) will have to*
(lui/lei/Lei)	dovrà	*he, she, you (pol.) will have to*
(noi)	dovremo	*we will have to*
(voi)	dovrete	*you will have to*
(loro)	dovranno	*they will have to*

potere / *to be able to*

(io)	potrò	*I will be able to*
(tu)	potrai	*you (fam.) will be able to*
(lui/lei/Lei)	potrà	*he, she, you (pol.) will be able to*
(noi)	potremo	*we will be able to*
(voi)	potrete	*you will be able to*
(loro)	potranno	*they will be able to*

sapere / *to know*

(io)	saprò	*I will know*
(tu)	saprai	*you (fam.) will know*
(lui/lei/Lei)	saprà	*he, she, you (pol.) will know*
(noi)	sapremo	*we will know*
(voi)	saprete	*you will know*
(loro)	sapranno	*they will know*

vedere / *to see*

(io)	vedrò	*I will see*
(tu)	vedrai	*you (fam.) will see*
(lui/lei/Lei)	vedrà	*he, she, you (pol.) will see*
(noi)	vedremo	*we will see*
(voi)	vedrete	*you will see*
(loro)	vedranno	*they will see*

dare / *to give*

(io)	darò	*I will give*
(tu)	darai	*you (fam.) will give*
(lui/lei/Lei)	darà	*he, she, you (pol.) will give*
(noi)	daremo	*we will give*
(voi)	darete	*you will give*
(loro)	daranno	*they will give*

dire / *to say, to tell, to speak*

(io)	dirò	*I will say*
(tu)	dirai	*you (fam.) will say*
(lui/lei/Lei)	dirà	*he, she, you (pol.) will say*
(noi)	diremo	*we will say*
(voi)	direte	*you will say*
(loro)	diranno	*they will say*

fare / *to do, to make*

(io)	farò	*I will make*
(tu)	farai	*you (fam.) will make*
(lui/lei/Lei)	farà	*he, she, you (pol.) will make*
(noi)	faremo	*we will make*
(voi)	farete	*you will make*
(loro)	faranno	*they will make*

stare / *to stay*

(io)	**starò**	*I will stay*
(tu)	**starai**	*you (fam.) will stay*
(lui/lei/Lei)	**starà**	*he, she, you (pol.) will stay*
(noi)	**staremo**	*we will stay*
(voi)	**starete**	*you will stay*
(loro)	**staranno**	*they will stay*

This leaves only a few verbs that are completely irregular in the future tense.

bere / *to drink*

(io)	**berrò**	*I will drink*
(tu)	**berrai**	*you (fam.) will drink*
(lui/lei/Lei)	**berrà**	*he, she, you (pol.) will drink*
(noi)	**berremo**	*we will drink*
(voi)	**berrete**	*you will drink*
(loro)	**berranno**	*they will drink*

essere / *to be*

(io)	**sarò**	*I will be*
(tu)	**sarai**	*you (fam.) will be*
(lui/lei/Lei)	**sarà**	*he, she, you (pol.) will be*
(noi)	**saremo**	*we will be*
(voi)	**sarete**	*you will be*
(loro)	**saranno**	*they will be*

rimanere / to remain

(io)	rimarrò	I will remain
(tu)	rimarrai	you (fam.) will remain
(lui/lei/Lei)	rimarrà	he, she, you (pol.) will remain
(noi)	rimarremo	we will remain
(voi)	rimarrete	you will remain
(loro)	rimarranno	they will remain

venire / to come

(io)	verrò	I will come
(tu)	verrai	you (fam.) will come
(lui/lei/Lei)	verrà	he, she, you (pol.) will come
(noi)	verremo	we will come
(voi)	verrete	you will come
(loro)	verranno	they will come

volere / to want to

(io)	vorrò	I will want to
(tu)	vorrai	you (fam.) will want to
(lui/lei/Lei)	vorrà	he, she, you (pol.) will want to
(noi)	vorremo	we will want to
(voi)	vorrete	you will want to
(loro)	vorranno	they will want to

QUICK PRACTICE 1

How do you say the following things in Italian?

1. That television program will start at 6 P.M. and end at 9 P.M.
2. There will be many people at the party.
3. I know that she will not go to see that movie.
4. I'm sure that they will call you, Alessandro.

5. We will pay at the Bar Roma if you (*fam., sing.*) will eat what (**quello che**) we say.

6. He said that she too will be there.

7. Tomorrow Maria and I will go out together.

8. I know for sure that the two of you will finish on time.

9. I will be leaving tomorrow for Italy.

Now, give the plural form.

Modello: tu verrai
           voi verrete

           il bambino comincerà
           i bambini cominceranno

10. io starò *noi staremo*
11. tu farai *voi farete*
12. quel ragazzo darà *daranno*
13. quella ragazza vedrà *vedranno.*
14. io saprò *sapremo*
15. tu potrai *potrete*
16. quel bambino dovrà *dovranno*
17. quella bambina avrà *avranno*
18. io cadrò *cadremo*
19. tu andrai *andrete*
20. lui mangerà *mangeremo*
21. lei cercherà *cercheranno*

Handwritten answers (margin):
5. Pagheremo alla Bar Roma si tu mangerei quello che diremo.
6. Ha detto lei anche sarà la.
8. Io so per certamente voi due finirete in orario.
7. Domani maria ed io usciremo insieme.
9. Lasciamo domani per Italia (or andremo fuori.)

Finally, fill in the chart appropriately with the future forms of the given verbs.

	essere	fare	dire	bere	volere	venire	rimanere
(io)	sarò	farò	dirò	berrò	vorrò	verrò	rimarrò
(tu)	sarai	farai	dirai	berrai	vorrai	verrai	rimarrai
(lui/lei)	sarà	farà	dirà	berrà	vorrà	verrà	rimarrà
(noi)	saremo	faremo	daremo	berremo	vorremo	verremo	rimarremo
(voi)	sarете	farete	daute	berete	vorете	verете	rimarrete
(loro)	saranno	faranno	daranno	beranno	vorranno	verranno	rimarrano

The Future Perfect
Il futuro anteriore

The *future perfect* is a compound tense (Chapter 4). Therefore, it is conjugated with the auxiliary verb, either **avere** / *to have* or **essere** / *to be* in the future tense, and the past participle of the verb, in that order. So, you know everything there is to know to form this tense, including irregular past participles (Chapter 4).

Examples:

Verbs Conjugated with avere			
First Conjugation: parlare / *to speak*			
(io)	avrò	parlato	*I will have spoken*
(tu)	avrai	parlato	*you (fam.) will have spoken*
(lui/lei/Lei)	avrà	parlato	*he, she, you (pol.) will have spoken*
(noi)	avremo	parlato	*we will have spoken*
(voi)	avrete	parlato	*you will have spoken*
(loro)	avranno	parlato	*they will have spoken*
Second Conjugation: vendere / *to sell*			
(io)	avrò	venduto	*I will have sold*
(tu)	avrai	venduto	*you (fam.) will have sold*
(lui/lei/Lei)	avrà	venduto	*he, she, you (pol.) will have sold*
(noi)	avremo	venduto	*we will have sold*
(voi)	avrete	venduto	*you (fam.) will have sold*
(loro)	avranno	venduto	*they will have sold*
Third Conjugation: finire / *to finish*			
(io)	avrò	finito	*I will have finished*
(tu)	avrai	finito	*you (fam.) will have finished*
(lui/lei/Lei)	avrà	finito	*he, she, you (pol.) will have finished*
(noi)	avremo	finito	*we will have finished*
(voi)	avrete	finito	*you will have finished*
(loro)	avranno	finito	*they will have finished*

Verbs Conjugated with essere

First Conjugation: arrivare / to arrive

(io)	sarò	arrivato/a	*I will have arrived*
(tu)	sarai	arrivato/a	*you (fam.) will have arrived*
(lui)	sarà	arrivato	
(lei)	sarà	arrivata	*he, she, you (pol.) will have arrived*
(Lei)	sarà	arrivato/a	
(noi)	saremo	arrivati/e	*we will have arrived*
(voi)	sarete	arrivati/e	*you will have arrived*
(loro)	saranno	arrivati/e	*they will have arrived*

Second Conjugation: cadere / to fall

(io)	sarò	caduto/a	*I will have fallen*
(tu)	sarai	caduto/a	*you (fam.) will have fallen*
(lui)	sarà	caduto	
(lei)	sarà	caduta	*he, she, you (pol.) will have fallen*
(Lei)	sarà	caduto/a	
(noi)	saremo	caduti/e	*we will have fallen*
(voi)	sarete	caduti/e	*you will have fallen*
(loro)	saranno	caduti/e	*they will have fallen*

Third Conjugation: uscire / to go out

(io)	sarò	uscito/a	*I will have gone out*
(tu)	sarai	uscito/a	*you (fam.) will have gone out*
(lui)	sarà	uscito	
(lei)	sarà	uscita	*he, she, you (pol.) will have gone out*
(Lei)	sarà	uscito/a	
(noi)	saremo	usciti/e	*we will have gone out*
(voi)	sarete	usciti/e	*you will have gone out*
(loro)	saranno	usciti/e	*they will have gone out*

The main use of this tense is in temporal subordinate clauses—clauses that start with **dopo che** / *after*, **quando** / *when*, and **appena** / *as soon as*—connected to clauses in the simple perfect:

Uscirò quando sarai arrivato. / *I will go out when you (will) have arrived.*
Appena avrò finito di lavorare, andrò al cinema. / *As soon as I (will) have finished working, I'll go to the movies.*

Like the simple future, it is also used to express probability:

Saranno usciti già. / *They must have already gone out.*
Quanto sarà costata quella casa? / *How much did that house (probably) cost?*

QUICK PRACTICE 2

Say the following sentences in Italian.

1. After they will have arrived, we will go to the movies together.
2. When they (will) have finished studying, they will go to Italy.
3. I will go out today, only after I (will) have studied a bit.
4. As soon as he (will) have finished reading that book, I am sure that he will start another one.
5. After that team (**quella squadra**) (will) probably have won the championship (**il campionato**), I will be very happy.
6. When you will have moved (**traslocare** / *to move*) into your new apartment, where will you be working, Mr. Smith?
7. That car must have cost (will have cost) a lot of money!
8. He must have already gone out.
9. When he comes, they will have already gone home.

[handwritten answers:]
1. Dopo sarano arrivati andremo ala cinema insieme
2. Quando avrono finito stadiando, andranno all'italia
3. Uscirò oggi, soltmente dopo studiai un po'.
4. Appena finito leggere la libro. certo cominscerebbe un altro.
5. Dopo quella squadra probalmente vincinto il campionato, paro molto contento
6. Quando avete trascolato a apartemento Nuovo dové avete lavorato, S. Smith
7. Auela mostrna, sarà costata molti saldi
8. Sarai uscito già!
9. Quando sarà arrivato

Stato piacere?
piacere mio?

The Conditional
Il condizionale presente

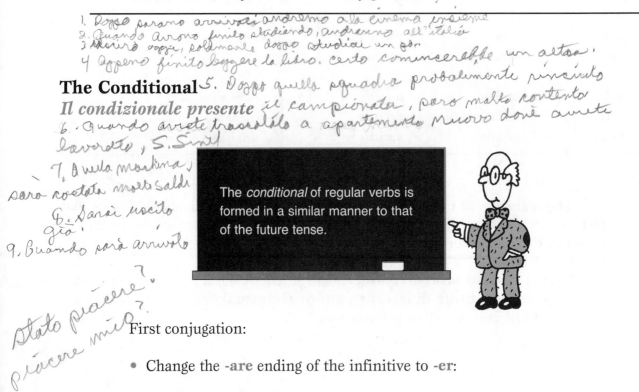

> The *conditional* of regular verbs is formed in a similar manner to that of the future tense.

First conjugation:

* Change the **-are** ending of the infinitive to **-er**:

  parlare / *to speak* → **parler-**

- Add the following endings to the stem according to person and number:

(io)	-ei
(tu)	-esti
(lui/lei/Lei)	-ebbe
(noi)	-emmo
(voi)	-este
(loro)	-ebbero

- Here's the result:

First Conjugation: parlare / *to speak*		
(io)	parlerei	*I would speak*
(tu)	parleresti	*you (fam.) would speak*
(lui/lei/Lei)	parlerebbe	*he, she, you (pol.) would speak*
(noi)	parleremmo	*we would speak*
(voi)	parlereste	*you would speak*
(loro)	parlerebbero	*they would speak*

- Note that the stress on the third person plural form is on the first vowel of the ending: parlerébbero.

- If the infinitive ending is -ciare or -giare, change it to -er:

cominciare / *to begin* → comincer-
mangiare / *to eat* → manger-

- Add the same endings to the stem:

First Conjugation: cominciare / *to begin* mangiare / *to eat*		
(io)	comincerei	*I would begin*
	mangerei	*I would eat*
(tu)	cominceresti	*you (fam.) would begin*
	mangeresti	*you (fam.) would eat*
(lui/lei/Lei)	comincerebbe	*he, she, you (pol.) would begin*
	mangerebbe	*he, she, you (pol.) would eat*
(noi)	cominceremmo	*we would begin*
	mangeremmo	*we would eat*
(voi)	comincereste	*you would begin*
	mangereste	*you would eat*
(loro)	comincerebbero	*they would begin*
	mangerebbero	*they would eat*

- If the infinitive ending is -**care** or -**gare** change it to -**er**, but add an "**h**" to the stem, so as to indicate that the hard sounds are to be retained:

  cercare / *to search for*   ➔   cercher-
  pagare / *to pay*   ➔   pagher-

- Add the same endings to the resulting stem:

First Conjugation: cercare / *to search for* pagare / *to pay*		
(io)	cercherei	*I would search for*
	pagherei	*I would pay*
(tu)	cercheresti	*you (fam.) would search for*
	pagheresti	*you (fam.) would pay*
(lui/lei/Lei)	cercherebbe	*he, she, you (pol.) would search for*
	pagherebbe	*he, she, you (pol.) would pay*
(noi)	cercheremmo	*we would search for*
	pagheremmo	*we would pay*
(voi)	cerchereste	*you would search for*
	paghereste	*you would pay*
(loro)	cercherebbero	*they would search for*
	pagherebbero	*they would pay*

Second and third conjugations:

- Drop the -**e** of the infinitive ending:

  scrivere / *to write*   ➔   scriver-
  finire / *to finish*   ➔   finir-

- Add the same endings to the stem according to person and number:

(io)	-ei
(tu)	-esti
(lui/lei/Lei)	-ebbe
(noi)	-emmo
(voi)	-este
(loro)	-ebbero

- Here's the result:

Second and Third Conjugations: scrivere / to write finire / to finish		
(io)	scriverei	*I would write*
(tu)	scriveresti	*you (fam.) would write*
(lui/lei/Lei)	scriverebbe	*he, she, you (pol.) would write*
(noi)	scriveremmo	*we would write*
(voi)	scrivereste	*you would write*
(loro)	scriverebbero	*they would write*
(io)	finirei	*I would finish*
(tu)	finiresti	*you (fam.) would finish*
(lui/lei/Lei)	finirebbe	*he, she, you (pol.) would finish*
(noi)	finiremmo	*we would finish*
(voi)	finireste	*you would finish*
(loro)	finirebbero	*they would finish*

As in the case of the future, most irregular verbs in the conditional are formed by dropping the first and last vowels of the infinitive ending. Take, for example, **andare** / *to go*:

- Drop both vowels of the ending:

  andare ➜ **andr-**

- Add the usual conditional endings:

Typical Irregular Conditional Tense: andare / to go		
(io)	andrei	*I would go*
(tu)	andresti	*you (fam.) would go*
(lui/lei/Lei)	andrebbe	*he, she, you (pol.) would go*
(noi)	andremmo	*we would go*
(voi)	andreste	*you would go*
(loro)	andrebbero	*they would go*

Other common verbs conjugated in this way are the same ones taken up previously. Just the first person singular forms are given here for convenience:

avere / *to have*	→	**avrei** / *I would have*	
cadere / *to fall*	→	**cadrei** / *I would fall*	
dovere / *to have to*	→	**dovrei** / *I would have to*	
potere / *to be able to*	→	**potrei** / *I would be able to, I could*	
sapere / *to know*	→	**saprei** / *I would know*	
vedere / *to see*	→	**vedrei** / *I would see*	

Again, with the verbs **dare**, **dire**, **fare**, **stare**, do what you already have learned to do with regular verbs. Drop the final vowel of the infinitive and add the usual endings:

dare	→	**dar-**	→	**darei** / *I would give*
dire	→	**dir-**	→	**direi** / *I would say*
fare	→	**far-**	→	**farei** / *I would do*
stare	→	**star-**	→	**starei** / *I would stay*

As in the case of the future, there are only a few verbs that are completely irregular in the conditional:

Impara questi verbi al condizionale presente.

bere / *to drink*		
(io)	berrei	*I would drink*
(tu)	berresti	*you (fam.) would drink*
(lui/lei/Lei)	berrebbe	*he, she, you (pol.) would drink*
(noi)	berremmo	*we would drink*
(voi)	berreste	*you would drink*
(loro)	berrebbero	*they would drink*

essere / to be

(io)	sarei	I would be
(tu)	saresti	you (fam.) would be
(lui/lei/Lei)	sarebbe	he, she, you (pol.) would be
(noi)	saremmo	we would be
(voi)	sareste	you would be
(loro)	sarebbero	they would be

rimanere / to remain

(io)	rimarrei	I would remain
(tu)	rimarresti	you (fam.) would remain
(lui/lei/Lei)	rimarrebbe	he, she, you (pol.) would remain
(noi)	rimarremmo	we would remain
(voi)	rimarreste	you would remain
(loro)	rimarrebbero	they would remain

venire / to come

(io)	verrei	I would come
(tu)	verresti	you (fam.) would come
(lui/lei/Lei)	verrebbe	he, she, you (pol.) would come
(noi)	verremmo	we would come
(voi)	verreste	you would come
(loro)	verrebbero	they would come

volere / to want to

(io)	vorrei	I would want to
(tu)	vorresti	you (fam.) would want to
(lui/lei/Lei)	vorrebbe	he, she, you (pol.) would want to
(noi)	vorremmo	we would want to
(voi)	vorreste	you would want to
(loro)	vorrebbero	they would want to

The conditional tense corresponds, generally, to the English conditional—*I would go, you would write,* etc. It is used, in essence, to convey a conjecture, hypothesis, or some action or event that *would, could,* or *might* take place under given conditions.

Uscirei, ma non ho tempo. / *I would go out, but I do not have time.*
Comprerebbero quella macchina, ma non hanno i soldi. / *They would buy that car, but they don't have the money.*

Specifically, it is used:

- To express a conditional, potential, or hypothetical action

    Andrei al cinema volentieri, ma non ho tempo. / *I would gladly go to the movies, but I don't have time.*
    Lo comprerei, ma non ho soldi. / *I would buy it, but I don't have any money.*

- To convey courtesy or politeness

    Mi potrebbe aiutare? / *Could you help me?*
    Vorrei un caffè, grazie. / *I would like a coffee, thanks.*

- To express an indirect quotation

    Maria ha detto che verrebbe domani. / *Mary said that she would be coming tomorrow.*

- To express probability

    Quanto costerebbe quel televisore? / *How much could that TV set (probably) cost?*

- To quote someone else's opinion

    Secondo lui, quella ragazza sarebbe spagnola. / *According to him, that girl is (probably) Spanish.*
    Nella loro opinione, l'Italia sarebbe il miglior paese del mondo. / *In their opinion, Italy is the best country in the world.*

13. vorrei un caffé, grazie
14. maria ha detto che verrebbe domani
15.

Stato piachere

Finally, note the meanings of **potere**, **dovere**, and **volere** in the conditional:

	Present		Conditional	
potere	Lo posso fare.	*I can do it.*	Lo potrei fare.	*I could do it.*
dovere	Lo devo fare.	*I have to do it.*	Lo dovrei fare.	*I should do it.*
volere	Lo voglio fare.	*I want to do it.*	Lo vorrei fare.	*I would like to do it.*

QUICK PRACTICE 3

Say the following phrases in Italian.

1. I would speak Italian more, but first I must study the verbs.
2. Is it true that you (*fam., sing.*) would study Spanish instead of (**anziché**) Italian?
3. My friend (*m.*) would start working earlier each day, but he is always very tired.
4. We would gladly pay for the coffee, but we have no money.
5. Would you (*fam., pl.*) help me learn Italian grammar (**la grammatica**), please?
6. I know that they would understand what you (*pl.*) are doing.
7. I would watch that TV program, but I don't have time.
8. She would eat those pastries for sure (**di sicuro**).
9. I could do it (**lo**), but I won't.
10. I should do it, and I will.
11. I would like to do it, but I can't.
12. Could you (*pol., sing.*) help me?
13. I would like a coffee, thanks.
14. Mary said that she would be coming tomorrow.
15. How much could that car cost?
16. According to him, that girl is (probably) Spanish.

1. Parlerei più italiano, ma prima devo studiare i verbi.
2. È vero che tu studeresti l'espagnol anziché l'italiano? molto
3. mi amico comincerebbe lavore tutti giorno, ma sempre Slanco.
4. volentieri pagheremmo Presto per il cafè ma abbiamo non soldi.
5. Aiuteresteni imparare la grammatica italiano per favore?
6. So capirobeno che avete fatto.
7. Guaderei quel program TV, ma non ho tempo.
8. mangerebbe questi pasticcini di sicuro.
9. Potrei fare lo, ma non voglio
10. dovrei fare lo. e farei.
11. Piacerei lo fare, ma non possi.
12. aiuteresteni? o mi potebbe aiutare?

Now, give the corresponding conditional forms.

Modello: io verrò
             io verrei

17. **io...**
    a. potrò — *potrei*
    b. verrò
    c. rimarrò — *rimarrei*
    d. sarò — *sarei*

18. **tu...**
    a. dovrai — *dovresti*
    b. berrai — *berresti*
    c. dirai — *diresti*
    d. farai — *faresti*

19. **lui/lei...**
    a. vorrà
    b. starà — *starebbe*
    c. vedrà — *vedrebbe*
    d. potrà — *potrebbe*

20. **noi...**
    a. avremo
  ? b. pagheremo — *pagheremmo*
  ? c. cercheremo — *cercheremmo*
    d. cominceremo — *cominceremmo*

21. **voi...**
    a. mangerete — *mangereste*
    b. leggerete — *leggereste*
    c. berrete — *berreste*
    d. sarete — *sareste*

22. **loro...**
    a. rimarranno — *rimarrebbero*
    b. vorranno — *vorrebbero*
    c. vedranno — *vedrebbero*
    d. verranno — *verrebbero*

The Past Conditional
Il condizionale passato

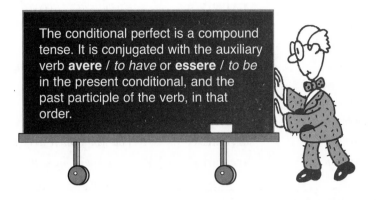

The conditional perfect is a compound tense. It is conjugated with the auxiliary verb **avere** / *to have* or **essere** / *to be* in the present conditional, and the past participle of the verb, in that order.

Examples:

Verbs Conjugated with avere			
First Conjugation: parlare / *to speak*			
(io)	avrei	parlato	*I would have spoken*
(tu)	avresti	parlato	*you (fam.) would have spoken*
(lui/lei/Lei)	avrebbe	parlato	*he, she, you (pol.) would have spoken*
(noi)	avremmo	parlato	*we would have spoken*
(voi)	avreste	parlato	*you would have spoken*
(loro)	avrebbero	parlato	*they would have spoken*
Second Conjugation: vendere / *to sell*			
(io)	avrei	venduto	*I would have sold*
(tu)	avresti	venduto	*you (fam.) would have sold*
(lui/lei/Lei)	avrebbe	venduto	*he, she, you (pol.) would have sold*
(noi)	avremmo	venduto	*we would have sold*
(voi)	avreste	venduto	*you would have sold*
(loro)	avrebbero	venduto	*they would have sold*
Third Conjugation: finire / *to finish*			
(io)	avrei	finito	*I would have finished*
(tu)	avresti	finito	*you (fam.) would have finished*
(lui/lei/Lei)	avrebbe	finito	*he, she, you (pol.) would have finished*
(noi)	avremmo	finito	*we would have finished*
(voi)	avreste	finito	*you would have finished*
(loro)	avrebbero	finito	*they would have finished*

Verbs Conjugated with essere

First Conjugation: arrivare / to arrive

(io)	sarei	arrivato/a	*I would have arrived*
(tu)	saresti	arrivato/a	*you (fam.) would have arrived*
(lui)	sarebbe	arrivato	
(lei)	sarebbe	arrivata	*he, she, you (pol.) would have arrived*
(Lei)	sarebbe	arrivato/a	
(noi)	saremmo	arrivati/e	*we would have arrived*
(voi)	sareste	arrivati/e	*you would have arrived*
(loro)	sarebbero	arrivati/e	*they would have arrived*

Second Conjugation: cadere / to fall

(io)	sarei	caduto/a	*I would have fallen*
(tu)	saresti	caduto/a	*you (fam.) would have fallen*
(lui)	sarebbe	caduto	
(lei)	sarebbe	caduta	*he, she, you (pol.) would have fallen*
(Lei)	sarebbe	caduto/a	
(noi)	saremmo	caduti/e	*we would have fallen*
(voi)	sareste	caduti/e	*you would have fallen*
(loro)	sarebbero	caduti/e	*they would have fallen*

Third Conjugation: uscire / to go out

(io)	sarei	uscito/a	*I would have gone out*
(tu)	saresti	uscito/a	*you (fam.) would have gone out*
(lui)	sarebbe	uscito	
(lei)	sarebbe	uscita	*he, she, you (pol.) would have gone out*
(Lei)	sarebbe	uscito/a	
(noi)	saremmo	usciti/e	*we would have gone out*
(voi)	sareste	usciti/e	*you would have gone out*
(loro)	sarebbero	usciti/e	*they would have gone out*

Generally, this tense corresponds to the English past conditional—*I would have spoken, you would have sold,* etc.

Therefore, it is used primarily to refer to an action that occurred before another simple conditional action:

> **Mi ha detto che sarebbe venuto.** / *He told me that he would (would have) come.*
> **Sapeva che io avrei capito.** / *He knew that I would have understood.*

Notice the meaning of **potere**, **volere**, and **dovere** in the present and past conditional tenses:

> **Lo potrei fare.** / *I could do it.*
> **Lo avrei potuto fare.** / *I could have done it.*

> **Lo vorrei fare.** / *I would like to do it.*
> **Lo avrei voluto fare.** / *I would like to have done it.*

> **Lo dovrei fare.** / *I should do it.*
> **Lo avrei dovuto fare.** / *I should have done it.*

QUICK PRACTICE 4

7-25

Say the following sentences in Italian.

1. I would have gone to the party, but I didn't have time.
2. My parents would have gone to Italy last year, but they didn't have the money.
3. I would have gone out with him, but I had to study.
4. Usually (**Di solito**) I would have done that myself (**io stesso/a**), but this time she decided to do it (**farlo**).
5. He would have bought that car, but it cost too much.
6. They told me that they would (would have) come.
7. He knew that I would have understood.
8. I could have done it (**la**), and I would like to have done it, and maybe I should have done it, but I didn't do it.

---

1. Andrei alla festa ma non avrei tempo
2. Mi genitori sarebbero andati in italia l'anno scorso, ma non ebbero la soldi.
3. Sarei uscita con lei ma avevo doruto studiare.
4. Di solito avrei fatto io stessa, ma questo tavolta decasi farlo.
5. Avrebbe comprato quela machina, ma costo troppo.
6. Avrebbero detto che sarebbero venuto!
7. Sapeva che io avrei capito!
8. Lo avrei potuto farela, e lo avrei voluto fare, e forse lo avrei dovuto farla ma non l'ho fatta

7.25

PUTTING IT ALL TOGETHER

A. *Match the two columns logically.*

1. Chi ... quella persona?
2. Tra un mese noi ... in vacanza al mare.
3. Loro ... domani alle sette dall'Italia.
4. Maria, io ti ... più tardi.
5. Alessandro, quanto pensi che ... quella macchina?
6. Signorina, che cosa ..., un caffè o un cappuccino?
7. Quale film ... domani al cinema?
8. Che tempo ... domani?
9. Sei sicuro che loro ... alla festa?

a. verranno
b. daranno
c. farà
d. arriveranno
e. sarà
f. andremo
g. chiamerò
h. costerà
i. prenderà

B. *Can you predict the future? Indicate what you think will happen, using the future tense.*

Modello: Chi vincerà il "World Series" di baseball quest'anno?
Secondo me (*in my opinion*) **i Milwaukee Brewers vinceranno il "World Series."**

1. Chi vincerà il "World Series" di baseball quest'anno?
2. Chi vincerà il premio "Oscar" quest'anno?
3. Chi sarà il prossimo Presidente degli Stati Uniti? *Spero non obama.*
4. Che tempo farà domani? *Spero il tempo non di pioggia*
5. Chi riceverà il "Premio Nobel" quest'anno? *forse Osama Bin laddn. postumo*

C. *Put the verb in parentheses into the future or future perfect according to sense.*

FP 1. Mangerò anche la pizza, appena che io (finire) *avrei finito* gli spaghetti.
FP 2. Sono quasi sicura che lui (uscire) *sarà uscito* già.
3. Mario (arrivare) *arriverà* domani verso il tardo pomeriggio.
FP 4. Quando (andare) *sarete andati* in Italia, tu e Sara?
5. È vero che (venire) *verranno* anche loro alla festa?
FP 6. A quest'ora Maria probabilmente (andare) *sarà andato* già a dormire.
FP 7. Appena (finire) *avranno finito* di lavorare, loro andranno direttamente a casa perché sono stanchi.
FP 8. Quando loro (vedere) *avranno visto* quel film, vorranno certamente vedere altri film di quel regista (*director*).
FP 9. Dopo che tu (assaggiare) *avrai assaggiato* questo cibo, sono sicuro che ne vorrai di più.

D. *Say the following in Italian.*

1. They would gladly (**volentieri**) go to the coffee bar (**al bar**), but they don't have time. *Sarebbero volentieri andare al bar, ma non hanno tempo.*
2. Mrs. Smith, could you help me? *Signora Smith potrebbe aiutarmi?*
3. Who would like a coffee? *Chi vorrebbe un cafè?*
4. Franco said that they would be arriving tomorrow. *Franco disse arriverato domani*
5. How much might that new car cost? *Quanto costarebbe quel macchina nuovo?*
6. In her opinion, that boy is (likely) Italian. *secondo lei, questa ragazza è l'italiano*
7. According to him, she is (likely) American. *Secondo lei, lei è americana probabilmente*
8. They could come a little later, no? *verrebbero un più tarde, no*
9. She shouldn't do that. *Lei non avrebbe*
10. Mr. Smith, would you like a cappuccino? *Signore Smith e vorebbe un cappuccino?*

E. **Cruciverba!**

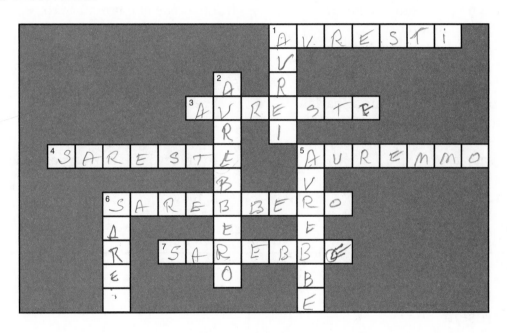

Missing from each verb, which is in the conditional perfect, is the auxiliary. Supply it.

Orizzontali
1. Tu … fatto
3. Voi … detto
4. voi … rimasti
5. Noi .., dato
6. Loro … stati
7. lei … andata

Verticali
1. Io … mangiato
2. Loro … bevuto
4. Lui … letto
5. Io mi … alzato

6

The Subjunctive

The Present
Il congiuntivo presente

The *subjunctive mood* is, as its name implies, a verb category that allows you
to convey your moods—point of view, fear, doubt, hope, possibility—in a phrase,
anything that is not a fact. In a way, the subjunctive is a counterpart to the indicative, the mood that allows you to convey facts and information.

To form the *present subjunctive* of regular verbs, do the following:

First conjugation:

- Drop the infinitive ending, **-are**:

    parlare / *to speak* ➔ **parl-**

- Add the following endings to the stem according to person and number:

(io)	-i
(tu)	-i
(lui/lei/Lei)	-i
(noi)	-iamo
(voi)	-iate
(loro)	-ino

TIP
Be careful once again when you pronounce the third person plural forms! The accent is *not* placed on the ending, but on a syllable before the ending:

párlino / *they speak*

- Here's the result:

First Conjugation: parlare / *to speak*		
(io)	parli	*I speak, I am speaking, I may speak*
(tu)	parli	*you (fam.) speak, you are speaking, you may speak*
(lui/lei/Lei)	parli	*he, she, you (pol.) speak(s), he, she, you is/are speaking, he, she, you may speak*
(noi)	parliamo	*we speak, we are speaking, we may speak*
(voi)	parliate	*you speak, you are speaking, you may speak*
(loro)	parlino	*they speak, they are speaking, they may speak*

If the first-conjugation infinitive ending is **-ciare** or **-giare**, drop the ending **-are**, retaining the **-i** of the ending, but do not write a "double -i" when adding on the present subjunctive endings:

cominciare / *to begin* → cominci-		
(io)	cominci	*I begin, I am beginning, I may begin*
(tu)	cominci	*you (fam.) begin, you are beginning, you may begin*
(lui/lei/Lei)	cominci	*he, she, you (pol.) begin(s), he, she, you is/are beginning, he, she, you may begin*
(noi)	cominciamo	*we begin, we are beginning, we may begin*
(voi)	cominciate	*you begin, you are beginning, you may begin*
(loro)	comincino	*they begin, they are beginning, they may begin*

mangiare / *to eat* ➜ mangi-		
(io)	mangi	*I eat, I am eating, I may eat*
(tu)	mangi	*you (fam.) eat, you are eating, you may eat*
(lui/lei/Lei)	mangi	*he, she, you (pol.) eat(s), he, she, you is/are eating, he, she, you may eat*
(noi)	mangiamo	*we eat, we are eating, we may eat*
(voi)	mangiate	*you eat, you are eating, you may eat*
(loro)	mangino	*they eat, they are eating, they may eat*

If the infinitive ends in **-iare**, the usual pattern of "not doubling the **-i**" applies, unless the **-i** is stressed during the conjugation, in which case it is retained before the **-i** ending only.

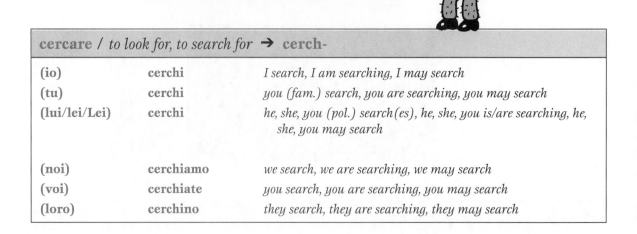

If the first-conjugation infinitive ending is **-care** or **-gare**, drop the ending **-are** but add "**h**" before the present subjunctive endings, indicating that the hard sound is to be retained:

cercare / *to look for, to search for* ➜ cerch-		
(io)	cerchi	*I search, I am searching, I may search*
(tu)	cerchi	*you (fam.) search, you are searching, you may search*
(lui/lei/Lei)	cerchi	*he, she, you (pol.) search(es), he, she, you is/are searching, he, she, you may search*
(noi)	cerchiamo	*we search, we are searching, we may search*
(voi)	cerchiate	*you search, you are searching, you may search*
(loro)	cerchino	*they search, they are searching, they may search*

pagare / to pay → pagh-		
(io)	paghi	*I pay, I am paying, I may pay*
(tu)	paghi	*you (fam.) pay, you are paying, you may pay*
(lui/lei/Lei)	paghi	*he, she, you (pol.) pay(s), he, she, you is/are paying, he, she, you may pay*
(noi)	paghiamo	*we pay, we are paying, we may pay*
(voi)	paghiate	*you pay, you are paying, you may pay*
(loro)	paghino	*they pay, they are paying, they may pay*

Second conjugation:

- Drop the infinitive ending, **-ere**:

  scrivere / *to write* ➔ **scriv-**

- Add the following endings to the stem according to person and number:

(io)	**-a**
(tu)	**-a**
(lui/lei/Lei)	**-a**
(noi)	**-iamo**
(voi)	**-iate**
(loro)	**-ano**

- Here's the result:

Second Conjugation: scrivere / *to write*		
(io)	scriva	*I write, I am writing, I may write*
(tu)	scriva	*you (fam.) write, you are writing, you may write*
(lui/lei/Lei)	scriva	*he, she, you (pol.) write(s), he, she, you is/are writing, he, she, you may write*
(noi)	scriviamo	*we write, we are writing, we may write*
(voi)	scriviate	*you write, you are writing, you may write*
(loro)	scrivano	*they write, they are writing, they may write*

Third conjugation:

As in the case of the present indicative (Chapter 3), there are two types of conjugation patterns that apply to third-conjugation verbs.

To form the present subjunctive of Type 1, do the same things you have been doing so far:

- Drop the infinitive ending, -**ire**:

  dormire / *to sleep* ➔ **dorm-**

- Add the following endings according to person and number:

(io)	-a
(tu)	-a
(lui/lei/Lei)	-a
(noi)	-iamo
(voi)	-iate
(loro)	-ano

- Here's the result:

Third Conjugation (Type 1): **dormire** / *to sleep*		
(io)	**dorma**	*I sleep, I am sleeping, I may sleep*
(tu)	**dorma**	*you (fam.) sleep, you are sleeping, you may sleep*
(lui/lei/Lei)	**dorma**	*he, she, you (pol.) sleep(s), he, she, you is/are sleeping, he, she, you may sleep*
(noi)	**dormiamo**	*we sleep, we are sleeping, we may sleep*
(voi)	**dormiate**	*you sleep, you are sleeping, you may sleep*
(loro)	**dormano**	*they sleep, they are sleeping, they may sleep*

To form the present subjunctive of Type 2 verbs, do the following:

- Drop the infinitive ending, -**ire**:

  finire / *to finish* ➔ **fin-**

- Add the following endings according to person and number:

(io)	-isca
(tu)	-isca
(lui/lei/Lei)	-isca
(noi)	-iamo
(voi)	-iate
(loro)	-iscano

- Here's the result:

Third Conjugation (Type 2): finire / *to finish*		
(io)	finisca	*I finish, I am finishing, I may finish*
(tu)	finisca	*you (fam.) finish, you are finishing, you may finish*
(lui/lei/Lei)	finisca	*he, she, you (pol.) finish(es), he, she, you is/are finishing, he, she, you may finish*
(noi)	finiamo	*we finish, we are finishing, we may finish*
(voi)	finiate	*you finish, you are finishing, you may finish*
(loro)	finiscano	*they finish, they are finishing, they may finish*

The verbs that are irregular in the present indicative are also irregular in the present subjunctive. Here is a list of such conjugations:

andare / *to go* — (io) vada, (tu) vada, (lui/lei/Lei) vada, (noi) andiamo, (voi) andiate, (loro) vadano

avere / *to have* — (io) abbia, (tu) abbia, (lui/lei/Lei) abbia, (noi) abbiamo, (voi) abbiate, (loro) abbiano

bere / *to drink* — (io) beva, (tu) beva, (lui/lei/Lei) beva, (noi) beviamo, (voi) beviate, (loro) bevano

dare / *to give* — (io) dia, (tu) dia, (lui/lei/Lei) dia, (noi) diamo, (voi) diate, (loro) diano

dire / *to tell, to say* — (io) dica, (tu) dica, (lui/lei/Lei) dica, (noi) diciamo, (voi) diciate, (loro) dicano

dovere / *to have to* — (io) deva (debba), (tu) deva (debba), (lui/lei/Lei) deva (debba), (noi) dobbiamo, (voi) dobbiate, (loro) devano (debbano)

essere / *to be* — (io) sia, (tu) sia, (lui/lei/Lei) sia, (noi) siamo, (voi) siate, (loro) siano

fare / *to do, to make* — (io) faccia, (tu) faccia, (lui/lei/Lei) faccia, (noi) facciamo, (voi) facciate, (loro) facciano

morire / *to die*	(io) muoia, (tu) muoia, (lui/lei/Lei) muoia, (noi) moriamo, (voi) moriate, (loro) muoiano
nascere / *to be born*	(io) nasca, (tu) nasca, (lui/lei/Lei) nasca, (noi) nasciamo, (voi) nasciate, (loro) nascano
potere / *to be able to*	(io) possa, (tu) possa, (lui/lei/Lei) possa, (noi) possiamo, (voi) possiate, (loro) possano
rimanere / *to remain*	(io) rimanga, (tu) rimanga, (lui/lei/Lei) rimanga, (noi) rimaniamo, (voi) rimaniate, (loro) rimangano
salire / *to climb*	(io) salga, (tu) salga, (lui/lei/Lei) salga, (noi) saliamo, (voi) saliate, (loro) salgano
sapere / *to know*	(io) sappia, (tu) sappia, (lui/lei/Lei) sappia, (noi) sappiamo, (voi) sappiate, (loro) sappiano
scegliere / *to choose*	(io) scelga, (tu) scelga, (lui/lei/Lei) scelga, (noi) scegliamo, (voi) scegliate, (loro) scelgano
stare / *to stay*	(io) stia, (tu) stia, (lui/lei/Lei) stia, (noi) stiamo, (voi) stiate, (loro) stiano
uscire / *to go out*	(io) esca, (tu) esca, (lui/lei/Lei) esca, (noi) usciamo, (voi) usciate, (loro) escano
valere / *to be worth*	(io) valga, (tu) valga, (lui/lei/Lei) valga, (noi) valiamo, (voi) valiate, (loro) valgano
venire / *to come*	(io) venga, (tu) venga, (lui/lei/Lei) venga, (noi) veniamo, (voi) veniate, (loro) vengano
volere / *to want*	(io) voglia, (tu) voglia, (lui/lei/Lei) voglia, (noi) vogliamo, (voi) vogliate, (loro) vogliano

The subjunctive is used in subordinate clauses, generally introduced by **che**. So, when expressing something that is a doubt, an opinion, etc. with a verb in the main clause (the verb to the left of **che**), then put the verb in the subordinate clause (the verb to the right of **che**) in the subjunctive.

> **Spero** che loro **parlino** italiano. / *I hope that they speak Italian.*
> **Credo** che voi **sappiate** parlare spagnolo, no? / *I believe you know how to speak Spanish, right?*

Because the endings are often the same, you will need to use the subject pronouns much more frequently with the subjunctive.

> **È necessario che tu finisca quel lavoro.** / *It is necessary that you finish that job.*
> **È necessario che lui finisca quel lavoro.** / *It is necessary that he finish that job.*

Keep in mind that not all verbs in subordinate clauses (those after **che**) are necessarily to be put in the subjunctive—only those connected to a main clause verb that expresses a "nonfact" (opinion, fear, supposition, anticipation, wish, hope, doubt, etc.):

Indicative	Subjunctive
Sa che è la verità. / *He knows it is the truth.*	Pensa che sia la verità. / *He thinks it is the truth.*
È certo che paga lui. / *It is certain that he will pay.*	È improbabile che paghi lui. / *It is improbable that he will pay.*

The best way to learn which main clause verbs require the subjunctive is to memorize the most commonly used ones. Here are a few of them:

Impersonal verbs and expressions also require that the subordinate clause verb be in the subjunctive:

È probabile che lui non ti riconosca più. / *It's probable that he may not recognize you anymore.*
Bisogna che voi studiate di più. / *It is necessary that you study more.*

Here are a few of these:

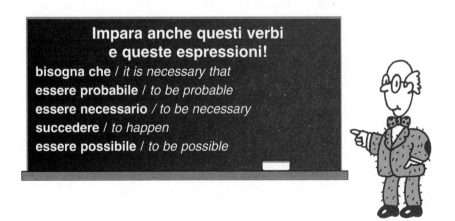

Superlative expressions also require the subjunctive:

Lei è la persona più intelligente che io conosca. / *She is the most intelligent person (that) I know.*

Certain conjunctions and indefinite structures also require the subjunctive:

Dovunque tu vada, io ti seguirò. / *Wherever you go, I will follow you.*
Benché piova, esco lo stesso. / *Although it is raining, I'm going out just the same.*

Here are the most common ones:

Impara queste forme!

a meno che...non / *unless*	**nonostante** / *despite*
affinché / *so that*	**perché** / *so that*
benché / *although*	**prima che** / *before*
chiunque / *whoever*	**purché** / *provided that*
dovunque / *wherever*	**qualunque** / *whichever*
nel caso che / *in the event that*	**sebbene** / *although*

Finally, the subjunctive is used in "wish" or "exhortation" expressions.

Che scriva lui! / *Let him write!*
Che piova, se vuole! / *Let it rain, if it wants to!*

QUICK PRACTICE 1

How do you say the following phrases in Italian?

1. He thinks (that) they are arriving tonight.
2. I imagine (that) she understands everything.
3. They doubt that you (*fam., sing.*) will finish in time.
4. You (*fam., sing.*) are the least elegant person I know.
5. Let it snow!
6. She wants me to call her tonight (She wants that I call her tonight).
7. It seems that you know Maria too.
8. I hope that Alessandro writes that e-mail.
9. Do you (*fam., sing.*) also believe that I speak Italian well?
10. We desire that they play soccer (**il calcio** / *soccer*) better.
11. It is necessary that he study more.
12. It is possible that they speak Italian.
13. It is probable that we will buy that car.

14. Although it is raining outside, I am going out just the same.

15. Unless she phones, we will not go to the movies.

16. So that you (*fam., sing.*) eat pasta, I will cook (**cucinare** / *to cook*) it myself (**io stesso/a**).

17. Whoever desires to do it, I agree!

18. Wherever she goes, I will also go.

19. In the event that he reads that e-mail, you (*fam., sing.*) should be ready (**pronto/a**) to call him.

20. Despite the fact that you (*fam., sing.*) never phone, I love you just the same.

21. Before you (*fam., pl.*) leave for Italy, you should save (**risparmiare** / *to save*) enough money.

22. I will do it, provided that you (*fam., sing.*) phone me first.

23. Whatever language they speak, I know that he will understand them.

Now, give the corresponding subjunctive form of each verb (which is in the indicative).

Modello: lui mangia
lui mangi

24. io...
    a. comincio
    b. mangio
    c. cerco
    d. pago

25. tu...
    a. hai
    b. bevi
    c. dai
    d. dici

26. lui/lei...
    a. va
    b. deve
    c. dice
    d. vuole

27. noi...
    a. siamo
    b. facciamo
    c. moriamo
    d. nasciamo

28. voi...
    a. potete
    b. rimanete
    c. salite
    d. sapete

29. loro...
    a. scelgono
    b. stanno
    c. escono
    d. vengono

The Past

Il congiuntivo passato

The *past subjunctive* is a compound tense. Therefore, it is conjugated with an auxiliary verb, either **avere** / *to have* or **essere** / *to be* in the present subjunctive, and the past participle of the verb, in that order. So, you know everything there is to know in order to conjugate verbs in this tense (for irregular past participles, see Chapter 4).

Examples:

Verbs Conjugated with avere			
First Conjugation: parlare / *to speak*			
(io)	abbia	parlato	*I have spoken, I spoke*
(tu)	abbia	parlato	*you (fam.) have spoken, you spoke*
(lui/lei/Lei)	abbia	parlato	*he, she, you (pol.) has/have spoken, he, she, you spoke*
(noi)	abbiamo	parlato	*we have spoken, we spoke*
(voi)	abbiate	parlato	*you have spoken, you spoke*
(loro)	abbiano	parlato	*they have spoken, they spoke*
Second Conjugation: vendere / *to sell*			
(io)	abbia	venduto	*I have sold, I sold*
(tu)	abbia	venduto	*you (fam.) have sold, you sold*
(lui/lei/Lei)	abbia	venduto	*he, she, you (pol.) has/have sold, he, she, you sold*
(noi)	abbiamo	venduto	*we have sold, we sold*
(voi)	abbiate	venduto	*you have sold, you sold*
(loro)	abbiano	venduto	*they have sold, they sold*
Third Conjugation: finire / *to finish*			
(io)	abbia	finito	*I have finished, I finished*
(tu)	abbia	finito	*you (fam.) have finished, you finished*
(lui/lei/Lei)	abbia	finito	*he, she, you (pol.) has/have finished, he, she, you finished*
(noi)	abbiamo	finito	*we have finished, we finished*
(voi)	abbiate	finito	*you have finished, you finished*
(loro)	abbiano	finito	*they have finished, they finished*

Verbs Conjugated with essere			

First Conjugation: arrivare / to arrive

(io)	sia	arrivato/a	*I have arrived, I arrived*
(tu)	sia	arrivato/a	*you (fam.) have arrived, you arrived*
(lui)	sia	arrivato	
(lei)	sia	arrivata	*he, she, you (pol.) has/have arrived, he,*
(Lei)	sia	arrivato/a	*she, you arrived*
(noi)	siamo	arrivati/e	*we have arrived, we arrived*
(voi)	siate	arrivati/e	*you have arrived, you arrived*
(loro)	siano	arrivati/e	*they have arrived, they arrived*

Second Conjugation: cadere / to fall

(io)	sia	caduto/a	*I have fallen, I fell*
(tu)	sia	caduto/a	*you (fam.) have fallen, you fell*
(lui)	sia	caduto	
(lei)	sia	caduta	*he, she, you (pol.) has/have fallen, he, she, you fell*
(Lei)	sia	caduto/a	
(noi)	siamo	caduti/e	*we have fallen, we fell*
(voi)	siate	caduti/e	*you have fallen, you fell*
(loro)	siano	caduti/e	*they have fallen, they fell*

Third Conjugation: uscire / to go out

(io)	sia	uscito/a	*I have gone out, I went out*
(tu)	sia	uscito/a	*you (fam.) have gone out, you went out*
(lui)	sia	uscito	
(lei)	sia	uscita	*he, she, you (pol.) has/have gone out, he, she,*
(Lei)	sia	uscito/a	*you went out*
(noi)	siamo	usciti/e	*we have gone out, we went out*
(voi)	siate	usciti/e	*you have gone out, you went out*
(loro)	siano	usciti/e	*they have gone out, they went out*

The past subjunctive corresponds to the present perfect in temporal usage and overall features (see Chapter 4). Essentially, it allows you to express a past action with respect to the main clause verb, which is usually in the present.

Non è possibile che lui abbia capito. / *It's not possible that he understood.*
Credo che loro siano già partiti. / *I think that they have already left.*
Sebbene sia venuta anche lei, lui non è felice. / *Although she too has come,*
    he is not happy.

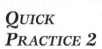

QUICK PRACTICE 2

Change the verb into the subjunctive by adding the indicated expression.

Modello: Maria ha mangiato gli spaghetti (Penso che…)
Penso che Maria abbia mangiato gli spaghetti.

1. Io ho cominciato a studiare l'italiano (Loro dubitano che…)
2. Tu hai letto quel romanzo già (Lei crede che…)
3. Mio fratello ha pagato il conto (Immagino che…)
4. Ha fatto bel tempo ieri (Penso che…)
5. Noi abbiamo bevuto il caffè al bar ieri (Lui crede che…)
6. Voi avete già visto quel film (Immagino che…)
7. Loro li hanno già comprati (Spero che…)
8. Io sono andata in Italia l'anno scorso (I miei amici pensano che…)
9. Tu sei uscito poco tempo fa (Lui pensa che…)
10. Mia sorella è arrivata qualche minuto fa (Penso che…)
11. Noi siamo venuti alla festa (Lui crede che…)
12. Voi siete tornati in Italia l'anno scorso (Mia madre crede che…)
13. Loro sono usciti tardi ieri (Lei pensa che…)
14. Tu sei andata in Italia l'anno scorso (Sembra che…)
15. Lui è venuto alla festa (Sembra che…)

The Imperfect
Il congiuntivo imperfetto

To form the *imperfect subjunctive* of regular verbs:

- Drop the **-re** from the infinitive endings **-are**, **-ere**, and **-ire**:

parlare / *to speak*	→	**parla-**
scrivere / *to write*	→	**scrive-**
finire / *to finish*	→	**fini-**

- Add the following endings to the stem according to person and number:

(io)	-ssi
(tu)	-ssi
(lui/lei/Lei)	-sse
(noi)	-ssimo
(voi)	-ste
(loro)	-ssero

- Here's the result:

First Conjugation: parlare / *to speak*

(io)	**parlassi**	*I was speaking, I used to speak*
(tu)	**parlassi**	*you (fam.) were speaking, you used to speak*
(lui/lei/Lei)	**parlasse**	*he, she, you (pol.) was/were speaking, he, she, you used to speak*
(noi)	**parlassimo**	*we were speaking, we used to speak*
(voi)	**parlaste**	*you were speaking, you used to speak*
(loro)	**parlassero**	*they were speaking, they used to speak*

Second Conjugation: scrivere / *to write*

(io)	**scrivessi**	*I was writing, I used to write*
(tu)	**scrivessi**	*you (fam.) were writing, you used to write*
(lui/lei/Lei)	**scrivesse**	*he, she, you (pol.) was/were writing, he, she, you used to write*
(noi)	**scrivessimo**	*we were writing, we used to write*
(voi)	**scriveste**	*you were writing, you used to write*
(loro)	**scrivessero**	*they were writing, they used to write*

Third Conjugation: finire / *to finish*

(io)	**finissi**	*I was finishing, I used to finish*
(tu)	**finissi**	*you (fam.) were finishing, you used to finish*
(lui/lei/Lei)	**finisse**	*he, she, you (pol.) was/were finishing, he, she, you used to finish*
(noi)	**finissimo**	*we were finishing, we used to finish*
(voi)	**finiste**	*you were finishing, you used to finish*
(loro)	**finissero**	*they were finishing, they used to finish*

The imperfect subjunctive corresponds to the imperfect indicative in temporal usage and overall features (see Chapter 4). Essentially, it allows you to convey the idea of repeated action in the past with respect to a main clause verb, which usually (although not necessarily) is in the past itself.

Non era possibile che lui capisse. / *It wasn't possible that he understood.*
Credevo che loro partissero. / *I thought that they were leaving.*
Mi sembrava che lui dicesse la verità. / *It seemed to me that he was telling the truth.*
Benché piovesse ieri, sono uscito lo stesso. / *Although it was raining yesterday, I went out just the same.*

> **TIP**
> Be careful again when you pronounce the third person plural forms! The accent is *not* placed on the ending, but on the syllable before the ending:
>
> parlássero
> scrivéssero
> finíssero

The imperfect subjunctive is also used after se / *if* in counterfactual statements when the main clause verb is in the conditional.

Se tu andassi a Roma, vedresti il Colosseo. / *If you were to go to Rome, you would see the Coliseum.*
Se potessimo, andremmo in Italia subito. / *If we could, we would go to Italy right away.*

It is also used in sentences beginning with magari / *I wish, if only*, expressing a wish or desire.

Magari non piovesse! / *I wish it wouldn't rain!*
Magari vincessi la lotteria! / *If only I would win the lottery!*

The same verbs that are irregular in the imperfect indicative (Chapter 4) are irregular in the corresponding subjunctive mood.

bere / *to drink*   (io) bevessi, (tu) bevessi, (lui/lei/Lei) bevesse, (noi) bevessimo, (voi) beveste, (loro) bevessero

dare / *to give*   (io) dessi, (tu) dessi, (lui/lei/Lei) desse, (noi) dessimo, (voi) deste, (loro) dessero

dire / *to say, to tell*	(io) dicessi, (tu) dicessi, (lui/lei/Lei) dicesse, (noi) dicessimo, (voi) diceste, (loro) dicessero
essere / *to be*	(io) fossi, (tu) fossi, (lui/lei/Lei) fosse, (noi) fossimo, (voi) foste, (loro) fossero
fare / *to do, to make*	(io) facessi, (tu) facessi, (lui/lei/Lei) facesse, (noi) facessimo, (voi) faceste, (loro) facessero
stare / *to stay*	(io) stessi, (tu) stessi, (lui/lei/Lei) stesse, (noi) stessimo, (voi) steste, (loro) stessero

QUICK PRACTICE 3

Change the verb into the subjunctive by adding the indicated expression.

Modello: Maria mangiava gli spaghetti (Pensavo che...)
   Pensavo che Maria mangiasse gli spaghetti.

1. Io cominciavo a studiare l'italiano (Loro dubitavano che...)
2. Tu leggevi quel romanzo (Lei credeva che...)
3. Mio fratello studiava a quest'ora (Io pensavo che...)
4. Lei usciva con Marco (Pensavo che...)
5. Noi guardavamo la televisione ogni sera da giovani (Lui credeva che...)
6. Pioveva ieri (Sembra che...)
7. Loro speravano di andare in Italia (Credo che...)
8. Io andavo in Italia ogni estate da bambino (I miei amici pensano che...)
9. Tu volevi uscire (Lui pensava che...)
10. Io bevevo il latte regolarmente (Loro dubitavano che...)
11. Tu dicevi sempre la verità (Lei credeva che...)
12. Mio fratello non faceva niente (Io pensavo che...)
13. Tu davi del tu al professore (Credevo che...)
14. Non piove (Magari...)
15. Nevicava, sono uscito lo stesso (Benché...)

Now, give the corresponding subjunctive form of each verb (which is in the indicative).

Modello: lui mangiava
            lui mangiasse

16. **io...**
    a. cominciavo
    b. mettevo
    c. capivo
    d. bevevo

17. **tu...**
    a. vendevi
    b. preferivi
    c. pagavi
    d. davi

18. **lui/lei...**
    a. era
    b. faceva
    c. stava
    d. finiva

19. **noi...**
    a. eravamo
    b. avevamo
    c. preferivamo
    d. facevamo

20. **voi...**
    a. stavate
    b. eravate
    c. avevate
    d. facevate

21. **loro...**
    a. erano
    b. avevano
    c. mangiavano
    d. capivano

The Pluperfect
Il congiuntivo trapassato

The *pluperfect subjunctive* is a compound tense. Therefore, it is conjugated with an auxiliary verb, either **avere** / *to have* or **essere** / *to be* in the imperfect subjunctive, and the past participle of the verb, in that order. So, you already know everything there is to know to conjugate this verb tense.

Examples:

Verbs Conjugated with avere			
First Conjugation: parlare / *to speak*			
(io)	avessi	parlato	*I had spoken*
(tu)	avessi	parlato	*you (fam.) had spoken*
(lui/lei/Lei)	avesse	parlato	*he, she, you (pol.) had spoken*
(noi)	avessimo	parlato	*we had spoken*
(voi)	aveste	parlato	*you had spoken*
(loro)	avessero	parlato	*they had spoken*
Second Conjugation: vendere / *to sell*			
(io)	avessi	venduto	*I had sold*
(tu)	avessi	venduto	*you (fam.) had sold*
(lui/lei/Lei)	avesse	venduto	*he, she, you (pol.) had sold*
(noi)	avessimo	venduto	*we had sold*
(voi)	aveste	venduto	*you had sold*
(loro)	avessero	venduto	*they had sold*
Third Conjugation: finire / *to finish*			
(io)	avessi	finito	*I had finished*
(tu)	avessi	finito	*you (fam.) had finished*
(lui/lei/Lei)	avesse	finito	*he, she, you (pol.) had finished*
(noi)	avessimo	finito	*we had finished*
(voi)	aveste	finito	*you had finished*
(loro)	avessero	finito	*they had finished*

Verbs Conjugated with essere			
First Conjugation: arrivare / *to arrive*			
(io)	fossi	arrivato/a	*I had arrived*
(tu)	fossi	arrivato/a	*you (fam.) had arrived*
(lui/lei/Lei)	fosse	arrivato	
	fosse	arrivata	*he, she, you (pol.) had arrived*
	fosse	arrivato/a	
(noi)	fossimo	arrivati/e	*we had arrived*
(voi)	foste	arrivati/e	*you had arrived*
(loro)	fossero	arrivati/e	*they had arrived*
Second Conjugation: cadere / *to fall*			
(io)	fossi	caduto/a	*I had fallen*
(tu)	fossi	caduto/a	*you (fam.) had fallen*
(lui/lei/Lei)	fosse	caduto	
	fosse	caduta	*he, she, you (pol.) had fallen*
	fosse	caduto/a	
(noi)	fossimo	caduti/e	*we had fallen*
(voi)	foste	caduti/e	*you had fallen*
(loro)	fossero	caduti/e	*they had fallen*
Third Conjugation: uscire / *to go out*			
(io)	fossi	uscito/a	*I had gone out*
(tu)	fossi	uscito/a	*you (fam.) had gone out*
(lui/lei/Lei)	fosse	uscito	
	fosse	uscita	*he, she, you (pol.) had gone out*
	fosse	uscito/a	
(noi)	fossimo	usciti/e	*we had gone out*
(voi)	foste	usciti/e	*you had gone out*
(loro)	fossero	usciti/e	*they had gone out*

This tense corresponds to the pluperfect indicative (Chapter 4) in usage and overall features. It allows you to express a past action that occurred before another past action.

Mi era sembrato che lui avesse detto la verità. / *It seemed to me that he had told the truth.*

Eravamo contenti che voi foste venuti. / *We were happy that you had come.*

Benché avesse piovuto tutto il mese, andavamo sempre fuori. / *Although it had rained the entire month, we went out just the same.*

As is the case with the imperfect subjunctive, the pluperfect subjunctive is also used after **se** / *if* in counterfactual statements. In this case, it is used when the main clause verb is in the conditional or conditional perfect, depending on sense:

> **Se avessi avuto i soldi, la avrei comprata.** / *If I had had the money, I would have bought it.*
>
> **Se tu avessi studiato ieri, oggi non ti preoccuperesti.** / *If you had studied yesterday, today you wouldn't worry.*

QUICK PRACTICE 4

*Choose either **a** (imperfect subjunctive) or **b** (pluperfect subjunctive) as the case may be.*

1. Se io ..., sarei andato in Italia l'anno scorso.
   a. potessi
   b. avessi potuto

2. Se tu ... quella pasta, ne avresti mangiata un'altra.
   a. mangiassi
   b. avessi mangiato

3. Se loro ... più soldi, comprerebbero una nuova casa.
   a. avessero
   b. avessero avuto

4. Se noi ... di più, oggi sapremmo parlare l'italiano meglio.
   a. studiassimo
   b. avessimo studiato

5. Se ... anche lui alla festa, tutti sarebbero stati più contenti.
   a. venisse
   b. fosse venuto

6. Se non ... ieri, io sarei uscita.
   a. nevicasse
   b. avesse nevicato

7. Se lui ... più velocemente ieri mattina, non sarebbe arrivato in ritardo.
   a. corresse
   b. avesse corso

8. Se ..., lo avrei fatto.
   a. potessi
   b. avessi potuto

Now, give the corresponding subjunctive form of each verb (which is in the indicative).

Modello: lui aveva capito
             lui avesse capito

9. **io…**
   a. avevo mangiato
   b. ero andato/a

10. **tu…**
    a. avevi fatto
    b. eri uscito/a

11. **lui/lei…**
    a. aveva detto
    b. era stato/a

12. **noi…**
    a. avevamo dato
    b. eravamo andati/e

13. **voi…**
    a. avevate parlato
    b. eravate usciti/e

14. **loro…**
    a. avevano detto
    b. erano usciti/e

PUTTING IT ALL TOGETHER

A. *Change the verbs into the subjunctive by adding the indicated expression to the given sentence. Follow the model.*

Modello: Giovanni va al cinema stasera (Dubito che…)
             Dubito che Giovanni vada al cinema stasera.

1. Loro vanno in Italia quest'anno (È probabile che…)
2. Tu hai trentatré anni (Penso che…)
3. Loro bevono il cappuccino (Sembra che…)
4. Lui dà la penna a Maria (Bisogna che…)
5. Voi dite la verità (Speriamo che…)
6. Loro devono studiare di più (Sembra che…)
7. C'è anche Alessandro (Immagino che…)

8. Fa bel tempo (Bisogna che...)
9. Nasce domani forse il bambino (Speriamo che...)
10. Marco può venire alla festa (Sembra che...)
11. Loro rimangono a casa domani (Penso che...)
12. La sua amica sa parlare l'italiano molto bene (Dubito che...)
13. Lui sceglie sempre lo stesso programma (Sembra che...)
14. Alessandro sta molto bene (Penso che...)
15. Loro escono insieme (Credo che...)
16. Quel film vale la pena di vedere (Dubito che...)
17. Loro vengono alla festa (Speriamo che...)
18. Lui vuole andare in Italia (Penso che...)

B. *Choose either* **a** *(present subjunctive) or* **b** *(past subjunctive) according to sense.*

1. Marco crede che tu ... con Maria tra qualche minuto.
   a. esca
   b. sia uscito

2. Marco crede che tu ... con Maria ieri sera.
   a. esca
   b. sia uscito

3. Loro pensano che voi ... in Italia l'anno prossimo.
   a. andiate
   b. siate andati

4. Loro pensano che voi ... in Italia l'anno scorso.
   a. andiate
   b. siate andati

5. Benché ..., esco lo stesso.
   a. piova
   b. abbia piovuto

6. Benché ..., sono uscita lo stesso.
   a. piova
   b. abbia piovuto

7. È probabile che lui ... la prossima settimana.
   a. venga
   b. sia venuto

8. È probabile che lui ... la settimana scorsa.
   a. venga
   b. sia venuto

Now, choose either **a** *(imperfect subjunctive) or* **b** *(present conditional) as the case may be.*

9. Se io ..., andrei subito in Italia.
   a. potessi
   b. potrei

10. Se loro ... più soldi, comprerebbero un nuovo televisore digitale.
    a. avessero
    b. avrebbero

11. Se noi studiassimo di più, ... parlare l'italiano meglio.
    a. sapessimo
    b. sapremmo

12. Magari ... anche lui alla festa!
    a. venisse
    b. verrebbe

13. Magari non ...!
    a. nevicasse
    b. nevicherebbe

14. Se lui ... più velocemente, non sarebbe sempre in ritardo ma in orario.
    a. camminasse
    b. camminerebbe

15. Se potessi, ... solo il mio cellulare per le chiamate telefoniche.
    a. usassi
    b. userei

C. *Say the following sentences in Italian.*

1. Although it snowed yesterday, I decided to go shopping just the same.
2. It's possible that they have already gone to the coffee shop.
3. He doesn't know who scored (**segnare** / *to score*) the goal yesterday.
4. He is the happiest person that I have ever known.
5. It seems that they have already seen that movie.
6. I think that my sister has already done that.
7. Everyone believes that I (*f.*) went to Italy last year.
8. Do you (*fam., sing.*) really think that he understood?
9. It is not true that I have eaten all the spaghetti.
10. I think that what he is saying is true.
11. It would be important that he study more.

12. If we could, we would go to the movies.

13. I wish it wouldn't be so hot!

14. If that were true, then I wouldn't be here.

D. **Cruciverba!**

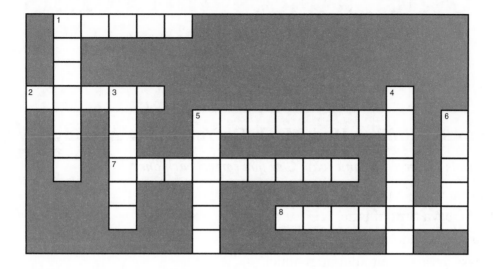

Change the verb into the imperfect subjunctive.

Pensavamo che...

Orizzontali
1. lui era italiano
2. tu davi del tu al professore
5. loro si amavano
7. loro sapevano parlare l'italiano
8. lei diceva la verità

Verticali
1. faceva bel tempo
3. tu stavi bene
4. lei poteva uscire
5. lei aveva 40 anni
6. lui dava del tu al professore

7

Other Tenses and Forms

Quanto Sai Già? — **How Much Do You Know Already?**

Each verb is incorrect in some way. Can you correct each one?

1. Signora, mangia la mela.   *mangi*
2. Marco, beva tutto il latte.   *bevi*
3. Cosa sei facendo in questo momento?
4. La casa avrà venduto dai miei amici.   *?*
5. Camminare per strada ieri, ho incontrato tuo fratello.   *Camminando*
6. Franco e Gina, mangino tutta la torta.   *mangiarono*
7. Signore e signori, desidera qualcosa?   *Desiderereste*
8. Maria, non leggi quel brutto libro.
9. Signorina, non ascoltare quella musica.   *ascolta*

The Imperative
L'imperativo

The *imperative* is the verb tense that allows you to give commands, issue requests, get things done for you, etc.

The imperative of regular verbs is formed as follows:

First conjugation:

- Drop the infinitive ending, **-are**:

    parlare / *to speak*   ➔   **parl-**

- Add the following endings according to person and number:

(io)	—
(tu)	-a
(lui/lei/Lei)	-i
(noi)	-iamo
(voi)	-ate
(loro)	-ino

- Here's the result:

First Conjugation: parlare / *to speak*		
(io)	—	—
(tu)	parla	*speak (fam.)*
(Lei)	parli	*speak (pol.)*
(noi)	parliamo	*let's speak*
(voi)	parlate	*speak (fam.)*
(Loro)	parlino	*speak (pol.)*

- Again, don't forget that the accent on third person plural forms does not fall on the last syllable: **párlino**.
- If the infinitive ending is **-ciare** or **-giare**, drop the **-are** and retain the **-i**, but do not write a "double **-i**" when adding on the endings **-i**, **-iamo**, and **-ino**:

cominciare / *to begin* ➔ cominci-		
(io)	—	—
(tu)	comincia	*begin (fam.)*
(Lei)	cominci	*begin (pol.)*
(noi)	cominciamo	*let's begin*
(voi)	cominciate	*begin (fam.)*
(Loro)	comincino	*begin (pol.)*

mangiare / *to eat* ➜ mangi-		
(io)	—	—
(tu)	mangia	*eat (fam.)*
(Lei)	mangi	*eat (pol.)*
(noi)	mangiamo	*let's eat*
(voi)	mangiate	*eat (fam.)*
(Loro)	mangino	*eat (pol.)*

- If the infinitive ending is -**care** or -**gare**, drop the -**are** but add "**h**" before the endings –**i**, -**iamo**, and -**ino**. As you know by now, this indicates that the hard sound is to be retained:

cercare / *to look for, to search for* ➜ cerc-		
(io)	—	—
(tu)	cerca	*look for (fam.)*
(Lei)	cerchi	*look for (pol.)*
(noi)	cerchiamo	*let's look for*
(voi)	cercate	*look for (fam.)*
(Loro)	cerchino	*look for (pol.)*

pagare / *to pay* ➜ pag-		
(io)	—	—
(tu)	paga	*pay (fam.)*
(Lei)	paghi	*pay (pol.)*
(noi)	paghiamo	*let's pay*
(voi)	pagate	*pay (fam.)*
(Loro)	paghino	*pay (pol.)*

First conjugation:

- Drop the infinitive ending, -**ere**:

  scrivere / *to write* ➜ scriv-

- Add the following endings according to person and number:

(io)	—
(tu)	-i
(lui/lei/Lei)	-a
(noi)	-iamo
(voi)	-ete
(loro)	-ano

- Here's the result:

Second Conjugation: scrivere / to write		
(io)	—	—
(tu)	scrivi	write (fam.)
(Lei)	scriva	write (pol.)
(noi)	scriviamo	let's write
(voi)	scvrivete	write (fam.)
(Loro)	scrivano	write (pol.)

For third conjugation verbs, a distinction between two types is once again applicable (see Chapter 3):

Third conjugation: Type 1

- Drop the infinitive ending, **-ire**:

  dormire / *to sleep*   ➔   **dorm-**

- Add the following endings according to person and number:

(io)	—
(tu)	-i
(Lei)	-a
(noi)	-iamo
(voi)	-ite
(Loro)	-ano

- Here's the result:

Third Conjugation (Type 1): dormire / to sleep		
(io)	—	—
(tu)	dormi	sleep (fam.)
(Lei)	dorma	sleep (pol.)
(noi)	dormiamo	let's sleep
(voi)	dormite	sleep (fam.)
(Loro)	dormano	sleep (pol.)

Third conjugation: Type 2

- Drop the infinitive ending, -ire:

  finire / *to finish* → fin-

- Add the following endings according to person and number:

(io)	—
(tu)	-isci
(Lei)	-isca
(noi)	-iamo
(voi)	-ite
(Loro)	-iscano

- Here's the result:

Third Conjugation (Type 2): finire / *to finish*		
(io)	—	—
(tu)	finisci	*finish (fam.)*
(Lei)	finisca	*finish (pol.)*
(noi)	finiamo	*let's finish*
(voi)	finite	*finish (fam.)*
(Loro)	finiscano	*finish (pol.)*

The imperative does not have the usual set of grammatical persons. It does not have a first person singular form (of course). The **voi** forms are used commonly as the plural forms of both **tu** (*familiar*) and **Lei** (*polite*) singular forms. The **Loro** (*polite*) forms are used in very formal situations:

Tu *form (sing.)*
Bambina, mangia la mela! / *Little girl, eat the apple!*

Voi *form (pl.)*
Bambine, mangiate le mele! / *Little girls, eat the apples!*

Lei *form (sing.)*
Signora, mangi la mela! / *Madam, eat the apple!*

Voi *form (pl.)*
Signore, mangiate le mele! / *Ladies, eat the apples!*

Loro *form (pl.)*
Signore, mangino le mele! / *Ladies, eat the apples!*

andare / *to go*	(io) —, (tu) va' (vai), (Lei) vada, (noi) andiamo, (voi) andate, (Loro) vadano
avere / *to have*	(io) —, (tu) abbi, (Lei) abbia, (noi) abbiamo, (voi) abbiate, (Loro) abbiano
bere / *to drink*	(io) —, (tu) bevi, (Lei) beva, (noi) beviamo, (voi) bevete, (Loro) bevano
dare / *to give*	(io) —, (tu) da' (dai), (Lei) dia, (noi) diamo, (voi) date, (Loro) diano
dire / *to tell, to say*	(io) —, (tu) di' (dici), (Lei) dica, (noi) diciamo, (voi) dite, (Loro) dicano
essere / *to be*	(io) —, (tu) sii, (Lei) sia, (noi) siamo, (voi) siate, (Loro) siano
fare / *to do, to make*	(io) —, (tu) fa' (fai), (Lei) faccia, (noi) facciamo, (voi) fate, (Loro) facciano
rimanere / *to remain*	(io) —, (tu) rimani, (Lei) rimanga, (noi) rimaniamo, (voi) rimanete, (Loro) rimangano
salire / *to climb*	(io) —, (tu) sali, (Lei) salga, (noi) saliamo, (voi) salite, (Loro) salgano
sapere / *to know*	(io) —, (tu) sappi, (Lei) sappia, (noi) sappiamo, (voi) sappiate, (Loro) sappiano
scegliere / *to choose*	(io) —, (tu) scegli, (Lei) scelga, (noi) scegliamo, (voi) scegliete, (Loro) scelgano
stare / *to stay*	(io) —, (tu) sta' (stai), (Lei) stia, (noi) stiamo, (voi) state, (Loro) stiano
uscire / *to go out*	(io) —, (tu) esci, (Lei) esca, (noi) usciamo, (voi) uscite, (Loro) escano
venire / *to come*	(io) —, (tu) vieni, (Lei) venga, (noi) veniamo, (voi) venite, (Loro) vengano

To form the negative imperative, add **non** before the verb (as always). But you must make one adjustment: change the second person singular form to the infinitive form of the verb.

Familiar Singular Forms

Affirmative	Negative
Parla! / *Speak!*	Non parlare! / *Don't speak!*
Scrivi! / *Write!*	Non scrivere! / *Don't write!*
Finisci! / *Finish!*	Non finire! / *Don't finish!*

Polite Singular Forms

Affirmative	Negative
Parli! / *Speak!*	Non parli! / *Don't speak!*
Scriva! / *Write!*	Non scriva! / *Don't write!*
Finisca! / *Finish!*	Non finisca! / *Don't finish!*

Plural Forms

Affirmative	Negative
Parliamo! / *Let's speak!*	Non parliamo! / *Let's not speak!*
Scrivete! / *Write (fam.)!*	Non scrivete! / *Don't write!*
Finiscano! / *Finish (pol.)!*	Non finiscano! / *Don't finish!*

QUICK PRACTICE 1

Give the following commands. This quick practice gives you practice with some of the verbs mentioned above. You will get more practice below in the Putting It All Together section.

Command Maria to do the following things:

Modello: Look for that book!
             Maria, cerca quel libro!

1. Speak Italian, please! *Maria, parla l'italiano, per favore*
2. Eat that cake (**la torta**)! *Maria, mangia la torta*
3. Close your mouth (**la bocca**)! *Maria Chiudi la boca*
4. Finish the spinach (**gli spinaci**)! *Maria finisci gli spinaci*
5. Go home! *Maria va acasa, or vai*
6. Have patience! *maria abbi pazienza*
7. Drink the coffee! *Maria bevi il caffe*
8. Give the pen to the teacher! *maria, da la penna al maestro.*
9. Tell the truth! *Maria, di verita.*
10. Be careful (**cauta**)! *maria sii cauta*

Now, give the same kinds of commands to Mr. Santini.

Modello: Look for that book!
Signor Santini, cerchi quel libro!

11. Speak Italian, please! *Signor Santini parli l'italiano per favore*
12. Eat that cake! *" " mangia la torta.*
13. Close your mouth! *" " chiuda sua bocca,*
14. Finish the spinach! *finisca gli spinaci*
15. Go home! *" " vada a casa*
16. Have patience! *" " abbia pazienza*
17. Drink the coffee! *" " beva il caffè*
18. Give the pen to the teacher! *" " dia la penna a maestra*
19. Tell the truth! *" " dica verità.*
20. Be careful (**cauto**)! *" " sia cauto.*

Now, give the same commands to both Maria and Marco.

Modello: Look for that book!
Maria e Marco, cercate quel libro!

21. Speak Italian, please! *Maria e Marco parlate l'italiano per favore*
22. Eat that cake! *mangiate le torta*
23. Close your mouth! *" " chiudete la bocca*
24. Finish the spinach! *" " finite gli spinaci*
25. Go home! *andate a casa*
26. Have patience! *abbiate gli pazienza*
27. Drink the coffee! *" " bevete il caffè*
28. Give the pen to the teacher! *date la penna a maestra*
29. Tell the truth! *dite verità*
30. Be careful (**cauti**)! *siate cauti.*

*Finally, give the same commands to Mr. and Mrs. Santini (use the **Loro** form).*

Modello: Look for that book!
Signore e signora Santini, cerchino quel libro!

31. Speak Italian, please! *Signore e signora Santini parlino l'italiano p. f.*
32. Eat that cake! *" " mangino la torta*
33. Close your mouth! *" " chiudano sua bocca.*
34. Finish the spinach! *" " finiscano gli spinaci*
35. Go home! *" " vadano a casa*
36. Have patience! *" " abbiano la pazienza*
37. Drink the coffee! *bevano il caffè*

38. Give the pen to the teacher!   *Diano la pena al professer*
39. Tell the truth!   *Diano la verda*
40. Be careful (cauti)!   *Diano Cauti.*

Now, someone tells Maria to do some things. You tell her not to do them.

Modello: Mangia la torta!
              Maria, non mangiare la torta!

41. Paga il conto!   *Marzo , non pagare il conto.*
42. Va' a casa!   *Marie non andar a casa*
43. Bevi il latte!   *" non bere il latte*
44. Da' a Marco la tua penna!   *Marie non dare*
45. Rimani a casa!   *Marie non remanere a case*
46. Scegli questo!   *non scegliere questo*
47. Sta' a casa tutto il giorno!   *non stare a casa tutto il giorno*
48. Esci con Marco!   *non uscire con marco*

The Progressive Tenses
I tempi progressivi

Progressive tenses are verb forms that allow you to zero in on an ongoing action, in the past, present, or future. The *present progressive* is an alternative to the present indicative, allowing you to zero in on a presently ongoing action.

> **In questo momento, mia sorella sta leggendo.** / *At this moment, my sister is reading.*
> **Marco sta scrivendo un'e-mail.** / *Mark is writing an e-mail.*
> **Loro stanno finendo di lavorare.** / *They are finishing work.*

The present progressive is formed with the present tense of the verb **stare** and the gerund of the verb, in that order. You already know how to conjugate **stare** (Chapter 3).

Here's how to form the gerund of regular verbs:

• Drop the infinitive ending of the verb:

> **parlare** / *to speak* ➔   parl-
> **vendere** / *to sell* ➔   vend-
> **finire** / *to finish* ➔   fin-

- Add the endings **-ando**, **-endo**, and **-endo** (respectively) to the resulting stems:

> parlando / *speaking*
> vendendo / *writing*
> finendo / *finishing*

The good news is that most verbs have regular gerunds. Even **essere** has a regular gerund (**essendo**)! Here are the four most common verbs with irregular ones:

Impara questi gerundi!

bere / *to drink*	→	**bevendo** / *drinking*
dare / *to give*	→	**dando** / *giving*
dire / *to tell, to say*	→	**dicendo** / *telling, saying*
fare / *to do, to make*	→	**facendo** / *doing*

Below are three verbs conjugated in the present progressive:

First Conjugation: parlare / *to speak*

(io)	sto	parlando	*I am speaking*
(tu)	stai	parlando	*you (fam.) are speaking*
(lui/lei/Lei)	sta	parlando	*he, she, you (pol.) is/are speaking*
(noi)	stiamo	parlando	*we are speaking*
(voi)	state	parlando	*you are speaking*
(loro)	stanno	parlando	*they are speaking*

Second Conjugation: vendere / *to sell*

(io)	sto	vendendo	*I am selling*
(tu)	stai	vendendo	*you (fam.) are selling*
(lui/lei/Lei)	sta	vendendo	*he, she, you (pol.) is/are selling*
(noi)	stiamo	vendendo	*we are selling*
(voi)	state	vendendo	*you are selling*
(loro)	stanno	vendendo	*they are selling*

Third Conjugation: finire / to finish			
(io)	sto	finendo	*I am finishing*
(tu)	stai	finendo	*you (fam.) are finishing*
(lui/lei/Lei)	sta	finendo	*he, she, you (pol.) is/are finishing*
(noi)	stiamo	finendo	*we are finishing*
(voi)	state	finendo	*you are finishing*
(loro)	stanno	finendo	*they are finishing*

This tense is an alternative to the present indicative when the action is ongoing.

Present Indicative	Present Progressive
In questo momento, Maria studia. / *At this moment, Maria is studying.*	**In questo momento, Maria sta studiando.** / *At this moment, Maria is studying.*
Che fa tuo fratello? / *What is your brother doing?*	**Che sta facendo tuo fratello?** / *What is your brother doing?*

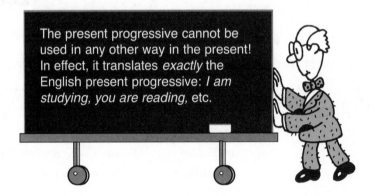

The present progressive cannot be used in any other way in the present! In effect, it translates *exactly* the English present progressive: *I am studying, you are reading,* etc.

The present subjunctive has a progressive form as well, allowing you to zero in on an ongoing action that is to be expressed in the subjunctive mood:

Penso che in questo momento, mia sorella stia mangiando. / *I think that at this moment, my sister is eating.*
Sembra che loro stiano guardando la televisione. / *It seems that they are watching TV.*

The present subjunctive progressive is formed with the present subjunctive of the verb **stare** (Chapter 6) and the gerund of the verb, in that order. Here are three verbs conjugated in the present progressive subjunctive:

TIP
The present progressive is often used with:

in questo momento / *in/at this moment, at this time*
mentre / *while*
adesso / ora *now*

First Conjugation: parlare / to speak

(io)	stia	parlando	I am speaking
(tu)	stia	parlando	you (fam.) are speaking
(lui/lei/Lei)	stia	parlando	he, she, you (pol.) is/are speaking
(noi)	stiamo	parlando	we are speaking
(voi)	stiate	parlando	you are speaking
(loro)	stiano	parlando	they are speaking

Second Conjugation: vendere / to sell

(io)	stia	vendendo	I am selling
(tu)	stia	vendendo	you (fam.) are selling
(lui/lei/Lei)	stia	vendendo	he, she, you (pol.) is/are selling
(noi)	stiamo	vendendo	we are selling
(voi)	stiate	vendendo	you are selling
(loro)	stiano	vendendo	they are selling

Third Conjugation: finire / to finish

(io)	stia	finendo	I am finishing
(tu)	stia	finendo	you (fam.) are finishing
(lui/lei/Lei)	stia	finendo	he, she, you (pol.) is/are finishing
(noi)	stiamo	finendo	we are finishing
(voi)	stiate	finendo	you are finishing
(loro)	stiano	finendo	they are finishing

The imperfect progressive is an alternative to the imperfect indicative, allowing you to zero in on an action in the past that was ongoing at the time (usually relative to another action):

Ieri mentre mia sorella stava mangiando, io stavo guardando la TV. / *Yesterday, while my sister was eating, I was watching TV.*

It is formed with the imperfect tense of the verb **stare** (Chapter 4) and the gerund of the verb, in that order.

action words use stare almost never essere

Here are three verbs conjugated in the present progressive:

First Conjugation: parlare / to speak			
(io)	stavo	parlando	I was speaking
(tu)	stavi	parlando	you (fam.) were speaking
(lui/lei/Lei)	stava	parlando	he, she, you (pol.) was/were speaking
(noi)	stavamo	parlando	we were speaking
(voi)	stavate	parlando	you were speaking
(loro)	stavano	parlando	they were speaking

Second Conjugation: vendere / to sell			
(io)	stavo	vendendo	I was selling
(tu)	stavi	vendendo	you (fam.) were selling
(lui/lei/Lei)	stava	vendendo	he, she, you (pol.) was/were selling
(noi)	stavamo	vendendo	we were selling
(voi)	stavate	vendendo	you were selling
(loro)	stavano	vendendo	they were selling

Third Conjugation: finire / to finish			
(io)	stavo	finendo	I was finishing
(tu)	stavi	finendo	you (fam.) were finishing
(lui/lei/Lei)	stava	finendo	he, she, you (pol.) was/were finishing
(noi)	stavamo	finendo	we were finishing
(voi)	stavate	finendo	you were finishing
(loro)	stavano	finendo	they were finishing

There is also a progressive form of the imperfect subjunctive, allowing you to zero in on an imperfect action to be expressed in the subjunctive mood:

Penso che mia sorella stesse mangiando, mentre io stavo guardando la TV ieri. / *I think that my sister was eating while I was watching TV yesterday.*

The imperfect subjunctive progressive is formed with the imperfect subjunctive of the verb **stare** (Chapter 6) and the gerund of the verb, in that order. Here are three verbs conjugated in this tense:

First Conjugation: parlare / to speak

(io)	stessi	parlando	*I was speaking*
(tu)	stessi	parlando	*you (fam.) were speaking*
(lui/lei/Lei)	stesse	parlando	*he, she, you (pol.) was/were speaking*
(noi)	stessimo	parlando	*we were speaking*
(voi)	steste	parlando	*you were speaking*
(loro)	stessero	parlando	*they were speaking*

Second Conjugation: vendere / to sell

(io)	stessi	vendendo	*I was selling*
(tu)	stessi	vendendo	*you (fam.) were selling*
(lui/lei/Lei)	stesse	vendendo	*he, she, you (pol.) was/were selling*
(noi)	stessimo	vendendo	*we were selling*
(voi)	steste	vendendo	*you were selling*
(loro)	stessero	vendendo	*they were selling*

Third Conjugation: finire / to finish

(io)	stessi	finendo	*I was finishing*
(tu)	stessi	finendo	*you (fam.) were finishing*
(lui/lei/Lei)	stesse	finendo	*he, she, you (pol.) was/were finishing*
(noi)	stessimo	finendo	*we were finishing*
(voi)	steste	finendo	*you were finishing*
(loro)	stessero	finendo	*they were finishing*

8–8

QUICK PRACTICE 2

Say the following phrases in Italian, using present progressive forms.

1. Franco, what are you drinking? Are you drinking an espresso coffee?
2. What movie are they showing at this time? *Stai levando Espresso cope*
3. Mrs. Marchi, what are you saying?

1. Franco rosa stai bevendo?
2. Che cosa stanno presentando a che ora?
3. Signora Marchi, che stai dicendo

4. What are they doing?

5. Marco and Maria are going out at this moment.

6. Where is Alessandro? He's sleeping.

7. What are they drinking? Are they drinking a cappuccino?

8. I believe that Franco is drinking an espresso coffee.

9. It's possible that they are leaving for Italy at this time.

10. She does not believe that you are saying that, Mrs. Marchi.

11. I think that they are doing nothing at this time.

12. I believe that Marco and Maria are shopping at this moment.

Now, give the equivalent imperfect subjunctive form as indicated by using the given expression. Follow the model.

Modello: (Pensavano che...) lui stava mangiando
           Pensavano che lui stesse mangiando.

Pensavano che...

13. io stavo leggendo

14. tu stavi bevendo il caffè

15. lei stava guardando la TV

16. noi stavamo facendo delle spese

17. voi stavate dicendo la verità

18. i loro genitori stavano guardando la TV

Finally, translate the following dialogue between Maria and Marco.

Maria: Hi, Marco, we haven't seen each other for years (**da anni**). What's up (**fare di bello** / *to be up*)?

Marco: Hi, Maria. It's true. Right now, I'm doing nothing. What about you?

Maria: I'm working in a bank. But I'm planning (**programmare** / *to plan*) to go back to university.

Marco: I'm planning the same thing.

Maria: You know, they are showing a new movie tonight. Do you want to come with my fiancé (**il fidanzato** / *fiancé*) and me?

Marco: No, thanks. Right now, I'm going out with Franca. We are planning to do something else. See you soon!

Maria: Bye!

162 Complete Italian Grammar Review

Reflexive Verbs
I verbi riflessivi

A verb is *reflexive* when it has an identical subject and direct object, as in *She dressed herself*. The object is expressed as a *reflexive pronoun* (**un pronome riflessivo**). Reflexive verbs are thus conjugated in exactly the same manner as nonreflexive verbs, but with reflexive pronouns.

Italian Reflexive Pronouns		
	Singular	Plural
(1st person)	**mi** / *myself*	**ci** / *ourselves*
(2nd person)	**ti** / *yourself* (fam.)	**vi** / *yourselves* (fam.)
(3rd person)	**si** / *himself, herself, yourself* (pol.)	**si** / *themselves, yourselves* (pol.)

Io mi lavo di solito alla mattina. / *I usually wash myself in the morning.*
Tu non ti diverti di solito al cinema, vero? / *You do not usually enjoy yourself at the movies, right?*

A reflexive infinitive is identifiable by the ending **-si** /*oneself*:

lavarsi / *to wash oneself*
mettersi / *to put on, to wear*
divertirsi / *to enjoy oneself*

Reflexive verbs are conjugated in exactly the same manner as other verbs with, of course, the addition of reflexive pronouns. Here's an example of verbs conjugated in the present tense (indicative and subjunctive).

- Drop the reflexive infinitive ending, **-arsi, -ersi, -irsi**:

lavarsi / *to wash oneself*	➜	**lav-**
mettersi / *to put on, to wear*	➜	**mett-**
divertirsi / *to enjoy oneself*	➜	**divert-**

- Add on the endings in the usual manner (Chapter 3).

lavarsi / *to wash oneself*			
(io)	mi	**lavo/lavi**	*I wash myself, I am washing myself*
(tu)	ti	**lavi/lavi**	*you (fam.) wash yourself, you are washing yourself*
(lui/lei/Lei)	si	**lava/lavi**	*he, she, you (pol.) wash(es) himself/herself/yourself, he, she, you is/are washing himself/herself/yourself*
(noi)	ci	**laviamo/laviamo**	*we wash ourselves, we are washing ourselves*
(voi)	vi	**lavate/laviate**	*you wash yourselves, you are washing yourselves*
(loro)	si	**lavano/lavino**	*they wash themselves, they are washing themselves*

mettersi / *to put on (oneself), to wear*			
(io)	mi	metto/metta	*I wear, I am wearing*
(tu)	ti	metti/metta	*you (fam.) wear, you are wearing*
(lui/lei/Lei)	si	mette/metta	*he, she, you (pol.) wear(s), he, she, you is/are wearing*
(noi)	ci	mettiamo/mettiamo	*we wear, we are wearing*
(voi)	vi	mettete/mettiate	*you wear, you are wearing*
(loro)	si	mettono/mettano	*they wear, they are wearing*

divertirsi / *to enjoy oneself*			
(io)	mi	diverto/diverta	*I enjoy myself, I am enjoying myself*
(tu)	ti	diverti/diverta	*you (fam.) enjoy yourself, you are enjoying yourself*
(lui/lei/Lei)	si	diverte/diverta	*he, she, you (pol.) enjoy(s) himself/herself/yourself, he, she, you is/are enjoying himself/herself/yourself*
(noi)	ci	divertiamo/divertiamo	*we enjoy ourselves, we are enjoying ourselves*
(voi)	vi	divertite/divertiate	*you enjoy yourselves, you are enjoying yourselves*
(loro)	si	divertono/divertano	*they enjoy themselves, they are enjoying themselves*

Here are some common reflexive verbs that will come in handy for basic communication purposes:

addormentarsi	*to fall asleep*
alzarsi	*to get up, to stand up*
andarsene	*to go away*
ammalarsi	*to get sick*
annoiarsi	*to become bored*
arrabbiarsi	*to become angry*
chiamarsi	*to call oneself, to be named*
dimenticarsi	*to forget*
divertirsi	*to enjoy oneself, to have fun*
farsi il bagno	*to take a bath*
lamentarsi	*to complain*
lavarsi	*to wash oneself*
mettersi	*to put on, to wear*
prepararsi	*to prepare oneself*
ricordarsi	*to remember*
sentirsi	*to feel*
sposarsi	*to marry, to get married*
svegliarsi	*to wake up*
vergognarsi	*to be ashamed*
vestirsi	*to get dressed*

Notice that a few of the verbs are not equivalently reflexive in English. Be careful! Some Italian reflexive verbs correspond to English verbal constructions made up with verbs such as *to get...* and *to become ...*:

alzarsi	=	*to get up*
ammalarsi	=	*to get sick*
annoiarsi	=	*to become bored*
sposarsi	=	*to get married*

Two of the verbs in the list on page 164 require special commentary. The first one is **andarsene**. Treat this verb as any reflexive verb, adding **ne** (which in this case means *away*) right after the pronouns. However, you must change the reflexive pronouns as shown. Recall that **andare** is an irregular verb (Chapter 4):

andarsene / *to go away*				
(io)	me	ne	vado	*I go away, I am going away*
(tu)	te	ne	vai	*you (fam.) go away, you are going away*
(lui/lei/Lei)	se	ne	va	*he, she, you (pol.) go(es) away, he, she, you is/are going away*
(noi)	ce	ne	andiamo	*we go away, we are going away*
(voi)	ve	ne	andate	*you go away, you are going away*
(loro)	se	ne	vanno	*they go away, they are going away*

The second verb that requires commentary is **chiamarsi**. This is rendered in English with expressions such as *my name is, your name is*, etc.:

(Io) mi chiamo Marcello. / *My name is Marcello.*
Come ti chiami? / *What's your name?*

Some verbs can be "converted" into reflexives. These allow you to express reciprocity (*to each other, to one another*, etc.):

vedere / *to see*	➔	vedersi / *to see one another*
telefonare / *to phone*	➔	telefonarsi / *to phone one another*
chiamare / *to call*	➔	chiamarsi / *to call one another*
parlare / *to speak*	➔	parlarsi / *to speak to each other*
capire / *to understand*	➔	capirsi / *to understand each other*

Examples:

Loro non si vedono da anni. / *They haven't seen each other for years.*
Voi vi telefonate spesso, vero? / *You phone each other often, right?*
Voi vi chiamate ogni giorno, no? / *You call each other every day, right?*
Noi non ci parliamo da molti anni. / *We haven't been talking to each other for many years.*

Notice that the preposition **da** followed by a time word or expression renders the idea of *since* and *for*...

> **Non si parlano da molto tempo.** / *They haven't been talking to each other for a long time.*
> **Non si vedono da mesi.** / *They haven't seen each other for months.*
> **Vivono qui dal 2005.** / *They have been living here since 2005.*

The progressive of reflexive verbs is formed in the usual fashion but with the addition of reflexive pronouns. Here is a brief overview:

Present Progressive (Indicative and Subjunctive) of *lavarsi* / *to wash oneself*

(io)	mi	sto/stia	lavando	*I am washing myself*
(tu)	ti	stai/stia	lavando	*you (fam.) are washing yourself*
(lui/lei/Lei)	si	sta/stia	lavando	*he, she, you (pol.) is/are washing himself/herself/yourself*
(noi)	ci	stiamo/stiamo	lavando	*we are washing ourselves*
(voi)	vi	state/stiate	lavando	*you are washing yourselves*
(loro)	si	stanno/stiano	lavando	*they are washing themselves*

Imperfect Progressive (Indicative and Subjunctive) of *lavarsi* / *to wash oneself*

(io)	mi	stavo/stessi	lavando	*I was washing myself*
(tu)	ti	stavi/stessi	lavando	*you (fam.) were washing yourself*
(lui/lei/Lei)	si	stava/stesse	lavando	*he, she, you (pol.) was/were washing himself/herself/yourself*
(noi)	ci	stavamo/stessimo	lavando	*we were washing ourselves*
(voi)	vi	stavate/steste	lavando	*you were washing yourselves*
(loro)	si	stavano/stiano	lavando	*they were washing themselves*

Future and Conditional of alzarsi / to get up

(io)	mi	alzerò/alzerei	I will/would get up
(tu)	ti	alzerai/alzeresti	you (fam.) will/would get up
(lui/lei/Lei)	si	alzerà/alzerebbe	he, she, you (pol.) will/would get up
(noi)	ci	alzeremo/alzeremmo	we will/would get up
(voi)	vi	alzerete/alzereste	you will/would get up
(loro)	si	alzeranno/alzerebbero	they will/would get up

Past Absolute of lavarsi / to wash oneself

(io)	mi	lavai	I washed myself
(tu)	ti	lavasti	you (fam.) washed yourself
(lui/lei/Lei)	si	lavò	he, she, you (pol.) washed himself/herself/yourself
(noi)	ci	lavammo	we washed ourselves
(voi)	vi	lavaste	you washed yourselves
(loro)	si	lavarono	they washed themselves

Imperfect (Indicative and Subjunctive) of lavarsi / to wash oneself

(io)	mi	lavavo/lavassi	I was washing myself, I used to wash myself
(tu)	ti	lavavi/lavassi	you (fam.) were washing yourself, you used to wash yourself
(lui/lei/Lei)	si	lavava/lavasse	he, she, you (pol.) was/were washing himself/herself/yourself, he, she, you used to wash himself/herself/yourself
(noi)	ci	lavavamo/lavassimo	we were washing ourselves, we used to wash ourselves
(voi)	vi	lavavate/lavaste	you were washing yourselves, you used to wash yourselves
(loro)	si	lavavano/lavassero	they were washing themselves, they used to wash themselves

In compound tenses, reflexive verbs are conjugated only with the auxiliary verb essere in the appropriate tense and mood:

Lui si è divertito in Italia. / *He enjoyed himself in Italy.*
Maria si è alzata tardi questa mattina. / *Mary got up late this morning.*

Present Perfect of lavarsi / to wash oneself

(io)	mi	sono	lavato/a	*I have washed myself, I washed myself*
(tu)	ti	sei	lavato/a	*you (fam.) have washed yourself, you washed yourself*
(lui)	si	è	lavato	*he has washed himself, he washed himself*
(lei)	si	è	lavata	*she has washed herself, she washed herself*
(Lei)	si	è	lavato/a	*you (pol.) have washed yourself, you washed yourself*
(noi)	ci	siamo	lavati/e	*we have washed ourselves, we washed ourselves*
(voi)	vi	siete	lavati/e	*you have washed yourselves, you washed yourselves*
(loro)	si	sono	lavati/e	*they have washed themselves, they washed themselves*

Past Subjunctive of divertirsi / to enjoy oneself, to have fun

(io)	mi	sia	divertito/a	*I have enjoyed myself, I enjoyed myself*
(tu)	ti	sia	divertito/a	*you (fam.) have enjoyed yourself, you enjoyed yourself*
(lui)	si	sia	divertito	
(lei)	si	sia	divertita	*he, she, you (pol.) has/have enjoyed himself/herself/*
(Lei)	si	sia	divertito/a	*yourself, he, she, you enjoyed himself/herself/yourself*
(noi)	ci	siamo	divertiti/e	*we have enjoyed ourselves, we enjoyed ourselves*
(voi)	vi	siate	divertiti/e	*you have enjoyed yourselves, you enjoyed yourselves*
(loro)	si	siano	divertiti/e	*they have enjoyed themselves, they enjoyed themselves*

Future Perfect and Past Conditional of divertirsi / to enjoy oneself

(io)	mi	sarò/sarei	divertito/a	*I will/would have enjoyed myself*
(tu)	ti	sarai/saresti	divertito/a	*you (fam.) will/would have enjoyed yourself*
(lui)	si	sarà/sarebbe	divertito	*he will/would have enjoyed himself*
(lei)	si	sarà/sarebbe	divertita	*she will/would have enjoyed herself*
(Lei)	si	sarà/sarebbe	divertito/a	*you (pol.) will/would have enjoyed yourself*
(noi)	ci	saremo/saremmo	divertiti/e	*we will/would have enjoyed ourselves*
(voi)	vi	sarete/sareste	divertiti/e	*you will/would have enjoyed yourselves*
(loro)	si	saranno/sarebbero	divertiti/e	*they will/would have enjoyed themselves*

Pluperfect Indicative and Subjunctive of divertirsi / *to enjoy oneself*				
(io)	mi	ero/fossi	divertito/a	*I had enjoyed myself*
(tu)	ti	eri/fossi	divertito/a	*you (fam.) had enjoyed yourself*
(lui)	si	era/fosse	divertito	*he, she, you (pol.) had enjoyed himself/herself/*
(lei)	si	era/fosse	divertita	*yourself*
(Lei)	si	era/fosse	divertito/a	
(noi)	ci	eravamo/fossimo	divertiti/e	*we had enjoyed ourselves*
(voi)	vi	eravate/foste	divertiti/e	*you had enjoyed yourselves*
(loro)	si	erano/fossero	divertiti/e	*they had enjoyed themselves*

Reflexive verbs are conjugated in the same manner as all other verbs in the imperative as well. However, the position of the reflexive pronoun varies.

- It is attached to familiar forms and to the **noi** form:

    Marco, alzati! / *Marco, get up!*
    Alziamoci! / *Let's get up!*
    Ragazzi, alzatevi! / *Guys, get up!*

- It goes before the polite forms:

    Signor Smith, si alzi! / *Mr. Smith, get up!*
    Signori, si alzino! / *Gentlemen, get up!*

Imperative of lavarsi / *to wash oneself* ➔ lav-		
(io)	—	—
(tu)	lavati	*wash yourself (fam.)*
(Lei)	si lavi	*wash yourself (pol.)*
(noi)	laviamoci	*let's wash ourselves*
(voi)	lavatevi	*wash yourselves (fam.)*
(Loro)	si lavino	*wash yourselves (pol.)*

In the case of the negative forms, remember that the infinitive is used in the second person singular. The pronoun can be attached or put before the verb. Note that attaching the pronoun to the infinitive requires that you drop the final -e of the infinitive:

Affirmative	**Negative**
Lavati! / *Wash yourself!*	Non lavarti! / *Don't wash yourself! (fam.)*
	Non ti lavare! / *Don't wash yourself! (fam.)*
Alzati! / *Get up!*	Non alzarti! / *Don't get up!*
	Non ti alzare! / *Don't get up!*

Notice that there are two possibilities for the negative of the **tu** forms. Also keep in mind that the accent is preserved on the stem: **álzati**, **méttiti**, etc.

QUICK
PRACTICE 3

Choose the correct verb form according to the sense.

1. Io generalmente ... quando guardo la televisione.
   a. mi addormento
   b. mi chiamo
   c. mi alzo

2. Tu ... sempre tutto!
   a. ti arrabbi
   b. ti diverti
   c. ti dimentichi

3. Sua cugina ... solo quando va al cinema.
   a. si chiama
   b. si diverte
   c. si sposa

4. Noi ... facilmente quando le cose non vanno bene.
   a. ci lamentiamo
   b. ci vestiamo
   c. ci laviamo

5. È vero che voi … facilmente tutto?
   a. vi ricordate
   b. vi vergognate
   c. vi sposate

6. Signore, come … Lei?
   a. si chiama
   b. si prepara
   c. si sveglia

7. Loro … il bagno ogni giorno.
   a. si lavano
   b. si annoiano
   c. si fanno

8. Io … alla festa ieri.
   a. mi sono divertito
   b. mi ero divertito
   c. mi divertivo

9. Tu … spesso quando eri bambina.
   a. ti sei annoiata
   b. ti eri annoiata
   c. ti annoiavi

10. Dopo che lui …, abbiamo deciso di andare a fare delle spese.
    a. si è alzato
    b. si era alzato
    c. si alzava

11. Noi … verso mezzogiorno ieri.
    a. ce ne siamo andati
    b. ce ne eravamo andati
    c. ce ne andavamo

12. Solo dopo che voi …, abbiamo guardato quel programma.
    a. vi siete addormentati
    b. vi eravate addormentati
    c. vi addormentavate

13. Da bambini, loro … sempre tardi il sabato.
    a. si sono alzati
    b. si erano alzati
    c. si alzavano

Missing from each of the following sentences is the verb. The missing verbs are given to you in their infinitive forms. Put each verb, in its correct form, in each sentence according to the sense.

annoiarsi, vedersi, capirsi, chiamarsi, sposarsi, parlarsi, alzarsi

14. Come ti chiami? _____ Claudia Corelli.
15. Marco, a che ora _____ generalmente la mattina?
16. Noi _____ spesso quando guardiamo la televisione.
17. Maria _____ questa primavera.
18. Quei due amici non _____ da mesi.
19. Io e tu non _____ mai!
20. È vero che voi non _____ da molto tempo?

Now, give the equivalent progressive form of the verb.

Modello: io mi lavo
             io mi sto lavando

21. io mi lamento
22. tu ti vesti
23. lei si diverte
24. noi ci arrabbiamo
25. voi ve ne andate
26. loro si annoiano
27. io mi ero annoiato
28. tu te ne eri andata

Now, say the following.

29. Giovanni, get up!
30. Mary don't get up yet!
31. I believe that he was feeling quite well.
32. Although he had fallen asleep, we still continued to watch TV.

Order Pietro to do (or not do) the following things.

33. Fall asleep!
34. Don't get angry!
35. Don't forget to write to your aunt!
36. Enjoy yourself in Italy!

Finally, make the following suggestions to Mrs. Rossi.

37. Don't complain!
38. Put on the new suit!
39. Don't worry!

Verbs Like *Dedurre* and *Porre*
Verbi tipo dedurre e porre

In addition to infinitives ending in -are, -ere, and ire, there is a fourth type ending in -rre; albeit very few of them:

> dedurre / *to deduce*
> indurre / *to induce*
> produrre / *to produce*
> tradurre / *to translate*
> porre / *to put*
> trarre / *to pull*
> attrarre / *to attract*

Those ending in -durre can be rendered hypothetically "regular" as follows:

- Change the ending in your mind to -cere:

  > tradurre / *to translate*   ➔   "traducere"

- Drop the -ere ending of the "hypothetical" verb stem:

  > traducere   ➔   traduc-

- Add the usual endings in the present (indicative and subjunctive), imperfect, and imperative:

  > *Present Indicative:*
  > (io) traduco, (tu) traduci, (lui/lei/Lei) traduce, (noi) traduciamo, (voi) traducete, (loro) traducono
  >
  > *Present Subjunctive:*
  > (io) traduca, (tu) traduca, (lui/lei/Lei) traduca, (noi) traduciamo, (voi) traduciate, (loro) traducano
  >
  > *Imperfect Indicative:*
  > (io) traducevo, (tu) traducevi, (lui/lei/Lei) traduceva, (noi) traducevamo, (voi) traducevate, (loro) traducevano
  >
  > *Imperfect Subjunctive:*
  > (io) traducessi, (tu) traducessi, (lui/lei/Lei) traducesse, (noi) traducessimo, (voi) traduceste, (loro) traducessero

Imperative:
—, (tu) traduci (non tradurre), (Lei) traduca, (noi) traduciamo, (voi) traducete, (Loro) traducano

To form the future and conditional, drop the -**e** and add the usual endings (Chapter 5):

Future:
(io) tradurrò, (tu) tradurrai, (lui/lei/Lei) tradurrà, (noi) tradurremo, (voi) tradurrete, (loro) tradurranno

Conditional:
(io) tradurrei, (tu) tradurresti, (lui/lei/Lei) tradurrebbe, (noi) tradurremmo, (voi) tradurreste, (loro) tradurrebbero

To conjugate these verbs in compound and progressive tenses, all you need to know is how to form the past participle and the gerund. Everything else remains the same:

Past Participle:	tradotto
Gerund:	traducendo

Note the past absolute of such verbs:

Past Absolute:
(io) tradussi, (tu) traducesti, (lui/lei/Lei) tradusse, (noi) traducemmo, (voi) traduceste, (loro) tradussero

The other types of -**rre** verbs show an irregular present (indicative and subjunctive) and imperative as follows:

porre / *to put, pose*
attrarre / *to attract*

Present Indicative:
(io) pongo, (tu) poni, (lui/lei/Lei) pone, (noi) poniamo, (voi) ponete, (loro) pongono

(io) attraggo, (tu) attrai, (lui/lei/Lei) attrae, (noi) attraiamo, (voi) attraete, (loro) attraggono

Present Subjunctive:
(io) ponga, (tu) ponga, (lui/lei/Lei) ponga, (noi) poniamo, (voi) poniate, (loro) pongano

(io) attragga, (tu) attragga, (lui/lei/Lei) attragga, (noi) attraiamo, (voi) attraiate, (loro) attraggano

Imperative:
—, (tu) **poni**, (Lei) **ponga**, (noi) **poniamo**, (voi) **ponete**, (Loro) **pongano**

—, (tu) **attrai**, (Lei) **attragga**, (noi) **attraiamo**, (voi) **attraiate**, (Loro) **attraggano**

For the imperfect (indicative and subjunctive), these verbs can also be rendered hypothetically "regular" as follows:

- Change the ending in your mind as follows:

  porre / *to pose* ➔ "ponere"
  attrarre / *to attract* ➔ "attraere"

- Drop the **-re** ending of the "hypothetical" verb stem:

  "ponere" ➔ "pon-"
  "attraere" ➔ "attra-"

- Add the usual endings:

  Imperfect Indicative:
  (io) **ponevo**, (tu) **ponevi**, (lui/lei/Lei) **poneva**, (noi) **ponevamo**, (voi) **ponevate**, (loro) **ponevano**

  Imperfect Subjunctive:
  (io) **attraessi**, (tu) **attraessi**, (lui/lei/Lei) **attraesse**, (noi) **attraessimo**, (voi) **attraeste**, (loro) **attraessero**

To form the future and conditional, drop the **-e** and add the usual endings (Chapter 5):

Future:
(io) **porrò**, (tu) **porrai**, (lui/lei/Lei) **porrà**, (noi) **porremo**, (voi) **porrete**, (loro) **porranno**

(io) **attrarrò**, (tu) **attrarrai**, (lui/lei/Lei) **attrarrà**, (noi) **attrarremo**, (voi) **attrarrete**, (loro) **attrarranno**

Conditional:
(io) **porrei**, (tu) **porresti**, (lui/lei/Lei) **porrebbe**, (noi) **porremmo**, (voi) **porreste**, (loro) **porrebbero**

(io) **attrarrei**, (tu) **attrarresti**, (lui/lei/Lei) **attrarrebbe**, (noi) **attrarremmo**, (voi) **attrarreste**, (loro) **attrarrebbero**

To conjugate these verbs in compound and progressive tenses, all you need to know is how to form the past participle and the gerund. Everything else remains the same:

Past Participle:	**posto** **attratto**
Gerund:	**ponendo** **attraendo**

Note the past absolute of such verbs:

Past Absolute:
(io) posi, (tu) ponesti, (lui/lei/Lei) pose, (noi) ponemmo, (voi) poneste, (loro) posero

(io) attrassi, (tu) attraesti, (lui/lei/Lei) attrasse, (noi) attraemmo, (voi) attraeste, (loro) attrassero

QUICK PRACTICE 4

Fill-in the chart with the correct forms of the indicated verb, in order of person (1st, 2nd, 3rd) and number (singular and plural), where applicable.

	Present Indic.	Present Subj.	Imperf. Indic.	Imperf. Subj.	Past Abs.	Future	Cond.	Imper.	Past Part.	Gerund
dedurre (io) (tu) (lui/lei) (noi) (voi) (loro)										
trarre (io) (tu) (lui/lei) (noi) (voi) (loro)										
porre (io) (tu) (lui/lei) (noi) (voi) (loro)										

Indefinite Tenses
I tempi indefiniti

The *indefinite tenses* allow you to express actions that refer to indefinite time relations.

For example, the *gerund* (**il gerundio**) is used to express an action simultaneous to another one, replacing **mentre** / *while* + imperfect when the subject of the two clauses is the same.

Mentre camminavo, ho visto Marco. / *While I was walking, I saw Marco.*
or
Camminando, ho visto Marco. / *While walking, I saw Marco.*

Object pronouns are attached to the gerund:

Vedendolo, l'ho salutato. / *Upon seeing him, I greeted him.*

There is also a *past gerund*, consisting of an auxiliary verb, **avere** / *to have* or **essere** / *to be*, in the gerund form, and the past participle of the verb, in that order:

avendo parlato / *having spoken*
essendo arrivato/a/i/e / *having arrived*
avendo venduto / *having sold*
essendo caduto/a/i/e / *having fallen*
avendo dormito / *having slept*
essendo partito/a/i/e / *having left*

Avendo mangiato tutto, siamo usciti. / *Having eaten everything, we went out.*
Essendo andati in Italia, visitarono tanti bei posti. / *Having gone to Italy, they visited many nice places.*

The *infinitive* (**l'infinito**) is used after certain constructions and can function as a substantive, in which case it is always assigned a masculine gender.

Prima di mangiare, abbiamo guardato la TV. / *Before eating, we watched TV.*
Il mangiare è necessario per sopravvivere. / *Eating is necessary to survive.*

When the subjects of two clauses are the same, then the infinitive is used.

Different Subjects	**The Same Subjects**
Lui crede che io scriva bene. /	**Lui crede di scrivere bene.** /
He believes that I write well.	*He believes that he (himself) writes well.*

There is also a *past infinitive* consisting of an auxiliary verb in the infinitive and a past participle.

aver(e) parlato / *having spoken*	**esser(e) arrivato/a** / *having arrived*
aver(e) venduto / *having sold*	**esser(e) caduto/a** / *having fallen*
aver(e) dormito / *having slept*	**esser(e) partito/a** / *having left*

Note that the final **-e** of the auxiliary may be dropped.

Dopo aver mangiato, uscirò. / *After having eaten, I will go out.*
Dopo esser arrivati, sono andati al cinema. / *After having arrived, they went to the movies.*

Object pronouns are also attached to infinitives:

Invece di mangiarlo, l'ho dato a lei. / *Instead of eating it, I gave it to her.*

QUICK PRACTICE 5

Say the following things in Italian.

1. While she was walking yesterday, she met me.
2. Seeing me, she got me to go with her.
3. Having done everything, they went out.
4. Having gone to Italy, they were able to travel around quite a bit (**assai**).
5. Drinking is necessary to survive (**per sopravvivere**).
6. He thinks that he (himself) knows everything.
7. After having gone out, they decided to go back home.
8. He was given a piece of cake. But instead of eating it, he put it down.

The Passive and Causative
Il passivo ed il causativo

Verbs can be in the *active* or *passive* voice (see Chapter 2). The active voice is used to indicate that the subject performs the action, whereas the passive voice, called the **passivo** in Italian, is used to indicate that the subject receives the action:

Active: **Alessandro mangia la mela.** / *Alexander is eating the apple.*
Passive: **La mela è mangiata da Alessandro.** / *The apple is eaten by Alexander.*

Passive sentences can be formed from corresponding active ones as follows:

- Change the order of the subject and the object:

> Alessandro mangia la mela. / *Alexander is eating the apple.*
>
> La mela (mangia) Alessandro

- Change the verb into the passive form by introducing the auxiliary verb **essere** / *to be* in the same tense and mood and changing the main verb into its past participle form. Recall that verbs conjugated with **essere** agree with the subject in number and gender:

> La mela è mangiata (Alessandro).

- Put **da** / *by* in front of the passive object:

> La mela è mangiata da Alessandro. / *The apple is eaten by Alexander.*

Here are a few other examples of "passivization":

Active	Passive
La ragazza legge quel libro. / *The girl reads that book.*	Quel libro è letto dalla ragazza. / *That book is read by the girl.*
Lui comprerà quella macchina. / *He will buy that car.*	Quella macchina sarà comprata da lui. / *That car will be bought by him.*

Always be sure to remember the rules above, and especially to transfer the tense and mood of the active verb to the auxiliary verb **essere**:

Active Verb		Passive Auxiliary
mangia	= *present indicative*	→ è (mangiato/a)
ha mangiato	= *present perfect*	→ è stato/a (mangiato/a)
mangiava	= *imperfect indicative*	→ era (mangiato/a)
aveva mangiato	= *pluperfect indicative*	→ era stato/a (mangiato/a)
mangiò	= *past absolute*	→ fu (mangiato/a)
mangerà	= *future*	→ sarà (mangiato/a)
avrà mangiato	= *future perfect*	→ sarà stato/a (mangiato/a)
mangerebbe	= *conditional*	→ sarebbe (mangiato/a)
avrebbe mangiato	= *conditional perfect*	→ sarebbe stato/a (mangiato/a)
mangi	= *present subjunctive*	→ sia (mangiato/a)
abbia mangiato	= *past subjunctive*	→ sia stato/a (mangiato/a)
mangiasse	= *imperfect subjunctive*	→ fosse (mangiato/a)
avesse mangiato	= *pluperfect subjunctive*	→ fosse stato/a (mangiato/a)

The verb **fare** / *to do, to make* can be used in causative constructions (**il causativo**). These allow you to express such things as *having* or *getting* someone to do something.

> **Maria fa lavare i piatti a suo fratello.**
> *Maria has her brother wash the dishes. / Maria gets her brother to wash the dishes.*
> **Maria li fa lavare a lui.**
> *Maria has him wash them. / Maria gets him to wash them.*
> **Maria ha fatto lavare i piatti a suo fratello.**
> *Maria had her brother wash the dishes. / Maria got her brother to wash the dishes.*
> **Maria li ha fatti lavare a lui.**
> *Maria had him wash them. / Maria got him to wash them.*
> **Maria farà lavare i piatti a suo fratello.**
> *Maria will have her brother wash the dishes. / Maria will get her brother to wash the dishes.*
> **Maria li farà lavare a lui.**
> *Maria will have him wash them. / Maria will get him to wash them.*

QUICK PRACTICE 6

Make each one of the following sentences passive.

1. Marco mangia la torta.
2. Quell'uomo ha bevuto il cappuccino.
3. Da bambina, mia sorella guardava regolarmente i cartoni animati *(cartoons)*.
4. Quando siamo arrivati, le tue amiche avevano già fatto la spesa.
5. Bocaccio scrisse *Il Decamerone*.
6. La mia amica comprerà quel computer portatile.
7. Giovanni avrà già fatto gli spaghetti.
8. Se potesse, lui comprerebbe quella Ferrari.
9. Se avesse potuto, lui avrebbe comprato quella Ferrari.
10. Penso che Marco desideri quel portatile.
11. Penso che loro abbiano già comprato quella casa.
12. Credevo che voi aveste già assaggiato i suoi spaghetti.

Now, how do you say the following things in Italian?

13. Maria has already gotten her brother to wash the dishes.
14. I will get her to study more.
15. They got me to go to the bar yesterday.
16. They also got me to drink a cappuccino.

PUTTING IT ALL TOGETHER

A. *Here's some more practice with the imperative.* Command Daniela to do (or not do) the following things.

Modello: Stay home today!
             Daniela, sta' a casa oggi!

 1. Taste the soup (**la minestra**)!
 2. Pay the bill!
 3. Sleep more!
 4. Make spaghetti!
 5. Pose that question (**quella domanda**) to the teacher!
 6. Remain at home!
 7. Choose this!
 8. Stay at home!
 9. Go out with them!
10. Come here!
11. Translate that book!
12. Don't go home yet!
13. Don't drink Coca-Cola!
14. Don't go out with them!
15. Get up early!
16. Put on a sweater (**una maglia**)!
17. Enjoy yourself at the party!

Command Mrs. Verdi to do (or not do) the same kinds of things.

Modello: Stay home today!
             Signora Verdi, stia a casa oggi!

18. Taste the soup!
19. Pay the bill!
20. Sleep more!
21. Make spaghetti!
22. Pose that question to the teacher!
23. Remain at home!
24. Choose this!
25. Stay at home!
26. Go out with them!
27. Come here!
28. Translate that book!

29. Don't go home yet!
30. Don't drink Coca-Cola!
31. Don't go out with them!
32. Get up early!
33. Put on a sweater!
34. Enjoy yourself at the party!

Finally, command Marco and Maria to do (or not do) the same kinds of things.

Modello: Stay home today!
           Marco e Maria, state a casa oggi!

35. Taste the soup!
36. Pay the bill!
37. Sleep more!
38. Make spaghetti!
39. Pose that question to the teacher!
40. Remain at home!
41. Choose this!
42. Stay at home!
43. Go out with them!
44. Come here!
45. Translate that book!
46. Don't go home yet!
47. Don't drink Coca-Cola!
48. Don't go out with them!
49. Get up early!
50. Put on a sweater!
51. Enjoy yourselves at the party!

B. *Choose the verb tense that is more appropriate. Note that in some cases both can be chosen.*

1. Che cosa stai facendo in questo momento, Giorgio?
    a. Sto bevendo un cappuccino.
    b. Bevo un cappuccino.

2. E tu che fai?
    a. Sto scrivendo un e-mail.
    b. Scrivo un'e-mail.

3. Generalmente che fa Maria quando ha tempo?
    a. Sta leggendo dei libri.
    b. Legge dei libri.

4. Che fa Marco in questo momento?
   a. Si sta alzando.
   b. Si alza.

5. Ogni estate noi ... in Italia.
   a. stiamo andando
   b. andiamo

6. Come ... loro generalmente per andare al lavoro?
   a. si stanno vestendo
   b. si vestono

7. Anche lui ... dei piselli e della frutta.
   a. sta comprando
   b. compra

8. Di solito noi ... solo un po' di carne in quel negozio di alimentari.
   a. stiamo comprando
   b. compriamo

9. Per che cosa ... ?
   a. ti stai preparando
   b. ti prepari

C. *Change the verbs into the subjunctive by adding the indicated expression to the given sentence. Follow the model.*

Modello: In questo momento mia sorella sta leggendo (Penso che...)
             Penso che in questo momento mia sorella stia leggendo.

In questo momento...

1. Giorgio sta mangiando (Penso che...)
2. voi stavate guardando un programma alla televisione (Maria credeva che...)
3. Marco sta dormendo (Sembra che...)
4. io stavo scrivendo (Lui credeva che...)
5. i miei amici stanno uscendo (Lei pensa che...)
6. noi stiamo bevendo un caffè (Loro credevano che...)
7. voi state leggendo (Dubito che...)
8. lui stava suonando il violoncello (Sembrava che...)
9. lei sta cantando (Sembra che...)

D. *Say the following sentences in Italian.*

1. Maria, why do you always dress elegantly?
2. I am not ashamed of anything!
3. Marco, at what time do you generally get up in the morning?
4. Alessandro and Sara, is it true that you are getting married this fall?
5. They always complain about everything!
6. Why are you becoming angry, Miss Gentile?
7. They always become bored when they watch TV.
8. I get sick very easily if it is cold outside.

E. **Cruciverba**

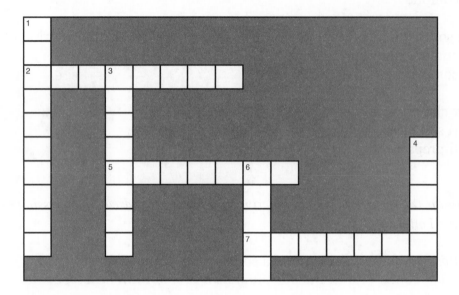

The required verbs are:

dire, guardare, tornare, fare, mangiare, camminare

Orizzontali
2. Prima di ..., bisogna aver appetito.
5. ... quello, si è rivelato bugiardo *(he revealed himself to be a liar)*.
7. Essendo ... a casa presto, hanno guardato la TV.

Verticali
1. ... ieri, mi ha visto.
3. Avendo ... la TV, ha deciso di studiare.
4. Li ho ... fare a lui.
6. Avendo ... quello, si è rivelato bugiardo.

Culture Capsule 2

Traditions
Tradizioni

Le principali feste italiane sono il Natale, l'Epifania, il Carnevale, la Pasqua e il Ferragosto.

Il Natale si celebra in maniera nordamericana con l'albero di Natale, con le tipiche giornate di shopping natalizio prima del 25 dicembre e con Babbo Natale che porta tanti bei regali ai bambini bravi.

> **VOCABOLARIO UTILE**
> la venuta / *the coming*
> il camino / *chimney*
> il dono / *gift*
> la Quaresima / *Lent*
> la colomba / *dove*

L'Epifania è caratterizzata dalla venuta della Befana, un personaggio mitico, una vecchia che la notte tra il 5 e il 6 gennaio passa per i camini e porta doni ai bambini, riempiendo le loro calze vuote.

Il Carnevale è il periodo festivo che precede la Quaresima, e si festeggia con balli, mascherate, e vari divertimenti. Il Carnevale più famoso in Italia è quello di Venezia. Dal Carnevale si passa alla Quaresima, che culmina nella celebrazione pasquale. La domenica di Pasqua in Italia si celebra con il classico pranzo di famiglia. Tradizionalmente durante questo periodo sono in vendita nei negozi le uova pasquali (quelle tradizionali di cioccolata) e la colomba pasquale (un dolce, chiamato così perché ha la forma di una colomba).

Il Ferragosto (15 agosto) è una festa nazionale in onore dell'Assunta (*Assumption*). Gli italiani approfittano di questa pausa estiva (che viene estesa ai giorni precedenti e seguenti il 15) per andare tutti in vacanza, abbandonare il caldo infernale delle grandi città, e cercare rifugio sulle spiagge, sulle montagne, e sui laghi.

CONTENT QUESTIONS
Vero o falso?

_____ 1. In Italia, il Natale non si celebra in maniera nordamericana.

_____ 2. La Befana porta doni ai bambini.

_____ 3. Il Carnevale segue la Quaresima.

_____ 4. Il Carnevale più famoso in Italia è quello di Venezia.

_____ 5. In Italia, a Pasqua nei negozi si vendono le colombe pasquali.

_____ 6. Per il Ferragosto gli italiani rimangono tutti in città.

PART III:
Reviewing and Practicing the Other Parts of Speech

8

Nouns

Quanto Sai Già? — **How Much Do You Know Already?** (?)
True or False?

_____ 1. **Mani** is the plural of **mano**.

_____ 2. **Amichi** is the plural of **amico**.

_____ 3. **Riso** does not have a plural form.

_____ 4. **Uva** does not have a plural form.

_____ 5. **Sport** is the plural of **sport**.

_____ 6. **Labbra** is the plural of **labbro**.

_____ 7. **Caporeparto** does not have a plural form.

_____ 8. **Uomi** is the plural of **uomo**.

_____ 9. **Amice** is the plural of **amica**.

Types of Noun
Tipi di nome

Common nouns (**nomi comuni**) are words that allow you to name and label the persons, objects, places, concepts, and things that make up the world. In Italian, a common noun can generally be recognized by its vowel ending, called a **desinenza**, which indicates its gender and number.

Masculine Singular	**Masculine Plural**
Quel bambin☐o è alto. /	Quei bambin☐i sono alti. /
That boy is tall.	*Those boys are tall.*

Feminine Singular	**Feminine Plural**
Quella ragazz☐a è alta. /	Quelle ragazz☐e sono alte. /
That girl is tall.	*Those girls are tall.*

Common nouns are not capitalized unless they occur at the beginning of a sentence. Also, unlike English, nouns referring to languages, speakers of a language, or inhabitants of an area normally are not capitalized.

189

L'italiano è una bella lingua. / *Italian is a beautiful language.*
Ci sono tanti spagnoli qui. / *There are lots of Spaniards here.*

Proper nouns (**nomi propri**) are the names given to people, places, and brands. They are always capitalized.

Il signor ⌐Rossi¬ è ricco. / *Mr. Rossi is rich.*
⌐Maria¬ è felice. / *Mary is happy.*
L'⌐Italia¬ è bella. / *Italy is beautiful.*
La ⌐FIAT¬ è una bella macchina. / *The FIAT is a beautiful car.*

There are two types of common nouns: count and mass. Count nouns refer to persons, things, etc. that can be counted. They have both singular and plural forms.

Singular	**Plural**
la penna / *the pen*	le penne / *the pens*
il libro / *the book*	i libri / *the books*

Mass nouns refer instead to things that cannot be counted, and therefore have only a singular form:

l'acqua / *water*
lo zucchero / *sugar*

Some mass nouns can, however, be used in a figurative or poetic way. In such cases they can be put in the plural.

le acque del mare / *the waters of the sea*
le morbide carni / *soft skins*

COMMON ITALIAN NAMES
Masculine
Alessandro / *Alexander*
Franco / *Frank*
Giorgio / *George*
Giovanni / *John*
Marco / *Mark*
Paolo / *Paul*
Renato / *Ron*

Feminine
Alessandra / *Alexandra*
Franca / *Franca*
Gina / *Gina*
Giovanna / *Joanne*
Maria / *Maria*
Paola / *Paula*
Renata / *Renata*

COMMON MASS NOUNS
l'acqua / *water*
la carne / *meat*
il latte / *milk*
il pane / *bread*
il riso / *rice*
l'uva / *grapes*
lo zucchero / *sugar*

QUICK PRACTICE 1

Classify each noun into its appropriate slot in the chart:

Gina, zucchero, Francia, carne, Spagna, Germania, Di Stefano, rivista, giornale, amico, amica, Da Vinci, libro, Paola, Marco, pane, Maria, latte, Renata, uva, Giovanni, Stati Uniti, italiano, Marconi, riso, Rossi, Ferrari (*twice*), FIAT, Franco, acqua, Rossini, Bellini, Italia, cane

Nomi comuni

COUNT	MASS	NAME	SURNAME	OTHER
		Gina		
	Zucchero			

Gender

Il genere

Italian nouns are classified as either masculine (**maschile**) or feminine (**femminile**). This is called _grammatical gender._ Gender is important because it determines the form of both the articles and adjectives that accompany nouns in sentences and phrases. Generally speaking, a noun's gender can be identified by looking at its ending.

Nouns ending with the vowel **-o** are normally masculine:

il ragazzo / _the boy_
il giorno / _the day_
l'aeroporto / _the airport_
Carlo / _Charles_
il Belgio / _Belgium_

Nouns ending with the vowel **-a** are normally feminine:

la ragazza / _the girl_
la carta / _the paper_
la valigia / _the suitcase_
Carla / _Carla_
l'Italia / _Italy_

> **TIP**
> A good dictionary will specify whether a noun ending in **-e** is masculine (_m._) or feminine (_f._)

Nouns ending with the vowel **-e** can be either masculine or feminine:

Masculine Nouns	**Feminine Nouns**
il dottore / _the doctor_	**la gente** / _people_
il padre / _the father_	**la madre** / _the mother_
il nome / _the name_	**la televisione** / _television_
Giuseppe / _Joseph_	**la notte** / _the night_

You can use the fact that noun modifiers such as articles and adjectives agree with the noun's gender to identify the gender itself.

il giornale italiano / _the Italian newspaper_
la notte lunga / _the long night_

The adjective form **italiano** tells you that the gender of **giornale** is masculine as does the article form **il**. Similarly, the adjective form **lunga** gives away the gender of **notte** as feminine, as does the article form **la**.

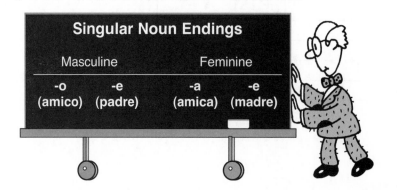

Singular Noun Endings			
Masculine		Feminine	
-o (amico)	-e (padre)	-a (amica)	-e (madre)

In the case of nouns referring to people, these endings usually refer to the biological gender of the people involved; that is, male beings are designated by nouns ending in **-o** or in **-e** (masculine endings), and female beings are designated by nouns ending in **-a** or **-e** (feminine endings).

EXCEPTIONS
- **Il soprano** *(soprano)* is a masculine noun referring to a female person.
- **La spia** *(spy)* is a feminine noun that refers to a male or female person.
- Male names ending in **-a**:
  Andrea / *Andrew*
  Luca / *Lucas*
  Nicola / *Nicholas*

Masculine

-o
il ragazzo / *the boy*
lo zio / *the uncle*
il figlio / *the son*

il gatto / *the cat (male)*
l'americano / *the American (male)*
Carlo / *Charles*
Paolo / *Paul*

-e
il francese / *the French man*
il canadese / *the Canadian man*
il cantante / *the male singer*
il nipote / *the nephew*

-e
l'infermiere / *the nurse (male)*
il cameriere / *the male waiter*

Feminine

-a
la ragazza / *the girl*
la zia / *the aunt*
la figlia / *the daughter*

la gatta / *the cat (female)*
l'americana / *the American (female)*
Carla / *Carla*
Paola / *Paula*

-e
la francese / *the French woman*
la canadese / *the Canadian woman*
la cantante / *the singer*
la nipote / *the niece*

-a
l'infermiera / *the nurse (female)*
la cameriera / *the waitress*

However, for most common nouns it is not possible to determine whether it will have a masculine or feminine ending on the basis of a noun's meaning. There are nevertheless some patterns that allow you to determine the gender of the noun.

- In general, the names of trees are masculine, but the names of the fruit they bear are feminine.

Masculine	Feminine
il melo / *the apple tree*	la mela / *the apple*
l'arancio / *the orange tree*	l'arancia / *the orange*
il pesco / *the peach tree*	la pesca / *the peach*
il pero / *the pear tree*	la pera / *the pear*
il ciliegio / *the cherry tree*	la ciliegia / *the cherry*

- If a masculine noun ends in **-tore** and refers to a male person, there generally exists a corresponding feminine noun ending in **-trice**, referring to a female person.

Masculine	Feminine
il genitore / *the male parent*	la genitrice / *the female parent*
il pittore / *the male painter*	la pittrice / *the female painter*
l'autore / *the male author*	l'autrice / *the female author*
l'attore / *the male actor*	l'attrice / *the female actor (actress)*
lo scultore / *the male sculptor*	la scultrice / *the female sculptor (sculptress)*

- However, for a number of masculine nouns referring to male beings there are instead corresponding feminine nouns ending in **-essa** referring to female beings.

Masculine	Feminine
il dottore / *the male doctor*	la dottoressa / *the female doctor*
il professore / *the male professor*	la professoressa / *the female professor*
l'avvocato / *the male lawyer*	l'avvocatessa / *the female lawyer*
l'elefante / *the male elephant*	l'elefantessa / *the female elephant*

- As in English, some of the feminine forms above are being eliminated, especially if they refer to professional people.

l'avvocato / *the male or female lawyer*
lo scultore / *the male or female sculptor*

- Nouns ending in **-ista** generally refer to persons (mainly professionals). They can be either masculine or feminine, according to whether they designate a male or female person.

Masculine	Feminine
il dentista / *the male dentist*	la dentista / *the female dentist*
il pianista / *the male pianist*	la pianista / *the female pianist*
il farmacista / *the male pharmacist*	la farmacista / *the female pharmacist*
il violinista / *the male violinist*	la violinista / *the female violinist*

- Nouns ending in an accented **-à** or **-ù** are generally feminine (with some exceptions); those ending in any other accented vowel (**-è, -ì, -ò**) are usually masculine.

Masculine	Feminine
il tè / *the tea*	la città / *the city*
il caffè / *the coffee*	l'università / *university*
il tassì / *the taxi*	la gioventù / *youth*
il lunedì / *Monday*	la virtù / *virtue*
il comò / *the dresser*	l'identità / *identity*

- Unless they refer to a female being, nouns that have been borrowed from other languages (**i prestiti**), such as English, are generally masculine.

lo sport / *sport*
il tram / *the streetcar, trolley*
il computer / *the computer*
il clacson / *the car horn*
il tennis / *tennis*
l'autobus / *the bus*
il compact disc / *the CD*

> **EXCEPTIONS**
> *Masculine rather than feminine:*
> il bambù / *bamboo*
> il cucù / *cuckoo bird*
> il gagà / *fop, dandy*
> il menù / *menu*
> il papà / *dad*
> il ragù / *ragu sauce*
>
> *Feminine rather than masculine:*
> la pansé / *pansy*

- There are some notable exceptions to this pattern in the area of cyber-communications. The following borrowed words, for example, are feminine.

la chat / *the chat room*
l'e-mail, la mail / *e-mail*

- Nouns ending in **-ema** and **-amma** are of Greek origin, corresponding to English nouns ending in **-em** and **-am**, respectively. They are all masculine.

il problema / *the problem*
il teorema / *the theorem*
il programma / *the program*
il telegramma / *the telegram*
il diagramma / *the diagram*

- Nouns ending in **-si** are also of Greek origin, corresponding to English nouns ending in **-sis**. They are feminine.

> **la crisi** / *the crisis*
> **la tesi** / *the thesis*
> **l'analisi** / *the analysis*
> **l'ipotesi** / *the hypothesis*

QUICK PRACTICE 2

Complete the chart by providing the missing corresponding masculine or feminine noun, as the case may be.

Maschile	Femminile
	arancia
autore	
	avvocato
cameriere	
	cantante
Carlo	
	ciliegia
dentista	
	dottoressa
elefante	
	fico
figlio	
	genitrice
limone	
	mandarino
melo	
	nipote
Paolo	
	pera
pesco	
	pianista
professore	
	ragazza
violinista	
	zia

Now, classify each of the following as masculine or feminine.

brindisi, città, tè, gente, notte, diagramma, università, ipotesi, e-mail, programma, gioventù, caffè, tassì, virtù, papà, pansé, valigia, televisione, gatta, identità, spia, analisi, crisi, problema, tesi, teorema, sport, computer, tram, clacson, tennis, menù, autobus, Andrea

Maschile	Femminile

Number

Il numero

A noun is said to be singular (**singolare**) when it refers to one person, thing, etc. It is said to be plural (**plurale**) when it refers to more than one person or thing. Recall that mass nouns have only a singular form, no matter what they refer to.

l'acqua / *water*
il pane / *bread*
la fame / *hunger*
la sete / *thirst*
il pepe / *pepper*
il sale / *salt*

Nouns referring to things made up of more than one part have only a plural form instead.

le forbici / *scissors*
gli occhiali / *(eye)glasses*
i pantaloni / *pants*
le mutande / *underwear*
i baffi / *mustache*

Regular common nouns are made plural by changing their vowel endings as follows.

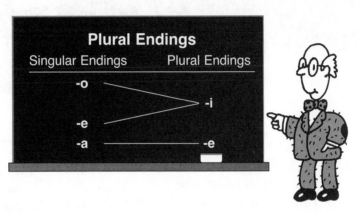

Masculine Singular

-o
il ragazzo / *the boy*
il giorno / *the day*
l'aeroporto / *the airport*

-e
il padre / *the father*
il cameriere / *the waiter*
l'attore / *the actor*

Masculine Plural

-i
i ragazzi / *the boys*
i giorni / *the days*
gli aeroporti / *the airports*

-i
i padri / *the fathers*
i camerieri / *the waiters*
gli attori / *the actors*

Feminine Singular

-a
la ragazza / *the girl*
la mela / *the apple*
la gonna / *the skirt*

-e
la madre / *the mother*
la notte / *the night*
l'attrice / *the actress*

Feminine Plural

-e
le ragazze / *the girls*
le mele / *the apples*
le gonne / *the skirts*

-i
le madri / *the mothers*
le notti / *the nights*
le attrici / *the actresses*

Be careful! The noun **gente** (*people*) is singular in Italian.

La gente parla troppo. / *People talk too much.*

Note that the plural ending -i is used when the noun refers to both male *and* female beings taken together as a group, whereas the plural ending -e refers only to females.

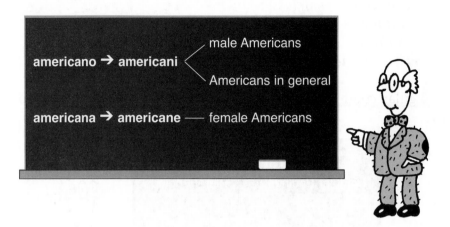

Spelling changes are required with certain noun endings involving soft and hard consonant sounds. Below is a list of patterns regarding such nouns.

As a "rule of thumb," if the noun ends in -co, then change it to -chi (which indicates a hard "k" sound) when -a, -o, -u, -uo, -ie, or a consonant precede; change it to -ci (which indicates a soft "c" sound) when -e or -i precede.

Note: This is just a rule of thumb, not a hard rule of grammar, but it seems to work for many nouns ending in -co. So, use it with some caution.

Singular	Plural
-co	**-chi**
il baco / *the silkworm*	i bachi / *the silkworms*
il fuoco / *the fire*	i fuochi / *the fires*
il buco / *the hole*	i buchi / *the holes*
il parco / *the park*	i parchi / *the parks*
il tedesco / *the German*	i tedeschi / *the Germans*
il cieco / *the blind person*	i ciechi / *the blind persons*
-co	**-ci**
il greco / *the Greek*	i greci / *the Greeks*
l'amico / *the friend*	gli amici / *the friends*
il medico / *the (medical) doctor*	i medici / *the (medical) doctors*
il cattolico / *the Catholic*	i cattolici / *the Catholics*

- If the noun ends in -go, change it to -ghi (to indicate that the hard "g" sound is to be retained):

Singular	Plural
-go	-ghi
il lago / *the lake*	i laghi / *the lakes*
l'albergo / *the hotel*	gli alberghi / *the hotels*
il catalogo / *the catalogue*	i cataloghi / *the catalogues*

- If the noun ends in -ca or -ga, change it to -che and -ghe respectively (indicating the hard consonant sounds are to be retained). There are no exceptions to this rule.

Singular	Plural
l'amica / *the female friend*	le amiche / *the female friends*
la greca / *the female Greek*	le greche / *the female Greeks*
la monaca / *the nun*	le monache / *the nuns*
l'oca / *the duck*	le oche / *the ducks*
la paga / *the pay (check)*	le paghe / *the pay (checks)*
la riga / *the ruler (drawing)*	le righe / *the rulers*
la lattuga / *lettuce*	le lattughe / *varieties of lettuce*
la toga / *the professional gown*	le toghe / *the professional gowns*

- If the -i in nouns ending in -cio, -gio, -cia, -gia, or -io is stressed, then it is retained in the plural. If it is not stressed, then it is dropped.

Singular Stressed	Plural Stressed
il fruscio / *the rustling sound*	i fruscii / *the rustling sounds*
il leggio / *music stand*	i legii / *music stands*
la farmacia / *the pharmacy*	le farmacie / *the pharmacies*
la bugia / *the lie*	le bugie / *the lies*
lo zio / *the uncle*	gli zii / *the uncles*

Singular Unstressed	Plural Unstressed
il bacio / *the kiss*	i baci / *the kisses*
l'orologio / *the watch, clock*	gli orologi / *the watches, clocks*
l'arancia / *the orange (fruit)*	le arance / *the oranges*
la valigia / *the suitcase*	le valige / *the suitcases*
il figlio / *the son*	i figli / *the sons*

Finally, here are a few other general patterns pertaining to the pluralization of nouns with special endings.

> **EXCEPTION**
> La camicia (*shirt*) is pluralized as le camicie even though the -i in the ending -cia is not stressed.

- If a noun ending in **-ista** refers to male persons, its plural form is **-isti**; if it refers to female persons, its plural form is **-iste**.

Masculine Singular	Masculine Plural
il **dentista** / *the male dentist*	i **dentisti** / *the male dentists (dentists in general)*
il **turista** / *the male tourist*	i **turisti** / *the male tourists (tourists in general)*
il **pianista** / *the male pianist*	i **pianisti** / *the male pianists (pianists in general)*

Feminine Singular	Feminine Plural
la **dentista** / *the female dentist*	le **dentiste** / *the female dentists*
la **turista** / *the female tourist*	le **turiste** / *the female tourists*
la **pianista** / *the female pianist*	le **pianiste** / *the female pianists*

- Nouns ending in **-ema** and **-amma** are masculine (as mentioned above). These endings are changed respectively to **-emi** and **-ammi** in the plural.

Singular	Plural
il **problema** / *the problem*	i **problemi** / *the problems*
il **programma** / *the program*	i **programmi** / *the programs*
il **diagramma** / *the diagram*	i **diagrammi** / *the diagrams*

- Borrowed nouns, as well as nouns ending in **-si** or in an accented vowel, do not undergo any changes in the plural.

Singular	Plural
il **computer** / *the computer*	i **computer** / *the computers*
lo **sport** / *sport*	gli **sport** / *sports*
la **crisi** / *the crisis*	le **crisi** / *the crises*
la **tesi** / *the thesis*	le **tesi** / *the theses*
la **città** / *the city*	le **città** / *the cities*
il **tè** / *the tea*	i **tè** / *the teas*

- Like the English nouns *memorandum* and *compendium*, which are pluralized by replacing the *-um* ending with *-a* (*memoranda* and *compendia*), Italian also has a few nouns whose plural forms end in **-a**. Such nouns derive from Latin neuter forms that were pluralized with this ending.

> **NOTE**
> In Italian, Latin neuter nouns are masculine in the singular but feminine in the plural!

Singular (masculine)	Plural (feminine)
il dito / *the finger*	le dita / *the fingers*
il braccio / *the arm*	le braccia / *the arms*
il paio / *the pair*	le paia / *the pairs*
il miglio / *the mile*	le miglia / *the miles*

- There are not too many of these nouns, and most refer to parts of the human body. A few of these have both plural forms, but with different meanings.

Singular (masculine)	Plural (masculine)	Plural (feminine)
il ciglio / *the eyebrow*	i cigli / *the edges*	le ciglia / *the eyebrows*
il labbro / *the lip*	i labbri / *the rims*	le labbra / *the lips*

- Nouns that are formed as abbreviations do not change in the plural:

Singular	Plural
l'auto / *the car* (from: l'automobile)	le auto / *the cars* (le automobili)
il cinema / *the movie theater* (from: il cinematografo)	i cinema / *the movie theaters* (i cinematografi)
la foto / *the photo* (from: la fotografia)	le foto / *the photos* (le fotografie)

- Some common nouns follow no pattern. Here are a few of them.

Singular	Plural
la mano / *the hand*	le mani / *the hands*
l'uomo / *the man*	gli uomini / *the men*
il bue / *the ox*	i buoi / *the oxen*
il vaglia / *the money order*	i vaglia / *the money orders*
il dio / *the god*	gli dei / *the gods*

QUICK
PRACTICE 3

Give the plural of the given nouns, as the case may be.

Singolare	Plurale	Singolare	Plurale
dio	gli dèi	vaglia	i vaglia
bue	buoi	uomo	uomini
mano	mani	foto	
cinema	i cinema	auto	
labbro	i labbri	ciglio	
paio	le paia	braccio	braccia
dito	le dita	tè	
città	le città	tesi	le tesi
computer	i computer	sport	
problema	i problemi	programma	programmi
dentista	le dentiste	pianista	
figlio	i figli	valigia	le valigie
bacio	i baci	zio	
leggio	i leggii	farmacia	
bugia	le bugie	camicia	
oca	le oche	riga	righe
teologo	i teologi	biologo	biologi
lago	i laghi	catalogo	
antropologo	gli antropogi	amico	
tedesco	i tedeschi	medico	
buco	i buchi	cattolico	
parco	i parchi	porco	
notte	le notti	fico	
mela	le mele	cameriere	
bambino		bambina	

Other
Altri tipi di nome

Italians use more titles than Americans do to address professionals. Here are a few common ones.

Masculine Title	Feminine Title	
signore	signora, signorina	*Mr., Mrs., Ms.*
dottore	dottoressa	*Doctor*
professore	professoressa	*Professor*
avvocato	avvocato	*Lawyer*
geometra	geometra	*Draftsperson*
ragioniere	ragioniera	*Accountant*
architetto	architetto	*Architect*

> **TIP**
>
> The title of Dottore / Dottoressa is used to address both a medical doctor and any university graduate.
>
> The title of Professore / Professoressa is used to address both a university professor and any junior and high school teacher.
>
> Titles may be written with small or large caps.

The final **-e** of a masculine title is dropped before a name.

Masculine Title	Used Before a Name
il signore / *the gentleman*	il signor Rossi / *Mr. Rossi*
il professore / *the professor*	il professor Verdi / *Professor Verdi*
il dottore / *the doctor*	il dottor Bianchi / *Dr. Bianchi*
l'avvocato / *the lawyer*	l'avvocato Tozzi / *the lawyer Tozzi*

Feminine Title	Used Before a Name
la signora / *the lady*	la signora Rossi / *Mrs. Rossi*
la professoressa / *the professor*	la professoressa Verdi / *Professor Verdi*
la dottoressa / *the doctor*	la dottoressa Bianchi / *Dr. Bianchi*

The article accompanies titles. But it is dropped when the title is used while addressing someone.

Title + Name	Direct Address
il signor Rossi / *Mr. Rossi*	Buonasera, signor Rossi! / *Good evening, Mr. Rossi!*
la dottoressa Fani / *Dr. Fani*	Buongiorno, dottoressa Fani! / *Good day, Dr. Fani!*

Prefixes (**i prefissi**) are forms that are attached to the beginning of words to modify their meaning. Here are the most common ones.

Noun	Prefix + Noun
gusto / *taste*	disgusto / *disgust*
accordo / *agreement*	disaccordo / *disagreement*
limitatezza / *limitation*	illimitatezza / *unlimitedness*
possibile / *possible*	impossibile / *impossible*
numero / *number*	innumere / *numberless*
realtà / *reality*	irrealtà / *unreality*
credente / *believer*	miscredente / *unbeliever*
annuncio / *announcement*	preannuncio / *preannouncement*
azione / *action*	reazione / *reaction*
esame / *examination*	riesame / *reexamination*

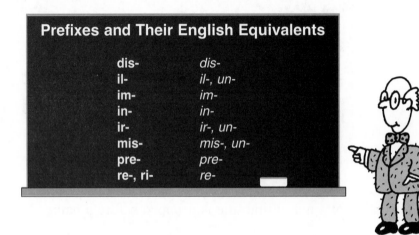

Prefixes and Their English Equivalents

dis-	*dis-*
il-	*il-, un-*
im-	*im-*
in-	*in-*
ir-	*ir-, un-*
mis-	*mis-, un-*
pre-	*pre-*
re-, ri-	*re-*

Suffixes (**i suffissi**) are forms that are attached to the end of words to modify their meaning. Here are some common ones.

- The suffixes -ino/-ina, -etto/-etta, and -ello/-ella can be used to add the nuance of "littleness" or "smallness" to the meaning of the noun.

il ragazzo / *the boy*	il ragazzino / *the little boy*
il piede / *the foot*	il piedino / *the small foot*
la ragazza / *the girl*	la ragazzina / *the little girl*
la bocca / *the mouth*	la bocchina / *the little mouth*
il ragazzo / *the boy*	il ragazzetto / *the small boy*
l'asino / *the donkey*	l'asinello / *the little donkey*

> **BE CAREFUL!**
> Be careful with these suffixes. There are a number of exceptions.
> For example:
>
> il libretto does not mean *small book* but *opera libretto* or *bank book*.
> The suffix in this case is il libricino / *the little book*.
>
> Also, la manina means *little hand* but la manetta means *handcuff*.

- The suffix **-one/-ona** can be used to add the nuance of "bigness" or "largeness" to the meaning of the noun.

il ragazzo / *the boy*	il ragazzone / *the big boy*
la ragazza / *the girl*	la ragazzona / *the big girl*
il libro / *the book*	il librone / *the big book*

- The suffix **-uccio/-uccia** (also **uzzo-/-uzza**) can be used to add the nuance of "smallness" with a tinge of criticism to the meaning of the noun.

l'affare / *the business transaction*	l'affaruccio / *the little/hollow business transaction*
il ragazzo / *the boy*	il ragazuccio / *the small and wretched boy*

- Finally, the suffix **accio/-accia** can be used to add the nuance of "badness" or "ugliness" to the meaning of the noun.

il ragazzo / *the boy*	il ragazzaccio / *the bad boy*
la ragazza / *the girl*	la ragazzaccia / *the bad girl*
l'uomo / *the man*	l'omaccio / *the bad man* (note the spelling change)
il corpo / *the body*	il corpaccio / *the ugly body*

Note: There is no steadfast rule as to when such suffixes can be used. Only through exposure, reading, and memorization will facility with them develop.

Compound nouns (**nomi composti**) are nouns that are made up of two parts of speech.

- Compound nouns made up of two nouns are pluralized by changing the ending of the second noun in the usual fashion.

Noun + Noun	Compound Noun	Plural Form
capo + luogo	il capoluogo / *capital of a region*	i capoluoghi / *capitals of regions*
capo + lavoro	il capolavoro / *the masterwork*	i capolavori / *the masterworks*
arco + baleno	l'arcobaleno / *the rainbow*	gli arcobaleni / *the rainbows*
ferro + via	la ferrovia / *the railroad*	le ferrovie / *the railroads*

There are a few exceptions to this rule.

Noun + Noun	Compound Noun	Plural Form
capo + reparto	il caporeparto / *the department head*	i capireparto / *the department heads*
capo + stazione	il capostazione / *the stationmaster*	i capistazione / *the stationmasters*

- Compound nouns made up of an adjective and a noun or two adjectives are pluralized by changing the ending of the second word in the usual fashion.

Two Parts	Compound Noun	Plural Form
piano + forte	il pianoforte / *the piano*	i pianoforti / *the pianos*
franco + bollo	il francobollo / *stamp*	i francobolli / *stamps*

- All other kinds of compound nouns do not change in the plural.

Two Parts	Compound Noun	Plural Form
caccia + vite	il cacciavite / *the screwdriver*	i cacciavite / *the screwdrivers*
salva + gente	il salvagente / *the life jacket*	i salvagente / *the life jackets*

- Again, there are exceptions to the above rules.

Noun + Adjective	Compound Noun	Plural Form
cassa + forte	la cassaforte / *the (money) safe*	le casseforti / *the safes*

As you can see, pluralizing compound nouns can be a complicated task. You would be wise to check a dictionary to be sure you have pluralized a compound noun correctly, as do most native speakers by the way!

6-15

QUICK PRACTICE 4

Give the Italian equivalent.

1. Dr. Bianchi *(a female)* Dottoressa Bianchi
2. Dr. Verdi *(a male)* Dottore
3. Professor Dini *(a female)*, how are you? Professoressa Dini, come sta?
4. Professor Giannetti *(a male)*, how are you? Professore Giannetti, "
5. She's a big girl. Lei è una ragazzona
6. That was a hollow business transaction. Era un l'affaruccio.

Give the opposite of each.

Modello: gusto
           disgusto

7. numero innumere
8. possibile impossibile

9. limitatezza *illimitatezza*
10. realtà *irrealtà*
11. azione *reazione*
12. annuncio *preannuncio*
13. ragazzone *ragazzo ragazzona*

Finally, give the plural form of each compound noun.

14. cassaforte *le casseforti*
15. cacciavite *i cacciavite*
16. francobollo *i francobolli*
17. capoluogo *i capoluoghi*
18. capolavoro *i capolavori*
19. ferrovia *le ferrovie*
20. caporeparto *i caporeparto*

PUTTING IT ALL TOGETHER

A. *Here is a straightforward exercise. Given the following nouns, simply identify them with check marks as common, proper, count, mass, masculine, or feminine. If a certain category does not apply to the noun, simply leave it blank in the chart.*

	COMMON	PROPER	COUNT	MASS	MASCULINE	FEMININE
italiano				✓		
ingegnere						
spagnola						
Renata		✓				
Andrea		✓				
Luca		✓				
carne						
riso						
uva						
Stati Uniti						
notte						
soprano						

B. *You are given either the masculine or feminine form of a noun. Provide the form of the other gender.*

Maschile	Femminile
ragazzo	*ragazza*
zio	zia
Giovanni	*Giovanna*
il gatto	gatta
cantante	*la cantante*
il cameriere	cameriera
pittore	*la pittrice*
dottore	dottoressa
farmacista	*la farmacista*
uomo	donna

C. *Change from the masculine to the feminine, or vice versa, as given by the noun in parentheses. Follow the model.*

Modello: Maria è un'amica. (Marco)
          Anche Marco è un amico.

1. Il signor Rossi è un mio collega. (la signora Betti) *La signora Betti è una mia collega*
2. Franco è un bambino intelligente. (Claudia) *Claudia è una bambina intelligente*
3. La mia amica Gina ha un nipote. (Mario) *Il mio amico Mario ha un nipote*
4. Mio fratello è studente. (tua sorella) *Tua sorella è studentessa*
5. Mia sorella ha un ragazzo. (tuo fratello) *Tuo fratello ha una ragazza*
6. La mia amica Gina ha tante amiche. (Angelo) *Il mio amico Angelo ha tanti amici*
7. Il mio collega Giorgio è un brav'uomo. (Maria) *La mia collega Maria è una brava donna*
8. Quell'uomo è professore. (quella donna) *Quella donna è professoressa*

D. *Now you are given either the singular or plural form of a noun. Provide the other form (singular or plural).*

Singolare	Plurale
attore	attori
giorno	giorni
mela	mele
notte	notti
buco	buchi
tedesco	tedeschi
monaco	monaci
greco	greci
porco	porci
medico	medici
albergo	gli alberghi
amica	amiche
camicia	le camicie
il fruscio	fruscii
problema	i problemi
il programma	programmi
foto	le foto
l'uomo	uomini

E. Cruciverba!

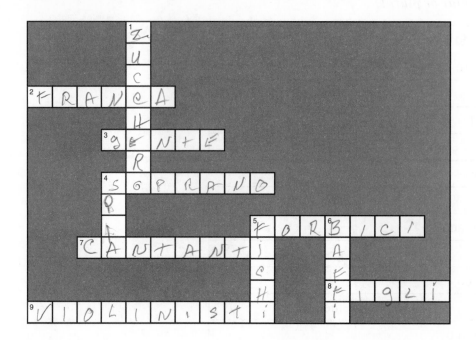

The crossword contains the following filled-in answers:

1. (down) Z U C C H E R O
2. (across) F R A N C A
3. (across) G E N T E
4. (across) S O P R A N O
5. (across) F O R B I C I
7. (across) C A N T A N T I
8. (across) F I G L I
9. (across) V I O L I N I S T I

Orizzontali

2. Nome di donna che corrisponde a Franco
3. Insieme di persone
4. Cantante d'opera con registro di voce alto
5. Strumento che si usa per tagliare
7. Persone che cantano
8. Plurale di "figlio"
9. Plurale di "violinista" (maschile)

Verticali

1. Si usa per rendere dolce il caffè.
4. Persona "segreta"
5. Plurale di "fico"
6. I peli lungo il labbro

F. *Can you explain the following in your own words? Use complete sentences.*

Modello: Che cosa è un pianoforte?
Il pianoforte è uno strumento musicale che si suona con tutte e due le mani.

Che cos'è?

1. un francobollo *e prendere a busta*
2. una cassaforte *mia cassaforte e vuoto (empty)*
3. un cacciavite *uso un cacciavite fare un scavare un fuco.*
4. un capoluogo *un capoluogo di NC. è Raleigh*
5. un ragioniere
6. un geometra *un geometra desegno progetti*
7. un monaco *un monaco da l'estrema unzione.*

9

Articles and Partitives

Quanto Sai Già? — How Much Do You Know Already?

Can you fill in each blank with the correct form of the indicated article?

Definite Article

1. ___i___ bambini
2. ___gli___ studenti
3. ___gli___ amici
4. ___le___ bambine

Indefinite Article

5. ___un___ libro
6. ___un___ amico
7. ___una___ finestra
8. ___un___ amica

Articles
Gli articoli

Articles are words used to signal nouns and to specify their application.

Specific
il libro / *the book*

Nonspecific
un libro / *a book*

The article that allows you to signal persons, objects, etc. in a specific way is called *definite* (**l'articolo determinativo**); the article that allows you to designate nonspecific persons, objects, etc. is called *indefinite* (**l'articolo indeterminativo**).

Demonstratives will be included in this chapter, even though you might find them listed as adjectives in other grammars. They are included here because they too have the function of specifying a noun in some way. More precisely, demonstratives allow us to specify whether someone or something is relatively near or far.

Near
questo libro / *this book*

Far
quel libro / *that book*

Definite and indefinite articles, as well as demonstratives, vary according to the noun's gender, number, and initial sound. It may help to remember that the English indefinite article also varies according to the initial sound of the following noun or adjective.

Before a Consonant   **Before a Vowel**
a boy   *an egg*
a friend   *an angel*

The forms of the definite article are:

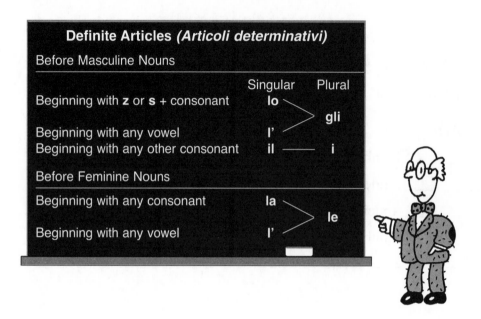

Definite Articles (Articoli determinativi)

Before Masculine Nouns

	Singular	Plural
Beginning with **z** or **s** + consonant	lo	gli
Beginning with any vowel	l'	gli
Beginning with any other consonant	il	i

Before Feminine Nouns

	Singular	Plural
Beginning with any consonant	la	le
Beginning with any vowel	l'	le

Examples:

Singular   **Plural**

lo   **gli**
lo zio / *the uncle*   gli zii / *the uncles*
lo zero / *the zero*   gli zeri / *the zeroes*
lo studente / *the student*   gli studenti / *the students*
lo specchio / *the mirror*   gli specchi / *the mirrors*
lo sbaglio / *the mistake*   gli sbagli / *the mistakes*

l'   **gli**
l'amico / *the friend*   gli amici / *the friends*
l'italiano / *the Italian*   gli italiani / *the Italians*
l'orologio / *the watch*   gli orologi / *the watches*

il   **i**
il padre / *the father*   i padri / *the fathers*
il fratello / *the brother*   i fratelli / *the brothers*
il nonno / *the grandfather*   i nonni / *the grandfathers*

la	le
la madre / *the mother*	le madri / *the mothers*
la sorella / *the sister*	le sorelle / *the sisters*
la nonna / *the grandmother*	le nonne / *the grandmothers*

l'	le
l'amica / *the (female) friend*	le amiche / *the (female) friends*
l'entrata / *the entrance*	le entrate / *the entrances*
l'uscita / *the exit*	le uscite / *the exits*

[handwritten marginal note: why not l'? l'amiche]

The masculine form **lo** (plural **gli**) is also used in front of forms beginning with **ps** or **gn** (and a few other unusual initial sounds).

lo psicologo / *the psychologist*	gli psicologi / *the psychologists*
lo gnocco / *the dumpling*	gli gnocchi / *the gnocchi*

Be careful! When an adjective precedes the noun, you will have to adjust the definite article according to its initial sound.

la zia / *the aunt*	la vecchia zia / *the old aunt*
lo studente / *the student*	l'altro studente / *the other student*
gli amici / *the friends*	i vecchi amici / *the old friends*
l'orologio / *the watch*	il bell'orologio / *the nice watch*

The forms of the indefinite article in the singular are:

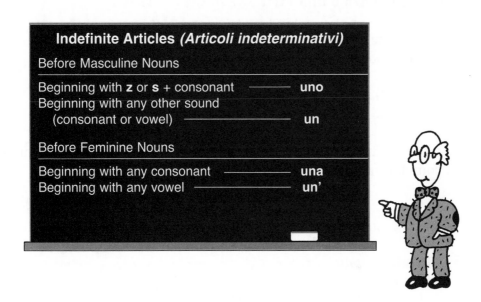

Indefinite Articles (*Articoli indeterminativi*)

Before Masculine Nouns

Beginning with **z** or **s** + consonant	**uno**
Beginning with any other sound (consonant or vowel)	**un**

Before Feminine Nouns

Beginning with any consonant	**una**
Beginning with any vowel	**un'**

Note that the apostrophe (**un'**) is used only when the indefinite article is in front of a feminine noun beginning with a vowel.

As in the case of the definite article form **lo**, the indefinite form **uno** is also used in front of nouns beginning with **ps** and **gn**.

Examples:

uno	un
uno zio / *an uncle*	un piede / *a foot*
uno sbaglio / *a mistake*	un braccio / *an arm*
uno psicologo / *a psychologist*	un occhio / *an eye*
uno gnocco / *a dumpling*	un orecchio / *an ear*

una	un'
una zia / *an aunt*	un'unghia / *a fingernail*
una bocca / *a mouth*	un'automobile / *an automobile*
una gamba / *a leg*	un'ora / *an hour*

Don't forget! When an adjective precedes the noun, you will have to adjust the indefinite article according to the beginning sound.

uno zio / *an uncle*	un caro zio / *a dear uncle*
un'amica / *a friend*	una cara amica / *a dear friend*

Note the following differences between English and Italian uses of articles.

- The definite article is used in front of mass nouns (Chapter 8) used as subjects (normally at the start of a sentence).

  L'acqua è un liquido. / *Water is a liquid.*
  Il cibo è necessario per vivere. / *Food is necessary to live.*
  La pazienza è una virtù. / *Patience is a virtue.*

- The definite article is also used with count nouns in the plural to express generalizations.

  Gli italiani sono simpatici. / *Italians are nice.*
  I libri ci aiutano a capire. / *Books help us understand.*

- As a guideline, just remember that you cannot start an Italian sentence with a common noun without its article.

- The definite article is used in front of geographical names (continents, countries, states, rivers, islands, mountains, etc.), except cities.

  l'Italia / *Italy*
  la Sicilia / *Sicily*
  gli Stati Uniti / *the United States*
  il Tevere / *the Tiber*
  la California / *California*
  il Mediterraneo / *the Mediterranean*
  il Belgio / *Belgium*
  le Alpi / *the Alps*
  il Piemonte / *Piedmont*

But:

>Roma / *Rome*
>Berlino / *Berlin*
>Parigi / *Paris*

- The definite article is usually dropped after the preposition in and before an unmodified geographical noun.

>Vado in Italia. / *I'm going to Italy.*
>Vivo in Francia. / *I live in France.*

- But when the noun is modified:

>Vado nell'Italia centrale. / *I'm going to central Italy.*
>Vivo nella Francia meridionale. / *I live in southern France.*

- The definite article is used with dates.

>Il 1492 è un anno importante. / *1492 is an important year.*
>Oggi è il tre novembre. / *Today is November third.*

- The definite article is commonly used in place of possessive adjectives when referring to family members (singular only), parts of the body, and clothing.

>Oggi vado in centro con la zia. / *Today I'm going downtown with my aunt.*
>Mi fa male la gamba. / *My leg hurts.*
>Mario non si mette mai la giacca. / *Mario never puts his jacket on.*

- The definite article is used with the days of the week to indicate an habitual action.

>Il lunedì gioco a tennis. / *On Mondays I play tennis.*
>La domenica vado in chiesa. / *On Sundays I go to church.*

- Note that the days of the week, except Sunday, are masculine. The definite article is not used when a specific day is intended.

>Il lunedì di solito gioco a tennis, ma lunedì prossimo vado via. / *On Mondays I usually play tennis, but next Monday I'm going away.*

The definite article is used with titles, unless the person mentioned is spoken to directly.

Speaking about	**Speaking to**
Il dottor Verdi è italiano. / *Dr. Verdi is Italian.*	Buon giorno, dottor Verdi. / *Hello, Dr. Verdi.*
La professoressa Bianchi è molto intelligente. / *Professor Bianchi is very intelligent.*	Professoressa Bianchi, dove abita?/ *Professor Bianchi, where do you live?*

- The definite article is used before the names of languages and nouns referring to school subjects.

  Stiamo imparando lo spagnolo. / *We are learning Spanish.*
  Studio la matematica. / *I am studying mathematics.*

- It is dropped after the prepositions **di** and **in**.

  Ecco il libro di spagnolo. / *Here is the Spanish book.*
  Sono bravo in matematica. / *I'm good in math.*

- The definite article is used with **scorso** / *last* and **prossimo** / *next* in time expressions.

  la settimana scorsa / *last week*
  il mese prossimo / *next month*

- Note that the definite article is not used in some common expressions.

  a destra / *to the right*
  a sinistra / *to the left*
  a casa / *at home*

- The indefinite article also means *one.*

  un'arancia / *an orange / one orange*
  un libro / *a book / one book*
  una penna / *a pen / one pen*

- The indefinite article is not used in exclamations starting with **Che...!** / *What...!*

  Che film! / *What a film!*
  Che bel vestito! / *What a beautiful dress!*

- Finally, remember to repeat the articles and demonstratives before every noun.

  un ragazzo e una ragazza / *a boy and girl*
  il ragazzo e la ragazza / *the boy and girl*

QUICK PRACTICE 1

Put both the definite and indefinite article in front of the following.

Modello: amico
           l'amico/un amico

1. zio *lo zio   uno zio*
2. zero *lo zero   uno zero*
3. studente *lo studente   uno studente*
4. sbaglio *lo sbaglio   uno sbaglio*
5. amico *l'amico   un'amico*
6. orologio *l'orologio   un orologio*
7. padre *il padre   uno padre*
8. fratello *il fratello   uno fratello*
9. nonno *il nonno   uno nonno*
10. madre *la madre   una madre*
11. sorella *la sorella   una sorella*
12. nonna *la nonna   una nonna*
13. amica *l'amica   un'amica*
14. entrata *l'entrata   un'entrata*
15. uscita *l'uscita   un'uscita*
16. psicologo *lo psicologo   uno psicologo*
17. gnocco *lo gnocco   uno gnocco*
18. zia *la zia   una zia*
19. altra zia *l'altra zia*
20. altro studente *l'altro studente   un l'altro studente*
21. nuovo orologio *l'orologio   il nuovo orologio*

Now, make the phrases with the definite article plural.

Modello: amico
           l'amico/gli amici

lo 22. zio *gli zii*
lo 23. zero *gli zero*
lo 24. studente *gli studenti*
lo 25. sbaglio *gli sbagli*
l' 26. amico *gli amici*
l' 27. orologio *gli orologi*
28. padre *i padri*

Write 10 sentences

No articolo 1. Che dolce arancia.

2. Vado in Italia, Germania, e Norvegia, e Inghilterra in prossimo vacanza.

3. Vado un festa per un bambino da settimana scorsa di Settembre.

4. Un volta ho pensato (ho sbagliato) ma ho sbagliato.

5. Sono la nonna per sei e mezzo bambini.

commettiamo Lui non mangia solo uno gnocco.

7. Noi diamo una mano, ma prendiamo un braccio e una gamba.

Articles and Partitives 217

il 29. fratello *i fratelli*

il 30. nonno *i nonni*

la 31. madre *le madre*

la 32. sorella *le sorele*

la 33. nonna *le nonne*

l' 34. amica *le amiche*

l' 35. entrata *le entrate*

l' 36. uscita *le uscite*

lo 37. psicologo *gli psicologi*

lo 38. gnocco *gli gnocchi*

la 39. zia *le zie*

l' 40. altra zia *l'altre zie*

l' 41. altro studente *gli altri studenti*

il 42. nuovo orologio *il nuovo orologi*

You will get a chance to practice differences in article usage between Italian and English in the Putting It All Together section at the end of the chapter.

8. Una brava l'amica è come d'oro or d'oro
9. I bambini devonno en la bocca e sculacciate, non alla corrisposta.
10. La settimana scorse è storia antica.

Demonstratives
I dimostrativi

The demonstrative forms are as follows:

how about pe o gn nouns? q z

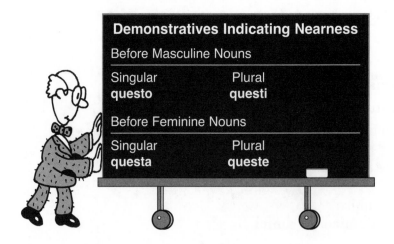

Demonstratives Indicating Nearness	
Before Masculine Nouns	
Singular	Plural
questo	**questi**
Before Feminine Nouns	
Singular	Plural
questa	**queste**

questo
questo sbaglio / *this mistake*
questo giornale / *this newspaper*
questo esercizio / *this exercise*

questi
questi sbagli / *these mistakes*
questi giornali / *these newspapers*
questi esercizi / *these exercises*

questa
questa stanza / *this room*
questa ora / *this hour*

queste
queste stanze / *these rooms*
queste ore / *these hours*

The form **quest'** can be used before singular nouns (or modifying adjectives) beginning with a vowel.

> **questo esercizio** or **quest'esercizio** /*this exercise*
> **questa ora** or **quest'ora** /*this hour*
> **questa ultima giornata** or **quest'ultima giornata** / *this last day*
> **questo incredibile giorno** or **quest'incredibile giorno** / *this incredible day*

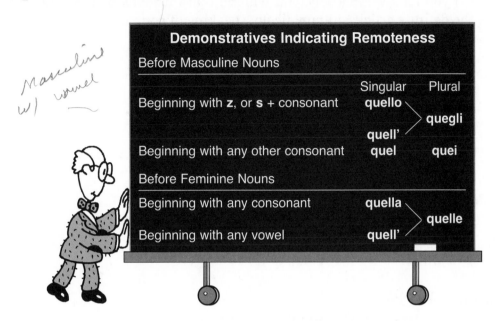

Demonstratives Indicating Remoteness

Before Masculine Nouns

	Singular	Plural
Beginning with **z**, or **s** + consonant	**quello** / **quell'**	**quegli**
Beginning with any other consonant	**quel**	**quei**

Before Feminine Nouns

	Singular	Plural
Beginning with any consonant	**quella**	**quelle**
Beginning with any vowel	**quell'**	**quelle**

(handwritten note:) Masculine w/ vowel

As with the article forms **lo** (plural **gli**) and **uno**, the form **quello** (plural **quegli**) is also used before those few nouns beginning with **ps** and **gn**.

quello
quello zingaro / *that gypsy*
quello spagnolo / *that Spaniard*
quello psicologo / *that psychologist*
quello gnocco / *that dumpling*

quegli
quegli zingari / *those gypsies*
quegli spagnoli / *those Spaniards*
quegli psicologi / *those psychologists*
quegli gnocchi / *those dumplings*

quell'
quell'albero / *that tree*
quell'esame / *that exam*

quegli
quegli alberi / *those trees*
quegli esami / *those exams*

quel
quel dottore / *that doctor*
quel tavolo / *that table*

quei
quei dottori / *those doctors*
quei tavoli / *those tables*

quella
quella porta / *that door*
quella finestra / *that window*

quelle
quelle porte / *those doors*
quelle finestre / *those windows*

quell'
quell'entrata / *that entrance*
quell'uscita / *that exit*

quelle
quelle entrate / *those entrances*
quelle uscite / *those exits*

Be careful! As with articles, when an adjective precedes a noun, you will have to change the demonstrative according to the adjective's initial sound.

quello zingaro / *that gypsy*   quel simpatico zingaro / *that nice gypsy*
quella porta / *that door*   quell'ultima porta / *that last door*
quegli amici / *those friends*   quei simpatici amici /*those nice friends*

If you look very closely, you will see that this demonstrative behaves exactly like the definite article, grammatically speaking of course!

quello zio   =   lo zio
quell'amico   =   l'amico
quei ragazzi   =   i ragazzi

QUICK PRACTICE 2

Put both types of demonstratives in front of each given noun, and then make the whole phrase plural.

Modello: sbaglio ^{this}   ^{that}
           questo sbaglio/quello sbaglio
           questi sbagli/quegli sbagli

1. zio   questo zio   quello
2. piede   questo   queste
3. psicologo   quello   quegli
4. occhio   questo   quello
5. gnocco   questo   quello
6. orecchio   questo   quello
7. unghia   questa   quella
8. bocca   questo   quella
9. ora   questa   quella
10. caro zio   questo   quello
11. cara amica questa   quella
12. giornale   questo   quello
13. esercizio   questo   quello
14. stanza   questa   quella
15. ultimo giorno   quest'   quell'
16. incredibile settimana   quest'   quel'
17. porta   questa   quella
18. finestra   queste   quella
19. entrata   questo   quel
20. tavolo

Partitives

I partitivi

 Partitives are structures placed before nouns that indicate a part of something to which the noun refers as distinct from its whole.

> dell'acqua / *some water*
> degli esami / *some exams*

Think of the partitive as translating only the "*of the*" portion of the English phrase "*some of the*":

(some) of the exams = degli esami

Before count nouns (Chapter 8), the partitive can, in effect, be considered to be the plural of the indefinite article. The most commonly used type of partitive in this case consists of the preposition **di** + the appropriate plural forms of the definite article.

Masculine Forms

di + i = dei   di + i libri = dei libri / *some books*
di + gli = degli   di + gli specchi = degli specchi / *some mirrors*

Feminine Form

di + le = delle   di + le penne = delle penne / *some pens*

Examples:

uno / un	degli
uno sbaglio / *a mistake*	degli sbagli / *some mistakes*
un albero / *a tree*	degli alberi / *some trees*

un	dei
un bicchiere / *a glass*	dei bicchieri / *some glasses*
un coltello / *a knife*	dei coltelli / *some knives*

una / un'	delle
una forchetta / *a fork*	delle forchette / *some forks*
una sedia / *a chair*	delle sedie / *some chairs*
un'automobile / *an automobile*	delle automobili / *some automobiles*

 In place of these forms, the pronouns **alcuni** (*m.*) and **alcune** (*f.*) can be used essentially to express the same kind of notion. The difference is that they render more the concept of *several* and *a few* than of *some*. They are used only in the plural.

degli zii / *some uncles*   alcuni zii / *several (a few) uncles*
dei bicchieri / *some glasses*   alcuni bicchieri / *several (a few) glasses*
delle forchette / *some forks*   alcune forchette / *several (a few) forks*
delle amiche / *some friends (f.)*   alcune amiche / *several (a few) friends (f.)*

Actually, these two types can be used together in expressions such as:

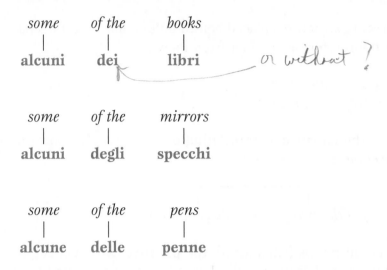

some	of the	books
alcuni	dei	libri

or without ?

some	of the	mirrors
alcuni	degli	specchi

some	of the	pens
alcune	delle	penne

The invariable pronoun **qualche** can also be used to express the partitive. But be careful with this one! It must be followed by a singular noun, even though the meaning is plural!

some	books	some	pens
qualche	**libro** (*sing.*)	**qualche**	**penna** (*sing.*)

Think of **qualche** as really translating "*whichever*," and then it will be easy to see why the noun is in the singular.

Some books	=	*whichever*	*book*
		qualche	**libro**

The pronoun forms (**qualche** or **alcuni/alcune**) are often used at the start of sentences, rather than the **degli/dei/delle** forms. Once again, be careful with **qualche**: It requires a singular verb!

Alcuni studenti studiano il francese. / *Some students study French.*
Qualche studente studia il francese. / *Some students study French.*

In colloquial Italian, it is not unusual to find that the partitive is omitted (when the noun is not the first word in a sentence).

Voglio della carne. = Voglio carne. / *I want (some) meat.*
Mangio degli spaghetti. = Mangio spaghetti. / *I'm eating (some) spaghetti.*

In negative sentences, the partitive is always omitted.

Affirmative Sentence	Negative Sentence
Ho dei biglietti. / *I have some tickets.*	Non ho biglietti. / *I don't have any tickets.*
Voglio delle paste. / *I want some pastries.*	Non voglio paste. / *I don't want any pastries.*

The negative partitive can also be rendered by **non...nessuno**. Think of **nessuno** as being made up of **"ness"** + indefinite article.

nessuno corresponds to **uno**:   **uno studente/nessuno studente**
nessun corresponds to **un**:   **un biglietto/nessun biglietto**
nessuna corresponds to **una**:   **una signora/nessuna signora**
nessun' corresponds to **un'**:   **un'automobile/nessun'automobile**

This means that the noun is always in the singular, even though the meaning is plural.

Affirmative Sentence	Negative Sentence
Carlo compra delle caramelle. / *Carlo is buying some candies.*	Carlo non compra nessuna caramella. / *Carlo is not buying any candies.*
Maria vuole dei libri nuovi. / *Maria wants some new books.*	Maria non vuole nessun libro nuovo. / *Maria doesn't want any new books.*

With mass nouns (Chapter 8), the partitive is rendered by either **di** + the singular forms of the definite article, or by the expression **un po' di** ("a bit of").

Masculine Forms
di + il = del   di + il vino = del vino /*some wine*
di + lo = dello   di + lo zucchero = dello zucchero / *some sugar*
di + l' = dell'   di + l'orzo = dell'orzo /*some barley*

Feminine Form
di + la = della   di + la pasta = della pasta /*some pasta*

Examples:

Voglio del pane. = Voglio un po' di pane. / *I want some bread.*
Lui vuole dello zucchero. = Lui vuole un po' di zucchero. / *He wants some sugar.*
Maria mangia dell'insalata. = Maria mangia un po' di insalata. / *Mary eats some salad.*
Preferisco mangiare della carne. = Preferisco mangiare un po' di carne. / *I prefer to eat some meat.*

The following chart summarizes the various partitive forms:

With Count Nouns

Singular Forms of the Indefinite Article	Corresponding Partitive Forms
Masculine	**Masculine**
un	dei, alcuni, qualche, nessun
un libro / *a book*	dei libri / *some books*
	alcuni libri / *several books*
	qualche libro / *some books*
	nessun libro / *no books*
un	degli, alcuni, qualche, nessun
un amico / *a friend*	degli amici / *some friends*
	alcuni amici / *several friends*
	qualche amico / *some friends*
	nessun amico / *no friends*
uno	degli, alcuni, qualche, nessuno
uno studente / *a student*	degli studenti / *some students*
	alcuni studenti / *several students*
	qualche studente / *some students*
	nessuno studente / *no students*
Feminine	**Feminine**
una	delle, alcune, qualche, nessuna
una penna / *a pen*	delle penne / *some pens*
	alcune penne / *several pens*
	qualche penna / *some pens*
	nessuna penna / *no pens*
un'	delle, alcune, qualche, nessun'
un'amica / *a friend*	delle amiche / *some friends*
	alcune amiche / *several friends*
	qualche amica / *some friends*
	nessun'amica / *no friends*

With Mass Nouns

Masculine	Equivalent Forms
del	
del riso / *some rice*	un po' di riso
dell'	
dell'orzo / *some barley*	un po' di orzo
dello	
dello zucchero / *some sugar*	un po' di zucchero
Feminine	Equivalent Forms
della	
della carne / *some meat*	un po' di carne
dell'	
dell'acqua / *some water*	un po' di acqua

Be careful! As in the case of articles and demonstratives, you may have to change the partitive forms when an adjective precedes the noun.

degli zii / *some uncles*   **dei simpatici zii** / *some nice uncles*
dell'acqua / *some water*   **della buon'acqua** / *some good water*

QUICK PRACTICE 3

g. 29

Make each phrase plural in three ways as shown in the model.

Modello: un libro
              dei libri
              alcuni libri
              qualche libro

1. uno studente   *dei studenti   alcuni studenti   qualche studente*
2. una studentessa *della studentessa   alcune   qualche*
3. un bicchiere   *dei   alcuni   qualche*
4. una sedia   *delle   alcuni   qualch*
5. un'automobile   *delle automobili   qualche*
6. un coltello   *dei cotelli alcuni   qualch*
7. uno sbaglio   *degli sbagli   alcuni   quale*
8. un albero   *degli alberi   "   .*
9. un simpatico amico   *dei simpatici amici*
10. un nuovo studente

PUTTING IT ALL TOGETHER

A. *Put the definite article in front of the following place names, if it is required.*

1. Italia   *l'Italia*
2. Francia   *la Francia*
3. Sicilia   *la*
4. Toscana   *la*
5. Stati Uniti *gli*
6. Po   *il*
7. Tevere   *il*
8. California *la*

9. Wisconsin *il*
10. Mediterraneo *il*
11. Adriatico *lo?*
12. Belgio *il*
13. Germania *la*
14. Alpi *le*
15. Appennini *gli*
16. Piemonte *il*
17. Roma
18. Venezia
19. Bari
20. Berlino
21. Madrid
22. Parigi

B. *Say the following sentences in Italian.*

1. Water is a liquid. *L'acqua è liquido*
2. Food is necessary to live. *Il cibo è necessario per vivere*
3. Meat is an important food. *La carne è un cibo importante*
4. Patience is a virtue. *La pazienza è una virtù*
5. Love is also a virtue. *L'amore anche è una virtù*
6. Italians are nice. *Gli italiani sono simpatici*
7. Americans are also very nice. *Gli Americani anche sono molto simpatici*
8. Books help us understand. *I libri aiutano a capire*
9. Videos are more enjoyable. *I video sono più divertenti*
10. She's going to Italy. *Lei va in Italia*
11. I live in France. *vivo en francia*
12. They live in the United States. *vivono negli E. U.*
13. He's going to central Italy. *va nel centro di Italia*
14. We live in southern France. *viviamo nella sud di francia*
15. 1776 is an important year. *Il 1776 è un anno importante*
16. Today is April the fourth. *Oggi è quattro aprile*
17. Today I'm going downtown with my uncle. *oggi vado centro con mio zio*
18. My hand hurts. *mi fa male la manno.*
19. Sara never puts her jacket on. *Sara*
20. On Tuesdays I have an Italian class (**la lezione** / *class, lesson*). *martedì ho la lezione di italiano*
21. On Saturdays I always go downtown. *Il sabato sempre vado in centro*
22. Dr. Smith is Italian, despite (**nonostante**) his name. *D.S. è italiano*
23. Good morning, Dr. Smith.

24. We are learning Italian.
25. My brother is studying mathematics. *mio fratello studia math* 4-27
26. Here is his math book. *Ecco suo libro di matematica*
27. Last week I went to the movies. *Scorsa settimana sono andato al cinema*
28. Next year we want to go to Italy. *L'anno prossimo vogliamo andare in Italia*
29. I would like only one coffee and one pastry, thanks. *vorrei solo una caffè e una pasta*
30. The boys and girls of the school are all very nice. *I ragazzi e le ragazze sono della scuola sono molto simpatici*

C. *Make each partitive negative.*

Modello: Voglio della carne.
   Non voglio carne.

   Voglio un libro.
   Non voglio libri. / Non voglio nessun libro.

Voglio… *do some of these*

1. un po' di carne *non voglio carne*
2. dell'acqua *non voglio acqua*
3. un po' zucchero *" " zucchero*
4. dell'orzo *" " orzo*
5. del riso *" " riso*
6. un'arancia *" " arancia*
7. delle pere *" " pere*
8. qualche libro
9. alcune cose
10. del pane
11. un po' d'insalata
12. qualche caramella
13. alcune paste
14. dei bicchieri
15. alcune forchette

D. *Odd one out! In each set of four there is an odd form. Can you detect it?*

1. il libro, un libro, la penna, gli zii
2. un amico, una stanza, uno zio, (quell'amico)
3. (degli amici), quello studente, quelle amiche, questo libro
4. un po' di carne, della pasta, la forchetta, qualche forchetta

do some

10

Adjectives and Information Words

Quanto Sai Già? — How Much Do You Know Already?

Match the items in the two columns correctly.

1. _B._ si chiama tuo fratello?   a. marrone
2. _F._ parli sempre così?   b. Come
3. _E._ è il tuo insegnante d'italiano?   c. Quanto
4. _G._ abitano i tuoi genitori?   d. italiani
5. _C._ costano quei CD?   e. Chi
6. Loro sono due ragazze _H._   f. Perché
7. E loro invece sono due ragazzi _D._   g. Dove
8. La mia giacca è …   h. francesi
9. I miei pantaloni sono …   i. grigia

Descriptive Adjectives
Gli aggettivi qualificativi

Adjectives are words that modify, or describe, nouns. They are placed before or after the noun they modify.

> **È una casa nuova.** / *It's a new house.*
> **È il mio libro.** / *It's my book.*

Descriptive adjectives are used specifically to describe nouns. They can be easily recognized. They are generally distinguishable by predictable changes in the final vowel:

> **il libro nuovo** / *the new book*
> **i libri nuovi** / *the new books*
> **la rivista nuova** / *the new magazine*
> **le riviste nuove** / *the new magazines*

These adjectives must agree with the nouns they modify. This means that an adjective must correspond in gender and number with the noun. Thus, the ending of an adjective depends on whether the noun is masculine or feminine, singular or plural.

There are two types of adjectives according to their endings.

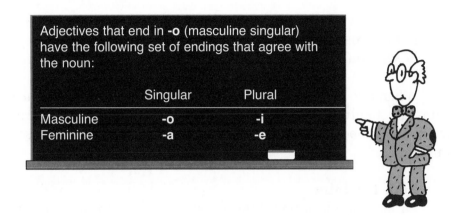

Adjectives that end in **-o** (masculine singular) have the following set of endings that agree with the noun:

	Singular	Plural
Masculine	**-o**	**-i**
Feminine	**-a**	**-e**

Singular

l'**uomo alto** / *the tall man*
il **figlio alto** / *the tall son*
la **donna alta** / *the tall woman*
la **madre alta** / *the tall mother*

Plural

gli **uomini alti** / *the tall men*
i **figli alti** / *the tall sons*
le **donne alte** / *the tall women*
le **madri alte** / *the tall mothers*

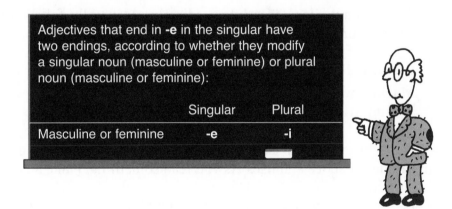

Adjectives that end in **-e** in the singular have two endings, according to whether they modify a singular noun (masculine or feminine) or plural noun (masculine or feminine):

	Singular	Plural
Masculine or feminine	**-e**	**-i**

Singular

il **medico elegante** / *the elegant doctor*
il **padre elegante** / *the elegant father*
la **donna elegante** / *the elegant woman*
la **madre elegante** / *the elegant mother*

Plural

i **medici eleganti** / *the elegant doctors*
i **padri eleganti** / *the elegant fathers*
le **donne eleganti** / *the elegant women*
le **madri eleganti** / *the elegant mothers*

A few adjectives are invariable; that is, their endings never change. The most common are the adjectives of color: **marrone** / *brown*, **arancione** / *orange*, **viola** / *violet, purple*, **rosa** / *pink*, and **blu** / *dark blue*.

Singular	Plural
il vestito marrone / *the brown suit*	i vestiti marrone / *the brown suits*
la giacca marrone / *the brown jacket*	le giacche marrone / *the brown jackets*
la matita arancione / *the orange crayon*	le matite arancione / *the orange crayons*
lo zaino viola /*the purple backpack*	gli zaini viola /*the purple backpacks*
l'abito rosa /*the pink dress*	gli abiti rosa /*the pink dresses*
la sciarpa blu /*the dark blue scarf*	le sciarpe blu /*the dark blue scarves*

When two nouns are modified, the adjective is always in the plural. If the two nouns are feminine, then the appropriate feminine plural form is used. If the two nouns are both masculine, or of mixed gender, then the masculine plural form is used.

Both Feminine
La maglia e la borsa sono rosse. / *The sweater and the purse are red.*

Both Masculine
Il cappotto e l'impermeabile sono rossi. / *The coat and the raincoat are red.*

Mixed Gender
La maglia e il cappotto sono rossi. / *The coat and the raincoat are red.*

As you have seen, descriptive adjectives generally follow the noun. Some, however, can come before or after.

È una bella camicia.	or	È una camicia bella. / *It's a beautiful shirt.*
Maria è una ragazza simpatica.	or	Maria è una simpatica ragazza. / *Mary is a nice girl.*

You will eventually learn which descriptive adjectives can come before the noun through practice and use. As you read something, make a note of the position of the adjective.

Be careful! As you know by now, you will have to change the form of the article, demonstrative, etc., when you put the adjective before a noun.

lo zio simpatico   but   il simpatico zio
    | |
  [before *z*]   [before *s*]

Some common descriptive adjectives that can come before or after a noun are:

bello / *beautiful*	cattivo / *bad*	piccolo / *small, little*
brutto / *ugly*	giovane / *young*	povero / *poor*
buono / *good*	grande / *big, large*	simpatico / *nice, charming*
caro / *dear*	nuovo / *new*	vecchio / *old*

But be careful! A few of these adjectives change meaning according to their position.

È un ragazzo povero.	=	*He is a poor boy (not wealthy).*
È un povero ragazzo.	=	*He is a poor boy (deserving of pity).*
È un amico vecchio.	=	*He is an old friend (in age).*
È un vecchio amico.	=	*He is an old friend (for many years).*

Descriptive adjectives can also be separated from the noun they modify by what is called a *linking* verb. The most common linking verbs are **essere** / *to be*, **sembrare** / *to seem*, and **diventare** / *to become*.

Quella casa è nuova. / *That house is new.*
Quell'uomo sembra giovane. / *That man seems young.*
Questa camicia sta diventando vecchia. / *This shirt is getting old.*

Adjectives used in this way are known as *predicate adjectives* because they occur in the predicate slot, *after* the verb that links them to the noun they modify.

When these adjectives are accompanied by an adverb, another adjective, or some other part of speech, they must *follow* the noun.

È un simpatico ragazzo. / *He is a pleasant boy.*
  but
È un ragazzo molto simpatico. / *He is a very pleasant boy.*
È un ragazzo simpatico e bravo. / *He is a pleasant and good boy.*

Descriptive adjectives specify a quality of the noun they modify. They make up the largest group of adjectives. As already discussed, they generally follow the noun.

È una strada lunga. / *It's a long road.*

Of the adjectives that can come before the noun, **buono** / *good*, **bello** / *beautiful*, **santo** *saint(ly)*, and **grande** / *big, large* change in form when they are placed before. Here are the forms of **buono**:

Before Masculine Nouns	Singular	Plural
Beginning with z, s + consonant, ps, gn	buono	buoni
Beginning with any other sound (vowel or consonant)	buon	buoni

Before Feminine Nouns	Singular	Plural
Beginning with any consonant	buona	buone
Beginning with any vowel	buon'	buone

When it is placed after the noun, **buono** is treated as a normal descriptive adjective ending in -o.

Singular
un **buono** zio or **uno** zio **buono** / *a good uncle*
un **buon** libro or un libro **buono** / *a good book*
un **buon** amico or un amico **buono** / *a good friend*
una **buona** macchina or una macchina **buona** / *a good car*
una **buon'**amica or un'amica **buona** / *a good friend*

Plural
dei **buoni** zii or degli zii **buoni** / *some good uncles*
dei **buoni** amici or degli amici **buoni** / *some good friends*
delle **buone** macchine or delle macchine **buone** / *some good cars*
delle **buone** amiche or delle amiche **buone** / *some good friends*

When referring to people, **buono** means *good*, mainly in the sense of *good in nature*. If *good at doing something* is intended, then you must use the adjective **bravo**.

È un **buon** ragazzo.   =   *He is a good (good-natured, well-behaved) boy.*
È un **bravo** ragazzo.   =   *He is a good student. (good at being a student)*

Here are the forms of **bello**:

Before Masculine Nouns	Singular	Plural
Beginning with z, s + consonant, **ps**, **gn**	bello	begli
Beginning with any vowel	bell'	begli
Beginning with any other consonant	bel	bei
Before Feminine Nouns		
Beginning with any consonant	bella	belle
Beginning with any vowel	bell'	belle

If placed after the noun, **bello** is treated like a normal descriptive adjective ending in -o.

Singular
un **bello** sport or **uno** sport **bello** / *a beautiful sport*
un **bell'**orologio or un orologio **bello** / *a beautiful watch*
un **bel** fiore or un fiore **bello** / *a beautiful flower*
una **bella** donna or una donna **bella** / *a beautiful woman*
una **bell'**automobile or un'automobile **bella** / *a beautiful automobile*

Plural
dei begli sport or degli sport belli / *some beautiful sports*
dei begli orologi or degli orologi belli / *some beautiful watches*
dei bei fiori or dei fiori belli / *some beautiful flowers*
delle belle automobili or delle automobili belle / *some beautiful automobiles*

Santo has the following forms:

Before Masculine Nouns	Singular	Plural
Beginning with z, s + consonant, ps, gn	santo	
Beginning with any vowel	sant'	santi
Beginning with any other consonant	san	
Before Feminine Nouns		
Beginning with any consonant	santa	sante
Beginning with any vowel	sant'	

Singular	**Plural**
Santo Stefano / *St. Stephen*	**i Santi Stefano e Antonio** / *Saints Stephen and Anthony*
San Pietro / *St. Peter*	**i Santi Pietro e Paolo** / *Saints Peter and Paul*
Santa Caterina / *St. Catharine*	**le Sante Caterina e Anna** / *Saints Catherine and Anne*
Sant'Anna / *Saint Anne*	**le Sante Anna e Caterina** / *Saints Anne and Catherine*

Grande has the optional forms **gran** (before a masculine singular noun beginning with any consonant except z, s + consonant, ps, and gn) and **grand'** (before any singular noun beginning with a vowel). Otherwise, it is treated as any adjective ending in -e. Notice that when it comes before a noun it generally means *great*.

un gran film or un grande film / *a great film*
un grand'amico or un grande amico / *a great friend*
un amico grande / *a big friend*

Those adjectives ending in -co, -go, -cio, and -gio manifest the same spelling peculiarities when pluralized as the nouns ending in these sounds (Chapter 8).

Singular	**Plural**
un uomo simpatico/ *a nice man*	degli uomini simpatici / *some nice men*
una strada lunga / *a long street*	delle strade lunghe / *some long streets*
un vestito grigio / *a gray suit*	dei vestiti grigi / *some gray suits*

QUICK PRACTICE 1

Give the equivalent masculine or feminine form of each phrase, as the case may be.

sentence for each

Maschile	**Femminile**
un uomo simpatico	*una donna simpatica*
un caro amico	una cara amica
un grande uomo	una grande donna
un simpatico zio	una simpatica zia
un ragazzo simpatico	*una ragazza simpatica*
un padre intelligente	una madre intelligente
un amico alto	*un'amica alta*

Now give the singular or plural form of each phrase, as the case may be.

Singolare	**Plurale**
un vestito grigio	*dei vestiti grigi*
quella strada lunga	quelle strade lunghe
una bella camicia	*delle belle camicie*
il cappotto rosso	i cappotti rossi
il vestito rosa	*dei vestiti rossi*
la sciarpa marrone	le sciarpe marrone
quello zaino viola	*quegli zaini viola*
quel ragazzo francese	quei ragazzi francesi
quella ragazza francese	*quelle ragazze francesi*

Information Words

Strutture interrogative

Information words (*How? Why?* etc.) allow you to ask content questions:

Quante scarpe hai comprato? / *How many shoes did you buy?*
Chi parla italiano qui? / *Who speaks Italian here?*
Dove abita Marco? / *Where does Marco live?*

Read

Impara queste espressioni!

Chi?	Who?
Che?/Cosa?/Che cosa?	What?
Come?	How?
Dove?	Where?
Perché?	Why?
Quale?	Which?
Quando?	When?
Quanto?	How much?

Note that che, quale, and quanto can also be used as adjectives. In the latter two cases, they agree with the noun they modify. This means their endings must agree in gender (masculine or feminine) and number (singular and plural) with the noun. Che is invariable.

Masculine Singular	Masculine Plural
Quale fratello arriva? / *Which brother is arriving?*	Quali fratelli arrivano? / *Which brothers are arriving?*
Quanto caffè desideri? / *How much coffee do you want?*	Quanti caffè desideri? / *How many coffees do you want?*
Che libro è? / *What book is it?*	Che libri sono? / *What books are they?*

Feminine Singular	Feminine Plural
Quale sorella arriva? / *Which sister is arriving?*	Quali sorelle arrivano? / *Which sisters are arriving?*
Quanta pasta desideri? / *How much pasta do you want?*	Quante paste desideri? / *How many pastries do you want?*
Che rivista è? / *What magazine is it?*	Che riviste sono? / *What magazines are they?*

Examples:

Singular	**Plural**
chi	chi
Chi è quell'uomo? / *Who is that man?*	Chi sono quegli uomini? / *Who are those men?*
Chi sei tu? / *Who are you?*	Chi siete voi? / *Who are you?*
che	che
Che libro leggi? / *What book are you reading?*	Che libri leggi? / *What books are you reading?*
Che strada è? / *What street is it?*	Che strade sono? / *What streets are they?*
Che è/Cosa è/Che cosa è? / *What is it?*	Che sono/Cosa sono/Che cosa sono? / *What are they?*

to someone you don't know

Note: cosa? and che cosa? cannot be used as adjectives.

come	come
Come ti chiami? / *What's your name?*	Come si chiamano loro? / *What are their names?*
Come stai? / *How are you?*	Come stanno loro? / *How are they?*
dove	dove
Dove abiti, Maria? / *Maria, where do you live?*	Dove abitano i tuoi amici? / *Where do your friends live?*

Adjectives and Information Words **235**

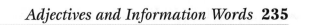

perché

Perché tu dici questo? / *Why are you saying this?*

perché

Perché loro dicono questo? / *Why are they saying this?*

quando

Quando arriva lui? / *When is he arriving?*

quando

Quando arrivano loro? / *When are they arriving?*

quale

Quale sport preferisci? / *Which sport do you prefer?*

Quale macchina hai comprato? / *Which car did you buy?*

quali

Quali sport preferisci? / *Which sports do you prefer?*

Quali macchine hai comprato? / *Which cars did you buy?*

quanto

Quanto zucchero vuoi? / *How much sugar do you want?*

quanti

Quanti soldi hai? / *How much money do you have?*

quanta

Quanta minestra vuoi? / *How much soup do you want?*

quante

Quante patate mangi? / *How many potatoes are you eating?*

Note that **Qual è...?** / *Which is...?* is typically (although not necessarily) written without an apostrophe before the verb form **è**.

Qual è il tuo compagno preferito? / *Which one is your favorite chum?*

QUICK PRACTICE 2

You are given statements that are responses to questions. Formulate the appropriate questions.

Modello: Ho mangiato tanta carne ieri.
Quanta carne hai mangiato ieri?

1. Ho solo ventidue euro. *Quanti euro hai?*
2. Voglio solo un po' di minestra. *Quanta minestra vuoi?*
3. Prendo solo una tazza di caffè, grazie. *Quanto café desidera?*
4. Loro vogliono tre o quattro biscotti. *Quanti biscotti desideri?*
5. Quel ragazzo è il mio nipotino. *chi è quel ragazzo?*
6. Quella ragazza è la mia nipotina. *Chi e quella ragazza*
7. Quelle due persone sono i miei amici. *chi sono quella due persone*
8. È un libro di fantascienza (*science fiction*). *Ch Qlibro è*

9. Sono due penne digitali. *Quante penne sono? chi cosa penne digitali*
10. Mi chiamo Marcello. *Como si chiama*
11. Noi stiamo molto bene, grazie. *come state*
12. Sono nato in Italia. *Dove sei nato?*
13. Anche loro sono nati in Italia. *Dove loro sono nati*
14. Preferisco questo DVD, non quello. *Quale DVD preferisci*
15. Vorrei queste scarpe, non quelle. *Quale scarpe preferisci*
16. Voglio vedere quel film perché Fellini è un grande regista. *Quale film vuole vedere?*
17. Voglio vederlo stasera. *quando vuole vederlo.*
18. Dico questo perché è la verità. *Perché dico questo.*

Possessive Adjectives

Gli aggettivi possessivi

Possessive adjectives allow us to indicate ownership of, or relationship to, something.

> **il mio libro** / *my book (ownership of)*
> **le nostre amiche** / *our (female) friends (relationship to)*

Like any other adjective, possessive adjectives agree in number and gender with the noun they modify.

Possessive Adjectives

	Before Masculine Nouns		Before Feminine Nouns	
	Singular	Plural	Singular	Plural
my	il mio	i miei	la mia	le mie
your (*fam., sing.*)	il tuo	i tuoi	la tua	le tue
his, her, its	il suo	i suoi	la sua	le sue
your (*pol. sing.*)	il Suo	i Suoi	la Sua	le Sue
our	il nostro	i nostri	la nostra	le nostre
your (*fam., pl.*)	il vostro	i vostri	la vostra	le vostre
their	il loro	i loro	la loro	le loro
Your (*pol., pl.*)	il Loro	i Loro	la Loro	le Loro

(handwritten: why caps)

Examples:

With Singular Nouns
il mio cappotto / *my coat*
la tua bicicletta / *your (fam.) bicycle*
il suo biglietto / *his, her ticket*
la nostra camera / *our bedroom*
il vostro passaporto / *your (pl.) passport*
la lora casa / *their house*
il Suo indirizzo / *your (pol.) address*
il Loro lavoro / *your (pol., pl.) job*

With Plural Nouns
i miei cappotti / *my coats*
le tue biciclette / *your bicycles*
i suoi biglietti / *his, her tickets*
le nostre camere / *our bedrooms*
i vostri passaporti / *your passports*
le loro case / *their houses*
i Suoi indirizzi / *your addresses*
i Loro lavori / *your jobs*

As you can see, possessives are adjectives that come before the noun and agree with it in gender and number. Notice that the definite article is part of the possessive adjective. It is, however, dropped for all forms except loro when the noun modified has the following characteristics.

- It is a kinship noun (i.e., it refers to family members or relatives).
- It is singular.
- It is unmodified (i.e., it is not accompanied by another adjective, or altered by a suffix).

Singular Kinship Noun	**Plural Kinship Noun**
tuo cugino / *your cousin*	i tuoi cugini / *your cousins*
mia sorella / *my sister*	le mie sorelle / *my sisters*
nostro fratello / *our brother*	i nostri fratelli / *our brothers*

Singular Kinship Noun	**Modified or Altered Kinship Noun**
tuo padre / *your father*	il tuo padre americano / *your American father*
mia sorella / *my sister*	la mia sorellina / *my little sister*
nostra cugina / *our cousin (f.)*	la nostra cugina italiana / *our Italian cousin*

- The article is always retained with loro.

il loro figlio / *their son*	i loro figli / *their children*
la loro figlia / *their daughter*	la loro figlia bella / *their beautiful daughter*
il loro fratello / *their brother*	il loro fratellino / *their little brother*

There are a few kinship nouns to which the above rules apply only optionally: e.g., mamma / mom and papà (babbo) / *dad*, nonno / *grandfather*, nonna / *grandmother*.

mia madre / *my mother*	la mia mamma / *my mom*
tuo padre / *your father*	il tuo papà / *your dad*

Notice that both *his* and *her* are expressed by the same possessive, which takes on the same form before the noun, agreeing with it in gender and number, of course.

His	**Her**
il suo libro / *his book*	il suo libro / *her book*
i suoi libri / *his books*	i suoi libri / *her books*
la sua penna / *his pen*	la sua penna / *her pen*
le sue penne / *his pens*	le sue penne / *her pens*

This can be confusing! Here's what to keep in mind. Make the possessive adjective agree with the noun first. Then worry about what it means in English. Otherwise, you will confuse its form with its meaning!

- If the noun is masculine singular, use **il suo**
- If the noun is feminine singular, use **la sua**
- If the noun is masculine plural, use **i suoi**
- If the noun is feminine plural, use **le sue**

This same form also means *its*:

la sua coda / *its tail*   **le sue zampe** / *its paws*

As you know, *your* is rendered in Italian with both *familiar* and *polite* forms. Note that the polite forms are identical to the *his, her* forms in the singular, and to the *their* forms in the plural. To keep the two types distinct in writing, the polite forms are often capitalized, as has been done here. But this is *not* an obligatory rule.

il suo amico / *his, her friend*   **il Suo amico** / *your friend*
le sue cose / *his, her things*   **le Sue cose** / *your things*
il loro amico / *their friend*   **il Loro amico** / *your (pl.) friend*
le loro cose / *their things*   **le Loro cose** / *your (pl.) things*

Thus, when you see or hear these forms, you will have to figure out what they mean from the context. For example:

il suo giornale
- *his newspaper* → **Mario non ha portato il suo giornale.** / *Mario didn't bring his newspaper.*
- *her newspaper* → **Maria non ha portato il suo giornale.** / *Mary didn't bring her newspaper.*
- *your newspaper* → **Professore, ha portato il suo giornale?** / *Professor, did you bring your newspaper?*

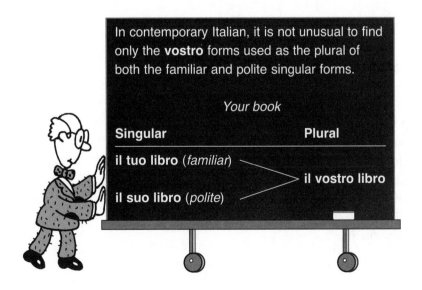

In contemporary Italian, it is not unusual to find only the **vostro** forms used as the plural of both the familiar and polite singular forms.

Your book

Singular	Plural
il tuo libro (*familiar*)	
	il vostro libro
il suo libro (*polite*)	

The possessive adjective can be put after the noun for emphasis.

È il mio cane. / *It's my dog.*   È il cane mio! / *It's my dog!*
Porta tuo cugino. / *Bring*   Porta il cugino tuo! / *Bring your cousin!*
   your cousin.

If the possessive adjective is preceded by the indefinite article, it allows you to express the equivalent of English *of mine, of yours,* etc.

un mio zio / *an uncle of mine*
una sua amica / *a friend of his, hers*

To express *own,* as in *my own dog,* use the adjective **proprio**.

il mio proprio cane / *my own dog*
la (sua) propria chiave / *his, her own key*

Notice, finally, that the article is dropped when speaking directly to someone.

Amico mio, che fai? / *My friend, what are you doing?*

QUICK PRACTICE 3

Provide the indicated forms of the possessive adjective.

1. *my…*
   a. amico il mio
   b. amica il mia
   c. amici i miei
   d. amiche le mei
   e. zio un mio zio ebbe parecchi cavalli da corsa
   f. zii i miei   quando era giovane.
   g. zio vecchio il mio

2. *your (fam., sing.)…*
   a. cappotto il suo.   Ho intenzione di sostituire il suo cappotto
   b. cappotti i suoi
   c. bicicletta la sua
   d. biciclette le sue
   e. fratello il suo.
   f. fratelli i suoi
   g. fratello grande suo

3. *your (pol., sing.)...*
   a. cappotto *il suo cappotto*
   b. cappotti *i suoi*   *La sua bicicletta è grosso quando la mia.*
   c. bicicletta *la sua*
   d. biciclette *le sue*
   e. fratello *il suo*
   f. fratelli *i suoi*
   g. fratello grande *il suo*

4. *your (fam., pl.)...*
   a. cappotto *il vostro*   *Sono questo cappotto?*
   b. cappotti *i vostri*
   c. bicicletta *la vostra*
   d. biciclette *le vostre*
   e. fratello *il vostro*
   f. fratelli *i vostri*
   g. fratello grande *il suo*

5. *your (pol., pl.)...*
   a. cappotto *il loro*
   b. cappotti *i loro*
   c. bicicletta *la loro*
   d. biciclette *le loro*   *I loro fratelli sono brava.*
   e. fratello *il loro*
   f. fratelli *i loro*
   g. fratello grande *il loro*   *i nostro passaporto sono americana*

6. *our...*
   a. passaporto *il nostro*
   b. passaporti *i nostri*
   c. camera *la nostra*
   d. camere *le nostre*
   e. zia *la nostra*
   f. zie *le nostre*
   g. simpatica zia *la nostra*

7. *his...*
   a. giornale *il suo*
   b. giornali *i suoi*
   c. rivista *la sua*   *La sua rivista è spinta*
   d. riviste *le sue*
   e. sorella *la sua*
   f. sorelle *le sue*
   g. sorellina *la sua*

8. *her* …
   a. giornale *il suo*
   b. giornali *i suoi*
   c. rivista *la sua*
   d. riviste *le sue*
   e. sorella *sua*
   f. sorelle *le sue*
   g. sorellina *la sua*   *La sua sorellina è una moccicosa.*

9. *their* …
   a. giornale *il loro*   *Il loro giornale è tardi.*
   b. giornali *i loro*
   c. rivista *la loro*
   d. riviste *le loro*
   e. sorella *la loro*
   f. sorelle *le loro*
   g. sorellina *la loro*

Indefinite Adjectives
Gli aggettivi indefiniti

There are a few other adjectives you should know about. The most of important of these are known as *indefinite* adjectives. The most common ones are listed below:

Indefinite Adjectives	
Invariable	Like adjectives ending in **-o**
abbastanza / *enough*	**altro** / *other*
~~**assai**~~ / *quite, enough*	**certo** / *certain*
ogni / *each, every*	**molto/tanto** / *much, many, a lot*
qualsiasi / *whichever, any*	**parecchio** / *quite a bit, a number*
qualunque / *whichever, any*	**poco** / *little, few*
	troppo / *too much*
	stesso / *the same*
	ultimo / *last*
	tutto / *all*

Examples:

Invariable
Non ho abbastanza soldi. / *I do not have enough money.*
Lui mangia assai carne. / *He eats quite a lot of meat.*
Ogni mattina leggiamo il giornale. / *Every morning we read the newspaper.*
In Italia puoi andare a qualsiasi (qualunque) ristorante. / *In Italy you can go to any restaurant.*

Treat it like adjectives ending in -o

Chi è l'altra ragazza? / *Who is the other girl?*

Conosco un certo signore che si chiama Roberto. / *I know a certain gentle-man named Robert.*

Ieri ho mangiato molti (tanti) dolci. / *Yesterday I ate a lot of sweets.*

Ci sono poche studentesse in questa classe. / *There are few female students in this class.*

Parecchi turisti visitano Venezia. / *Quite a number of tourists visit Venice.*

Abbiamo mangiato troppo gelato. / *We ate too much ice cream.*

Questa è l'ultima volta che ti telefonerò. / *This is the last time I'm going to call you.*

Questi sono gli stessi studenti. / *These are the same students.*

Notice that **tutto** is separated from the noun by the definite article.

Lei ha mangiato tutto il riso. / *She ate all the rice.*

Mario ha mangiato tutta la minestra. / *Mario ate all the soup.*

Molto, **tanto**, **poco**, and **troppo** are also used as adverbs, in which case there is no agreement (Chapter 12).

QUICK PRACTICE 4

Say the following phrases in Italian.

1. I do not have enough money. *non ho abbastanza soldi*
2. He eats quite a lot of pasta. *Lui mangia assai pasta*
3. Every afternoon we watch TV. *ogni pomeriggio guardiamo TV*
4. In Italy you can go to any coffee bar. *In Italia puoi andare al qualunque bar*
5. Who are the other girls? *Chi è l'altre ragazze?*
6. I know a certain doctor named Elena. *Conosco un certo dottore che si chiama Elena*
7. Yesterday I ate a lot of candies. *Ieri ho mangiato molti dolci.*
8. There are few female students in this class. *Ci sono poche studentesse in questa classe*
9. Quite a number of tourists visit Florence. *Parecchi turisti visitano Firenza*
10. We ate too much ice cream. *abbiamo mangiato troppo gelato.*
11. This is the last time I'm going to call you. *Questa è l'ultima volta che te telefonerò*
12. These are the same women. *Questi sono gli donne –*
13. She ate all the rice. *Lei ha mangiato tutti il riso.*
14. Alessandro ate all the soup. *Alessandro ha mangiato tutta la minestra*
15. All my friends *(m.)* will come to the party. *Tutti miei amici verrano a la festa*
16. All their friends *(f.)* will also come to the party.

Comparison of Adjectives
La comparazione degli aggettivi

Adjectives can be used to indicate that something or someone has a relatively equal, greater, or lesser degree of some quality. The three degrees of comparison are called: *positive*, *comparative*, and *superlative*.

- For the positive degree use either così. . . come or tanto. . .quanto, if two nouns are compared by one adjective.

  > Paola è così felice come sua sorella. / *Paula is as happy as her sister.*
  > Quei ragazzi sono tanto noiosi quanto gli altri. / *Those boys are as boring as the others.*

- The first words (così or tanto) are optional.

  > Paola è felice come sua sorella.
  > Quei ragazzi sono noiosi quanto gli altri.

- With any other structure, or when two adjectives are used to compare the same noun, only tanto...quanto can be used. In this case agreement patterns apply as shown:

With nouns (agreement is made with the nouns):

Maria ha tanta audacia quanto senso. / *Mary has as much audaciousness as she has good sense.*

With adjectives referring to the same noun (no agreement):

Maria è tanto bella quanto simpatica. / *Mary is as beautiful as she is nice.*

With other structures (no agreement):

Io studio tanto quanto te. / *I study as much as you do.*

- For the comparative degree simply use più / *more* or meno / *less*, as the case may be, in front of the adjective.

  > Maria è più studiosa di sua sorella. / *Mary is more studious than her sister.*
  > Maria è meno alta di suo fratello. / *Mary is shorter than her brother.*
  > Quei ragazzi sono più generosi degli altri. / *Those boys are more generous than the others.*
  > Quei ragazzi sono meno intelligenti di quelle ragazze. / *Those boys are less intelligent than those girls.*

- For the superlative degree use the definite article (in its proper form, of course!) followed by **più** or **meno**, as the case may be.

> **Maria è la più studiosa della sua classe.** / *Mary is the most studious in her class.*
> **Quel ragazzo è il più simpatico della famiglia.** / *That boy is the nicest in the family.*
> **Le patate sono le meno costose.** / *Potatoes are the least expensive.*

- The definite article is never repeated.

> **Maria è la ragazza più studiosa della classe.** / *Mary is the most studious girl in the class.*
> **Lui è il ragazzo meno intelligente della classe.** / *He is the least intelligent boy in the class.*

- Notice that the superlative is followed by **di** + definite article (if needed), not *in* (as in English).

> **Gina è la più elegante della scuola.** / *Gina is the most elegant in the school.*
> **Lui è il meno generoso dei miei amici.** / *He is the least generous of my friends.*
> **È il ristorante più caro di Roma.** / *It's the most expensive restaurant in Rome.*

In comparative constructions, the structure corresponding to English *than* is rendered as follows:

- If two structures (e.g., nouns, substantives, or noun phrases) are compared by one adjective, **di** is used.

> Giovanni **è più alto di** Pietro. / *John is taller than Peter.*
> Questo signore **è meno elegante dell'**altro signore. / *This gentleman is less elegant than the other gentleman.*

- If two adjectives are used to compare the same structure (e.g., a noun, a substantive, or a noun phrase), **che** is used instead.

> **Giovanni è più elegante che bello.** / *John is more elegant than handsome.*
> **Questa ragazza è più simpatica che bella.** / *This girl is more friendly than beautiful.*

- If a subordinate clause follows, **quello che/quel che/ciò che** is used.

> **È più intelligente di quel che crediamo.** / *He is more intelligent than we believe.*
> **Noi siamo meno stanchi di quello che pensate.** / *We are less tired than you think.*
> **Io sono più ricco di ciò che pensi.** / *I am richer than you think.*

Some adjectives have both regular and irregular comparative and superlative forms.

Adjective	Comparative	Superlative
buono / *good*	più buono migliore	il più buono il migliore
cattivo / *bad*	più cattivo peggiore	il più cattivo il peggiore
grande / *big, large*	più grande maggiore	il più grande il migliore
piccolo / *small*	più piccolo minore	il più piccolo il minore

Before nouns, the -e may be dropped.

È il miglior vino della Toscana. / *It's the best wine in Tuscany.*
Questo è il peggior caffè che abbia mai bevuto. / *This is the worst coffee I have ever drunk.*

There is another type of superlative. It is constructed by dropping the final vowel of the adjective and adding the suffix **-issimo**. Don't forget to make this newly formed adjective agree with the noun! In actual fact this is another way of exaggerating. It is equivalent to *very very big, very very tall*, etc.

buono	→	buon-	→	buonissimo / *very very good*
alto	→	alt-	→	altissimo / *very very tall*
grande	→	grand-	→	grandissimo / *very very big*
facile	→	facil-	→	facilissimo / *very very easy*

Giovanni è intelligentissimo. / *John is very very intelligent.*
Anche Maria è intelligentissima. / *Mary is also very very intelligent.*
Quei ragazzi sono bravissimi. / *Those boys are very very good.*
Quelle lezioni sono facilissime. / *Those classes are very very easy.*

QUICK PRACTICE 5

Compare Maria, Marco, Gino, and Claudia as indicated in the model, following the same pattern for each given trait.

Modello: intelligente
Maria è intelligente.
Marco è più intelligente.
Gino, invece, è meno intelligente.
Ma Claudia è la più intelligente.

1. elegante
2. studioso
3. alto
4. generoso
5. forte

Now, compare Maria and Marco in terms of the following traits. Follow the model.

Modello: intelligente
Maria è intelligente.
Marco è più intelligente di Maria. / Marco è meno intelligente di Maria.
No, Marco è tanto intelligente quanto Maria.

6. elegante
7. forte
8. alto
9. generoso

Now, indicate which trait Maria has more or less of. Follow the model.

Modello: intelligente/bello
Maria è più intelligente che bella. / Maria è meno intelligente che bella.

10. forte/piccolo
11. alto/forte
12. generoso/studioso
13. elegante/interessante

Finally, say the following things in Italian.

14. Maria is more intelligent than they think.
15. My friends *(m.)* are very very intelligent.

16. And my friends *(f.)* are very very studious.

17. Italian is a very very easy language.

18. Tuscan wines are very very good.

19. Maria is smaller than Sara.

20. Giovanni is a big boy. Marco is bigger. Alessandro is the biggest.

21. She is my best friend.

22. He is the best student in the class.

PUTTING IT ALL TOGETHER

A. *Put the adjective before the noun, making all necessary changes.*

Modello: un film grande
   un gran film

1. un amico grande

2. uno studioso *(scholar)* grande

3. Stefano (un santo)

4. Stefano e Giovanni (due santi)

5. Maria (una santa)

6. Maria e Anna (due sante)

7. Antonio (un santo)

8. Anna (una santa)

9. una ragazza bella

10. quelle ragazze belle

11. un ragazzo bello

12. quei ragazzi belli

13. un orologio bello

14. quegli anelli *(rings)* belli

15. lo sport bello

16. quel fiore bello

17. quell'amico buono

18. quella caramella buona

19. uno zio buono

20. degli amici buoni

21. un amico caro

22. una situazione brutta

B. *Say the following in Italian.*

1. He is a good student. He studies all the time.
2. He is a good boy. He always obeys (**obbedire** / *to obey*).
3. That is a big book.
4. That is a great book.
5. He is a very good boy.
6. She is a nice and beautiful girl.
7. My dress is getting old.
8. That woman seems very young.
9. He is an old friend. I've known him for many years.
10. They are a poor family. Maybe they'll get rich by winning the lottery (**la lotteria** / *lottery*).
11. The coat and raincoat are green.
12. The sweater and purse are blue.
13. She's a friend of theirs.
14. And he is a friend of ours.
15. My dear friend, what are you doing?

C. *Provide the questions that produced the following statements.*

Modello: Ho bevuto due espressi.
               Quanti espressi hai/ha bevuto?

1. Ho mangiato tante patatine fritte.
2. Ho letto i libri che ci ha suggerito l'insegnante.
3. Siamo arrivati ieri.
4. Sto abbastanza bene grazie.
5. Lo faccio perché mi piace.
6. Lei è la sorella di Alessandro.
7. Sto mangiando un pezzo di torta.

D. *Now, fill in the blanks with the appropriate structures.*

1. La mia gatta è bella, ma la tua è più bella. La tua è _____ bella _____ mia.
2. Il tuo cane è intelligente, come il suo. Il tuo è _____ intelligente _____ il suo.
3. Mi piace camminare col cane e mi piace anche guardare la TV la sera. Mi piace _____ camminare col cane _____ guardare la TV la sera.
4. Ho comprato la stessa quantità di carne e di latte per il mio gatto. Ho comprato _____ carne _____ latte.
5. La mia gatta è simpatica, ma non è poi così tanto simpatica. La mia gatta è _____ simpatica di _____ pensate.

6. La mia gatta è furba, ma è meno intelligente. La mia gatta è _____ furba _____ intelligente.

7. Il mio cane è il cane _____ intelligente _____ tutti i cani del mondo.

E. *There are 10 adjectives hidden in the word search puzzle. Can you find them?*

B	I	A	N	C	O	G	U	N	E	R	O	N	O	M	R	O	S	S	O	E
H	Q	A	S	E	D	I	A	B	C	D	E	F	G	H	U	N	G	F	D	S
I	Q	A	S	E	D	A	G	H	J	U	T	I	O	P	A	D	R	A	N	A
E	Q	A	S	V	D	G	H	A	A	E	I	Q	V	G	N	N	G	F	D	R
S	R	T	Y	E	I	I	D	Z	A	N	R	U	V	G	T	D	R	A	N	A
A	O	C	S	R	C	A	L	Z	O	O	U	E	V	G	O	D	R	A	N	N
A	S	I	4	D	R	L	R	U	N	R	M	S	V	G	C	V	G	D	G	C
C	A	N	T	E	R	L	O	R	H	E	T	T	O	R	C	H	I	U	S	I
E	B	Q	E	E	E	O	R	R	N	R	R	V	I	O	L	A	A	A	D	O
D	B	U	E	E	W	A	B	O	D	E	F	G	H	B	E	I	C	B	R	N
F	C	E	E	E	Q	G	H	J	U	M	A	R	R	O	N	E	C	A	D	E
V	D	A	U	U	A	A	B	C	D	E	F	G	H	V	O	P	A	B	R	T

11

Pronouns

Quanto Sai Già? — How Much Do You Know Already?

Which of the two options is the correct one?

1. Perché non vieni con ... ?
   a. me
   b. io

2. Signora Binni, viene anche ...
   a. Lei
   b. tu

3. Paola, vieni anche ...
   a. Lei
   b. tu

4. Gli spaghetti? ... ho già mangiati?
   a. li
   b. gli

5. Maria? ... ho già telefonato.
   a. gli
   b. le

6. Paolo, vedi quella torta?
   a. La mangia!
   b. Mangiala!

Subject
I pronomi in funzione di soggetto

Pronouns are words used in place of nouns, substantives (words taking on the function of nouns), or noun phrases (nouns accompanied by articles, demonstratives, adjectives, etc.).

> **Giovanni è siciliano.** / *John is Sicilian.*
> ↓
> **Lui è siciliano.** / *He is Sicilian.*

> **Quel disco nuovo è di Maria.** / *That new record belongs to Mary.*
> ↓
> **Quello è di Maria.** / *That one belongs to Mary.*

Personal pronouns refer to a person (*I, you, we*, etc.). They can be classified as subject, object, or reflexive. They are also classified according to the person(s) speaking (= first person), the person(s) spoken to (= second person), or the person(s) spoken about (= third person). The pronoun can, of course, be in the singular (= referring to one person) or in the plural (= referring to more than one person).

As you have already seen, *subject* pronouns are used as the subject of a verb.

Io studio il francese. / *I study French.*
Loro studiano la matematica. / *They study mathematics.*

The Italian subject pronouns are listed again here for your convenience.

Person	Italian Forms	English Equivalents	Examples
1st sing.	io	*I*	**Io non capisco.** / *I do not understand.*
2nd sing.	tu	*you (familiar)*	**Tu sei simpatico.** / *You are nice.*
3rd sing.	lui	*he*	**Lui è americano.** / *He is American.*
	lei	*she*	**Lei è americana.** / *She is American.*
	Lei	*you (polite)*	**Come si chiama, Lei?** / *What is your name?*
1st pl.	noi	*we*	**Noi non lo conosciamo.** / *We do not know him.*
2nd pl.	voi	*you*	**Voi arrivate sempre in ritardo.** / *You always arrive late.*
3rd pl.	loro	*they*	**Loro vanno in Italia.** / *They are going to Italy.*
	Loro	*you (formal)*	**Come si chiamano, Loro?** / *What is your name?*

Again, keep in mind that **io** is not capitalized (unless it is the first word of a sentence).

Subject pronouns are optional in simple affirmative sentences because it is easy to tell from the verb ending which person is the subject.

Io non capisco or **Non capisco.** / *I do not understand.*
Loro vanno in Italia or **Vanno in Italia.** / *They are going to Italy.*

Sometimes, however, the way a sentence is constructed makes it impossible to avoid using pronouns. This is particularly true when you want to emphasize or allude to the subject.

Devi parlare tu, non io! / *You have to speak, not I!*
Non è possibile che l'abbiano fatto loro. / *It's not possible that they did it.*

These pronouns must also be used to avoid confusion when more than one person is being referred to. Needless to say, they must also be specified in compound constructions (constructions with **e** and **o**).

Mentre lui guarda la TV, lei ascolta la radio. / *While he watches TV, she listens to the radio.*
Lui e io vogliamo che tu dica la verità. / *He and I want you to tell the truth.*

They are used after the words **anche** / *also, too* and **neanche** / *neither, not even* (whose synonyms are **neppure** and **nemmeno**), and **proprio** / *really*.

Anche tu devi venire alla festa. / *You too must come to the party.*
Non è venuto neanche lui. / *He didn't come either.*
Signor Bianchi, è proprio Lei? / *Mr. Bianchi, is it really you?*

The subject pronoun *it* usually is not stated in Italian.

È vero. / *It is true.*
Pare che sia corretto. / *It appears to be correct.*

However, if you should ever need to express this subject, use **esso** *(m.)*, **essa** *(f.)*; and plural forms **essi** *(m.)*, **esse** *(f.)*.

È una buona scusa, ma neanche essa potrà aiutarti adesso. / *It's a good excuse, but not even it can help you now.*

As you know, there are both polite and familiar forms of address in Italian. The familiar forms (and their corresponding verb forms) are used, as the name suggests, with people with whom you are on familiar terms: that is, members of the family, friends, etc. If you call someone by a first name, then you are obviously on familiar terms.

> **TIP**
> Using polite forms is important to Italians. If you address someone incorrectly, it might be taken as rudeness! So, be careful.

Maria, anche tu studi l'italiano? / *Mary, are you studying Italian too?*
Signora Bianchi, anche Lei studia l'italiano? / *Mrs. Bianchi, are you studying Italian too?*

In writing, the polite forms (**Lei**, **Loro**) are typically capitalized in order to distinguish them from **lei** / *she* and **loro** / *they*. In the plural, there is a strong tendency to use **voi** as the plural of both **tu** and **Lei**. **Loro** is restricted to formal situations when addressing a few people, not a crowd.

The forms **lui** / *he* and **lei** / *she* are used in ordinary conversation. However, there are two more formal pronouns: **egli** / *he* and **ella** / *she* that are used to refer to historical personages or in formal writing contexts. The plural forms are, respectively, **essi** and **esse**.

Everyday Italian

Giovanni è italiano, ma neanche lui capisce i pronomi! / *John is Italian, but not even he understands pronouns!*
Maria studia sempre, ma neanche lei capisce i pronomi! / *Maria always studies, but she doesn't understand pronouns either.*

Formal (Usually Written) Italian

Dante scrisse *La Divina Commedia.* **Egli era fiorentino.** / *Dante wrote The Divine Comedy. He was Florentine.*
Natalia Ginzburg scrisse molto. Ella era una grande scrittrice. / *Natalia Ginzburg wrote a lot. She was a great writer.*

QUICK PRACTICE 1

Provide the missing pronoun.

1. Pina, sei proprio _____?
2. Signora Bianchi, è proprio _____?
3. Marco e Maria, andrete alla festa anche _____?
4. Signor e Signora Bianchi, andranno alla festa anche _____ due?
5. Di solito, neanche _____ prendiamo il caffè forte.
6. Sì, sono proprio _____, le mie sorelle!
7. Quella teoria è incorretta, perché anche _____ non è basata sulla matematica.
8. Non so come risolvere quel problema. Anche _____ è troppo difficile.
9. Vengo anche _____ al cinema, va bene?
10. Galileo era un grande scienziato. _____ inventò il telescopio, se non sbaglio.
11. Lucrezia Borgia era una grande donna. _____ era conosciuta in tutto il mondo durante il Rinascimento.

Object

I pronomi in funzione di complemento

Object pronouns are used as objects of verbs, prepositions, and other structures. As you know (Chapter 2), the object can be direct or indirect.

> **Maria chiama suo fratello.** / *Mary calls her brother.*
> |
> direct object

> **Maria sta parlando a suo fratello.** / *Mary is speaking to her brother.*
> |
> indirect object

The corresponding pronouns are also known as direct and indirect. Italian object pronouns generally come right *before* the verb.

Maria chiama suo fratello. / *Mary calls her brother.*
Maria lo chiama. / *Mary calls him.*

Maria sta parlando a suo fratello. / *Mary is speaking to her brother.*
Maria gli sta parlando. / *Mary is speaking to him.*

The Italian object pronouns are detailed in the chart below.

Person	Object Pronouns		Examples
	Direct	Indirect	
1st sing.	mi / *me*	mi / *to me*	Maria mi chiama. / *Mary calls me.*
			Maria mi scrive. / *Mary writes (to) me.*
2nd sing.	ti / *you*	ti / *to you*	Ti chiamo fra mezz'ora. / *I'll call you in a half hour.*
			Ti scrivo fra un mese. / *I'll write (to) you in a month.*
3rd sing.	lo (m.) / *him*	gli (m.) / *to him*	Maria lo chiama. / *Mary calls him.*
			Maria gli scrive spesso. / *Mary writes (to) him often.*
	la (f.) / *her*	le (f.) / *to her*	Maria la chiama. / *Mary calls her.*
			Maria le scrive spesso. / *Mary writes (to) her often.*
	La / *you*	Le / *to you*	Signore, La chiamo domani. / *Sir, I'll call you tomorrow.*
			Signore, Le scrivo presto. / *Sir, I'll write (to) you soon.*
1st pl.	ci / *us*	ci / *to us*	Perché non ci chiami? / *Why don't you call us?*
			Perché non ci scrivi? / *Why don't you write to us?*
2nd pl.	vi / *you*	vi / *to you*	Domani vi chiamo. / *Tomorrow I'll call you.*
			Vi scrivo dall'Italia. / *I'll write (to) you from Italy.*
3rd pl.	li (m.) / *them*	gli (m.) / *to them*	Li chiamo dopo. / *I'll call them (m.) after.*
	le (f.) / *them*	gli (f.) / *to them*	Le chiamo dopo. / *I'll call them (f.) after.*
			Non gli scrivo più. / *I don't write to them (m./f.) anymore.*

Notice that the plural of the indirect object pronouns gli / *to him* and le / *to her* is gli / *to them*. This is very common in current Italian. However, in more formal situations, some Italians prefer to use loro / *to them*, which goes after the verb.

Normal Usage	Very Formal Usage
I ragazzi? Gli parlo domani. / *The boys? I'll speak to them tomorrow.*	I signori? Parlo loro domani. / *The gentlemen? I'll speak to them tomorrow.*
Le ragazze? Gli parlo domani. / *The girls? I'll speak to them tomorrow.*	Le signore? Parlo loro domani. / *The ladies? I'll speak to them tomorrow.*

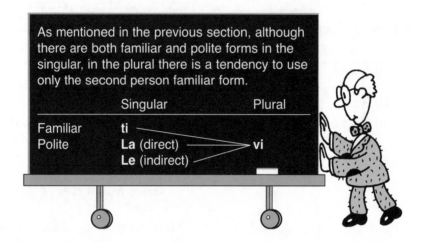

As mentioned in the previous section, although there are both familiar and polite forms in the singular, in the plural there is a tendency to use only the second person familiar form.

	Singular	Plural
Familiar	**ti**	**vi**
Polite	**La** (direct)	
	Le (indirect)	

These pronouns function as objects, as mentioned.

Maria mi chiama ogni sera. / *Mary calls me every night.*
Maria non mi dà mai niente. / *Mary never gives anything to me.*

Maria ti chiama ogni sera. / *Mary calls you every night.*
Maria non ti dà mai niente. / *Mary never gives anything to you.*

Maria ci chiama ogni sera. / *Mary calls us every night.*
Maria non ci dà mai niente. / *Mary never gives anything to me.*

They also replace entire object noun phrases.

Maria chiama suo fratello. / *Mary is calling her brother.*
Maria lo chiama. / *Mary is calling him.*

Maria sta parlando a suo fratello. / *Mary is speaking to her brother.*
Maria gli sta parlando. / *Mary is speaking to him.*

Maria chiama sua sorella. / *Mary is calling her sister.*
Maria la chiama. / *Mary is calling her.*

Maria sta parlando a sua sorella. / *Mary is speaking to her sister.*
Maria le sta parlando. / *Mary is speaking to her.*

Note the following.

- The English direct object pronoun *it* (plural *them*) is expressed by the third person direct object pronoun forms listed previously. Be careful! Choose the pronoun according to the gender and number of the noun that it replaces.

  Giovanni compra il biglietto. / *John is buying the ticket.*
  Giovanni lo compra. / *John is buying it.*

  Giovanni compra i biglietti. / *John is buying the tickets.*
  Giovanni li compra. / *John is buying them.*

  Giovanni compra la rivista. / *John is buying the magazine.*
  Giovanni la compra. / *John is buying it.*

  Giovanni compra le riviste. / *John is buying the magazines.*
  Giovanni le compra. / *John is buying them.*

- In compound tenses, the past participle of the verb must be made to agree in gender and number with the four third-person direct object pronouns (lo, la, li, le):

  Giovanni ha comprato il biglietto. / *John bought the ticket.*
  Giovanni lo ha comprato. / *John bought it.*

  Giovanni ha comprato i biglietti. / *John bought the tickets.*
  Giovanni li ha comprati. / *John bought them.*

  Giovanni ha comprato la rivista. / *John bought the magazine.*
  Giovanni la ha comprata. / *John bought it.*

  Giovanni ha comprato le riviste. / *John bought the magazines.*
  Giovanni le ha comprate. / *John bought them.*

- Note that only the singular forms lo and la can be elided with the auxiliary forms of avere: ho, hai, ha, hanno:

  Giovanni lo ha comprato.   or   Giovanni l'ha comprato. /
                                     John bought it.
  Giovanni la ha comprata.   or   Giovanni l'ha comprata. /
                                     John bought it.

- Agreement with the other direct object pronouns mi, ti, ci, vi is optional:

  Giovanni ci ha chiamato. / *John called us.*
     or
  Giovanni ci ha chiamati. / *John called us.*

- There is no agreement with indirect object pronouns.

> **Giovanni gli ha scritto.** / *John wrote (to) him, (to) them.*
> **Giovanni le ha scritto.** / *John wrote (to) her.*

- But be very careful! The pronoun form **le** has two meanings.

Direct Object

---

le = *them*

Giovanni ha mangiato le pere. / *John ate the pears.*

Giovanni le **ha mangiate.** / *John ate them.*

Indirect Object

---

le = *to her*

Giovanni ha parlato a Maria. / *John spoke to Mary.*

Giovanni le **ha parlato.** / *John spoke to her.*

Now comes the complicated task of sequencing indirect and direct objects. Just remember the following, and you won't have too much difficulty.

- The indirect object always precedes the direct object (**lo**, **la**, **li**, or **le**).

> **Giovanni me lo dà.** / *John gives it to me.*

- Change the indirect forms **mi**, **ti**, **ci**, and **vi** to **me**, **te**, **ce**, and **ve**, respectively.

> **Giovanni mi dà l'indirizzo.** / *John gives me the address.*
> **Giovanni me lo dà.** / *John gives it to me.*

> **Giovanni ti manda sempre i francobolli.** / *John always sends you the stamps.*
> **Giovanni te li manda sempre.** / *John always sends them to you.*

> **Giovanni ci scrive sempre una cartolina.** / *John always writes us a card.*
> **Giovanni ce la scrive sempre.** / *John always writes it to us.*

> **Giovanni non vi scrive mai una cartolina.** / *John never writes you a card.*
> **Giovanni non ve la scrive mai.** / *John never writes it to you.*

- Change the indirect forms **gli** and **le** to **glie**, and combine this with **lo**, **la**, **li**, or **le** to form one word: **glielo**, **glieli**, **gliela**, **gliele**.

> **Lo studente gli porta gli esercizi.** /*The student brings the exercises to him/them.*
> **Lo studente glieli porta.** / *The student brings them to him/them.*

> **Lo studente le porta le dispense.** / *The student brings the course notes to her.*
> **Lo studente gliele porta.** / *The student brings them to her.*

- And do not forget that when **lo**, **la**, **li**, **le** are put before a past participle, there must be agreement.

> **Lo studente giele ha portate.** / *The student brought them to her.*

- The forms **glielo** and **gliela** can be elided with the auxiliary verb.

> **Gliel'hanno portato.** / *They brought it to him/her/them.*

Object pronouns can be put before the modals or attached to the infinitive. Notice that in the latter case, the **-e** of the infinite is dropped.

Maria non può mangiare il pollo. / *Mary can't eat chicken.*
Maria non lo può mangiare. / *Mary can't eat it.*
or
Maria non può mangiarlo. / *Mary can't eat it.*

Voglio dare quel regalo a mio fratello. / *I want to give my brother that gift.*
Glielo voglio dare. / *I want to give it to him.*
    or
Voglio darglielo. / *I want to give it to him.*

With verbs in the imperative (Chapter 7), the pronouns are attached to the familiar forms.

Polite Forms
Signor Binni, mi telefoni! / *Mr. Binni, phone me!*
Signora Dini, gliela scriva! / *Mrs. Dini, write it to him!*
Signori, ce li mandino! / *Gentlemen, send them to us!*

Familiar Forms
Sara, telefonami! / *Sarah, phone me!*
Alessandro, scrivigliela! / *Alexander, write it to him!*
Amici, mandateceli! / *Friends, send them to us!*

With the second person singular negative infinitive form, you can either attach the pronouns to the infinitive or else put them before it. Notice that the final -e of the infinitive is dropped when attaching pronouns.

Affirmative	Negative
Mangialo! / *Eat it!*	Non mangiarlo! or Non lo mangiare! / *Don't eat it!*
Scrivigliela! /*Write it to him!*	Non scrivergliela! or Non gliela scrivere! / *Don't write it to him!*

As you know, the second person singular imperative forms of dare / *to give*, dire / *to say*, fare / *to do*, andare / *to go*, and stare / *to stay* are written with an apostrophe (Chapter 7):

Da' la penna a me! / *Give the pen to me!*
Di' la verità! / *Tell the truth!*
Fa' qualcosa! / *Do something!*
Va' via! / *Go away!*
Sta' qui! / *Stay here!*

When attaching pronouns to these forms, you must double the consonant of the pronoun:

Dammi la penna! / *Give me the pen!*
Dilla! / *Tell it* (la verità)!
Fallo! / *Do it!*
Dammela! / *Give it to me!*
Diccela! / *Tell it to us!*

There is, of course, no double "gl":

Digli la verità! / *Tell him the truth!*

The pronouns are also attached to the form ecco / *here is, here are, there is, there are.*

Ecco la ricetta. / *Here is the recipe.*
Eccola. / *Here it is.*
Ecco i nostri genitori. / *Here are our parents.*
Eccoli. / *Here they are.*

There is a second type of object pronoun that goes after the verb. It is known as a *stressed* or *tonic* pronoun (un pronome tonico):

Impara i pronomi tonici!

BEFORE THE VERB	AFTER THE VERB	TRANSLATION
mi	me	*me*
mi	a me	*to me*
ti	te	*you (fam., sing.)*
ti	a te	*to you (fam., sing.)*
lo	lui	*him*
gli	a lui	*to him*
la	lei	*her*
lei	a lei	*to her*
Lei	a Lei	*to you (pol., sing.)*
ci	noi	*us*
ci	a noi	*to us*
vi	voi	*you (pl.)*
vi	a voi	*to you (pl.)*
li	loro	*them (m.)*
gli	loro	*to them (m.)*
le	loro	*them (f.)*
gli	loro	*to them (f.)*

These allow you to put greater emphasis on the object.

Normal Speech

Maria mi chiama. / *Mary calls me.*

Giovanni gli dice la verità. / *John tells him the truth.*

Emphasis

Maria chiama me, non te! / *Mary calls me, not you!*

Giovanni dice la verità a lui, non a loro! / *John tells him, not them, the truth!*

They also allow you to be precise and clear about the person you are referring to.

Giovanni glielo dà. = Giovanni lo dà a lui. / *John gives it to him.*
Giovanni lo dà a lei. / *John gives it to her.*
Giovanni lo dà a loro. / *John gives it to them.*

These are the only object pronouns you can use after a preposition.

Maria viene con noi. / *Mary is coming with us.*
Il professore parla di te. / *The professor is speaking of you.*
L'ha fatto per me. / *He did it for me.*

Replace the objects in italics with direct object pronouns, making all necessary adjustments.

Modello: Maria ha chiamato *noi.*
Maria ci ha chiamato/Maria ci ha chiamati.

Maria ha comprato *gli stivali a suo fratello.*
Maria glieli ha comprati.

1. Paolo ha sempre detto *la verità*!
2. Bruno ha chiamato *voi* ieri, vero?
3. Hanno invitato *me* alla festa!
4. Paola ha chiamato *te* poco tempo fa.
5. Io ho comprato *quel vestito* in quel negozio in via Nazionale.
6. Anche tu hai comprato *quei guanti* nello stesso negozio, vero?
7. Lui ha mangiato *quella mela* volentieri *(gladly)*.
8. Lei ha già assaggiato *quelle mele.*
9. Noi abbiamo letto *quella rivista.*
10. Loro hanno dato *quella rivista a me.*
11. Tu hai chiamato *la ragazza.*
12. Tu hai telefonato *alla ragazza.*
13. Giovanni mi ha dato *il giornale.*
14. Nostro fratello ci ha portato *gli spaghetti.*
15. Lei ti ha dato *quelle riviste.*
16. Loro gli hanno dato *quelle riviste.*
17. Noi le abbiamo portato *quei giornali.*
18. Voglio comprare *quel cappotto a mio fratello.*
19. Ecco *i miei genitori.*
20. Marco, da' *la penna a me*!
21. Maria, da' *le penne a loro*!
22. Maria, non dare *la penna a lui*!

Say the following sentences in Italian.

23. Giovanni, eat the cake! Eat it!
24. Maria, don't drink the coffee! Don't drink it!
25. Mrs. Smith, pay the bill! Please pay it!
26. Giorgio, phone her!
27. Claudia, give me the spaghetti!

28. Bruno, give us your address!
29. Pasquale, tell the truth! Tell it to us!
30. Maria, where is your pen? Give it to me!
31. Do it (lo), Maria!
32. Do it (lo), Mrs. Smith!

Reflexive
I pronomi riflessivi

Reflexive pronouns "reflect" the subject of a verb, as you know (Chapter 7). Like object pronouns, they generally come before the verb.

La ragazza si lava prima di andare a dormire. / *The girl washes herself before going to sleep.*

They are listed here again for your convenience.

Person	Italian Forms	English Equivalents	Examples
1st sing.	mi	*myself*	**Io mi lavo.** / *I wash myself.*
2nd sing.	ti	*yourself*	**Tu ti diverti.** / *You enjoy yourself.*
3rd sing.	si	*himself, herself, oneself, itself*	**Lui si diverte.** / *He enjoys himself.* **Anche lei si diverte.** / *She enjoys herself too.*
3rd sing.	Si	*yourself (pol.)*	**Si diverte, Lei?** / *Are you enjoying yourself?*
1st pl.	ci	*ourselves*	**Anche noi ci divertiamo.** / *We too are enjoying ourselves.*
2nd pl.	vi	*yourselves*	**Vi divertite, voi?** / *Are you enjoying yourselves?*
3rd pl.	si	*themselves*	**Loro si divertono sempre.** / *They always enjoy themselves.*
3rd pl.	Si	*yourselves (pol.)*	**Si divertono, Loro?** / *Are you enjoying yourselves?*

Notice that the third person polite forms of address are often capitalized to distinguish them from the other third person forms in writing.

These pronouns are also used as reciprocal forms: *to each other, to themselves,* etc.

Si telefonano ogni sera. / *They phone each other every night.*
Noi ci scriviamo ogni mese. / *We write each other every month.*

After prepositions (especially **da**), the stressed form **sé** is used instead.

Lo farà da sé. / *He'll do it by himself.*

Notice that **sé** is written with an accent. However, in the expression **se stesso** / *by oneself* the accent is omitted.

Ci andrà se stesso. / *He'll go by himself.*
Maria gli scriverà se stessa. / *Mary will write to him herself.*

When used with direct object pronouns, the reflexives are changed to **me**, **te**, **se**, **ce**, and **ve**. In compound tenses, the agreement between object pronoun and past participle takes precedence over the agreement between the past participle and the subject.

Maria si è messa il cappotto. / *Mary put on her coat.*
Maria se lo è messo. / *Mary put it on.*

Quella donna non si è lavata le mani. / *That woman did not wash her hands.*
Quella donna non se le è lavate. / *That woman did not wash them.*

With modal verbs the reflexive pronoun can be put before or attached to the infinitive.

Maria si vuole divertire in Italia. / *Mary wants to enjoy herself in Italy.*
  or
Maria vuole divertirsi in Italia. / *Mary wants to enjoy herself in Italy.*

Note that in compound tenses when the reflexive pronoun precedes, the verb is conjugated with **essere**, and when it is attached the verb is conjugated with **avere**.

Precedes	**Attached**
Maria non si è potuta divertire. / *Mary was unable to enjoy herself.*	**Maria non ha potuto divertirsi.** / *Mary was unable to enjoy herself.*

As a final feature, note that the reflexive pronouns, like the object pronouns, are attached to the familiar and **noi** forms of the imperative.

Affirmative Familiar Forms
Sara, telefonami! / *Sara, phone me!*
Amici, chiamateci! / *Friends, call us!*

Negative Familiar Forms
Sara, non telefonarmi! or Sara, non mi telefonare!/ *Sara, don't phone me!*
Amici, non chiamateci! / *Friends, don't call us!*

Polite Forms
Signora Smith, mi telefoni! / *Mrs. Smith, phone me!*
Signori, ci chiamino! / *Gentlemen, call us!*

*Q*UICK
*P*RACTICE *3*

Say the following in Italian.

1. I (*f.*) washed myself this morning.
2. You (*fam., sing.*) never enjoy yourself downtown.
3. He put on that new sweater. He put it on yesterday.
4. She put on those new shoes. She too put them on yesterday.
5. Marco wanted to enjoy himself in Italy, but he wasn't able to (enjoy himself).
6. Alessando, phone me! But don't phone me late!
7. Professor Verdi, call us! But don't call us late!

Relative
I pronomi relativi

As discussed in Chapter 2, a relative clause is introduced into a main sentence by means of a *relative* pronoun, which serves as a subject or an object in the clause. The relative pronouns in Italian are as follows:

che / *that, which, who*

cui / *of whom, to whom, etc.*

chi / *he who, she who, they who*

quel che / *what = that which*
quello che / *what = that which*
ciò che / *what = that which*

Examples:

che

Quella donna che legge il giornale è mia sorella. / *That woman who is reading the newspaper is my sister.*

Il vestito che ho comprato ieri è molto bello. / *The dress I bought yesterday is very beautiful.*

Mi piace la poesia che stai leggendo. / *I like the poem (that) you are reading.*

cui

Il ragazzo a cui ho dato il regalo è mio cugino. / *The boy to whom I gave the gift is my cousin.*

Non trovo il cassetto in cui ho messo il mio anello. / *I can't find the drawer in which I put my ring.*

Ecco la rivista di cui ho parlato. / *Here is the magazine of which I spoke.*

chi

Chi va in Italia si divertirà. / *He/she who goes to Italy will enjoy himself/ herself.*

C'è chi dorme e c'è chi lavora. / *Some sleep, some work! (lit., There is he who sleeps and there is he who works!)*

quel che / quello che / ciò che

Quello che dici è vero. / *What (that which) you are saying is true.*

Non sai quel che dici. / *You don't know what you are saying.*

Ciò che dici non ha senso. / *What you are saying makes no sense.*

Both che and cui can be replaced by il quale, if there is an antecedent. This changes in form according to the noun it refers to and is always preceded by the definite article.

L'uomo che legge il giornale è italiano. / *The man who is reading the newspaper is Italian.*
  or
L'uomo il quale legge il giornale è italiano. / *The man who is reading the newspaper is Italian.*

Le donne che leggono il giornale sono italiane. / *The women who are reading the newspapers are Italian.*
  or
Le donne le quali leggono il giornale sono italiane. / *The women who are reading the newspapers are Italian.*

Il ragazzo a cui ho dato il regalo è mio cugino. / *The boy to whom I gave the gift is my cousin.*
  or
Il ragazzo al quale ho dato il regalo è mio cugino. / *The boy to whom I gave the gift is my cousin.*

Ecco la rivista di cui ho parlato. / *Here is the magazine of which I spoke.*
  or
Ecco la rivista della quale ho parlato. / *Here is the magazine of which I spoke.*

The form **il cui** is used to convey possession. It is the equivalent of English *whose*. The article varies according to the gender and number of the noun modified.

Ecco il professore il cui corso è molto interessante. / *Here is the professor whose course is very interesting.*
Ecco gli scrittori i cui romanzi sono celebri. / *Here are the writers whose novels are famous.*
Ecco la ragazza la cui intelligenza è straordinaria. / *Here is the girl whose intelligence is extraordinary.*
Ecco la ragazza le cui amiche sono italiane. / *Here is the girl whose friends are Italian.*

QUICK PRACTICE 4

Put in the missing relative form in each sentence.

1. La persona _____ legge il giornale è mio fratello.
2. Il film _____ ho visto ieri è molto interessante.
3. Il ragazzo a _____ ho dato il regalo è mio nipote.
4. Non trovo il cassetto in _____ ho messo le mie chiavi.
5. Quello è il film di _____ ti ho parlato.
6. _____ andrà a quella festa si divertirà.
7. _____ dici è proprio vero.
8. La persona la _____ legge il giornale è mia sorella.
9. Il ragazzo al _____ ho dato il giornale è mio cugino.
10. Quella è la rivista della _____ ti ho parlato.
11. Quello è il professore il _____ corso è molto interessante.
12. Ecco la ragazza i _____ amici sono tutti interessanti.

Demonstrative and Possessive
I pronomi dimostrativi e possessivi

Demonstrative pronouns replace a noun phrase containing a demonstrative structure (Chapter 9).

Quel ragazzo è italiano. / *That boy is Italian.*

↓

Quello è italiano. / *That one is Italian.*

Demonstrative pronouns preserve the gender and number of the noun in the noun phrase they replace.

Demonstratives of Nearness	Corresponding Demonstrative Pronouns
this/these	*this one/these (ones)*
	With Masculine Nouns **Singular**
questo quest'	questo
	Plural
questi	questi
	With Feminine Nouns **Singular**
questa quest'	questa
	Plural
queste	queste

Demonstratives of Remoteness	Corresponding Demonstrative Pronouns
that/those	*that one/those (ones)*
	With Masculine Nouns **Singular**
quello quell' quel	quello
	Plural
quegli quei	quelli
	With Feminine Nouns **Singular**
quella quell'	quella
	Plural
quelle	quelle

Examples:

Questo fiore è bello. / *This flower is beautiful.*
Questo è bello. / *This one is beautiful.*

Quest'amico è russo. / *This friend is Russian.*
Questo è russo. / *This one is Russian.*

Questi CD sono costosi. / *These CDs are expensive.*
Questi sono costosi. / *These are expensive.*

Questa maglia è nuova. / *This sweater is new.*
Questa è nuova. / *This one is new.*

Queste banche sono nuove. / *These banks are new.*
Queste sono nuove. / *These are new.*

Quello studente è canadese. / *That student is Canadian.*
Quello è canadese. / *That one is Canadian.*

Quell'amico si chiama Gino. / *That friend is called Gino.*
Quello si chiama Gino. / *That one is called Gino.*

Quel ragazzo è spagnolo. / *That boy is Spanish.*
Quello è spagnolo. / *That one is Spanish.*

Quegli studenti sono inglesi. / *Those students are English.*
Quelli sono inglesi. / *Those are English.*

Quei ragazzi sono italiani. / *Those boys are Italian.*
Quelli sono italiani. / *Those are Italian.*

Quella ragazza è francese. / *That girl is French.*
Quella è francese. / *That one is French.*

Quelle studentesse sono francesi. / *Those students are French.*
Quelle sono francesi. / *Those are French.*

A possessive pronoun replaces a noun phrase containing a possessive adjective (Chapter 10) and a noun. The Italian possessive pronouns correspond to the English forms *mine, yours, his, hers, ours, theirs.*

Il mio fidanzato è bello. / *My fiancé is handsome.*
↓
Il mio è bello. / *Mine is handsome.*

There is a perfect match between the adjective and pronoun forms of the possessive. So, just go over the appropriate section in Chapter 10, since it will give you the pronoun forms as well.

La sua casa è in Italia. / *His/her house is in Italy.*
La sua è in Italia. / *His/hers is in Italy.*

Non mi piacciono i tuoi guanti. / *I do not like your gloves.*
Non mi piacciono i tuoi. / *I do not like yours.*

I nostri nonni sono italiani. / *Our grandparents are Italian.*
I nostri sono italiani. / *Ours are Italian.*

The article is always used with the pronoun forms, even when it replaces noun phrases containing singular, unmodified, kinship nouns.

Sua sorella è antipatica. / *His/her sister is unpleasant.*
La sua è antipatica. / *His/hers is unpleasant.*

Nostro zio è amichevole. / *Our uncle is friendly.*
Il nostro è amichevole. / *Ours is friendly.*

The article can be dropped if the pronoun occurs as a predicate, i.e., if it occurs after the verb **essere** / *to be*, or some other linking verb.

Questo denaro è mio. / *This money is mine.*
È tua questa borsa? / *Is this purse yours?*
Quei biglietti sono suoi. / *Those tickets are his/hers.*

QUICK PRACTICE 5

Substitute each noun phrase with its appropriate pronoun. Follow the model.

Modello: Questo libro è di Alessandro.
Questo è di Alessandro.

1. La mia amica vive in Italia.
2. Quel ragazzo è italiano.
3. Le tue sorelle sono simpatiche.
4. Questi bambini sono intelligenti.
5. Quegli studenti sono pigri.
6. Quell'uomo è molto forte.
7. La loro amica è alta.
8. Tua zia è simpatica.
9. Quelle bambine sono pigre, ma queste bambine sono energiche.
10. Quel ragazzo parla francese.

11. Quei ragazzi studiano matematica.

12. Quest'uomo è un amico.

13. Le nostre amiche sono tutte intelligenti.

14. La vostra macchina è proprio bella.

15. Suo cugino è molto intelligente.

Other Pronouns
Altri pronomi

Indefinite adjectives have corresponding pronoun functions (Chapter 10).

Lui mangia assai. / *He eats quite a lot.*
Tuo fratello dorme molto, no? / *Your brother sleeps a lot, doesn't he?*
Ieri ho mangiato troppo. / *Yesterday I ate too much.*

When referring to people in general, use the plural forms **molti, alcuni, tanti, pochi, parecchi, tutti,** etc.

Molti vanno in Italia quest'anno. / *Many are going to Italy this year.*
Alcuni dormono alla mattina, ma parecchi lavorano già. / *Some sleep in the morning, but quite a few are working already.*
Tutti sanno quello. / *Everyone knows that.*

Use the corresponding feminine forms (**molte, alcune,** etc.) when referring only to females.

Di quelle ragazze, molte sono italiane. / *Of those girls, many are Italian.*
Di tutte quelle donne, alcune sono americane. / *Of all those women, some are American.*

Note the expression **alcuni... altri** / *some... others.*

Alcuni andranno in Italia; altri, invece, andranno in Francia. / *Some will go to Italy; others, instead, will go to France.*

Like most object pronouns, it is usually placed before the verb (except in those cases discussed previously in the section pertaining to the object pronouns).

Examples:

ne = *some* (replacing partitives)
Domani scriverò delle cartoline. / *Tomorrow I'm going to write some postcards.*
Domani ne scriverò. / *Tomorrow I'm going to write some.*

Anch'io devo comprare della carne. / *I too have to buy some meat.*
Anch'io ne devo comprare. / *I too have to buy some.*

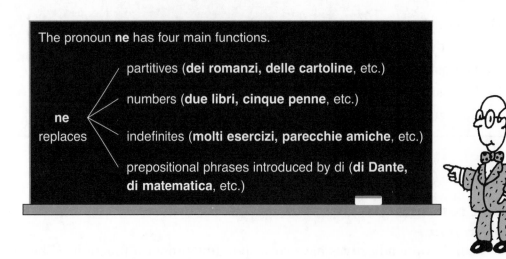

The pronoun **ne** has four main functions.

ne replaces →
- partitives (**dei romanzi, delle cartoline**, etc.)
- numbers (**due libri, cinque penne**, etc.)
- indefinites (**molti esercizi, parecchie amiche**, etc.)
- prepositional phrases introduced by di (**di Dante, di matematica**, etc.)

ne = *of them* (replacing numbers)

Domani comprerò tre matite. / *Tomorrow I will buy three pencils.*
Domani ne comprerò tre. / *Tomorrow I will buy three (of them).*

Voglio comprare quattro CD. / *I want to buy four CDs.*
Ne voglio comprare quattro. / *I want to buy four (of them).*

ne = *of them* (replacing indefinites)

Domani vedrò molte amiche. / *Tomorrow I'm going to see many (female) friends.*
Domani ne vedrò molte. / *Tomorrow I'm going to see many of them.*

Devo comprare parecchi regali. / *I have to buy quite a few presents.*
Ne devo comprare parecchi. / *I have to buy quite a few of them.*

ne = *of it, them* (replacing phrases)

Il professore parlerà di matematica. / *The professor will speak about mathematics.*
Il professore ne parlerà. / *The professor will speak about it.*

Lei parlerà del suo amico. / *She will speak about her friend.*
Lei ne parlerà. / *She will speak about him.*

When **ne** replaces partitives, numbers, and indefinites, there is agreement between **ne** and the past participle. This is not the case when **ne** replaces a prepositional phrase introduced by **di**.

Ha comprato dei dolci. / *He bought some sweets.*
Ne ha comprati. / *He bought some.*

Ha visto tre film. / *He saw three films.*
Ne ha visti tre. / *He saw three (of them).*

Ha mangiato molta pasta. / *He ate a lot of pasta.*
Ne ha mangiata molta. / *He ate a lot (of it).*

But:

Ha parlato di quella ragazza. / *He spoke about that girl.*
Ne ha parlato. / *He spoke about her.*

Finally, the only indefinite ne cannot replace is qualche. In this case, replace it with alcuni/e, as shown:

Mario ha comprato qualche libro. / *Mario bought some books.*
Mario ha comprato alcuni libri. / *Mario bought some.*
Mario ne ha comprati alcuni. / *Mario bought some.*

The particle ci has many meanings, as you have seen. It also means *there*, replacing locative (place) phrases. Like the object pronouns, it goes before the verb (except in the cases mentioned above).

ci = *there*
Andiamo in Inghilterra domani. / *We are going to England tomorrow.*
Ci andiamo domani. / *We are going there tomorrow.*

Chi abita in quella città? / *Who lives in that city?*
Chi ci abita? / *Who lives there?*

However, to express *from there*, ne is used instead.

Tu vai in Italia, e io vengo dall'Italia. / *You are going to Italy, and I'm coming from Italy.*
Tu ci vai, e io ne vengo. / *You are going there, and I'm coming from there.*

In these cases, there is no agreement between ci and ne and the past participle. And both ci and ne can occur in combination with object pronouns.

- Ci is changed to ce, preceding other pronouns.

    Io metto il portafoglio nel cassetto. / *I put my wallet in the drawer.*
    Chi ce lo mette? / *Who is putting it there?*

- Ne is placed after the indirect object pronouns.

    Giovanni mi dà delle rose. / *John gives me some roses.*
    Giovanni me ne dà. / *John gives some to me.*

    Il medico gli dà delle pillole. / *The doctor gives him some pills.*
    Il medico gliene dà. / *The doctor gives some to him.*

And now for the last pronoun to be discussed! The impersonal si / *one in general, we, they,* etc. has the following peculiar characteristics:

- The verb agrees with what appears to be the predicate.

> **Si compra quel libro solo in Italia.** / *One buys that book only in Italy.*
> **Si comprano quei libri solo in Italia.** / *One buys those books only in Italy.*

- When used in compound tenses the only auxiliary allowed is **essere** / *to be*, with the past participle agreeing, obviously, with the predicate!

> **Si sono visti quei film solo in Italia.** / *One saw those films only in Italy.*

- When followed by a predicate adjective, the adjective is always in the plural.

> **Sì è contenti in Italia.** / *One is happy in Italy.*

- Direct object pronouns are placed before it!

> **La si deve dire.** / *One has to tell it* (**la verità**).

- In front of the reflexive **si** / *oneself*, it changes to **ci**!

> **Ci si diverte in Italia.** / *One enjoys oneself in Italy.*

QUICK PRACTICE 6

Replace the italicized parts with appropriate pronouns, making any and all necessary changes.

Modello: Giovanni non è mai andato *in Inghilterra*.
      Giovanni non ci è mai andato.

1. Ieri ho mangiato *delle mele*.
2. Lui ha comprato *otto camicie* ieri.
3. Forse ci saranno *molti amici* alla festa.
4. Mi hanno portato *qualche libro nuovo* ieri.
5. Chi ha parlato *di politica* ieri?
6. Chi è stato *in quella città*?
7. Chi è tornato *dall'Italia* ieri?
8. Lui ha messo *il portafoglio nel cassetto*.

Now, say the following phrases in Italian using the pronoun si.

9. They sell those books only in Italy.
10. One saw those films only in Italy.
11. One is always happy in Italy.
12. Giovanni, tell the truth! One should always tell it.
13. Is it true that one enjoys oneself in Italy?

PUTTING IT ALL TOGETHER

A. *Say the following sentences in Italian.*

1. Gina, are you also coming with us?
2. Mrs. Verdi, is it really you?
3. She and I are going out with them tonight.
4. Have you read Dante? He was a truly great poet (**poeta**).
5. Marco, did you put on a new sweater? When did you put it on?
6. Sara, enjoy yourself!
7. He'll do it by himself.
8. He enjoys himself.
9. He eats quite a lot.
10. Yesterday I ate too much.
11. One eats well in Italy.
12. Some sleep in the morning; others go to work.
13. Of all those women, some are Italian.

B. *Replace each italicized part of each sentence with an appropriate pronoun or pronouns, making any and all necessary changes.*

Modello: Maria, ci porti *della minestra?*
             Maria, ce ne porti (un po')?

1. Paolo, mi compri *la carne?*
2. Vi hanno portato *la verdura?*
3. Ci hai già preparato *il caffè?*
4. Scusi, quando mi porta *gli spaghetti?*
5. Quando mi compri *il gelato?*
6. Posso dare *il latte a Pierino?*
7. Posso fare *gli spaghetti ai bambini* stasera?

8. Ti sei mangiata *tutta la pasta*?

9. Ti ha offerto *il pranzo*?

10. Mi hai comprato *delle fragole*?

11. Avete già dato *i pomodori al nonno*?

12. Hai già preparato *il caffè alla mamma*?

13. Mi compri *un po' di gelato* oggi?

14. *Questo fiore* è bello.

15. *Quest'amico* è francese.

16. *Quello studente* è americano.

17. *Quel ragazzo* è intelligente.

18. Anche *quei ragazzi* sono intelligenti.

19. *La sua casa* è in Toscana.

20. *I nostri nonni* sono canadesi.

21. *Sua sorella* è molto simpatica.

22. *Quel denaro* è *il mio denaro*.

C. *Insert the appropriate relative pronoun in each blank.*

1. L'articolo ____ ho letto ieri è molto interessante.

2. La persona ____ ha detto quello ha ragione.

3. L'articolo di ____ ti ho parlato è molto interessante.

4. La persona a ____ ho parlato ha ragione.

5. Quella è la ragazza con la ____ sono uscito.

6. ____ ha detto quello, ha detto una bugia.

7. ____ parla bene le lingue, ha buone possibilità di lavoro.

8. C'è ____ preferisce il lavoro alle vacanze.

9. ____ che dici è assolutamente vero.

10. Ecco la ragazza, la ____ intelligenza è ben nota.

D. *Odd one out! Which of the four phrases does not belong?*

1. il mio, il nostro, molti, la sua

2. mi, ti, ci, noi

3. glielo, gliela, ne, ce lo

4. si diverte, si alza, si mette, si dice

12

Other Parts of Speech

> ## *Quanto Sai Già?* — How Much Do You Know Already?
>
> *Each sentence is incorrect in some way. Can you correct each one?*
>
> 1. L'ho visto nella televisione.
> 2. L'ho sentito sulla radio.
> 3. Lui guida molto buono.
> 4. Lei sta un po' cattivo.
> 5. Giovanni cammina più lento di te.
> 6. Non mi piace anche quella torta.

Adverbs
Gli avverbi

    Adverbs are words that modify verbs, adjectives, or other adverbs. They allow you to convey notions of time, place, degree of intensity, and manner.

    Mara guida lentamente. / *Mara drives slowly.*
    Questa casa è molto bella. / *This house is very beautiful.*

    Adverbs of manner *(slowly, easily,* etc.) are formed in the following way. Notice that the ending **-mente** corresponds to the English ending *-ly*.

- Change the **-o** ending of the descriptive adjective to **-a**:

        certo / *certain*   →   certa
        lento / *slow*   →   lenta

- Add -mente:

certa	➔	certamente /*certainly*
lenta	➔	lentamente /*slowly*

- If the adjective ends in -e instead of -o, then simply add -mente:

elegante / *elegant*	➔	elegantemente / *elegantly*
semplice / *simple*	➔	semplicemente /*simply*

- However, if the adjective ends in -le or -re and is preceded by a vowel, then the -e is dropped:

facile / *easy*	➔	facilmente /*easily*
popolare / *popular*	➔	popolarmente / *popularly*

A few exceptions to these rules are:

benevolo / *benevolent*	➔	benevolmente / *benevolently*
leggero / *light*	➔	leggermente / *lightly*
violento / *violent*	➔	violentemente / *violently*

Examples:

Adjective	**Adverb of Manner**
enorme / *enormous*	enormemente / *enormously*
felice / *happy*	felicemente / *happily*
preciso / *precise*	precisamente / *precisely*
raro / *rare*	raramente /*rarely*
regolare / *regular*	regolarmente / *regularly*
speciale / *special*	specialmente / *specially*
triste / *sad*	tristemente / *sadly*
utile / *useful*	utilmente / *usefully*
vero / *true*	veramente /*truly*

These adjectives normally follow the verb, but may begin a sentence for emphasis.

Lui manda e-mail ai suoi amici regolarmente. / *He sends his friends e-mails regularly.*
Regolarmente, lui manda e-mail ai suoi amici. / *Regularly, he sends his friends e-mails.*

Below is a list of other kinds of adverbs.

abbastanza / *enough*
allora / *then*
anche / *also, too*
ancora / *still, yet, again*
anzi / *as a matter of fact*
appena / *just, barely*
di nuovo / *again*
domani / *tomorrow*
finora / *until now*
fra (tra) poco / *in a little while*
già / *already*
in fretta / *in a hurry*
insieme / *together*
invece / *instead*
lì / là / *there*
lontano / *far*
male / *bad(ly)*
qui/qua / *here*

nel frattempo / *in the meanwhile*
oggi / *today*
oggigiorno / *nowadays*
ormai / *by now*
per caso / *by chance*
piuttosto / *rather*
poi / *then, after*
presto / *early*
prima / *first*
purtroppo / *unfortunately*
quasi / *almost*
solo / *only*
stamani / *this morning*
stasera / *this evening*
subito / *right away*
tardi / *late*
vicino / *near(by)*
davvero / *really*

Examples:

Noi andiamo spesso al cinema. / *We often go to the movies.*
L'ha fatto ancora una volta. / *He did it again (one more time).*
Lei abita lontano, e lui vicino. / *She lives far, and he nearby.*
Sono quasi le tre. / *It's almost three o'clock.*
Ho appena finito di lavorare. / *I have just finished working.*
Prima mangio e poi studio. / *First I will eat, and then I will study.*

In compound tenses, some of these adverbs should be put between the auxiliary verb and the past participle. The ones most commonly placed in this way are: **ancora**, **appena**, and **già**.

> **Sono già usciti.** / *They went out already.*
> **Ha appena telefonato.** / *She has just phoned.*
> **Non abbiamo ancora finito di lavorare.** / *We haven't yet finished working.*

The adjectives **molto**, **tanto**, **poco**, **troppo**, and **parecchio** can also be used as adverbs. But be careful! In this case, there is no agreement to be made!

Adjectives	**Adverbs**
Lei ha molti soldi. / *She has a lot of money.*	**Lei è molto intelligente.** / *She is very intelligent.*
Lei ha molta fame. / *She is very hungry.*	**Lei è molto famosa.** / *She is very famous.*
Ci sono pochi studenti qui. / *There are few students here.*	**Loro studiano poco.** / *They study little.*

To determine if a word such as **molto** is an adjective or adverb, check the following word. If it is a noun, then **molto** is an adjective, agreeing with the noun. Otherwise, it can be either an adverb or pronoun. In either case, no agreement pattern is required.

Adverbs are compared in the same manner as adjectives (Chapter 10). So, you know everything there is to know about the comparison of adjectives.

lentamente / *slowly*	**più lentamente** / *more slowly*
facilmente / *easily*	**meno facilmente** / *less easily*
lontano / *far*	**il più lontano** / *the farthest*

Tricky Comparative Forms

Adjectives

buono / *good*	→	più buono = migliore / *better*	→	il migliore / *the best*
cattivo / *bad*	→	più cattivo = peggiore / *worse*	→	il peggiore / *the worst*

Adverbs

bene / *well*	→	più bene = meglio / *better*	→	il meglio / *the best*
male / *bad(ly)*	→	più male = peggio / *worse*	→	il peggio / *the worst*

Given that both the adjectives **buono** and **cattivo** and their corresponding adverb forms **bene** and **male** are rendered in English by *better* and *worse*, you might become confused about which form to use. Follow the tip.

QUICK PRACTICE 1

Give the adverb form of each adjective. Then give both the comparative forms of the adverb. You will be able to practice other adverbs and other features related to adverbs in the Putting It All Together section.

Modello: lento
             lentamente
             più/meno lentamente

1. semplice
2. felice
3. preciso
4. vero
5. facile
6. popolare
7. benevolo
8. violento
9. utile

Now, give the equivalent Italian adverb or adverbial expression.

10. enough
11. in the meanwhile
12. then
13. today
14. also, too
15. nowadays
16. still, yet, again
17. by now
18. as a matter of fact
19. by chance
20. just, barely
21. rather
22. again
23. then, after
24. tomorrow
25. early
26. until now
27. first
28. in a little while
29. unfortunately
30. already
31. almost
32. in a hurry
33. only
34. together
35. this morning
36. instead
37. this evening
38. there
39. right away
40. far
41. late
42. bad(ly)
43. near(by)
44. here
45. really

Prepositions
Le preposizioni

A *preposition* is a word that comes before some other part of speech, generally a noun, substantive, or noun phrase, to show its relationship to other parts of the sentence.

La bicicletta di Maria è nuova. / *Mary's bicycle is new.*
Lui era in macchina. / *He was in the car.*

When the prepositions **a** / *to, at*, **di** / *of*, **da** / *from*, **in** / *in*, and **su** / *on* immediately precede a definite article form, they contract with it to form one word:

Questo è il libro del cugino di Francesca. / *That is the book of Francesca's cousin.*
del cugino = di + il (cugino)

Ci sono due dollari nella scatola. / *There are two dollars in the box.*
nella = in + la (scatola)

Arrivano dall'Italia domani. / *They are arriving from Italy tomorrow.*
dall' = da + l' (Italia).

The chart below summarizes the contracted forms (**le preposizioni articolate**).

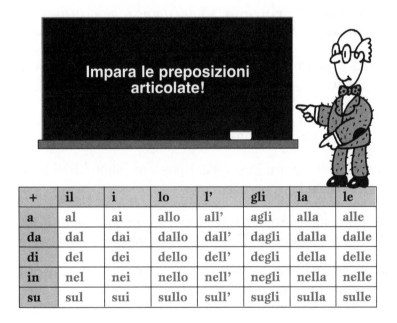

Impara le preposizioni articolate!

+	il	i	lo	l'	gli	la	le
a	al	ai	allo	all'	agli	alla	alle
da	dal	dai	dallo	dall'	dagli	dalla	dalle
di	del	dei	dello	dell'	degli	della	delle
in	nel	nei	nello	nell'	negli	nella	nelle
su	sul	sui	sullo	sull'	sugli	sulla	sulle

Examples:

I gioielli sono nel casssetto. / *The jewels are in the drawer.*
Ecco gli indirizzi elettronici degli amici miei. / *Here are the electronic addresses of my friends.*
Le forchette sono sulla tavola. / *The forks are on the table.*
Domani mio cugino andrà dal medico. / *Tomorrow my cousin is going to the doctor's.*
Arrivano alle nove di sera. / *They are arriving at 9 P.M.*

Contraction with the preposition **con** / *with* is optional:

con il = col
con i = coi
con lo = collo
con gli = cogli
con la = colla
con l' = coll'
con le = colle

Examples:

Lui parlerà col direttore domani. / *He will speak with the director tomorrow.*
Loro ariveranno coll'Alitalia. / *They will arrive with Alitalia.*

Other prepositions do not contract.

tra, fra / *between, among*
per / *for, through*
sopra / *above, on top*
sotto / *under, below*

Examples:

Lo faccio per il principio. / *I am doing it on principle.*
L'ho messo tra la tavola e la sedia. / *I put it between the table and the chair.*

The article is dropped in expressions that have a high degree of usage or have become idiomatic.

Sono a casa. / *I am at home.*
Vado in macchina. / *I'm going by car.*

However, if the noun in such expressions is modified in any way whatsoever, then the article must be reinserted.

Sono alla casa nuova di Michele. / *I am at Michael's new home.*
Vado nella macchina di Luigi. / *I'm going in Louis's car.*

Prepositions have many, many uses. All of them cannot be mentioned here. The more important ones are listed below.

- **A** is used in front of a city name.

    Abito a Roma. / *I live in Rome.*
    Andiamo a Parigi. / *We are going to Paris.*

- Otherwise, **in** is used (generally speaking).

    Vivo in Italia. / *I live in Italy.*
    Andremo nell'Italia centrale. / *We will be going to central Italy.*

- **Di** is used to indicate possession or relationship.

> **È la macchina nuova di Alessandro.** / *It's Alexander's new car.*
> **Come si chiama la figlia del professore?** / *What's the name of the professor's daughter?*

- **Da** is translated as *from* and *to* in "place expressions" such as the following.

> **Vado dal medico.** / *I'm going to the doctor's.*
> **Vengo dalla farmacia.** / *I'm coming from the pharmacy.*

- It is translated as both *since* and *from* in temporal constructions.

> **Vivo qui dal 1998.** / *I have been living here since 1998.*
> **Vivo qui da dodici anni.** / *I have been living here for 12 years.*

- It is also translated with the English expression *as a …*

> **Te lo dico da amico.** / *I'm telling you as a friend.*
> **Da piccolo, navigavo spesso Internet.** / *As a kid, I used to navigate the Internet often.*

- In expressions consisting of a noun + infinitive it is translated in various ways.

> **una macchina da vendere** / *a car to sell*
> **un abito da sera** / *an evening dress*

- **Per** is used in time expressions when "future duration" is implied.

> **Abiterò in questa città per tre anni.** / *I will live in this city for three years.*

Some verbs are followed by **a** before an infinitive.

Cominciano a capire. / *They are starting to understand.*
Devo imparare ad usare il computer. / *I must learn how to use the computer.*

Some are followed instead by **di**.

Finiranno di lavorare alle sei. / *They will finish working at six o'clock.*
Cercheremo di rientrare presto. / *We will try to get back home early.*

Others are not followed by any preposition.

Voglio capire meglio. / *I want to understand better.*
Desiderano andare in Italia. / *They want to go to Italy.*
Preferisco rimanere a casa stasera. / *I prefer staying home tonight.*

Missing from the blanks is a preposition or prepositional contraction. Supply one or the other, as the case may be.

1. Finirò _____ guardare la TV stasera molto presto.
2. Anche loro vogliono imparare _____ parlare italiano bene.
3. Starò _____ casa domani _____ tutta la giornata.
4. Anche loro hanno una macchina _____ vendere.
5. _____ bambini, noi giocavamo sempre insieme.
6. Abito _____ quella casa _____ 2001.
7. Anche loro abitano _____ loro casa _____ nove anni.
8. Domani devo andare _____ dentista.
9. Questo è il nuovo televisore digitale _____ miei genitori.
10. Voglio andare _____ Firenze _____ qualche anno.
11. Preferirei andare _____ Toscana settentrionale.
12. Di solito vado _____ centro in macchina, ma oggi vado _____ autobus.
13. La forchetta è caduta _____ il tavolo.
14. Che cosa ci metti _____ spaghetti?
15. Io non metto mai niente _____ caffè.
16. Quella è la macchina _____ amici _____ mia sorella.
17. Io non scrivo mai _____ zii.
18. A che ora arrivano loro _____ Italia domani?

Other Grammatical Points
Altre questioni grammaticali

    Negatives are words and expressions that allow you to deny, refuse, or oppose something.

> **Non conosco nessuno qui.** / *I do not know anyone here.*
> **Non lo faccio più.** / *I won't do it anymore.*

    The following are some common negative adverbs. Notice that **non** is retained before the predicate.

Impara gli avverbi negativi!

non...mai / *never*
non...nessuno / *no one*
non...niente, nulla / *nothing*
non...più / *no more, no longer*
non...neanche, nemmeno, neppure / *not even*
non...né...né / *neither...nor*
non...mica / *not really, quite*

Examples:

Affirmative	**Negative**
Lui canta sempre. / *He always sings.*	Lui non canta mai. / *He never sings.*
Lui sta chiamando qualcuno. / *He is calling someone.*	Lui non sta chiamando nessuno. / *He is calling no one.*
Ci vado spesso. / *I go there a lot.*	Non ci vado mai. / *I never go there.*

These can be put at the beginning of a sentence for emphasis. In this case, **non** is dropped.

Nessuno parla! / *No one is speaking.*
Mai capirò i verbi! / *Never will I understand verbs!*

The conjunctions **e** / *and* and **o** / *or* allow you to combine similar parts of speech (two nouns, two phrases, etc.).

Marco e Carlo sono amici. / *Mark and Charles are friends.*
Non so se Marco studi o lavori / *I do not know if Marco works or studies.*

The conjunction **e** and the preposition **a** can be changed to **ed** and **ad**, respectively, before a word beginning with a vowel. This makes the pronunciation smoother.

Gina ed Elena sono buone amiche. / *Gina and Helen are good friends.*
Noi vivamo ad Atene. / *We live in Athens.*

Be careful with the following confusingly similar structures!

Singular	**Plural**
Che cosa è? / *What is it?*	Che cosa sono? / *What are they?*
È un libro. / *It's a book.*	Sono dei libri. / *They are books.*
C'è Alessandro? / *Is Alex there?*	Ci sono Alessandro e Sara? / *Are Alex and Sarah there?*
Sì, c'è. / *Yes, he is (here).*	Sì, ci sono. / *Yes, they are (here).*
Dov'è Alessandro? / *Where is Alex?*	Dove sono Alessandro e Sara? / *Where are Alex and Sara?*
Ecco Alessandro. / *Here's Alex.*	Eccoli. / *Here they are.*

QUICK PRACTICE 3

Make each statement negative.

1. Io conosco tutti qui.
2. Lo farò ancora.
3. Lui cammina sempre a scuola.
4. Voglio tutto!
5. Ho mangiato anche la pizza.
6. Voglio la minestra e la pasta.
7. Marco lavora e studia sempre.
8. È un libro o una rivista.
9. Sì, Marco c'è.

PUTTING IT ALL TOGETHER

A. *Say the following in Italian.*

1. I have just finished working.
2. It's almost three o'clock.
3. He did it again (one more time).
4. She lives far, and he nearby.
5. We often go to the movies.
6. First I will eat, and then I will study.
7. She went out already.
8. He has just phoned.
9. They haven't yet finished working.
10. Maria, do you have a lot of money?
11. My sister is very intelligent.
12. They are very hungry.
13. My sister is very famous.
14. There are few students here.
15. They study little.
16. Your book is better than mine.
17. I am feeling better than you are.
18. They are feeling worse than we.

B. *Missing from the following advertisement are the prepositions, simple or in contracted form. Supply them.*

Abitate ____ città, ____ centro, ____ periferia? Non importa dove abitiate, avrete bisogno ____ Carta Visa. Tenetela sempre ____ voi, quando siete ____ casa, ____ ufficio, ____ cinema, ____ teatro, ____ spiaggia, ____ montagna, insomma, dappertutto! Se dovete andare ____ medico, ____ avvocato, portatevela *(bring it)* ____ voi. Se dovete andare ____ Roma, ____ Siena, ____ Spagna, ____ Francia, dovunque, portatevela sempre dietro! Se andate ____ Italia meridionale o ____ Francia centrale, ____ grandi centri di turismo o ____ periferie ____ grandi città, portate la Carta Visa! ____ tutti questi posti accettano sicuramente la Carta Visa. E quando siete ____ casa, non buttatela *(throw it)* ____ tavolo, ____ cassetto *(drawer)*, o ____ scaffali *(bookshelves)*, ma conservatela ____ un posto sicuro. La Carta Visa è molto preziosa.

C. **Cruciverba!**

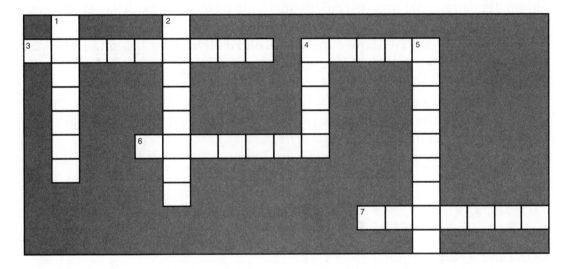

Orizzontali
3. Forma avverbiale di "vero"
4. Il contrario di "tanti"
6. Il participio passato di "coprire"
7. Equivalente di "sono sufficienti"

Verticali
1. Il contrario di "tutti"
2. Il contrario di "migliore"
4. Il contrario di "vuoto"
5. *Interest* in italiano.

Culture Capsule 3

Cuisine
La cucina

La cucina italiana è conosciuta in tutto il mondo. Tuttavia non esiste veramente una cucina comune a tutti, ma molte cucine che riflettono le diverse tradizioni delle regioni italiane. I ristoranti, perciò, vengono indicati come toscani, lombardi, emiliani, e così via. Per esempio, tra molte altre cose, la Lombardia è famosa per il panettone (pane dolce con frutta candita e uva secca), la Liguria per la pasta al pesto (salsa a base di aglio, olio e basilico), l'Emilia Romagna per i tortellini, le tagliatelle e le lasagne, la Toscana per il castagnaccio (torta fatta con farina di castagne), la Campania per la pizza e la Sicilia per i cannoli.

Studi condotti sia negli Stati Uniti che in Italia durante gli ultimi vent'anni hanno dimostrato che una delle diete più «sane e corrette» è quella «mediterranea». Con la parola «dieta mediterranea» si vogliono indicare gli alimenti consumati tradizionalmente dagli italiani: pane, pasta, olio d'oliva, vino, legumi secchi, verdura e frutta fresca, pesce e piccole quantità di carne.

Oggi anche in Italia c'è il fast-food e i locali più popolari tra i giovani si notano nomi come McDonald's e Wendy's. Oltre ai ristoranti e alle trattorie, ci sono anche locali come le paninoteche (dove si vendono i panini), le pizzerie, i self-service (*cafeterias*) e le rosticcerie (*take-out/rotisseries*).

CONTENT QUESTIONS
Vero o falso?

_____ 1. Chi segue la dieta mediterranea mangia molta carne.

_____ 2. McDonald's e Wendy's non sono popolari tra i giovani.

_____ 3. Le rosticcerie sono ristoranti di lusso.

_____ 4. La Lombardia è famosa per i cannoli.

_____ 5. La Sicilia è famosa per il panettone.

_____ 6. La Toscana è famosa per il castagnaccio.

_____ 7. La Liguria è famosa per la pasta al pesto.

PART IV:
Special Topics

13

The Verb *Piacere*

> ## *Quanto Sai Già?* — How Much Do You Know Already?
>
> *Choose the correct form of* **piacere***.*
>
> 1. Mi … quelle mele.
>   a. piace
>   b. piacciono
>
> 2. Le … quelle mele?
>   a. è piaciuta
>   b. sono piaciute
>
> 3. Marco non è mai … a Maria.
>   a. piaciuto
>   b. piaciuta
>
> 4. Maria pure non è mai … a Marco.
>   a. piaciuto
>   b. piaciuta
>
> 5. Marco, … nuotare?
>   a. ti piace
>   b. Le piace
>
> 6. Signor Rossi, … nuotare?
>   a. ti piace
>   b. Le piace

Forms
Forme verbali

The verb **piacere** / *to be pleasing to, to like* is an important but pesky verb. Its present (indicative and subjunctive) and past absolute forms are irregular. They are given on the next page:

piacere / *to be pleasing to, to like*

Present Indicative

(io)	piaccio	*I am pleasing to*
(tu)	piaci	*you (fam.) are pleasing to*
(lui/lei/Lei)	piace	*he, she, you (pol.) is/are pleasing to*
(noi)	piacciamo	*we are pleasing to*
(voi)	piacete	*you are pleasing to*
(loro)	piacciono	*they are pleasing to*

Present Subjunctive

(io)	piaccia	*I am pleasing to*
(tu)	piaccia	*you (fam.) are pleasing to*
(lui/lei/Lei)	piaccia	*he, she, you (pol.) is/are pleasing to*
(noi)	piacciamo	*we are pleasing to*
(voi)	piacciate	*you are pleasing to*
(loro)	piacciano	*they are pleasing to*

Past Absolute

(io)	piacqui	*I was pleasing to*
(tu)	piacesti (regular)	*you (fam.) were pleasing to*
(lui/lei/Lei)	piacque	*he, she, you (pol.) was/were pleasing to*
(noi)	piacemmo (regular)	*we were pleasing to*
(voi)	piaceste (regular)	*you were pleasing to*
(loro)	piacquero	*they were pleasing to*

It is regular in the other tenses. Notice that in order to use it, you will have to "rephrase it in your mind" as shown below:

I will not like that restaurant.

Non mi	piacerà	quel ristorante.
↓	↓	↓
Not to me	*will be pleasing*	*that restaurant.*

She will not like us.

Non le	piaceremo	(noi).
↓	↓	↓
Not to her	*will be pleasing*	*we.*

I would like to go to Italy.

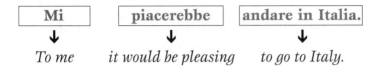

Mi	piacerebbe	andare in Italia.
↓	↓	↓
To me	*it would be pleasing*	*to go to Italy.*

In compound tenses, **piacere** is conjugated with **essere**. This means, of course, that the past participle agrees with the subject—no matter where it occurs in the sentence:

I didn't like her.

Non mi	è piaciuta	(lei).
↓	↓	↓
Not to me	*has been pleasing*	*she.*

She didn't like us.

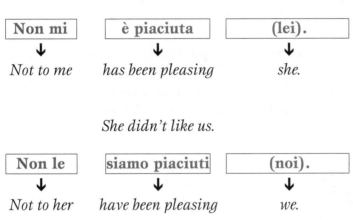

Non le	siamo piaciuti	(noi).
↓	↓	↓
Not to her	*have been pleasing*	*we.*

I hadn't liked the pizza.

Non mi	era piaciuta	la pizza.
↓	↓	↓
Not to me	*had been pleasing*	*the pizza.*

As you can see, this verb allows you to express what you *like* in Italian. But it is a tricky verb because it really means *to be pleasing to*:

- In order to use it appropriately, you will need to use the indirect object pronouns *to me, to you*, etc. (Chapter 11).
- The best initial learning strategy is to rephrase the English expression in your mind as shown above. Notice that object pronouns precede the verb:

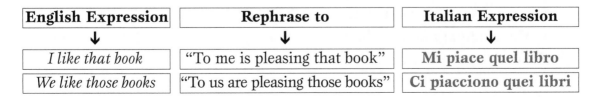

English Expression	Rephrase to	Italian Expression
↓	↓	↓
I like that book	"To me is pleasing that book"	**Mi piace quel libro**
We like those books	"To us are pleasing those books"	**Ci piacciono quei libri**

- If the object is not a pronoun, use the preposition **a** before the noun or noun phrase:

English Expression ↓	Rephrase to ↓	Italian Expression ↓
John likes Mary	"Mary is pleasing to John"	**Maria piace a Giovanni**
My friends like your teacher	"Your teacher is pleasing to my friends"	**Il tuo/La tua insegnante piace ai miei amici**
Mary likes me	"I am pleasing to Mary"	**Io piaccio a Maria**

You might need to use the stressed forms of the indirect object pronouns (**a me, a te,** etc.) (Chapter 11). These are used for emphasis or clarity.

> **Quella musica è piaciuta solo a me, non a loro!** / *Only I like that music, not they!*

Also, keep in mind what the verb means in Italian, even when it is used in tenses such as the present subjunctive:

> **Dubito che gli piacciano gli spaghetti.** / *I doubt that he likes spaghetti ("spaghetti are pleasing to him").*
> **Penso che anche a lei piaccia andare al cinema.** / *I think that she also likes to go to the movies ("going to the movies is pleasing to her").*

QUICK PRACTICE 1

*Do the following: (1) give the missing form of **piacere** in the tense and mood indicated; (2) translate the sentence into English; and (3) provide an alternative form of the sentence in Italian.*

Modello: Io ... a lei (*present indicative*)
   a. **Io piaccio a lei.**
   b. **She likes me** *("I am pleasing to her").*
   c. **Io le piaccio.**

1. Tu ... a me. *(future)*
2. Io ... a te. *(present indicative)*
3. Lei ... a noi. *(past absolute)*
4. Noi ... a lei. *(imperfect indicative)*
5. Lei ... a noi. *(present perfect)*
6. Voi ... a lui. *(present perfect)*
7. Lui ... a voi. *(future perfect)*

8. Loro … a me. *(pluperfect indicative)*

9. Io … a loro. *(conditional)*

Now, say the following phrases in Italian.

10. Maria, did you like that new movie?

11. I didn't like it at all!

12. I have always liked spaghetti!

13. She used to like Paolo a lot, but he didn't like her.

14. They liked me, but they didn't like my sister.

Rule of Thumb
Regola pratica

As you can see, **piacere** can be very confusing for anyone accustomed to the English verb *to like*. The following rule of thumb might help you use this important verb more readily.

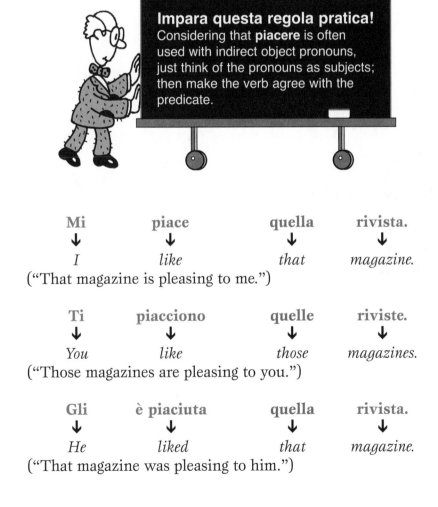

Impara questa regola pratica!
Considering that **piacere** is often used with indirect object pronouns, just think of the pronouns as subjects; then make the verb agree with the predicate.

Mi	**piace**	**quella**	**rivista.**
↓	↓	↓	↓
I	*like*	*that*	*magazine.*

("That magazine is pleasing to me.")

Ti	**piacciono**	**quelle**	**riviste.**
↓	↓	↓	↓
You	*like*	*those*	*magazines.*

("Those magazines are pleasing to you.")

Gli	**è piaciuta**	**quella**	**rivista.**
↓	↓	↓	↓
He	*liked*	*that*	*magazine.*

("That magazine was pleasing to him.")

Le	sono piaciute	quelle	riviste.
↓	↓	↓	↓
She	*liked*	*those*	*magazines.*

("Those magazines were pleasing to her.")

Ci	piacerà	la	frutta.
↓	↓	↓	↓
We	*will like*	*(the)*	*fruit.*

("The fruit will be pleasing to us.")

Vi	piacciono	i	formaggi italiani.
↓	↓	↓	↓
You	*like*	*(the)*	*Italian cheeses.*

("Italian cheeses are pleasing to you.")

Gli	piace	la	verdura.
↓	↓	↓	↓
They	*like*	*(the)*	*vegetables.*

("Vegetables are pleasing to them.")

Remember that this is merely a rule of thumb. If you are unsure, you must go through the process described above.

QUICK PRACTICE 2

Say the following phrases in Italian, as indicated.

Modello: I like…
quel libro
Mi piace quel libro.

They will like…
quei libri
Gli piaceranno quei libri.

I like…

1. Beethoven's music
2. spaghetti

You (*fam., sing.*) will like...

  3. that movie
  4. those magazines (**la rivista** / *magazine*)

You (*pol., sing.*) did like...

  5. my friend (*m.*)
  6. my friends (*m.*)

He used to like...

  7. your car
  8. those cars

She liked... (*past absolute*)

  9. that book
10. those books

We like...

11. that newspaper
12. those persons

You (*fam., pl.*) had liked...

13. my friend (*f.*)
14. my friends (*f.*)

They would like...

15. that new magazine
16. those new magazines

Expressing Likes and Dislikes
Esprimere i propri gusti

To say that you do not like something, simply put **non** before the predicate in the normal fashion:

> **Non mi piace quella rivista.** / *I do not like that magazine.*
> **Non le piacciono gli spaghetti.** / *She doesn't like spaghetti.*

Be careful! The verb **dispiacere** is not used to express the same thing. This verb is used in the following ways:

Mi dispiace. / *I'm sorry.*
Ti dispiace. / *You are sorry.*
Gli dispiace. / *He is sorry.*

QUICK
PRACTICE 3

Say the following sentences in Italian.

1. I do not like to play the piano.
2. They like everyone in this city.
3. I don't like that movie.
4. I am sorry, but I know that she doesn't like you *(fam., sing.)*.
5. We're sorry, but we don't like that pastry.
6. We didn't like that cheese.
7. You *(fam., sing.)* didn't like that new book, did you?
8. I'm sorry, but I didn't like that new movie.
9. She will not like my new car.

Similar Verbs
Verbi simili

The following verbs exhibit the same "grammatical behavior" of **piacere**—that is, they require frequent usage of indirect object pronouns and they have to be rephrased mentally in analogous ways:

affascinare	*to fascinate, to be fascinated by*
apparire	*to appear*
bastare	*to be sufficient, to suffice, to be enough*
dolere	*to be painful, to ache*
importare	*to be important, to matter*
interessare	*to interest, to be interested by*
mancare	*to lack, to miss*
rimanere	*to be left over, to remain*
sembrare	*to seem*

The irregular verb forms of **rimanere** have been covered in previous chapters. Note the following irregular forms of **apparire** and **dolere**:

apparire / *to appear*		
Present Indicative/Subjunctive		
(io)	appaio/appaia	*I appear*
(tu)	appari/appaia	*you (fam.) appear*
(lui/lei/Lei)	appare/appaia	*he, she, you (pol.) appear(s)*
(noi)	appaiamo/appaiamo	*we appear*
(voi)	apparite/appariate	*you appear*
(loro)	appaiono/appaiano	*they appear*
Past Participle:	apparso	

dolere / *to suffer*		
Present Indicative/Subjunctive		
(io)	dolgo/dolga	*I suffer*
(tu)	duoli/dolga	*you (fam.) suffer*
(lui/lei/Lei)	duole/dolga	*he, she, you (pol.) suffer(s)*
(noi)	dogliamo/dogliamo	*we suffer*
(voi)	dolete/dogliate	*you suffer*
(loro)	dolgono/dolgano	*they suffer*
Future		
(io)	dorrò	*I will suffer*
(tu)	dorrai	*you (fam.) will suffer*
(lui/lei/Lei)	dorrà	*he, she, you (pol.) will suffer*
(noi)	dorremo	*we will suffer*
(voi)	dorrete	*you will suffer*
(loro)	dorranno	*they will suffer*
Past Absolute		
(io)	dolsi	*I suffered*
(tu)	dolesti (regular)	*you (fam.) suffered*
(lui/lei/Lei)	dolse	*he, she, you (pol.) suffered*
(noi)	dolemmo (regular)	*we suffered*
(voi)	doleste (regular)	*you suffered*
(loro)	dolsero	*they suffered*

The best initial learning strategy is, once again, to rephrase the English expression in your mind:

English Expression ↓	Rephrase to ↓	Italian Expression ↓
I am fascinated by that book	"That book is fascinating to me"	**Quel libro mi affascina**
There are two days left	"Two days are lacking"	**Mancano due giorni**
We miss you	"You are lacking to us"	**Tu ci manchi**

QUICK PRACTICE 4

Say the following phrases in Italian.

1. Does that restaurant seem good?
2. The only thing left is to write to Maria.
3. That movie didn't interest me at all.
4. The spaghetti was enough for me.
5. My bones (**le mie ossa**) are aching.
6. Those things will matter a lot in the future.
7. Did you (*fam., sing.*) miss me?

PUTTING IT ALL TOGETHER

A. *Choose the appropriate answer, **a** or **b**, to each question.*

1. Marco, ti piace il formaggio italiano?
   a. Sì, mi piace molto.
   b. Sì, mi piacciono molto.

2. Piacete anche a loro?
   a. Sì, gli piacciamo.
   b. Sì, gli piacete.

3. Piacciamo a te?
   a. Sì, mi piacete.
   b. Sì, mi piacciono.

4. A chi piace la musica di Beethoven?
   a. Piace a noi.
   b. Piacete a noi.

5. Signora Dini, Le piace quella macchina nuova?
   a. Sì, mi piace.
   b. Sì, Le piace.

6. Quale macchina vi piace?
   a. Vi piace quella macchina.
   b. Ci piace quella macchina.

7. Tu piaci ai genitori di Paolo?
   a. Sì, loro mi piacciono.
   b. Sì, io gli piaccio.

8. Ti piacciono i genitori di Paolo?
   a. No, non gli piaccio.
   b. No, non mi piacciono.

9. A chi piaci tu?
   a. Ti piaccio.
   b. Piaccio a lei.

B. *You are given each sentence in the present. First, rephrase each sentence as shown, and then give its Italian equivalent.*

Modello: I like the book.
              "The book is pleasing to me."
              Il libro mi piace / Mi piace il libro.

1. I like Maria.
2. Maria used to like me.
3. You *(fam., sing.)* liked only those books.
4. Those girls will like you *(fam., sing.)*.
5. We think that she likes that boy.
6. That boy would like her, but he doesn't know her yet.
7. My parents don't like that restaurant.
8. We don't like cheese (**il formaggio**).
9. I believe that they liked us.
10. I thought that he used to like fruit.
11. She used to like him, but she doesn't like him any longer now.
12. You *(fam., pl.)* did like that newspaper, didn't you?

13. My parents like you *(fam., pl.)*.

14. They will like those magazines.

15. I like them.

C. **Vero o falso?** *Indicate whether the following things are true ("V") or false ("F")
from your personal perspective.*

A me...

____ 1. piace il cinema.

____ 2. piacciono i film di Fellini.

____ 3. piace suonare il pianoforte.

____ 4. piacciono gli gnocchi.

A tua sorella/A tuo fratello...

____ 5. piace la televisione.

____ 6. piacciono gli spaghetti.

____ 7. piace la musica classica.

____ 8. piacciono le riviste di moda.

Ai tuoi genitori...

____ 9. piace il film *Cinema paradiso.*

____ 10. piacciono i film italiani.

____ 11. piace la musica italiana.

____ 12. piacciono i formaggi italiani.

D. *Now, answer each question with* **sì** *or* **no** *from your personal perspective.*

____ 1. Ti affascinano gli sport?

____ 2. Al tuo amico/alla tua amica appaiono interessanti i film italiani?

____ 3. Alla tua famiglia basta una macchina?

____ 4. Ti dolgono spesso le ossa *(your bones)*?

____ 5. Per te, importano le feste?

____ 6. Alla tua famiglia interessa parlare l'italiano?

____ 7. Ti mancano soldi in questo momento?

____ 8. Ti sembra importante studiare molto?

E. Cruciverba!

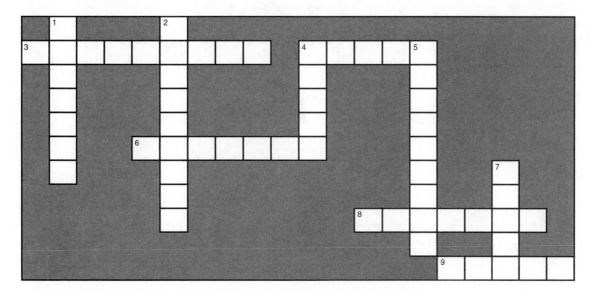

All answers are forms of the verb **piacere** *or of a similar type of verb.*

Orizzontali

3. Ti … gli spaghetti?
4. Tu … anche a me.
6. Voi … ai miei genitori.
8. Non gli … gli spaghetti.
   Ha molta fame.
9. Ti … quel libro?

Verticali

1. Io … alla tua amica.
2. Noi … ai tuoi amici.
4. Gli … la frutta.
5. Il cinema non mi … affatto!
7. Lei mi … molto.

14

Idiomatic Expressions

Quanto Sai Già? — How Much Do You Know Already?

How do you say the following in Italian?

1. I am hungry.
2. Maria, are you sleepy?
3. It doesn't depend on me.
4. Heed what I say, Giovanni!
5. Did you get your plane ticket yet?
6. She is about to go to the store.

Expressions with *Avere*
Expressioni col verbo avere

An idiomatic expression is a phrase that is relatively fixed in form and whose meaning cannot always be determined by the meanings of the separate words in it. For example, the English expression *He kicked the bucket* cannot be understood as the sum of the meanings of the separate words. Moreover, it cannot be altered in any way; otherwise, it would lose its idiomatic meaning (*He kicks the buckets; He kicks a bucket;* etc.).

There are many idiomatic expressions in a language—too many to list in a simple textbook. So, in this chapter a selection has been made on the basis of those that occur frequently in common conversations.

The following common expressions are made up of **avere** + noun, contrasting with their English equivalents, as shown below.

Ho fame. / *I am hungry (literally: "I have hunger").*
Non ha paura. / *He is not afraid (literally: "He does not have fear").*

Expressions with **avere**

avercela con qualcuno	*to be angry with someone*
avere bisogno (di)	*to need*
avere caldo	*to be hot*
avere fame	*to be hungry*
avere freddo	*to be cold*
avere fretta	*to be in a hurry*
avere l'occasione di	*to have the opportunity to*
avere paura	*to be afraid*
avere ragione	*to be right*
avere sete	*to be thirsty*
avere sonno	*to be sleepy*
avere torto	*to be wrong*
avere vergogna	*to be ashamed*
avere voglia (di)	*to feel like*

Examples:

Ieri avevamo fame e allora abbiamo mangiato molto. / *Yesterday we were hungry, so we ate a lot.*
Scusa, ma ho fretta. / *Excuse me, but I'm in a hurry.*
Penso che tu abbia torto. / *I believe you are wrong.*
Stasera non ho voglia di uscire. / *Tonight, I don't feel like going out.*
Gli studenti hanno bisogno di tanta pazienza. / *The students need a lot of patience.*
Perché ce l'hai con Franca? / *Why are you angry with Franca?*

When using **molto**, **tanto**, or **poco** with such expressions make sure you treat them as adjectives (Chapter 12). They must agree with the gender of the noun:

Ho molta fame. / *I am very hungry* (**la fame** = feminine).
Hanno tanto sonno. / *They are very sleepy* (**il sonno** = masculine).
Abbiamo poca voglia di uscire. / *We have little desire to go out* (**la voglia** = feminine).

QUICK PRACTICE 1

Write a character sketch of Giovanni. Say that Giovanni…

1. is very hungry and thirsty.
2. is very sleepy today because he fell asleep late last night.
3. had little desire to go out yesterday because he was tired.
4. was angry with his friend *(m.)* because he didn't call him last night.
5. is not ashamed to ask questions in class.
6. needs to study more.

7. is never cold but always hot, even in winter.

8. is always in a hurry.

9. had an opportunity yesterday to meet a famous soccer player (**giocatore**).

10. is never afraid to be wrong.

Expressions with *Fare, Dare,* and *Stare*
Espressioni con i verbi fare, dare, e stare

A number of common expressions are constructed with the verbs **fare**, **dare**, and **stare**. If you have forgotten how to conjugate these irregular verbs, just look them up in the *Verb Charts* section at the back of this book.

Expressions with **fare**

fare a meno	*to do without*
fare attenzione	*to pay attention to*
fare finta di	*to pretend*
fare il biglietto	*to buy a (transportation) ticket*
fare senza	*to do without*
fare una domanda a	*to ask a question*
fare una passeggiata	*to go for a walk*
farsi la barba	*to shave*
farsi vivo	*to show up*
Faccia pure!	*Go ahead! (Please do!)*
Faccio io!	*I'll do it!*
Non fa niente!	*It doesn't matter!*
Non fa per me.	*It doesn't suit me.*

Examples:

Ho fatto il biglietto con Alitalia. / *I bought my ticket with Alitalia.*
Ogni mattina mi faccio la barba. / *I shave every morning.*
Giovanni, perché non ti fai mai vivo? / *John, why don't you come more often?*

Expressions with **dare**

dare fastidio a	*to bother (someone)*
dare la mano	*to shake hands*
dare retta a	*to heed (pay attention to)*
darsi da fare	*to get busy*

Examples:

Tutto mi dà fastidio. / *Everything bothers me.*
Dare la mano a qualcuno è un segno di cortesia. / *Shaking someone's hand is a sign of courtesy.*
Da' retta a me! / *Heed what I say!*

Expressions with **stare**

stare a qualcuno	*to be up to someone*
stare attento	*to be careful*
stare bene	*to be well*
stare calmo	*to stay calm*
stare fermo	*to stay still*
stare male	*to be not well*
stare per	*to be about to*
stare zitto	*to be quiet*

Examples:

Marco, sta' zitto! / *Marco, be quiet!*
Sta alla signora Rossi scrivere. / *It's up to Mrs. Rossi to write.*
Ieri stavo per uscire quando sono arrivati alcuni amici. / *Yesterday I was about to go out when some friends arrived.*
Come sta? (*pol., sing.*) / *How are you?*
Come stai? (*fam., sing.*) / *How are you?*
Sto bene. / *I am well.*

QUICK
PRACTICE 2

Match the parts in the left and right columns to make complete sentences.

1. Ragazzi, state…	a. mangiare quando sei arrivata.
2. Marco, come …	b. da fare, altrimenti non finirai!
3. Lui non sta mai…	c. zitti!
4. Dino, devi stare…	d. da' retta solo a me!
5. Marco, ti devi dare…	e. hai dato la mano?
6. Maria, …	f. stai?
7. Noi stavamo per…	g. meno di guardare la televisione.
8. Pino, devi sempre fare…	h. fermo quando guarda la TV.
9. Io non posso fare a…	i. attenzione in classe.
10. Chi è quella persona alla quale…	j. calmo, altrimenti diventerai nervoso!
11. Ieri lui ha fatto finta…	k. il biglietto per partire?
12. L'hai fatto ancora…	l. la televisione!
13. Stasera ho deciso di fare senza…	m. una bella passeggiata insieme.
14. Ieri abbiamo fatto…	n. di non vedermi.
15. Marco, fa'…	o. per me!
16. Non ti preoccupare! Non…	p. fa niente.
17. Quello non fa…	q. pure quello che vuoi!

Miscellaneous Expressions
Espressioni varie

Below is a collection of miscellaneous expressions that seem to be used constantly in common everyday speech.

Espressioni varie	
a destra	*to the right*
a lungo andare	*in the long run*
a sinistra	*to the left*
Auguri!	*All the best! / Congratulations!*
Che combinazione!	*What a coincidence!*
Che guaio!	*What a mess (to be in)!*
dipendere da	*to depend on*
est	*east*
farlo apposta	*to do it on purpose*
in ogni caso	*in any case*
niente di buono	*nothing good*
non poterne più	*to not be able to stand it anymore*
nord	*north*
ovest	*west*
prendere in giro	*to pull one's leg*
qualcosa di buono	*something good*
sud	*south*
Ti piace? Altro che!	*Do you like it? I'll say!*
valere la pena	*to be worthwhile*
volerci tempo	*to take time*

Examples:

Quel negozio si trova a destra. / *That store is to the right.*
Davvero? Non mi prendere in giro! / *Really? Don't pull my leg!*
Tutto dipende da te. / *Everything depends on you.*
Non ne posso più! / *I can't stand it anymore!*
Ci vuole molto tempo! / *It takes a long time!*
L'ha fatto apposta! / *He did it on purpose!*

QUICK PRACTICE 3

Choose the appropriate expression, according to situation.

1. Marco, ti piace il mio nuovo cellulare digitale?
   a. Altro che!
   b. Che combinazione!

2. Claudia, devi avere pazienza.
   a. Lo devi fare apposta!
   b. Ci vuole molto tempo per fare tutto!

3. Io non posso fare più niente.
   a. Adesso tutto dipende da te.
   b. Che guaio!

4. Sara, ha suonato il pianoforte fantasticamente!
   a. Auguri!
   b. Non ne posso più!

5. Non devi sempre preoccuparti di tutto!
   a. L'ha fatto apposta!
   b. Non vale la pena!

6. Anch'io ho visto Maria ieri nello stesso negozio.
   a. Non mi prendere sempre in giro!
   b. Che combinazione!

PUTTING IT ALL TOGETHER

A. *Complete each sentence with the appropriate form of the verb* avere, dare, fare, *or* stare, *according to sense.*

1. Marco non (_____) paura di niente. È molto coraggioso.
2. Maria, (_____) zitta! Parli troppo!
3. Marco, (_____) a te telefonare ai tuoi genitori.
4. Mentre io (_____) per uscire ieri, sono arrivati alcuni amici.
5. Ieri i miei amici ed io (_____) molta fame e allora abbiamo mangiato più del normale.
6. Maria, come (_____)? (_____) abbastanza bene grazie. E tu come (_____)? Io invece (_____) male oggi.
7. Tutto ti (_____) fastidio, Franco!
8. Chi è quella signora a cui hai (_____) la mano?
9. Alessandro, devi (_____) retta a me!
10. Non è possibile che tu (_____) torto.
11. Per andare in Italia conviene (_____) il biglietto con Alitalia.
12. Ogni giorno mi (_____) la barba, altrimenti sembrerei un gorilla.
13. Maria, perché non ti (_____) mai viva?
14. Maria, hai voglia di uscire stasera? (_____) un bel film al cinema.
15. Bruna, è vero che tu ce l'(_____) con la tua migliore amica?

B. *Say the following in Italian.*

1. My house is to the right of Via Rossini, not to the left.
2. Maria, do your relatives (**parenti**) live north or south?
3. Claudia, do you like my new car? I'll say!
4. In the long run, it is worthwhile to have patience.
5. All the best!
6. In any case, I will continue to study Italian.
7. What a mess!
8. I can't stand it anymore!
9. Maria, you shouldn't always pull my leg like this!
10. It takes a long time!
11. They did it on purpose!
12. What a coincidence!
13. It all depends on them!
14. Let's hope that something good will happen.

C. **Cruciverba!**

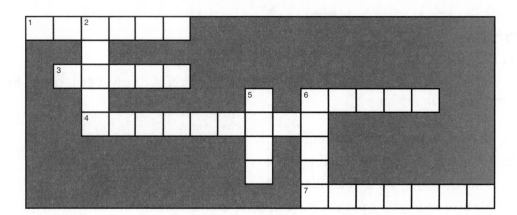

Orizzontali
1. Non ho … di uscire stasera.
3. Loro non hanno … di niente.
4. Non ho mai avuto l'… di andare in Italia.
6. Devi sempre … zitto in classe.
7. Quando guidi devi sempre stare ….

Verticali
2. Che …!
5. No, stasera ho … fame!
6. Non posso fare … lo sport!

15

Numbers

Quanto Sai Già? — How Much Do You Know Already?

Match the items in the two columns correctly.

1. first
2. one
3. twelve
4. twelfth
5. half
6. three-fourths
7. three hundred and four

a. dodicesimo
b. tre quarti
c. metà
d. trecento e quattro
e. dodici
f. primo
g. uno

Cardinal Numbers
I numeri cardinali

Cardinal numbers are used for counting (*one, two, three,* etc.). *Ordinal numbers* are used to indicate order (*first, second, third,* etc.). The first twenty cardinal numbers in Italian require that you memorize them, for they will be needed to form the remaining numbers. They are listed for you on the next page.

Impara i numeri cardinali!

Zero to Twenty

0	zero	11	undici
1	uno	12	dodici
2	due	13	tredici
3	tre	14	quattordici
4	quattro	15	quindici
5	cinque	16	sedici
6	sei	17	diciassette
7	sette	18	diciotto
8	otto	19	diciannove
9	nove	20	venti
10	dieci		

The numbers from twenty on are formed by adding the first nine numbers to each new category of tens, keeping the following adjustments in mind:

- In front of **uno** and **otto** (the two numbers that start with a vowel), drop the final vowel of the tens number:

21	venti	→	vent- + uno	→	ventuno
31	trenta	→	trent- + uno	→	trentuno
38	trenta	→	trent- + otto	→	trentotto
98	novanta	→	novant- + otto	→	novantotto
108	cento	→	cent- + otto	→	centotto

- When **tre** is added on, it must be written with an accent (to show that the stress is on the final vowel):

23	venti + tre	→	ventitré
33	trenta + tre	→	trentatré
43	quaranta + tre	→	quarantatré
73	settanta + tre	→	settantatré
103	cento + tre	→	centotré

20	venti		60	sessanta
21	ventuno		61	sessantuno
22	ventidue		62	sessantadue
23	ventitrè		63	sessantatrè
24	ventiquattro		...	
25	venticinque		70	settanta
26	ventisei		71	settantuno
27	ventisette		72	settantadue
28	ventotto		73	settantatrè
29	ventinove		...	
30	trenta		80	ottanta
31	trentuno		81	ottantuno
32	trentadue		82	ottantadue
...			83	ottantatrè
40	quaranta		...	
41	quarantuno		90	novanta
42	quarantadue		91	novantuno
43	quarantatrè		92	novantadue
...			93	novantatrè
50	cinquanta		94	novantaquattro
51	cinquantuno		95	novantacinque
52	cinquantadue		96	novantasei
53	cinquantatrè		...	
...			100	cento

The same method of construction applies to the remaining numbers. Note that in Italy the divisions in a whole number digit are shown by periods, not commas (as in the U.S.):

U.S.	Italy
2,345	**2.345**
45,678	**45.678**

101	centuno	2000	duemila
102	centodue	3000	tremila
...		...	
200	duecento	100.000	centomila
300	trecento	200.000	duecentomila
...		...	
900	novecento	1.000.000	un milione
...		2.000.000	due milioni
1000	mille	3.000.000	tre milioni
1001	milleuno	...	
1002	milledue	1.000.000.000	un miliardo

Notice that the plural of **mille** is **mila**, whereas **un milione** and **un miliardo** are pluralized in the normal way.

cinquemila / *five thousand*
due milioni / *two million*
tre miliardi / *three billion*

Cardinal numbers normally are placed before a noun.

tre persone / *three persons*
cinquantotto minuti / *fifty-eight minutes*

When you put **uno** (or any number constructed with it, e.g., **ventuno, trentuno,** etc.) before a noun, then you must treat it exactly like the indefinite article (Chapter 9).

uno zio / *one uncle*
ventun anni / *twenty-one years*
trentuna ragazze / *thirty-one girls*

Milione and **miliardo** are always followed by **di** before a noun.

un milione di dollari / *a million dollars*
due milioni di abitanti / *two million inhabitants*
tre miliardi di euro / *three billion euros*

The cardinal numbers may be written as one word. But for large numbers, it is better to separate them logically, so that they can be read easily.

30.256 = **trentamila duecento cinquantasei**
(rather than **trentamiladuecentocinquantasei!**)

QUICK PRACTICE 1

Imagine being an accountant for a large firm. You are asked to estimate the value of certain acquisitions that various people and institutions are about to make. Write down what you think each item or set of items might cost in words. Follow the model.

Modello: 2 camicie/€350
          Due camicie potrebbero costare trecentocinquanta euro.

1. 1 CD / €33
2. 2 cellulari / €598
3. 11 radio digitali / €4.679
4. 9 computer portatili / €29.345
5. 3 abitazioni in periferia / €957.209
6. 15 case in centro / €18.234.567
7. 18 metropolitane *(subways)* / €290.256.543

Ordinal Numbers
I numeri ordinali

As mentioned previously, *ordinal* numbers are used to indicate order (*first, second, third, fourth,* etc.). You will have to memorize the first ten ordinal numbers.

First to Tenth

1st	primo	6th	sesto
2nd	secondo	7th	settimo
3rd	terzo	8th	ottavo
4th	quarto	9th	nono
5th	quinto	10th	decimo

The remaining numerals are easily constructed in the following manner.

- Take the corresponding cardinal number, drop its vowel ending, and then add **-esimo**:

11th	undici	→	undic- + -esimo	→	undicesimo
40th	quaranta	→	quarant- + -esimo	→	quarantesimo

- The exceptions are numbers ending in **-sei**, in which case the vowel is not dropped:

26th	ventisei	→	ventisei + -esimo	→	ventiseiesimo

- In the case of numbers ending in **-tré**, remove the accent mark, but keep the final **-e**.

23rd	ventitré + -esimo	→	ventitreesimo
33rd	trentatré + -esimo	→	treantatreesimo

Unlike the cardinal numbers, ordinals are adjectives that precede the noun. Therefore, they agree with the noun in the normal fashion.

i primi giorni / *the first days*
la ventesima volta / *the twentieth time*
l'ottavo capitolo / *the eighth chapter*

> **CULTURE NOTE**
> In Italy, the ground floor is called the pianterreno. The floor above it is not called the *second floor*, but il primo piano.

As in English, ordinals are used to express the denominator of fractions, whereas the numerator is expressed by cardinals.

tre quarti   **un diciasettesimo**

$$\frac{3}{4}$$ → tre $$\frac{1}{17}$$ → un
        → quarti (*pl.*)   → diciassettesimo (*sing.*)

Be careful!

1/2 = **mezzo/metà**

mezzo litro / *a half liter*
la metà di tutto / *half of everything*

The definite article is not used with a proper name, as shown below.

Papa Giovanni XXIII (= Ventitreesimo) / *Pope John (the) XXIII*
Luigi XIV (= Quattordicesimo) / *Louis (the) XIV*

QUICK
PRACTICE 2

Express the following in Italian using words for the number concepts.

1. Elizabeth II
2. Pope Benedict XVI
3. ½ liter
4. ¼
5. ⅝
6. 23rd chapter
7. 12th floor
8. 5th time
9. 112th time
10. 1st numbers
11. 2nd floor
12. 86th trip to Italy
13. The 3rd, 4th, 6th, 7th, 8th, 9th, 15th, 16th, and 21st person will win a prize (**un premio**).
14. the ground floor
15. the second floor (in Italy)

Arithmetical Expressions
Espressioni aritmetiche

There are a small number of numerical expressions that will come in handy in everyday situations, especially if they involve arithmetical concepts.

Arithmetic

L'addizione / *Addition*
23 + 36 = 59   **ventitrè più trantasei fa cinquantanove**

La sottrazione / *Subtraction*
8 − 3 = 5   **otto meno tre fa cinque**

La moltiplicazione / *Multiplication*
7 × 2 = 14   **sette per due fa quattordici**

La divisione / *Division*
16 ÷ 2 = 8   **sedici diviso per due fa otto**

Age

Quanti anni ha? (*pol.*)	*How old are you?*
Quanti anni hai? (*fam.*)	*How old are you?*
Ho ventidue anni.	*I am twenty-two years old (lit.: "I have 22 years")*
Ho trentanove anni.	*I am thirty-nine years old (lit.: "I have 39 years")*

Impara queste espressioni numeriche!

A Few Useful Expressions

il doppio	*double*
una dozzina	*a dozen*
una ventina, una trentina, ...	*about twenty, about thirty, ...*
un centinaio, due centinaia, tre centinaia, ...	*about a hundred, about two hundred, about three hundred, ...*
centinaia di ...	*hundreds of ...*
un migliaio, due migliaia, tre migliaia, ...	*about a thousand, about two thousand, about three thousand, ...*
migliaia di ...	*thousands of ...*

QUICK PRACTICE 3

Say the following in Italian.

1. There are hundreds of people here.
2. Yesterday there were thousands of people.
3. I need a double espresso, thanks.
4. How old is your brother?
5. I am too old.
6. How much does twenty-two minus eight make?
7. Can you (Do you know how to) divide eighty-five by five?
8. What is five times nineteen?
9. I need two dozen eggs, please.

PUTTING IT ALL TOGETHER

A. *How do you say…?*

1. eighty-one books
2. four million dollars
3. two billion people
4. ninety-four years
5. ninety-eight houses
6. twelve thousand inhabitants (**abitanti**)
7. two hundred thousand inhabitants

B. *Rephrase each statement in an equivalent fashion.*

Modello: Ho bisogno di dodici rose.
Ho bisogno di una dozzina di rose.

Ci sono quasi 20 studenti in questa classe.
Ci sono una ventina di studenti in questa classe.

1. Conosco quasi 30 studenti in questa classe.
2. Bruno ha circa venti orologi!
3. In questo corso ci sono dodici studenti.
4. Per quell'orologio ho pagato due volte di più!
5. Alla festa sono venute quasi cento persone.
6. Al concerto c'erano circa mille persone.
7. Ho quasi 60 anni.

C. *Giochi matematici! Figure out the next number in each sequence. Write every number as a word.*

Modello: 34, 36, 38...
quaranta

$3 + 9 =$
Tre più nove fa dodici.

1. 1, 3, 5 ...
2. 2, 4, 6 ...
3. 12, 15, 18 ...
4. 25, 35, 45 ...
5. 123, 223, 323 ...
6. 3.002, 5.002, 7.002 ...
7. $34 \times 20 =$
8. $90.000 \div 90 =$
9. $78 + 45 =$
10. $4.567 + 1.111 =$
11. $560 \times 3 =$
12. $456 - 234 =$

16

Telling Time

Quanto Sai Già? — How Much Do You Know Already?

Choose the correct response.

1. Che ore sono?
   a. Sono le due.
   b. È due.

2. Che ore sono?
   a. Sono l'una.
   b. È l'una.

3. A che ora arrivano?
   a. Le quattordici.
   b. Alle quattordici.

4. Che ore sono?
   a. Sono le otto meno dieci.
   b. Sono le otto più dieci.

5. Sono veramente le sedici?
   a. Sì, sono le quattro precise.
   b. Sì, sono le cinque precise.

Hours

Le ore

You can ask the time in the singular or the plural:

Che ora è? / *What time is it?*
Che ore sono? / *What time is it?*

The word **ora** literally means *hour*. The abstract concept of *time* is expressed by **il tempo**.

Come passa il tempo! / *How time flies!*

To be able to tell time, you must know, of course, how to name the hours. Just use the cardinal numbers (Chapter 15).

The hours are feminine. Therefore, they are preceded by the feminine forms of the definite article.

È l'una. / *It's one o'clock* (= the only singular form).
Sono le due. / *It's two o'clock.*
Sono le tre. / *It's three o'clock.*
Sono le quattro. / *It's four o'clock.*
...
Sono le sette. / *It's seven o'clock.*

Officially, telling time in Italian is on the basis of the twenty-four hour clock. Thus, after the noon hour (le dodici), official hours are as follows:

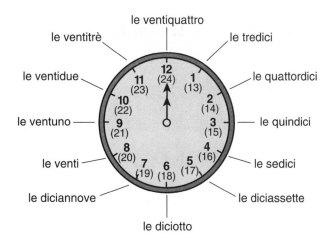

Examples:

Sono le quindici. / *It's 3 P.M.*
Sono le venti. / *It's 8 P.M.*
Sono le ventiquattro. / *It's (twelve) midnight.*

However, in common conversations, Italians often employ the same system used in the U.S.

Sono le quattordici = Sono le due. / *It's two* P.M.
Sono le venti = Sono le otto. / *It's eight* P.M.

The morning, afternoon, and evening hours are referred to colloquially as follows:

di mattina (della mattina)	*in the morning*
di pomeriggio (del pomeriggio)	*in the afternoon*
di sera (della sera)	*in the evening*
di notte (della notte)	*in the night/at night*

Sono le otto di mattina. / *It's eight o'clock in the morning.*
Sono le nove di sera. / *It's nine o'clock in the evening.*

QUICK PRACTICE 1

Give an equivalent for each time.

Modello: Sono le nove A.M.
   Sono le nove di mattina/del mattino.

   Arrivano alle venti.
   Arrivano alle otto di sera/della sera.

1. È l'una A.M.
2. È l'una P.M.
3. Sono le ventiquattro.
4. Arriveremo alle due P.M.
5. Loro, invece, arriveranno alle due A.M.
6. Usciremo verso le tre P.M.
7. Spesso mi alzo alle tre A.M.
8. Sono le quindici.
9. Partiranno alle sedici.
10. Sono le diciassette.
11. Mi sono alzato alle quattro A.M.
12. Sono le diciannove.

Minutes
I minuti

To indicate minutes, simply add them to the hour with the conjunction **e** / *and*.

Sono le tre e venti. / *It's three twenty.*
Sono le quattro e dieci. / *It's ten after four.*
È l'una e quaranta. / *It's one forty.*
Sono le sedici e cinquanta. / *It's 4:50 P.M.*
Sono le ventidue e cinque. / *It's 10:05 P.M..*
Loro arriveranno all'una. / *They will arrive at one.*
Quel programma inizia alle ventidue. / *That show is starting at 10 P.M.*

As the next hour approaches, an alternative way of expressing the minutes is: the next hour minus (**meno**) the number of minutes left to go.

8:58	=	**le otto e cinquantotto** or **le nove meno due**
10:50	=	**le dieci e cinquanta** or **le undici meno dieci**

The expressions **un quarto** (*a quarter*), and **mezzo/mezza** (*half*) can be used for the quarter and half hour.

3:15	=	**le tre e quindici** or **le tre e un quarto**
4:30	=	**le quattro e trenta** or **le quattro e mezzo/mezza**
5:45	=	**le cinque e quarantacinque** or **le sei meno un quarto** or **le cinque e tre quarti** (*three quarters*)

QUICK PRACTICE 2

Give the time in all possible ways.

Modello: 3:45 P.M.

> **le tre e quarantacinque del pomeriggio/di pomeriggio**
> **le tre e tre quarti del pomeriggio/di pomeriggio**
> **le quattro meno quindici del pomeriggio/di pomeriggio**
> **le quattro meno un quarto del pomeriggio/di pomeriggio**
> **le quindici e quarantacinque**
> **le quindici e tre quarti**
> **le sedici meno quindici**
> **le sedici meno un quarto**

1. 1:10 P.M.

2. 2:15 P.M.

3. 3:20 A.M.

4. 4:30 A.M.

5. 5:40 P.M.

6. 6:45 A.M.

7. 7:50 P.M.

8. 8:59 A.M.

Time Expressions
Espressioni di tempo

Finally, as you can see, the following expressions will come in handy when talking about time.

Time Expressions	
il mezzogiorno	*noon/midday*
la mezzanotte	*midnight*
È mezzogiorno e un quarto.	*It's a quarter past noon.*
È mezzanotte e mezzo.	*It's half past midnight.*
il secondo	*second*
l'orologio	*watch, clock*
L'orologio va avanti.	*The watch is fast.*
L'orologio va indietro.	*The watch is slow.*
l'orario	*schedule*
preciso	*exactly*
È l'una precisa.	*It's exactly one o'clock.*
Sono le tre e mezzo precise.	*It's three-thirty exactly.*
in punto	*on the dot*
È l'una in punto.	*It's one o'clock on the dot.*
Sono le tre e mezzo in punto.	*It's three-thirty on the dot.*

Say the following in Italian.

1. It's midnight, according to my watch.
2. There are twenty seconds to go before noon. (Use **mancare** / *to be lacking*, i.e., "Twenty seconds are lacking to noon.")
3. My watch is fast, but I believe that the bus is on schedule.
4. It's exactly two P.M.
5. It is exactly one on the dot.
6. I think that your watch is slow.

PUTTING IT ALL TOGETHER

A. *Give alternative ways of saying each of the following.*

Modello: Di solito mi alzo alle sette precise.
   Di solito mi alzo alle sette in punto.

1. Sono le undici in punto.
2. Sono le dodici del pomeriggio.
3. Sono andato a dormire alle dodici di notte.
4. Siamo usciti alle nove e quindici.
5. Quel programma inizia alle sette e trenta.
6. Sono le dieci meno un quarto.

B. *Domande personali. Answer each question.*

1. A che ora ti alzi generalmente ogni giorno?
2. A che ora vai a dormire generalmente?
3. A che ora cominci a lavorare/studiare/ecc.?
4. A che ora finisci a lavorare/studiare/ecc.?
5. A che ora ceni generalmente?

C. Cruciverba!

Orizzontali

3. Sono le tre …
4. Sono le sette e tre …
6. Arrivano alle nove e un …
8. Il mio orologio va sempre …
9. Sono le otto … due minuti.

Verticali

1. Non vado mai a dormire prima di …
2. Sono le otto e … precise.
3. Sono le cinque in …
5. Il suo orologio va …
7. È l'… in punto.

17

Dates and the Weather

Days, Months, and Seasons
I giorni, i mesi e le stagioni

In order to be able to speak about dates, years, etc., you will need to know (or review) the words for the days of the week (**i giorni della settimana**), the months of the year (**i mesi dell'anno**), and the seasons (**le stagioni**).

Impara queste parole!

Days of the Week

lunedì	*Monday*
martedì	*Tuesday*
mercoledì	*Wednesday*
giovedì	*Thursday*
venerdì	*Friday*
sabato	*Saturday*
domenica	*Sunday*

Months of the Year		The Seasons	
gennaio	*January*	la primavera	*spring*
febbraio	*February*	l'estate	*summer*
marzo	*March*	l'autunno	*fall, autumn*
aprile	*April*	l'inverno	*winter*
maggio	*May*		
giugno	*June*		
luglio	*July*		
agosto	*August*		
settembre	*September*		
ottobre	*October*		
novembre	*November*		
dicembre	*December*		

Notice that the days are masculine, except for **domenica**, which is feminine. The formula *on Mondays, on Tuesdays,* etc. is rendered with the definite article:

il martedì / *on Mondays*
il sabato / *on Saturdays*
la domenica / *on Sundays*

Notice that the days and months are not capitalized (unless, of course, they are the first word of a sentence).

The preposition **di** is often used with a month to indicate something habitual or permanent.

Di febbraio andiamo spesso al mare. / *Every February we often go to the sea.*
Di maggio c'è sempre tanto sole. / *In May there is always lots of sunshine.*
Di settembre andiamo sempre via. / *In September we always go away.*

The preposition **a** is used to indicate that something will take place.

Verrò a giugno. / *I will come in May.*
Torneranno a luglio. / *They will return in July.*
Ci andiamo sempre a febbraio. / *We always go there in February.*

The preposition **tra (fra)** is used to convey *in how much time* something will be done or take place.

Maria andrà in Italia tra due mesi. / *Mary is going to Italy in two months time.*
Arriveremo fra otto ore. / *We will arrive in eight hours' time.*
Partiremo tra qualche minuto. / *We're leaving in a few minutes.*

The following expressions and ways of speaking will come in handy in common conversation.

Time Expressions	
prossimo	*next*
la settimana prossima	*next week*
il mese prossimo	*next month*
scorso	*last*
la settimana scorsa	*last week*
il mese scorso	*last month*
a domani, a giovedì, etc.	*till tomorrow, till Thursday, etc.*
domani a otto, domenica a otto, etc.	*a week from tomorrow, a week from Sunday, etc.*
il giorno	*the day*
la giornata	*the whole day (long)*
la sera	*the evening*
la serata	*the whole evening (long)*
oggi	*today*
ieri	*yesterday*
domani	*tomorrow*
avantieri	*the day before yesterday*
dopodomani	*the day after tomorrow*

QUICK PRACTICE 1

Choose the appropriate response.

1. È il giorno in cui si celebra il *Mardi Gras.*
   a. lunedì
   b. martedì

2. È il giorno tradizionalmente «del riposo».
   a. mercoledì
   b. domenica

3. È il giorno in cui tradizionalmente non c'è scuola.
   a. giovedì
   b. sabato

4. È un mese di primavera.
   a. aprile
   b. luglio

5. Per le persone superstiziose il tredici di questo giorno porta sfortuna.
   a. sabato
   b. venerdì

6. È un mese di estate.
   a. agosto
   b. ottobre

7. È un mese di autunno.
   a. settembre
   b. marzo

8. È un mese di inverno.
   a. giugno
   b. dicembre

9. È il mese di «San Valentino».
   a. febbraio
   b. gennaio

10. È il mese del Natale.
    a. gennaio
    b. dicembre

11. Di solito, vado in centro …
    a. sabato
    b. il sabato

12. Questo … non andrò in centro perché devo studiare molto.
    a. sabato
    b. il sabato

13. … andiamo spesso in vacanza.
    a. Di agosto
    b. Agosto

14. … andremo in Italia.
    a. A dicembre
    b. In dicembre

15. Partiremo … qualche giorno.
    a. tra
    b. in

16. Andremo al cinema la settimana …
    a. prossima
    b. scorsa

17. Siamo andati al cinema la settimana …
   a. prossima
   b. scorsa

18. Il mio compleanno è …
   a. oggi
   b. la serata

19. Non devi venire domani, ma …
   a. dopodomani
   b. avantieri

20. Arriveranno sabato a …
   a. otto
   b. giornata

Dates
La data

In addition to **Che giorno è?**, literally, *What day is it?* the following expression is also used to ask for the date.

Quanti ne abbiamo oggi? / *(literally) How many of them (= days of the month) do we have today?*
Ne abbiamo quindici. / *It's the fifteenth.*

If you want to find out the complete date (day, month, and, if needed, year), then you would ask:

Che data è? / *What date is it?*
È il ventuno settembre. / *It's September twenty-first.*

As a rule of thumb, use **Che giorno è?** unless you want specific information on the month or year.

Dates are expressed with the following formula:

Masculine definite article	Cardinal number	Month
↓	↓	↓
il	tre	maggio
il	quattro	aprile
il	ventitré	giugno
il	ventuno	settembre

Examples:

Oggi è il ventinove gennaio. / *Today is January 29.*
Oggi è il quindici settembre. / *Today is September 15.*
Oggi è lunedì, il sedici marzo. / *Today is Monday, March 16.*
Oggi è mercoledì, il quattro dicembre. / *Today is Wednesday, December 4.*

The exception to this formula is the first day of every month, for which you must use the ordinal number **primo**.

È il primo ottobre. / *It's October 1.*
È il primo giugno. / *It's June 1.*

Years are always preceded by the definite article.

È il 2006. / *It's 2006.*
Sono nato nel 1994. / *I was born in 1994.*

Notice also that the definite article is used with dates:

Il 1492 è un anno importante. / *1492 is an important year.*

However, in complete dates, the article is omitted before the year.

Oggi è il cinque febbraio, 2006. / *Today is February 5, 2006.*

QUICK
PRACTICE 2

Choose the answer that is grammatically correct.

1. Quando è nata?
   a. È nata il ventun settembre, 1998.
   b. È nata ventun settembre, 1998.

2. Quale anno è importante per gli Stati Uniti?
   a. Il 1776 è un anno importante per gli Stati Uniti.
   b. 1776 è un anno importante per gli Stati Uniti.

3. In che anno è nato tuo fratello?
   a. È nato nel 1994.
   b. È nato il 1994.

4. Che giorno è?
   a. È il primo ottobre.
   b. È l'uno ottobre.

5. Che data è?
   a. È il ventisette luglio.
   b. È ventisette luglio.

6. Quanti ne abbiamo?
   a. È ventuno.
   b. Ne abbiamo ventuno.

The Weather
Il tempo

Knowing how to talk about the weather is basic in any language. Here are frequently used weather expressions in Italian.

Che tempo fa?	How's the weather?
Fa bel tempo (verb: **fare**).	*It's beautiful (weather).*
Fa brutto (cattivo) tempo.	*It's bad (awful) weather.*
Fa caldo.	*It's hot.*
Fa freddo.	*It's cold.*
Fa molto caldo (freddo).	*It's very hot (cold).*
Fa un po' caldo (freddo).	*It's a bit hot (cold).*
Fa fresco.	*It's cool.*
Il caldo (freddo) è insopportabile.	*The heat (cold) is unbearable.*

Le previsioni del tempo	The Weather Forecast
Piove (verb: **piovere**).	*It is raining.*
Nevica (verb: **nevicare**).	*It is snowing.*
Tira vento (verb: **tirare**).	*It is windy.*
È nuvoloso.	*It is cloudy.*
la pioggia	*rain*
la neve	*snow*
il vento	*wind*
la grandine	*hail*
l'alba	*dawn*
il tramonto	*twilight*
il temporale	*storm*
il tuono (verb: **tuonare**)	*clap of thunder*
il lampo (verb: **lampeggiare**)	*flash of lightning*

Use the appropriate verb tense when referring to the weather in the past or the future.

Ieri pioveva. / *It was raining yesterday.*
Domani nevicherà. / *Tomorrow it will snow.*
La settimana scorsa faceva molto freddo. / *It was very cold last week.*
Quest'anno ha fatto bel tempo. / *This year the weather has been beautiful.*

When referring to climate conditions in general, use **essere** instead of **fare**:

In Sicilia l'inverno è sempre bello. / *Winter is always beautiful in Sicily.*
L'estate è fresca in Piemonte. / *Summer is cool in Piedmont.*

*Q*UICK
*P*RACTICE 3

Vero o falso?

____ 1. In estate nevica sempre in Florida.

____ 2. L'inverno è una stagione molto calda in Alaska.

____ 3. Quando fa bel tempo, ci cono molti lampi e molti tuoni.

____ 4. Quando fa brutto tempo, c'è il sole.

____ 5. Quando c'è la tempesta, di solito tira tanto vento.

____ 6. Nel Wisconsin usualmente fa freddo d'inverno.

____ 7. In autunno, fa generalmente un po' fresco nell'Italia settentrionale.

____ 8. In Florida il caldo è generalmente insopportabile d'estate.

____ 9. A dicembre non nevica mai in Canada.

____ 10. Quando è nuvoloso, molte volte c'è la pioggia.

____ 11. Quando fa bel tempo, c'è sempre la grandine.

____ 12. All'alba spunta il sole.

____ 13. Al tramonto, il sole scompare.

____ 14. A gennaio di solito fa caldo a Milwaukee.

____ 15. A gennaio di solito fa caldo a Miami.

*P*UTTING *I*T
*A*LL *T*OGETHER

A. *Quiz storico! Scegli la riposta giusta.*

1. Cristoforo Colombo partì dalla Spagna per le Americhe...
   a. il 3 agosto 1492.
   b. il 3 settembre 1592.
   c. il 3 luglio 1452.

2. Colombo raggiunse l'isola di San Salvador...
   a. il 12 ottobre 1592.
   b. il 12 ottobre 1492.
   c. il 22 ottobre 1529.

3. Due astronauti americani sono scesi sulla luna...
   a. il 20 luglio 1969.
   b. il 20 agosto 1979.
   c. il 20 aprile 1959.

4. Il telefono fu inventato in America dall'italiano Antonio Meucci...
   a. nel 1857.
   b. nel 1957.
   c. nel 1557.

5. Guglielmo Marconi riuscì a trasmettere messaggi a distanza senza l'aiuto dei fili...
   a. nel 1685.
   b. nel 1985.
   c. nel 1895.

6. L'americano Edison inventò la lampadina elettrica...
   a. nel 1960.
   b. nel 1579.
   c. nel 1879.

7. Negli Stati Uniti i fratelli Wright riuscirono a volare con un apparecchio a motore...
   a. nel 1703.
   b. nel 1903.
   c. nel 1945.

8. Il primo orologio fu costruito intorno al...
   a. 1360.
   b. 1660.
   c. 1860.

B. *Give the correct answer.*

1. È il primo mese dell'anno.

2. Ha 28 giorni.

3. Ha inizio il 21 marzo.

4. È l'ultimo mese dell'anno.

5. Ultimo giorno della settimana dedicato tradizionalmente al riposo.

6. È la stagione più calda in Italia.

7. È la stagione più fredda in Italia.

C. *In the word search puzzle there are 10 days and months in total. Find them.*

```
S  I  L  U  G  L  I  O  G  I  O  S  E  T  T  E  M  B  R  E  E
A  Q  A  S  E  D  I  A  B  C  D  E  F  G  H  U  N  G  F  D  S
B  Q  A  S  E  D  A  G  H  J  U  T  I  O  P  A  D  R  A  N  G
A  Q  D  S  E  A  P  R  I  L  E  I  Q  V  G  N  O  G  F  D  I
T  R  I  Y  U  I  C  D  R  A  N  R  U  V  G  T  T  R  A  N  U
O  A  C  S  E  C  A  L  D  O  O  U  E  V  G  O  T  R  A  N  G
A  S  E  4  5  R  D  R  A  N  R  M  S  V  G  C  O  G  D  G  N
C  A  M  T  A  R  D  O  M  E  N  I  C  A  R  C  B  I  U  S  O
E  B  B  E  E  E  D  R  A  N  R  E  O  V  G  I  R  A  A  D  F
D  B  R  E  E  W  A  B  C  D  E  F  G  H  B  E  E  C  B  R  T
F  C  E  E  M  A  G  G  I  O  T  I  O  P  F  L  O  C  A  D  F
V  D  A  U  U  A  A  B  C  D  E  F  G  A  G  O  S  T  O  R  T
```

18

Conversation Techniques

Quanto Sai Già? — How Much Do You Know Already? (?)

True or False?

_____ 1. **Buongiorno** can mean *Hello.*

_____ 2. **Buonasera** can mean *Good afternoon.*

_____ 3. **Buona giornata** can mean *Have a good day.*

_____ 4. **Buona serata** can mean *Have a good evening.*

_____ 5. **Buona notte** can mean *Have a good night.*

_____ 6. **Ciao** is a polite greeting.

_____ 7. **Arrivederci** is a polite greeting.

Basic Conversation
La conversazione di base

A *conversation* is a spoken exchange of thoughts, opinions, and feelings. Knowing how to converse involves knowing which words, phrases, expressions, and types of sentences apply to a given situation. By knowing grammar, you already know quite a bit about how to converse—for instance, you'll need interrogative words to ask questions; imperative verb forms to give commands; subjunctive tenses to express opinion, doubt, wishes, etc.

However, there are some aspects of communication that are purely formulaic or idiomatic. The following are a few common formulas that occur frequently in conversations.

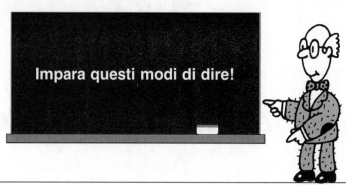

Impara questi modi di dire!

Saying Hello/Responding in Polite Speech

Buon giorno, signor Verdi, come va?	*Hello/Good morning Mr. Verdi, how's it going?*
Bene, grazie, e Lei?	*Well, thanks, and you?*
Buon pomeriggio, signora Verdi, come sta?	*Hello/Good afternoon, Mrs. Verdi, how are you?*
Non c'è male, grazie.	*Not bad, thanks.*
Buona sera, signora Rossi, come sta?	*Hello/Good evening, Mrs. Rossi, how are you?*
Abbastanza bene, grazie, e Lei?	*Quite well, thanks, and you?*

Saying Hello/Responding in Informal Speech

Ciao, come va?	*Hi, how's it going?*
Benissimo, e tu?	*Very well, and you?*
Salve, come stai?	*Greetings, how are you?*
Così, così.	*So, so.*

On the Phone

Pronto.	*Hello.*
Chi parla?	*Who's speaking?/Who is it?*
Con chi parlo?	*With whom am I speaking?*
Sono Dino Franceschi.	*This is Dino Franceschi.*
C'è il signor Marchi?	*Is Mr. Marchi there?*

Ending Conversations/Phone Calls

Buona giornata!	*Have a good day!*
Buona serata!	*Have a good evening!*
ArrivederLa (polite)!	*Good-bye!*
Arrivederci (familiar)!	*Good-bye!*
Ciao!	*Bye!*
A presto!	*See you soon!*
Ci vediamo!	*See you!*
A più tardi!	*See you later!*

In polite address, *hello* is expressed as **buon giorno**, also written as one word **buongiorno** until noon, as **buon pomeriggio** in the afternoon, and **buona sera**, also written as one word **buonasera**, in the evening. In familiar address, **ciao** is used at any time of the day.

When approached by waiters, store clerks, etc., you will often hear:

Desidera? (*sing.*) / **Desiderano?** (*pl.*) / *May I help you?*

When meeting, running into, and introducing people, the following expressions are essential to know.

Impara anche questi
modi di dire!

Meeting Someone

Come si chiama, Lei? *(pol.)*	*What is your name?*
Come ti chiami? *(fam.)*	*What's your name?*
Mi chiamo Mara Fratti.	*My name is Mara Fratti.*
Le presento la signora Gentile *(pol.).*	*Allow me to introduce you to Mrs. Gentile.*
Ti presento Alessandro Dini *(fam.).*	*Let me introduce you to Alexander Dini.*
Piacere di fare la Sua conoscenza *(pol.).*	*A pleasure to make your acquaintance.*
Piacere di fare la tua conoscenza *(fam.).*	*A pleasure to make your acquaintance.*
Scusi *(pol.).*	*Excuse me.*
Scusi *(fam.).*	*Excuse me.*
Permesso.	*Excuse me (used when making one's way through people).*
Grazie molto.	*Thanks a lot.*
Grazie mille.	*Thanks a million (literally "a thousand").*

QUICK
PRACTICE 1

Choose the appropriate phrase, sentence, etc.

1. Buongiorno, ..., come va?
   a. signor Verdi
   b. Marco

2. Come sta?
   a. Buonasera.
   b. Bene grazie, e Lei?

3. ... signor Rossi, come sta?
   a. Buon pomeriggio
   b. Ciao

4. ..., Marco, come stai?
   a. Buonasera
   b. Ciao

5. Maria, salve, ...?
   a. come sta
   b. come stai?

6. E tu come stai?
   a. Benissimo.
   b. Salve.

7. Pronto.
   a. Chi parla?
   b. Così, così.

8. Con chi parlo?
   a. Sono il professor Verdi.
   b. C'e il professor Verdi?

9. Arrivederci!
   a. Ciao!
   b. ArrivederLa!

10. Ci vediamo!
    a. Abbastanza bene!
    b. A presto!

11. ArrivederLa!
    a. Buona giornata!
    b. Desidera?

12. Come si chiama?
    a. Mi chiamo Franco Torelli.
    b. Si chiama Franco Torelli.

13. ..., devo uscire.
    a. Permesso
    b. Piacere

14. Scusa, come...?
    a. si chiama
    b. ti chiami

15. Ti presento Marco Stradivario.
    a. Piacere di fare la tua conoscenza.
    b. Piacere di fare la Sua conoscenza.

16. Le presento Maria Bernini.
    a. Piacere di fare la tua conoscenza.
    b. Piacere di fare la Sua conoscenza.

17. Ecco a Lei!
    a. Grazie mille.
    b. Permesso.

18. Ciao!
    a. Arrivederci!
    b. ArrivederLa!

Expressing Feelings
Esprimere i sentimenti

Expressing how you feel is another important communication technique. Here are some useful expressions to help you do so.

Surprise

Vero? / Davvero? / No!	*Really?*
Come?	*How come?*
Scherza? (*pol.*) / **Scherzi?** (*fam.*)	*Are you kidding?*
Incredibile!	*Unbelievable! / Incredibile!*

Agreement / Disagreement

Buon'idea!	*Good idea!*
D'accordo. / Va bene.	*OK.*
Non va bene.	*It's not OK.*
Non sono d'accordo.	*I don't agree.*

Pity / Resignation

Peccato.	*Too bad. / It's a pity.*
Mi dispiace.	*I'm sorry.*
Che triste!	*How sad!*
Non c'è niente da fare.	*There's nothing to do.*
Pazienza!	*Patience!*

Indifference / Boredom

Non importa.	*It doesn't matter.*
Per me è lo stesso.	*It's all the same to me.*
Fa lo stesso.	*It's all the same thing to me.*
Uffa!	*Exclamation similar to "Ugh!"*
Basta!	*Enough!*
Che noia!	*What a bore!*

QUICK
PRACTICE 2

Give the equivalent Italian expressions.

It doesn't matter. _____

It's all the same to me. _____

It's all the same thing to me. _____

Exclamation similar to "Ugh!" _____

Enough! _____

What a bore! _____

Too bad. / It's a pity. _____

I'm sorry. _____

How sad! _____

There's nothing to do. _____

Patience! _____

Good idea! _____

OK. _____

It's not OK. _____

I don't agree. _____

Really? _____

How come? _____

Are you kidding? _____

Unbelievable! / Incredible! _____

Speaking About Oneself
Parlare di sé

Obviously, you'll have to know how to talk about yourself in any given conversation. Here are a few tips.

Personal Data	
Mi chiamo…	*My name is…*
il nome	*first name/name in general*
il cognome	*surname/family name*
chiamarsi	*to be called*
Abito in via…, numero…	*I live at (number, street)*
l'indirizzo	*address*
la via	*street*
il corso	*avenue*
la piazza	*square*

Personal Data (continued)

Il mio numero di telefono...	*My phone number is...*
il telefono	*phone*
il numero telefonico	*phone number*
il prefisso	*area code*
formare/fare il numero	*to dial*
l'e-mail	*e-mail*
il sito personale	*personal Web site*
Ho...anni	*I am...years old*
la data di nascita	*date of birth*
il luogo di nascita	*place of birth*
l'età	*age*
Sono nato/a il 15 settembre	*I was born on September 15*
lo stato civile	*marital status*
sposato/a	*married*
celibe *(m)*/nubile *(f)*	*single, unmarried*
figli	*children*

QUICK PRACTICE 3

Supply the missing word from each statement.

1. Sono sposato e ho due _____.
2. Lui non è sposato. È ancora _____.
3. Il mio _____ di nascita è New York.
4. La mia _____ di nascita è il quattro dicembre.
5. Ho quarantacinque _____.
6. Il mio indirizzo _____ è n.franchi@simpatico.it.
7. Non ho ancora un _____ personale.
8. Ho fatto quel _____ già cinque volte, ma nessuno risponde.
9. Qual è il _____ di Roma? Devo telefonare alla mia amica.
10. Il suo numero _____ è 21-34-46.
11. Abito in _____ Donizetti, numero 14.

PUTTING IT ALL TOGETHER

A. *Do the following.*

Modello: Greet Mr. Verdi in the morning.
Buongiorno, signor Verdi.

Greet Mr. Verdi…

1. in the afternoon
2. in the evening

Ask him…

3. how he is
4. how it's going

Phone Mrs. Rossini…

5. saying hello
6. asking with whom you are talking
7. asking her if her daughter is in
8. wishing her a good evening

Say good-bye to Carlo…

9. in the morning
10. in the afternoon

Introduce…

11. Mr. Verdi to Mrs. Rossini
12. Carlo to Maria

Say that…

13. you're sorry
14. it doesn't matter
15. you agree

B. *Give the following information about yourself, by answering each question.*

1. Come ti chiami?

2. Dove abiti?

3. Qual e il tuo numero telefonico?

4. Qual è il tuo indirizzo e-mail?

5. Hai un sito personale?

6. Quanti anni hai?

7. Qual è la tua data di nascita?

8. Qual è il tuo luogo di nascita?

9. Qual è il tuo stato civile?

C. **Cruciverba!**

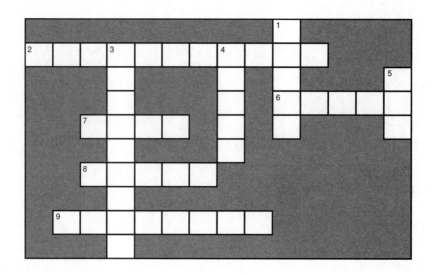

Orizzontali

2. … Marco. A più tardi.

6. … signora Verdi. Non La avevo vista.

7. … Maria, come va?

8. Grazie …!

9. …! Non c'è nente da fare.

Verticali

1. … Maria, Non ti avevo vista.

3. Qual è il tuo …?

4. Eccoti il mio indirizzo …

5. Abito in … Paganini.

19

Synonyms, Antonyms, and Cognates

> **Quanto Sai Già? — How Much Do You Know Already?**
>
> *Do you know...?*
>
> *Synonyms for:*
>
> 1. per piacere
> 2. adesso
> 3. l'abito
> 4. la strada
>
> *Antonyms for:*
>
> 5. buono
> 6. grande
> 7. alto
> 8. simpatico

Synonyms
I sinonimi

Synonyms are words or expressions that have the same or approximate meaning (for many intents and purposes). *Antonyms* are words or expressions that have an opposite, contrary, or contrastive meaning. Being able to relate words as synonyms or antonyms will help you learn and remember vocabulary.

Synonyms allow you to say the same thing in a different way, thus increasing your communicative competence. Keep in mind, however, that no two words or expressions have the exact same meaning in every situation.

English	Italian	Italian Synonyms
to ask	chiedere	domandare
crazy	pazzo	matto
dress/suit	l'abito	il vestito
face	la faccia	il viso
gladly	volentieri	con piacere
much/many/a lot	molto	tanto
near	vicino	presso
nothing	niente	nulla
now	ora	adesso
only	solo	solamente, soltanto
please	per piacere	per favore
quick(ly)	veloce(mente)	svelto
the same	lo stesso	uguale
slowly	lentamente	piano
street/road	la strada	la via
therefore	quindi	dunque, perciò
truly/really	veramente	davvero
to understand	capire	comprendere
unfortunately	purtroppo	sfortunatamente

As you know, the verbs **conoscere** and **sapere** both mean *to know*. But they are used in specific ways.

- *To know someone* is rendered by **conoscere**.

    Maria non conosce quell'avvocato. / *Mary doesn't know that lawyer.*
    Chi conosce la dottoressa Verdi? / *Who knows Dr. Verdi?*

- *To know how to do something* is rendered by **sapere**.

    Mia sorella sa pattinare molto bene. / *My sister knows how to skate very well.*
    Sai cucire? / *Do you know how to sew?*

- *To know something* is rendered by **sapere**.

    Marco non sa la verità. / *Mark doesn't know the truth.*
    Chi sa come si chiama quella donna? / *Who knows what that woman's name is?*

- *To be familiar with something* is rendered by **conoscere**.

    Conosci Roma? / *Are you familiar with Rome?*
    Conosco un bel ristorante qui vicino. / *I know a good restaurant nearby.*

In reference to *knowledge*, **sapere** implies complete knowledge; **conoscere**, partial knowledge, although the two are often used interchangeably.

Lo sai l'italiano? / *Do you know Italian?*
Conosco/So qualche parola. / *I know a few words.*

QUICK PRACTICE 1

Simply give the synonym of each of the following.

domandare _____

matto _____

il vestito _____

il viso _____

con piacere _____

tanto _____

presso _____

nulla _____

adesso _____

solamente, soltanto _____

per piacere _____

veloce(mente) _____

lo stesso _____

lentamente _____

la strada _____

quindi _____

veramente _____

capire _____

purtroppo _____

Antonyms

I contrari

Antonyms allow you to say the opposite or the counterpart of something. This type of knowledge will also increase your communicative competence. Keep in mind, however, that no two words have the exact opposite meaning in every situation.

Impara i contrari!

Italian	English	Italian Antonym	English Antonym
l'alba	*sunrise*	il tramonto	*sunset*
alto	*tall*	basso	*short*
aperto	*open*	chiuso	*closed*
l'atterraggio	*landing*	il decollo	*take-off*
bello	*beautiful*	brutto	*ugly*
bene	*well*	male	*bad*
bianco	*white*	nero	*black*
buono	*good*	cattivo	*bad*
chiaro	*clear, light*	scuro	*dark*
dentro	*inside*	fuori	*outside*
l'entrata	*entrance*	l'uscita	*exit*
facile	*easy*	difficile	*difficult*
magro	*thin, skinny*	grasso	*fat*
presto	*early*	tardi	*late*
pulito	*clean*	sporco	*dirty*
piccolo	*small*	grande	*big*
primo	*first*	ultimo	*last*
ricco	*rich*	povero	*poor*
simpatico	*nice, pleasant*	antipatico	*unpleasant*
spesso	*often*	mai	*never*
tanto, molto	*much, a lot*	poco	*little, a bit*
trovare	*to find*	perdere	*to lose*
tutto	*everything*	niente, nulla	*nothing*
vecchio	*old*	giovane	*young*
vendere	*to sell*	comprare	*to buy*
venire	*to come*	andare	*to go*
vicino	*near*	lontano	*far*
vuoto	*empty*	pieno	*full*

QUICK PRACTICE 2

Simply give the opposite of each of the following.

l'alba _____

l'atterraggio _____

bello _____

bianco _____

buono _____

dentro _____

l'entrata _____

facile _____

magro _____

presto _____

pulito _____

primo _____

ricco _____

simpatico _____

trovare _____

vecchio _____

vicino _____

vuoto _____

Cognates

Le voci di simile origine

Another good way to learn and remember vocabulary is to recognize *cognates*—Italian words that look very similar to English words because they are related in origin. They are, so to speak, "friends." But just like friends, they can be "true" or "false."

Cognates that have the same meaning are, of course, true friends. Generally speaking, true cognates can be recognized by their endings. Needless to say, you must always be wary of spelling differences!

English Endings	Cognate Italian Endings
-tion	**-zione**
action	l'azione
admiration	l'ammirazione
attention	l'attenzione
condition	la condizione
conversation	la conversazione
implication	l'implicazione
nation	la nazione
operation	l'operazione
-sion	**-sione**
conclusion	la conclusione
delusion	la delusione
occasion	l'occasione
tension	la tensione
-ty	**-tà**
city	la città
rarity	la rarità
society	la società
university	l'università
-ce	**-za**
appearance	l'apparenza
difference	la differenza
importance	l'importanza
violence	la violenza
-or	**-ore**
actor	l'attore
doctor	il dottore
professor	il professore
-ary	**-ario**
arbitrary	arbitrario
ordinary	ordinario
vocabulary	il vocabolario
-ist	**-ista**
dentist	il/la dentista
pianist	il/la pianista
tourist	il/la turista
violinist	il/la violinista

English Endings	Cognate Italian Endings
-logy	**-logia**
anthropology	**l'antropologia**
archeology	**l'archeologia**
biology	**la biologia**
psychology	**la psicologia**
zoology	**la zoologia**
-ical	**-ico**
typical	**tipico**
political	**politico**
practical	**pratico**
economical	**economico**
-al	**-ale**
animal	**l'animale**
central	**centrale**
social	**sociale**
special	**speciale**
-ect	**-etto**
correct	**corretto**
direct	**diretto**
perfect	**perfetto**
-ous	**-oso**
famous	**famoso**
generous	**generoso**
-phy	**-fia**
geography	**la geografia**
philosophy	**la filosofia**
photography	**la fotografia**

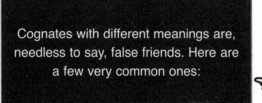

Cognates with different meanings are, needless to say, false friends. Here are a few very common ones:

English Word	False Friend	Correct Word
accident	**l'accidente** = *unexpected event*	**l'incidente**
argument	**l'argomento** = *topic (of discussion)*	**la discussione, la lite**
to assist	**assistere** = *to be present*	**aiutare**
brave	**bravo** = *good*	**coraggioso**
complexion	**la complessione** = *constitution of things*	**la carnagione**

conductor (musical)	il conduttore = bus/train conductor, driver	il direttore
to confront	confrontare = to compare	affrontare
contest	il contesto = context	il concorso
disgrace	la disgrazia = misfortune	la vergogna
effective	effettivo = actual	efficace
factory	la fattoria = farm	la fabbrica
firm	la firma = signature	la ditta, l'azienda
large	largo = wide	grande
lecture	la lettura = reading	la conferenza
magazine	il magazzino = warehouse, department store	la rivista
sensible	sensibile = sensitive	sensato
stamp	la stampa = the press	il francobollo

Do not assume that cognates have the same meanings. For example, the word **finalmente** means both *finally* and *at last*.

It is always wise to keep a good dictionary on hand to check for differences in meaning or usage!

QUICK PRACTICE 3

Choose the word that means the same as the English one.

1. accident
   a. accidente
   b. incidente
   c. violenza

2. stamp
   a. stampa
   b. francobollo
   c. apparenza

3. sensible
   a. rarità
   b. sensato
   c. sensibile

4. magazine
   a. magazzino
   b. tensione
   c. rivista

5. lecture
   a. occasione
   b. conferenza
   c. lettura

6. large
   a. grande
   b. largo
   c. delusione

7. argument
   a. discussione
   b. conclusione
   c. argomento

8. brave
   a. bravo
   b. coraggioso
   c. operazione

9. complexion
   a. complessione
   b. carnagione
   c. nazione

10. orchestra conductor
    a. implicazione
    b. conduttore
    c. direttore

11. to confront
    a. confrontare
    b. conversazione
    c. affrontare

12. factory
    a. fattoria
    b. fabbrica
    c. condizione

13. effective
    a. efficace
    b. effettivo
    c. attenzione

14. disgrace
    a. vergogna
    b. disgrazia
    c. ammirazione

15. to assist
    a. aiutare
    b. assitere
    c. azione

PUTTING IT ALL TOGETHER

A. *Say the following phrases in Italian.*

1. John doesn't know that lawyer.
2. Who knows a good doctor?
3. My brother knows how to play the piano very well.
4. Maria, do you know how to play tennis?
5. They don't know the truth.
6. Who knows what the instructor's name is?
7. I know Italy quite well.

B. *Say the same thing in an equivalent way.*

Modello: Lui lavora vicino a casa mia.
           Lui lavora presso casa mia.

1. Che cosa ti ha chiesto il professore?
2. Tu sei matta!
3. Che bel vestito che hai comprato!
4. Lei ha un bel viso.
5. Lo faccio con piacere.
6. Bisogna guidare molto piano in quella strada.
7. Dunque, che c'è di nuovo?
8. Non si capisce niente.

C. *Now, choose the word or expression with an opposite meaning.*

1. alto
   a. basso
   b. aperto

2. simpatico
   a. antipatico
   b. ricco

3. spesso
   a. mai
   b. tardi

4. presto
   a. tardi
   b. spesso

5. dentro
   a. mai
   b. fuori

6. bene
   a. chiuso
   b. male

7. bianco
   a. molto
   b. nero

8. vendere
   a. conoscere
   b. comprare

9. venire
   a. andare
   b. vicino

10. tutto
    a. tanto
    b. niente

D. *In the word search puzzle, you will find cognates of:*

1. actor
2. difference
3. arbitrary
4. ordinary
5. vocabulary
6. pianist
7. anthropology
8. psychology
9. typical
10. geography

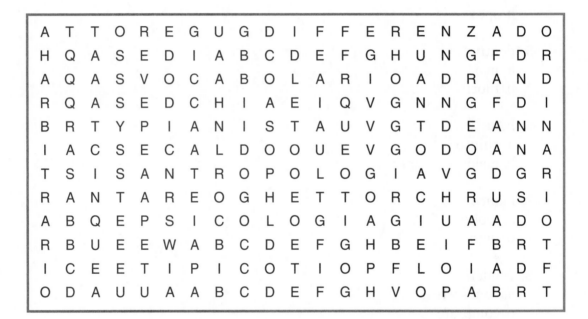

A	T	T	O	R	E	G	U	G	D	I	F	F	E	R	E	N	Z	A	D	O
H	Q	A	S	E	D	I	A	B	C	D	E	F	G	H	U	N	G	F	D	R
A	Q	A	S	V	O	C	A	B	O	L	A	R	I	O	A	D	R	A	N	D
R	Q	A	S	E	D	C	H	I	A	E	I	Q	V	G	N	N	G	F	D	I
B	R	T	Y	P	I	A	N	I	S	T	A	U	V	G	T	D	E	A	N	N
I	A	C	S	E	C	A	L	D	O	O	U	E	V	G	O	D	O	A	N	A
T	S	I	S	A	N	T	R	O	P	O	L	O	G	I	A	V	G	D	G	R
R	A	N	T	A	R	E	O	G	H	E	T	T	O	R	C	H	R	U	S	I
A	B	Q	E	P	S	I	C	O	L	O	G	I	A	G	I	U	A	A	D	O
R	B	U	E	E	W	A	B	C	D	E	F	G	H	B	E	I	F	B	R	T
I	C	E	E	T	I	P	I	C	O	T	I	O	P	F	L	O	I	A	D	F
O	D	A	U	U	A	A	B	C	D	E	F	G	H	V	O	P	A	B	R	T

20

Written Communication

Quanto Sai Già? — How Much Do You Know Already?

In the following sentences there are errors of punctuation, style, or spelling. Correct them.

1. loro abitano lontano
2. perche sei in ritardo
3. sono in ritardo perche avevo molto da fare
4. marco conosci maria
5. si la conosco

Punctuation
La punteggiatura

Punctuation is the use of marks and signs in writing and printing to separate words into sentences, clauses, and phrases in order to clarify meaning. For example, there are three ways to end a sentence:

With a period:	**Ho mangiato tutta la minestra.**
With a question mark:	**Chi ha mangiato tutta la minestra?**
With an exclamation mark:	**Maria, mangia tutta la minestra!**

A *comma* (**la virgola**) is used to indicate a separation of ideas or of elements within the structure of a sentence.

It is used…

- when more than one modifier is employed to describe a noun:

    Sara è alta, bella, e simpatica. / *Sara is tall, beautiful, and nice.*

- with introductory structures:

    Dopo aver lavorato tutto il giorno, io mi sento stanco. / *After working hard all day, I feel tired.*

- after interjections or before tags:

  Uffa, sono stanca! / *Heck, I'm tired!*
  Vieni anche tu, no? / *You're coming too, aren't you?*

- before and after transitional or parenthetical forms:

  Lui è, credo, assai vecchio. / *He is, I believe, rather old.*

- with direct quotations:

  «Chiamami», mi ha detto. / *"Call me," he said.*

- in dates with years:

  il 23 ottobre, 1958 / *October 23, 1958*

- after yes and no in responses:

  Sì, vengo anch'io. / *"Yes, I'm coming too."*

A *semicolon* is used to connect clauses in order to indicate a closer relationship between the clauses than a period does:

Leggere libri è importante; guardare la TV non lo è. / *Reading is important; watching TV is not.*

It is also used before a connecting word or expression such as *then, hence, that is, in fact, still, thus,* etc.:

Vorrei venire anch'io; comunque, sono al lavoro a quell'ora. / *I would like to come too; however, I am working at that time.*

A *colon* used after a word introduces a quotation, an explanation, an example, or a series.

Lui aveva un solo obiettivo nella sua vita: di giocare a calcio. / *He had only one goal in life: to play soccer.*
Lei ha detto: «Vengo anch'io». / *She said: "I am coming too."*

The *apostrophe* is used in Italian to form a few specific types of contractions, as you have seen in previous chapters.

anch'io = anche io
l'ha fatto = lo ha fatto

For the rules of capitalization, refer to Chapter 1.

Quick Practice 1

The following sentences lack all punctuation and capitalization. Rewrite them correctly.

1. maria e andata al negozio ieri
2. carlo dove sei andato ieri
3. state zitti
4. alessandro e alto intelligente e molto simpatico
5. ti piace la pizza non e vero
6. tua sorella e penso molto intelligente
7. telefonami stasera mi ha detto
8. verrebbe anche lui comunque non ha tempo

Letter Writing
Scrivere le lettere

    An important aspect of written communication is letter writing, whether traditional (mail-delivered) or electronic (e-mail). There are two main kinds of letters; *formal* (used when applying for a job, when writing to someone in authority, etc.) and *informal* (used when writing to friends, acquaintances, etc.).

    The main parts of a formal letter are shown below:

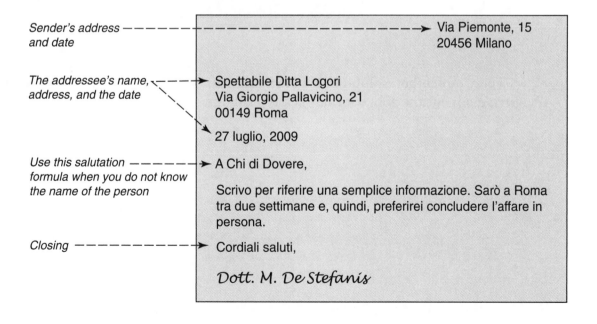

Notice that:

- The number is put after the street and the postal code before the city (this is standard practice in all kinds of letters and envelopes).
- **Spettabile...** is the formula used when writing to businesses, companies, etc.
- **A Chi di Dovere** is the equivalent of *To Whom It May Concern*.
- If the person is known then use: **Gentile...**
- There are other closings, but **"Cordiali saluti"** is the most common one.

The above format is a standard one. There are, of course, many variations.

The main parts of an informal letter are shown below:

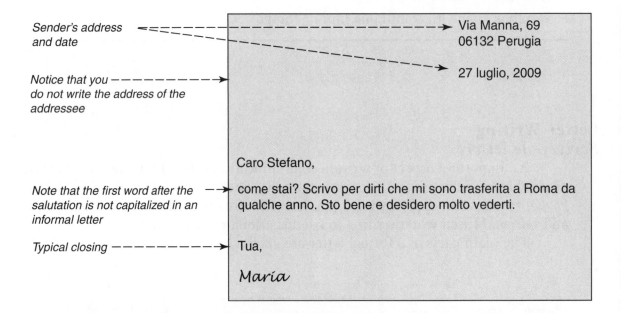

There are other salutations (**Carissimo/a**) and closings (**Un abbraccio, Auguri,** etc.), but the above format is a typical one.

Indicate (with a check mark ✔) if you think the salutation or greeting belongs to a formal or informal letter.

	FORMAL	INFORMAL
A Chi di Dovere		
Con i più cordiali saluti		
Ciao		
Gentile signor Brunetti		
Un abbraccio		
Il tuo amico		
Carissimo Marco		
Un bacione		
Con distinti saluti		

E-mails

Le e-mail

The parts of an e-mail are named as follows in Italian.

anna@dini.provider.it
↓   ↓   ↓↓   ↓   ↓
1   2   3 4   5   6

1	**nome utente**	*user name*
2	**chiocciola**	*at*
3/5	**nome di dominio**	*domain name*
4	**punto**	*dot*
6	**Italia**	*Italy*

And here is important computer vocabulary pertaining to the whole system of e-mailing.

Impara queste parole!

Allegato	*Attachment*
Elimina	*Delete*
Inoltra	*Forward*
Invia	*Send*
Nuovo messaggio	*New message*
Ricevi	*Receive*
Rispondi	*Reply*
Rubrica	*Addresses/Nicknames*
Stampa	*Print*
Trova	*Find*

QUICK
PRACTICE 3

Give the Italian equivalent of each of the following.

1. Print
2. •
3. @
4. maria.rossini
5. Find
6. Addresses
7. Reply
8. Receive
9. New message
10. Send
11. Delete
12. Attachment

**PUTTING IT
ALL TOGETHER**

A. *Set up a formal letter in Italian to the indicated person and address, given to you in English.*

1. Mr. Marco Verdi
2. who works for the **Banca Nazionale del Lavoro**
3. at **25 Via Nazionale, Rome 00194**

In it, indicate…

4. that you think there is a mistake in one of your accounts (**il conto** / *account*)
5. that you would like to set up a meeting (**un incontro**) as soon as possible

B. *Now, write an informal e-mail in Italian to your friend Maria Rossini. In it, indicate that you would like to ask her if she wants to go out with you this evening. Say that there is a magnificent new movie that you believe will be very enjoyable. After the movie suggest going to a coffee bar nearby to catch up on things.*

C. **Cruciverba!**

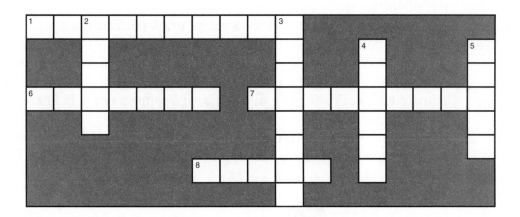

Orizzontali
1. @
6. delete
7. Nuovo …
8. •

Verticali
2. send
3. attachment
4. print
5. find

Culture Capsule 4

Geography
La geografia

L'Italia è una penisola che ha la forma di uno stivale. È situata al centro del Mar Mediterraneo ed è circondata dal Mar Adriatico, dal Mar Ionio, dal Mar Tirreno e dal Mar Ligure. La sua superficie è costituita per il 42% da colline, per il 35% da montagne e per il 23% da pianure.

Le catene di montagne più importanti sono le Alpi, gli Appennini e le Dolomiti. Il Monte Bianco è la montagna più alta. (4810 m di altezza). Il principale fiume italiano è il Po. Il Po è lungo 652 km e attraversa la città di Torino. Altri fiumi importanti sono l'Adige (che bagna le cittá di Trento e Bolzano), il Tevere (che attraversa Roma) e l'Arno (che attraversa Firenze e Pisa). Tra i laghi più famosi sono da menzionare il lago di Garda, il lago Maggiore e il lago di Como. Ci sono anche due vulcani, l'Etna in Sicilia e il Vesuvio vicino a Napoli.

Genova:	è il più importante porto italiano.
Torino:	è la sede della FIAT (Fabbrica Italiana Automobili Torino).
Milano:	è il più importante centro industriale e commerciale d'Italia.
Venezia:	è la città con oltre 120 isolotti (islets) e 170 canali collegati tra loro da più di 400 ponti.
Bologna:	è la città dove è nata nel 1158 la prima università europea.
Firenze:	è la culla della lingua italiana; in questa città è nato Dante Alighieri, il primo grande poeta in lingua italiana, autore della *Divina Commedia*.
Roma:	è la capitale d'Italia ed è una delle città più ricche di storia del mondo.
Napoli:	è una città ricca di storia e di cultura ed è famosa per le bellezze del suo paesaggio naturale.
Palermo:	è il capoluogo della Sicilia, la più grande e importante isola del Mediterraneo e la più grande regione d'Italia.

CONTENT QUESTIONS

Vero o falso? *Indicate whether each statement is true or false.*

_____ 1. L'Italia è una penisola che ha la forma di uno stivale.

_____ 2. È situata al centro del Mar Pacifico.

_____ 3. Le catene di montagne più importanti sono le Alpi, gli Appennini e le Dolomiti.

_____ 4. Tra i laghi più famosi c'è il lago di Garda.

_____ 5. Genova è il più importante porto italiano.

_____ 6. Bologna è la città dove è nata nel 1158 la prima università europea.

_____ 7. Roma è la capitale d'Italia.

The Most Frequently Used Words and Expressions in Italian

A

a	at
a che ora	at what time
a meno che	unless
a otto	a week from
a più tardi	later
a presto	see you soon
abbastanza	enough
abbracciare	to hug
abitare	to live
accendere	to turn on
l'acqua	water
addormentarsi	to fall asleep
adesso	now
affascinare	to fascinate, to be fascinating to
affinché	so that
affittare	to rent (a place)
africano	African
agosto	August
aiutare	to help
alcuni (-e)	some
gli alimentari	food (store)
allacciare	to fasten
allora	then, therefore, thus, so
alto	tall
altrimenti	otherwise
altro	other
alzarsi	to get up, to stand up
amare	to love
ambizioso	ambitious
americano	American
l'amica (l'amico)	friend
ammalarsi	to get sick
anche	also, too
ancora	yet, still

andare	to go
andarsene	to go away
l'anno	year
annoiarsi	to become bored
annunciare	to announce
l'annunciatore (m.), l'annunciatrice (f.)	TV announcer, host
ansioso	anxious
apparire	to appear
l'appartamento	apartment
appena	just (barely), as soon as
l'appetito	appetite
l'appuntamento	appointment, date
l'appunto	note
aprile	April
aprire	to open
arrabbiarsi	to become angry
arrivare	to arrive
arrivederci	good-bye (fam.)
arrivederLa	good-bye (pol.)
ascoltare	to listen to
aspettare	to wait for
assaggiare	to taste
assai	quite, rather
assicurare	to ensure
attento	careful
l'attenzione (f.)	attention
attrarre	to attract
attraversare	to cross
attuale	current
australiano	Australian
l'autobus (m.)	bus
l'automobile (f.)	automobile
l'autunno	autumn, fall
avere	to have
avere bisogno (di)	to need
avere caldo	to be hot

avere fame	to be hungry	il calcio	soccer
avere freddo	to be cold	caldo	hot, warm
avere fretta	to be in a hurry	calmo	calm
avere mal di...	to have a sore...	cambiare	to change
avere paura	to be afraid	cambiare idea	to change one's mind
avere ragione	to be right		
avere sete	to be thirsty	la camera	bedroom
avere sonno	to be sleepy	la camicetta	blouse
avere torto	to be wrong	la camicia	shirt
avere vergogna	to be ashamed	camminare	to walk
avere voglia (di)	to feel like	il campionato	championship
avere...anni	to be...years old	canadese	Canadian
l'avvocato	lawyer	cantare	to sing
		i capelli	hair (head)

B

		capire	to understand
baciare	to kiss	il capolavoro	masterwork
ballare	to dance	il cappuccino	cappuccino coffee
il bambino (la bambina)	child	la caramella	candy
		la carne	meat
la banca	bank	caro	dear
il bar	espresso bar	la carta	card
la barzelletta	joke	il cartone animato	cartoon
basso	short	la casa	house
bastare	to be sufficient, to suffice, to be enough	cattivo	bad
		il cellulare	cell phone
		la cena	dinner
il bel tempo	beautiful/nice weather	cercare	to look for, to search for
bello	beautiful, handsome	certo	certainly, of course
		che	that, which, who
benché	although	che, cosa, che cosa	what
bene	well, good	chi	who
bere	to drink	chiacchierare	to chat
bere alla salute	to drink to health	chiamare	to call
bere forte	to drink heavily	chiamarsi	to call oneself, to be named
biondo	blond		
bisogna che	it is necessary that	la chiamata	call
la bocca	mouth	chiedere	to ask
bravo	good	la chiromante	fortune-teller
brutto	ugly	chissà	who knows, I wonder
la bugia	lie		
buon divertimento	have fun	la chitarra	guitar
buongiorno	good day, good morning	chiudere	to close
		chiunque	whoever
buono	good	ci vediamo	see you later
		ciao	bye, hi (fam.)
		ciascuno	each one

C

		il cibo	food
cadere	to fall	il cinema	cinema, movies
il caffè	coffee		

cinese	Chinese	dare del tu	to be on familiar terms
la cintura di sicurezza	seatbelt	dare la mano	to shake hands
la città	city	dare un film	to show a movie
il cittadino (la cittadina)	citizen	dare via	to give away
		davvero	really, truly
la classe	class	decidere	to decide
il/la cliente (m./f.)	customer	decisione	decision
la cognata	sister-in-law	dedurre	to deduce
il cognato	brother-in-law	il/la dentista (m./f.)	dentist
la colazione	breakfast	desiderare	to want, to desire
come	how, like, as	deviare	to deviate
come va?	how's it going?	di	of
cominciare	to begin	di me	than I/me
la commessa, il commesso	store clerk	di nuovo	again
		di più	more, most
comporre	to compose	di solito	usually
comprare	to buy	dicembre	December
comprendere	to comprehend	digitale	digital
il computer	computer	dimenticarsi	to forget
comunicare	to communicate	dipingere	to paint
comunque	however	dire	to say, to tell, to speak
con	with		
conoscere	to know someone, to be familiar with	dire di no	to say no
		dire di sì	to say yes
		dire la verità	to tell the truth
contento	happy	dire una bugia/la bugia	to tell a lie, to lie
il conto	bill		
controllare	to control	dispiacere	to feel sorry
copiare	to copy	la ditta	company, firm
coprire	to cover	diventare	to become
correre	to run	divertimento	enjoyment, fun
cortese	courteous	divertirsi	to enjoy oneself, to have fun
cosa	thing		
così, così	so, so	dolce	sweet
costare	to cost	dolere	to be painful, to ache
costruire	to build, to make		
credere	to believe	la domanda	question
criticare	to criticize	domani	tomorrow
cucinare	to cook	domenica	Sunday
il cugino (la cugina)	cousin	la donna	woman
		dopo	after
D		dopo che	after (conjunction)
d'ora in poi	from now on	dormire	to sleep
da	from	dove	where
dappertutto	everywhere	dovere	to have to
dare	to give	dovunque	wherever
dare del Lei	to be on polite terms	dubitare	to doubt
		dunque	thus, therefore

durante	*during*	il formaggio	*cheese*
durare	*to last*	forse	*maybe*
		forte	*strong, heavily*
		fortunato	*fortunate, lucky*
E		fra	*within (equivalent*
e	*and*		*to **tra**)*
ecco	*here is, here are*	francese	*French*
elegante	*elegant*	il fratello	*brother*
entrare	*to enter*	frattempo	*meanwhile*
l'espresso	*espresso coffee*	il freddo	*cold*
esserci	*to be there*	fresco	*cool*
essere	*to be*	la frutta	*fruit*
essere d'accordo	*to agree*	i fumetti	*comic books*
l'estate (f.)	*summer*	fuori	*outside*
		il futuro	*future*
F			
fa	*ago*	**G**	
la faccenda	*house chore*	garantire	*to guarantee*
facile	*easy*	il generale	*general*
il fagiolo	*bean*	il genitore	*parent*
la famiglia	*family*	gennaio	*January*
famoso	*famous*	la gente	*people*
la fantascienza	*science fiction*	gentile	*kind*
fantastico	*fantastic*	già	*already*
fare	*to do, to make*	la giacca	*jacket*
fare del bene	*to do good (things)*	giapponese	*Japanese*
fare del male	*to do bad (things)*	giocare	*to play*
fare delle spese	*to shop (in*	il giocattolo	*toy*
	general)	il giornale	*newspaper*
fare il medico/	*to be a doctor/a*	la giornata	*day (all day)*
l'avvocato/...	*lawyer/...*	il giorno	*day*
farsi il bagno	*to take a bath*	giovane	*young*
farsi la barba	*to shave*	giovedì	*Thursday*
farsi la doccia	*to take a shower*	giù	*down*
il fatto	*fact*	giugno	*June*
febbraio	*February*	giusto	*right, correct*
la febbre	*fever, temperature*	lo gnocco	*dumpling*
felice	*happy*	godere	*to enjoy*
fermo	*still, motionless*	il gol	*goal*
la festa	*holiday, feast,*	la gola	*throat*
	party	la grammatica	*grammar*
la fidanzata, il	*fiancée, fiancé*	grande	*great, big*
fidanzato		grasso	*fat*
la figlia, il figlio	*daughter, son*	grazie	*thank you*
il film	*film, movie*	il guanto	*glove*
finalmente	*finally*	guardare	*to look at, to watch*
la fine	*end*	la guerra	*war*
finire	*to finish*		
fino a	*until*		

I

l'idea	idea
ieri	yesterday
ieri sera	last night
immaginare	to imagine
imparare	to learn
importante	important
importare	to be important, to matter
in	in
in giro	around
in orario	on time
in punto	on the dot
in ritardo	late
incontrarsi	to encounter
indicare	to indicate
indipendente	independent
indirizzo	address
indovinare	to guess
indurre	to induce
infatti	in fact
l'informatica	computer science
l'ingegnere (m./f.)	engineer
ingenuo	naïve, ingenuous
inglese (m.)	English
l'insegnante (m./f.)	teacher
insieme	together
intelligente	intelligent
interessante	interesting
interessare	to interest, to be interested by
introdurre	to introduce
invece	instead
inventare	to invent
l'inverno	winter
inviare	to send
invitare	to invite
l'invitato	guest
l'Italia	Italy
italiano	Italian

L

lamentarsi	to complain
la lampadina	lightbulb
lanciare	to throw
lasciare	to let, to leave (behind)
il latte	milk
lavare	to wash
lavarsi	to wash oneself
lavorare	to work
il lavoro	work, job
legare	to tie
leggere	to read
la lezione	class, lesson
lì	there
libero	free
il libro	book
la lingua	language
lo stesso	the same
luglio	July
la luna	moon
lunedì	Monday

M

ma	but
la macchina	car
la madre	mother
magari	perhaps
maggio	May
magro	skinny
male	bad, evil
Mamma mia!	Egad! (lit.: My mother!)
mancare	to lack, to miss
mangiare	to eat
la mano (le mani)	hand (hands)
il mare	sea, ocean
il marito	husband
martedì	Tuesday
marzo	March
la matita	pencil, crayon
il matrimonio	matrimony, wedding
la mattina	morning
il meccanico (la meccanica)	mechanic
il medico	doctor
il medioevo	medieval period
meglio	better
la mela	apple
il membro	member
meno	less, minus
mentre	while
mercoledì	Wednesday
il mese	month

il messaggio	message	oggi	today
messicano	Mexican	oggi come oggi	nowadays, these days
mettere	to put		
mettersi	to put on, to wear	ogni	every
la mezzanotte	midnight	olandese	Dutch
mezzo	half	l'opera	opera
il mezzogiorno	noon	opinione (f.)	opinion
migliore	better, best	l'ora	hour, time
la minestra	soup	ora	now
il minuto	minute	l'orologio	watch
mio	my	l'osso (le ossa)	bone (bones)
la moda	fashion	ottobre	October
il modo	manner, way	ovvio	obvious
la moglie	wife		
molto	very, much, a lot	**P**	
il mondo	world	il padre	father
morire	to die	il paese	country
la musica	music	pagare	to pay (for)
		la palla	ball
N		il panino	bun, sandwich
nascere	to be born	i pantaloni	pants
la nazione	nation	parcheggiare	to park
necessario	necessary	il/la parente	relative
negare	to deny	parlare	to speak
il negozio	store	la parola	word
nel caso che	in the event that	partire	to leave, to depart
nessuno	no one, nobody	la partita	game, match
la neve	snow	passare	to pass, to go by
nevicare	to snow	il passato	past
niente	nothing	la passeggiata	stroll, walk
il/la nipote (m./f.)	nephew, grandchild	la pasta	pasta, pastry
		la pasticca	lozenge
noleggiare	to rent (car, movie, etc.)	la pazienza	patience
		il peccato	sin, too bad, a pity
il nome	name	la penna	pen
non c'è di che	don't mention it	pensare	to think
non c'è male	not bad	per	for
la nonna	grandmother	per favore	please
il nonno	grandfather	perché	why, because, so that
nonostante	despite		
normale	normal	il pericolo	danger
novembre	November	però	but
il numero	number	la persona	person
nuovo	new	il pesce	fish
		il pezzo	piece
O		piacere	to be pleasing to, to like
o	or		
occupato	busy	il pianoforte	piano

il piatto	plate, dish	pulire	to clean
piccolo	small	punire	to punish
la pioggia	rain	purché	provided that
piovere	to rain	purtroppo	unfortunately
il pisello	pea		
più	more, plus	**Q**	
la poesia	poem	qualche	a few, some
poi	then	qualcosa	something
poiché	since	qualcuno	someone
il Polo Nord	North Pole	quale	which
il Polo Sud	South Pole	qualunque	whatever, whichever
il pomeriggio	afternoon		
porre	to pose, to put	quando	when
il portafoglio	wallet	quanto	how, how much
portare	to wear, to carry	il quarto	quarter
portatile	portable (laptop)	quasi	almost
possibile	possible	quello	that
il posto	place	questo	this
potere	to be able to	qui	here
povero	poor		
il pranzo	lunch	**R**	
preciso	exactly, precisely	la radio	radio
preferire	to prefer	il raffreddore	cold (illness)
preferito	favorite	la ragazza	girl, young female
pregare	to pray	il ragazzo	boy, young male
prego	you're welcome	rapido	rapid
il premio	prize	il/la regista	director
prendere	to take	regolare	regular
preoccuparsi	to worry	ricco	rich
preparare	to prepare	ricordarsi	to remember
prepararsi	to prepare oneself	ridere	to laugh
presto	early	ridurre	to reduce
prima	before	rimanere	to be left over, to remain
la primavera	spring		
probabile	probable	riposarsi	to relax
produrre	to produce	rispondere	to answer
il professore (la professoressa)	professor	la risposta	answer
		ristorante	restaurant
il programma	program	rivelare	to reveal
programmare	to plan	la rivista	magazine
promettere	to promise	il romanzo	novel
pronto	hello (answering the phone), ready	rompere	to break
pronunciare	to pronounce		
proprio	really	**S**	
prossimo	next (week, year, etc.)	sabato	Saturday
		salire	to climb, to go up
provarsi	to try on	salutarsi	to greet (one another)
lo psicologo	psychologist		

Italian	English	Italian	English
la salute	health	solo	only
sapere	to know something, how to do something	sopravvivere	to survive
		la sorella	sister
		gli spaghetti	spaghetti
la scala, le scale	stair, staircase	spagnolo	Spanish
la scarpa	shoe	specialmente	especially
scegliere	to choose	spedire	to send, to mail
sciare	to ski	sperare	to hope
la sciarpa	scarf	la spesa	food shopping
scoprire	to discover	spesso	often
scorso	last (week, month, etc.)	la spiaggia	beach
		spiegare	to explain
scrivere	to write	gli spinaci	spinach
lo scudetto	sports cup, prize	lo sport	sport
la scuola	school	sposarsi	to marry, to get married
scusa, scusi	excuse me (fam.), excuse me (pol.)	la squadra	team
scusarsi	to excuse oneself	squisito	delicious
se	if	stamani, stamane	this morning
sebbene	although	la stampa	printing, printing press
il secondo	second		
secondo	according to	stanco	tired
sedurre	to seduce	stare	to stay, to be
segnare	to score	stare per	to be about to
la segreteria telefonica	answering machine	stasera	tonight
		gli Stati Uniti	United States
sembrare	to seem	lo stile	style
semplice	simple	lo stivale	boot
sempre	always	la storia	story, history
sentire	to feel, to hear	la strada	road
sentirsi	to feel	strano	strange
senza	without	lo studente, la studentessa	student
la sera	evening		
sette	seven	studiare	to study
settembre	September	studioso	studious
la settimana	week	su	on
sicuro	sure	subito	right away
la signora	Mrs., Ms.	succedere	to happen
il signore	Mr., Sir	suonare	to play an instrument
la signorina	Ms., Miss		
simile	similar	svedese	Swedish
simpatico	nice, pleasant	svegliarsi	to wake up
il sintomo	symptom	svizzero	Swiss
smettere	to stop, to quit		
il soffitto	ceiling	**T**	
soffrire	to suffer	tanto	much, a lot
il sogno	dream	la tappa	stage
i soldi	money	tardi	late

tardo	late (adjective)	**V**	
la tasca	pocket	**va bene**	OK
tedesco	German	**la vacanza**	vacation
telefonare	to phone	**valere**	to be worth
telefonico	phone (adjectival)	**valere la pena**	to be worthwhile
il telefono	phone	**vaso**	vase
il telequiz	TV quiz show	**vecchio**	old
il telescopio	telescope	**vedere**	to see
il telespettatore	TV viewer	**veloce**	fast, quick
la televisione	television	**vendere**	to sell
televisivo	(of) television	**venerdì**	Friday
il televisore	television set	**venire**	to come
temere	to fear	**venti**	twenty
il tempo	time, weather	**il vento**	wind
tenere	to keep, to hold	**veramente**	truly
il termometro	thermometer	**il verbo**	verb
la testa	head	**la verdura**	vegetables, greens
il tipo	type	**vergognarsi**	to be ashamed
tirare vento	to be windy	**la verità**	truth
tornare	to go back, to return	**vero**	true
la torta	cake	**verso**	around, toward
tra	in, within	**vestirsi**	to get dressed
tra poco	in a little while	**il vestito**	dress, suit
tra qualche minuto	in a few minutes	**via**	street
tradurre	to translate	**viaggiare**	to travel
trarre	to draw (pull)	**vicino a**	near
traslocare	to move (residence)	**vincere**	to win
		il vino	wine
triste	sad	**il violino**	violin
troppo	too much	**il violoncello**	cello
trovare (trovarsi)	to find (to find oneself)	**la visita**	visit
		visitare	to visit
tuo	your (fam., sing.)	**la vita**	life
il/la turista (m./f.)	tourist	**vivace**	lively, active
tutti (tutte)	everyone	**vivere**	to live
tutto	everything, entire, whole	**la voglia**	desire, urge
		volentieri	gladly
		volere	to want to
		la volta	time, occasion
U			
ultimo	last	**Z**	
un po'	a bit	**la zia**	aunt
unire	to unite	**lo zio**	uncle
l'università (f.)	university	**zitto**	quiet
l'uomo (gli uomini)	man (men)		
usare	to use		
uscire	to go out		

Verb Charts

accadere (conjugated like **cadere**)

accendere
Past Participle	acceso
Past Absolute	(io) accesi, (tu) accendesti, (Lei) accese, (lui/lei) accese, (noi) accendemmo, (voi) accendeste, (loro) accesero

accludere (conjugated like **concludere**)

aggiungere (conjugated like **piangere**)

alludere (conjugated like **concludere**)

ammettere (conjugated like **mettere**)

andare
Present Indicative	(io) vado, (tu) vai, (Lei) va, (lui/lei) va, (noi) andiamo, (voi) andate, (loro) vanno
Future	(io) andrò, (tu) andrai, (Lei) andrà, (lui/lei) andrà, (noi) andremo, (voi) andrete, (loro) andranno
Conditional	(io) andrei, (tu) andresti, (Lei) andrebbe, (lui/lei) andrebbe, (noi) andremmo, (voi) andreste, (loro) andrebbero
Present Subjunctive	(io) vada (tu) vada, (Lei) vada, (lui/lei) vada, (noi) andiamo, (voi) andiate, (loro) vadano
Imperative	(tu) va', (Lei) vada, (noi) andiamo, (voi) andate, (Loro) vadano

apprendere (conjugated like **prendere**)

aprire
Past Participle	aperto

assolvere (conjugated like **risolvere**)

assumere
Past Participle	assunto
Past Absolute	(io) assunsi, (tu) assumesti, (Lei) assunse, (lui/lei) assunse, (noi) assumemmo, (voi) assumeste, (loro) assunsero

astrarre

Present Indicative	(io) astraggo, (tu) astrai, (Lei) astrae, (lui/lei) astrae, (noi) astraiamo, (voi) astraete, (loro) astraggono
Past Participle	astratto
Imperfect	(io) astraevo, (tu) astraevi, (Lei) astraeva, (lui/lei) astraeva, (noi) astraevamo, (voi) astraevate, (loro) astraevano
Past Absolute	(io) astrassi, (tu) astraesti, (Lei) astrasse, (lui/lei) astrasse, (noi) astraemmo, (voi) astraeste, (loro) astrassero
Present Subjunctive	(io) astragga, (tu) astragga, (Lei) astragga, (lui/lei) astragga, (noi) astraiamo, (voi) astraiate, (loro) astraggano
Imperfect Subjunctive	(io) astraessi, (tu) astraessi, (Lei) astraesse, (lui/lei) astraesse, (noi) astraessimo, (voi) astraeste, (loro) astraessero
Imperative	(tu) astrai, (Lei) astragga, (noi) astraiamo, (voi) astraete, (Loro) astraggano
Gerund	astraendo

attendere

Past Participle	atteso
Past Absolute	(io) attesi, (tu) attendesti, (Lei) attese, (lui/lei) attese, (noi) attendemmo, (voi) attendeste, (loro) attesero

avere

Present Indicative	(io) ho, (tu) hai, (Lei) ha, (lui/lei) ha, (noi) abbiamo, (voi) avete, (loro) hanno
Past Absolute	(io) ebbi, (tu) avesti, (Lei) ebbe, (lui/lei) ebbe, (noi) avemmo, (voi) aveste, (loro) ebbero
Future	(io) avrò, (tu) avrai, (Lei) avrà, (lui/lei) avrà, (noi) avremo, (voi) avrete, (loro) avranno
Conditional	(io) avrei, (tu) avresti, (Lei) avrebbe, (lui/lei) avrebbe, (noi) avremmo, (voi) avreste, (loro) avrebbero
Present Subjunctive	(io) abbia (tu) abbia, (Lei) abbia, (lui/lei) abbia, (noi) abbiamo, (voi) abbiate, (loro) abbiano
Imperative	(tu) abbi, (Lei) abbia, (noi) abbiamo, (voi) abbiate, (Loro) abbiano

avvenire (conjugated like **venire**)

benedire (conjugated like **dire**)

bere

Present Indicative	(io) bevo, (tu) bevi, (Lei) beve, (lui/lei) beve, (noi) beviamo, (voi) bevete, (loro) bevono
Past Participle	bevuto
Past Absolute	(io) bevvi (bevetti), (tu) bevesti, (Lei) bevve (bevette), (lui/lei) bevve (bevette), (noi) bevemmo, (voi) beveste, (loro) bevvero (bevettero)
Future	(io) berrò, (tu) berrai, (Lei) berrà, (lui/lei) berrà, (noi) berremo, (voi) berrete, (loro) berranno

Conditional	(io) berrei, (tu) berresti, (Lei) berrebbe, (lui/lei) berrebbe, (noi) berremmo, (voi) berreste, (loro) berrebbero
Present Subjunctive	(io) beva, (tu) beva, (Lei) beva, (lui/lei) beva, (noi) beviamo, (voi) beviate, (loro) bevano
Imperfect	(io) bevevo, (tu) bevevi, (Lei) beveva, (lui/lei) beveva, (noi) bevevamo, (voi) bevevate, (loro) bevevano
Imperative	(tu) bevi, (Lei) beva, (noi) beviamo, (voi) bevete, (Loro) bevano
Gerund	bevendo

cadere

Past Absolute	(io) caddi, (tu) cadesti, (Lei) cadde, (lui/lei) cadde, (noi) cademmo, (voi) cadeste, (loro) caddero
Future	(io) cadrò, (tu) cadrai, (Lei) cadrà, (lui/lei) cadrà, (noi) cadremo, (voi) cadrete, (loro) cadranno
Conditional	(io) cadrei, (tu) cadresti, (Lei) cadrebbe, (lui/lei) cadrebbe, (noi) cadremmo, (voi) cadreste, (loro) cadrebbero
Present Subjunctive	(io) cada, (tu) cada, (Lei) cada, (lui/lei) cada, (noi) cadiamo, (voi) cadiate, (loro) cadano

chiedere

Past Participle	chiesto
Past Absolute	(io) chiesi, (tu) chiedesti, (Lei) chiese, (lui/lei) chiese, (noi) chiedemmo, (voi) chiedeste, (loro) chiesero

chiudere

Past Participle	chiuso
Past Absolute	(io) chiusi, (tu) chiudesti, (Lei) chiuse, (lui/lei) chiuse, (noi) chiudemmo, (voi) chiudeste, (loro) chiusero

comporre (conjugated like **porre**)

comprendere (conjugated like **prendere**)

concludere

Past Participle	concluso
Past Absolute	(io) conclusi, (tu) concludesti, (Lei) concluse, (lui/lei) concluse, (noi) concludemmo, (voi) concludeste, (loro) conclusero

concorrere (conjugated like **correre**)

conoscere

Past Absolute	(io) conobbi, (tu) conoscesti, (Lei) conobbe, (lui/lei) conobbe, (noi) conoscemmo, (voi) conosceste, (loro) conobbero

contenere (conjugated like **tenere**)

contraddire (conjugated like **dire**)

convincere (conjugated like **vincere**)

convivere (conjugated like **vivere**)

correggere
Past Participle	corretto
Past Absolute	(io) corressi, (tu) correggesti, (Lei) corresse, (lui/lei) corresse, (noi) correggemmo, (voi) correggeste, (loro) corressero

correre
Past Participle	corso
Past Absolute	(io) corsi, (tu) corresti, (Lei) corse, (lui/lei) corse, (noi) corremmo, (voi) correste, (loro) corsero

crescere
Past Absolute	(io) crebbi, (tu) crescesti, (Lei) crebbe, (lui/lei) crebbe, (noi) crescemmo, (voi) cresceste, (loro) crebbero

cuocere
Past Participle	cotto
Past Absolute	(io) cossi, (tu) cocesti, (Lei) cosse, (lui/lei) cosse, (noi) cocemmo, (voi) coceste, (loro) cossero

dare
Present Indicative	(io) do, (tu) dai, (Lei) dà, (lui/lei) dà, (noi) diamo, (voi) date, (loro) danno
Past Participle	dato
Imperfect	(io) davo, (tu) davi, (Lei) dava, (lui/lei) dava, (noi) davamo, (voi) davate, (loro) davano
Past Absolute	(io) diedi, (tu) desti, (Lei) diede, (lui/lei) diede, (noi) demmo, (voi) deste, (loro) diedero
Future	(io) darò, (tu) darai, (Lei) darà, (lui/lei) darà, (noi) daremo, (voi) darete, (loro) daranno
Conditional	(io) darei, (tu) daresti, (Lei) darebbe, (lui/lei) darebbe, (noi) daremmo, (voi) dareste, (loro) darebbero
Present Subjunctive	(io) dia, (tu) dia, (Lei) dia, (lui/lei) dia, (noi) diamo, (voi) diate, (loro) diano
Imperfect Subjunctive	(io) dessi, (tu) dessi, (Lei) desse, (lui/lei) desse, (noi) dessimo, (voi) deste, (loro) dessero
Imperative	(tu) da', (Lei) dia, (noi) diamo, (voi) date, (Loro) diano
Gerund	dando

darsi (conjugated like **dare**)

decidere
Past Participle	deciso
Past Absolute	(io) decisi, (tu) decidesti, (Lei) decise, (lui/lei) decise, (noi) decidemmo, (voi) decideste, (loro) decisero

deludere (conjugated like **concludere**)

deporre (conjugated like **porre**)

descrivere (conjugated like **scrivere**)

detenere (conjugated like **tenere**)

difendere
Past Participle	difeso
Past Absolute	(io) difesi, (tu) difendesti, (Lei) difese, (lui/lei) difese, (noi) difendemmo, (voi) difendeste, (loro) difesero

difendersi (conjugated like **difendere**)

diffondere
Past Participle	diffuso
Past Absolute	(io) diffusi, (tu) diffondesti, (Lei) diffuse, (lui/lei) diffuse, (noi) diffondemmo, (voi) diffondeste, (loro) diffusero

dipingere
Past Participle	dipinto
Past Absolute	(io) dipinsi, (tu) dipingesti, (Lei) dipinse, (lui/lei) dipinse, (noi) dipingemmo, (voi) dipingeste, (loro) dipinsero

dire
Present Indicative	(io) dico, (tu) dici, (Lei) dice, (lui/lei) dice, (noi) diciamo, (voi) dite, (loro) dicono
Past Participle	detto
Imperfect	(io) dicevo, (tu) dicevi, (Lei) diceva, (lui/lei) diceva, (noi) dicevamo, (voi) dicevate, (loro) dicevano
Past Absolute	(io) dissi, (tu) dicesti, (Lei) disse, (lui/lei) disse, (noi) dicemmo, (voi) diceste, (loro) dissero
Future	(io) dirò, (tu) dirai, (Lei) dirà, (lui/lei) dirà, (noi) diremo, (voi) direte, (loro) diranno
Conditional	(io) direi, (tu) diresti, (Lei) direbbe, (lui/lei) direbbe, (noi) diremmo, (voi) direste, (loro) direbbero
Present Subjunctive	(io) dica, (tu) dica, (Lei) dica, (lui/lei) dica, (noi) diciamo, (voi) diciate, (loro) dicano
Imperfect Subjunctive	(io) dicessi, (tu) dicessi, (Lei) dicesse, (lui/lei) dicesse, (noi) dicessimo, (voi) diceste, (loro) dicessero
Imperative	(tu) di', (Lei) dica, (noi) diciamo, (voi) dite, (Loro) dicano
Gerund	dicendo

discutere
Past Participle	discusso
Past Absolute	(io) discussi, (tu) discutesti, (Lei) discusse, (lui/lei) discusse, (noi) discutemmo, (voi) discuteste, (loro) discussero

dissuadere (conjugated like **persuadere**)

distruggere

Past Participle	distrutto
Past Absolute	(io) distrussi, (tu) distruggesti, (Lei) distrusse, (lui/lei) distrusse, (noi) distruggemmo, (voi) distruggeste, (loro) distrussero

dividere

Past Participle	diviso
Past Absolute	(io) divisi, (tu) dividesti, (Lei) divise, (lui/lei) divise, (noi) dividemmo, (voi) divideste, (loro) divisero

dovere

Present Indicative	(io) devo, (tu) devi, (Lei) deve, (lui/lei) deve, (noi) dobbiamo, (voi) dovete, (loro) devono
Future	(io) dovrò, (tu) dovrai, (Lei) dovrà, (lui/lei) dovrà, (noi) dovremo, (voi) dovrete, (loro) dovranno
Conditional	(io) dovrei, (tu) dovresti, (Lei) dovrebbe, (lui/lei) dovrebbe, (noi) dovremmo, (voi) dovreste, (loro) dovrebbero
Present Subjunctive	(io) deva (debba), (tu) deva (debba), (Lei) deva (debba), (lui/lei) deva (debba), (noi) dobbiamo, (voi) dobbiate, (loro) devano (debbano)

eleggere (conjugated like **leggere**)

emettere (conjugated like **mettere**)

espandere

Past Participle	espanso
Past Absolute	(io) espansi, (tu) espandesti, (Lei) espanse, (lui/lei) espanse, (noi) espandemmo, (voi) espandeste, (loro) espansero

esprimere

Past Participle	espresso
Past Absolute	(io) espressi, (tu) esprimesti, (Lei) espresse, (lui/lei) espresse, (noi) esprimemmo, (voi) esprimeste, (loro) espressero

esprimersi (conjugated like **esprimere**)

essere

Present Indicative	(io) sono, (tu) sei, (Lei) è, (lui/lei) è, (noi) siamo, (voi) siete, (loro) sono
Past Participle	stato
Imperfect	(io) ero, (tu) eri, (Lei) era, (lui/lei) era, (noi) eravamo, (voi) eravate, (loro) erano
Past Absolute	(io) fui, (tu) fosti, (Lei) fu, (lui/lei) fu, (noi) fummo, (voi) foste, (loro) furono
Future	(io) sarò, (tu) sarai, (Lei) sarà, (lui/lei) sarà, (noi) saremo, (voi) sarete, (loro) saranno

Conditional	(io) sarei, (tu) saresti, (Lei) sarebbe, (lui/lei) sarebbe, (noi) saremmo, (voi) sareste, (loro) sarebbero
Present Subjunctive	(io) sia, (tu) sia, (Lei) sia, (lui/lei) sia, (noi) siamo, (voi) siate, (loro) siano
Imperfect Subjunctive	(io) fossi, (tu) fossi, (Lei) fosse, (lui/lei) fosse, (noi) fossimo, (voi) foste, (loro) fossero
Imperative	(tu) sii, (Lei) sia, (noi) siamo, (voi) siate, (Loro) siano

estinguere

Past Participle	estinto
Past Absolute	(io) estinsi, (tu) estinguesti, (Lei) estinse, (lui/lei) estinse, (noi) estinguemmo, (voi) estingueste, (loro) estinsero

estrarre (conjugated like **astrarre**)

fare

Present Indicative	(io) faccio, (tu) fai, (Lei) fa, (lui/lei) fa, (noi) facciamo, (voi) fate, (loro) fanno
Past Participle	fatto
Imperfect	(io) facevo, (tu) facevi, (Lei) faceva, (lui/lei) faceva, (noi) facevamo, (voi) facevate, (loro) facevano
Past Absolute	(io) feci, (tu) facesti, (Lei) fece, (lui/lei) fece, (noi) facemmo, (voi) faceste, (loro) fecero
Future	(io) farò, (tu) farai, (Lei) farà, (lui/lei) farà, (noi) faremo, (voi) farete, (loro) faranno
Conditional	(io) farei, (tu) faresti, (Lei) farebbe, (lui/lei) farebbe, (noi) faremmo, (voi) fareste, (loro) farebbero
Present Subjunctive	(io) faccia, (tu) faccia, (Lei) faccia, (lui/lei) faccia, (noi) facciamo, (voi) facciate, (loro) facciano
Imperfect Subjunctive	(io) facessi, (tu) facessi, (Lei) facesse, (lui/lei) facesse, (noi) facessimo, (voi) faceste, (loro) facessero
Imperative	(tu) fa', (Lei) faccia, (noi) facciamo, (voi) fate, (Loro) facciano
Gerund	facendo

farsi (conjugated like **fare**)

fondere

Past Participle	fuso
Past Absolute	(io) fusi, (tu) fondesti, (Lei) fuse, (lui/lei) fuse, (noi) fondemmo, (voi) fondeste, (loro) fusero

friggere

Past Participle	fritto
Past Absolute	(io) frissi, (tu) friggesti, (Lei) frisse, (lui/lei) frisse, (noi) friggemmo, (voi) friggeste, (loro) frissero

indurre (conjugated like **riprodurre**)

interrompere (conjugated like **rompere**)

leggere
- *Past Participle*   letto
- *Past Absolute*   (io) lessi, (tu) leggesti, (Lei) lesse, (lui/lei) lesse, (noi) leggemmo, (voi) leggeste, (loro) lessero

maledire (conjugated like **dire**)

mettere
- *Past Participle*   messo
- *Past Absolute*   (io) misi, (tu) mettesti, (Lei) mise, (lui/lei) mise, (noi) mettemmo, (voi) metteste, (loro) misero

mettersi (conjugated like **mettere**)

morire
- *Present Indicative*   (io) muoio, (tu) muori, (Lei) muore, (lui/lei) muore, (noi) moriamo, (voi) morite, (loro) muoiono
- *Past Participle*   morto
- *Present Subjunctive*   (io) muoia, (tu) muoia, (Lei) muoia, (lui/lei) muoia, (noi) moriamo, (voi) morite, (loro) muoiano

muovere
- *Past Participle*   mosso
- *Past Absolute*   (io) mossi, (tu) movesti, (Lei) mosse, (lui/lei) mosse, (noi) movemmo, (voi) moveste, (loro) mossero

muoversi (conjugated like **muovere**)

nascere
- *Past Participle*   nato
- *Past Absolute*   (io) nacqui, (tu) nascesti, (Lei) nacque, (lui/lei) nacque, (noi) nascemmo, (voi) nasceste, (loro) nacquero

offendere
- *Past Participle*   offeso
- *Past Absolute*   (io) offesi, (tu) offendesti, (Lei) offese, (lui/lei) offese, (noi) offendemmo, (voi) offendeste, (loro) offesero

offrire
- *Past Participle*   offerto

ottenere (conjugated like **tenere**)

perdere
- *Past Participle*   perso
- *Past Absolute*   (io) persi, (tu) perdesti, (Lei) perse, (lui/lei) perse, (noi) perdemmo, (voi) perdeste, (loro) persero

persuadere

Past Participle	persuaso
Past Absolute	(io) persuasi, (tu) persuadesti, (Lei) persuase, (lui/lei) persuase, (noi) persuademmo, (voi) persuadeste, (loro) persuasero

piacere

Present Indicative	(io) piaccio, (tu) piaci, (Lei) piace, (lui/lei) piace, (noi) piacciamo, (voi) piacete, (loro) piacciono
Past Absolute	(io) piacqui, (tu) piacesti, (Lei) piacque, (lui/lei) piacque, (noi) piacemmo, (voi) piaceste, (loro) piacquero
Present Subjunctive	(io) piaccia, (tu) piaccia, (Lei) piaccia, (lui/lei) piaccia, (noi) piacciamo, (voi) piacciate, (loro) piacciano

piangere

Past Participle	pianto
Past Absolute	(io) piansi, (tu) piangesti, (Lei) pianse, (lui/lei) pianse, (noi) piangemmo, (voi) piangeste, (loro) piansero

porre

Present Indicative	(io) pongo, (tu) poni, (Lei) pone, (lui/lei) pone, (noi) poniamo, (voi) ponete, (loro) pongono
Past Participle	posto
Imperfect	(io) ponevo, (tu) ponevi, (Lei) poneva, (lui/lei) poneva, (noi) ponevamo, (voi) ponevate, (loro) ponevano
Past Absolute	(io) posi, (tu) ponesti, (Lei) pose, (lui/lei) pose, (noi) ponemmo, (voi) poneste, (loro) posero
Future	(io) porrò, (tu) porrai, (Lei) porrà, (lui/lei) porrà, (noi) porremo, (voi) porrete, (loro) porranno
Conditional	(io) porrei, (tu) porresti, (Lei) porrebbe, (lui/lei) porrebbe, (noi) porremmo, (voi) porreste, (loro) porrebbero
Present Subjunctive	(io) ponga, (tu) ponga, (Lei) ponga, (lui/lei) ponga, (noi) poniamo, (voi) poniate, (loro) pongano
Imperfect Subjunctive	(io) ponessi, (tu) ponessi, (Lei) ponesse, (lui/lei) ponesse, (noi) ponessimo, (voi) poneste, (loro) ponessero
Imperative	(tu) poni, (Lei) ponga, (noi) poniamo, (voi) ponete, (Loro) pongano
Gerund	ponendo

potere

Present Indicative	(io) posso, (tu) puoi, (Lei) può, (lui/lei) può, (noi) possiamo, (voi) potete, (loro) possono
Future	(io) potrò, (tu) potrai, (Lei) potrà, (lui/lei) potrà, (noi) potremo, (voi) potrete, (loro) potranno
Conditional	(io) potrei, (tu) potresti, (Lei) potrebbe, (lui/lei) potrebbe, (noi) potremmo, (voi) potreste, (loro) potrebbero
Present Subjunctive	(io) possa, (tu) possa, (Lei) possa, (lui/lei) possa, (noi) possiamo, (voi) possiate, (loro) possano

prendere
Past Participle　preso
Past Absolute　(io) presi, (tu) prendesti, (Lei) prese, (lui/lei) prese, (noi) prendemmo, (voi) prendeste, (loro) presero

prescrivere (conjugated like **scrivere**)

promettere (conjugated like **mettere**)

proporre (conjugated like **porre**)

proteggere
Past Participle　protetto
Past Absolute　(io) protessi, (tu) proteggesti, (Lei) protesse, (lui/lei) protesse, (noi) proteggemmo, (voi) proteggeste, (loro) protessero

pungere
Past Participle　punto
Past Absolute　(io) punsi, (tu) pungesti, (Lei) punse, (lui/lei) punse, (noi) pungemmo, (voi) pungeste, (loro) punsero

raccogliere
Present Indicative　(io) raccolgo, (tu) raccogli, (Lei) raccoglie, (lui/lei) raccoglie, (noi) raccogliamo, (voi) raccogliete, (loro) raccolgono
Past Participle　raccolto
Past Absolute　(io) raccolsi, (tu) raccogliesti, (Lei) raccolse, (lui/lei) raccolse, (noi) raccogliemmo, (voi) raccoglieste, (loro) raccolsero
Present Subjunctive　(io) raccolga, (tu) raccolga, (Lei) raccolga, (lui/lei) raccolga, (noi) raccogliamo, (voi) raccogliete, (loro) raccolgono
Imperative　(tu) raccogli, (Lei) raccolga, (noi) raccogliamo, (voi) raccogliete, (Loro) raccolgono

raggiungere
Past Participle　raggiunto
Past Absolute　(io) raggiunsi, (tu) raggiungesti, (Lei) raggiunse, (lui/lei) raggiunse, (noi) raggiungemmo, (voi) raggiungeste, (loro) raggiunsero

redigere
Past Participle　redatto
Past Absolute　(io) redassi, (tu) redigesti, (Lei) redasse, (lui/lei) redasse, (noi) redigemmo, (voi) redigeste, (loro) redassero

riassumere (conjugated like **assumere**)

richiedere (conjugated like **chiedere**)

ridere
Past Participle	riso
Past Absolute	(io) risi, (tu) ridesti, (Lei) rise, (lui/lei) rise, (noi) ridemmo, (voi) rideste, (loro) risero

ridurre (conjugated like **riprodurre**)

rimanere
Present Indicative	(io) rimango, (tu) rimani, (Lei) rimane, (lui/lei) rimane, (noi) rimaniamo, (voi) rimanete, (loro) rimangono
Past Participle	rimasto
Past Absolute	(io) rimasi, (tu) rimanesti, (Lei) rimase, (lui/lei) rimase, (noi) rimanemmo, (voi) rimaneste, (loro) rimasero
Future	(io) rimarrò, (tu) rimarrai, (Lei) rimarrà, (lui/lei) rimarrà, (noi) rimarremo, (voi) rimarrete, (loro) rimarranno
Conditional	(io) rimarrei, (tu) rimarresti, (Lei) rimarrebbe, (lui/lei) rimarrebbe, (noi) rimarremmo, (voi) rimarreste, (loro) rimarrebbero
Present Subjunctive	(io) rimanga, (tu) rimanga, (Lei) rimanga, (lui/lei) rimanga, (noi) rimaniamo, (voi) rimaniate, (loro) rimangano
Imperative	(tu) rimani, (Lei) rimanga, (noi) rimaniamo, (voi) rimanete, (Loro) rimangano

rimettere/rimettersi (conjugated like **mettere**)

riprodurre
Present Indicative	(io) riproduco, (tu) riproduci, (Lei) riproduce, (lui/lei) riproduce, (noi) riproduciamo, (voi) riproducete, (loro) riproducono
Past Participle	riprodotto
Imperfect	(io) riproducevo, (tu) riproducevi, (Lei) riproduceva, (lui/lei) riproduceva, (noi) riproducevamo, (voi) riproducevate, (loro) riproducevano
Past Absolute	(io) riprodussi, (tu) riproducesti, (Lei) riprodusse, (lui/lei) riprodusse, (noi) riproducemmo, (voi) riproduceste, (loro) riprodussero
Future	(io) riprodurrò, (tu) riprodurrai, (Lei) riprodurrà, (lui/lei) riprodurrà, (noi) riprodurremo, (voi) riprodurrete, (loro) riprodurranno
Conditional	(io) riprodurrei, (tu) riprodurresti, (Lei) riprodurrebbe, (lui/lei) riprodurrebbe, (noi) riprodurremmo, (voi) riprodurreste, (loro) riprodurrebbero
Present Subjunctive	(io) riproduca, (tu) riproduca, (Lei) riproduca, (lui/lei) riproduca, (noi) riproduciamo, (voi) riproduciate, (loro) riproducano
Imperfect Subjunctive	(io) riproducessi, (tu) riproducessi, (Lei) riproducesse, (lui/lei) riproducesse, (noi) riproducessimo, (voi) riproduceste, (loro) riproducessero

Imperative	(tu) riproduci, (Lei) riproduca, (noi) riproduciamo, (voi) riproducete, (Loro) riproducano
Gerund	riproducendo

riscuotere

Past Participle	riscosso
Past Absolute	(io) riscossi, (tu) riscotesti, (Lei) riscosse, (lui/lei) riscosse, (noi) riscuotemmo, (voi) riscoteste, (loro) riscossero

risolvere

Past Participle	risolto
Past Absolute	(io) risolsi, (tu) risolvesti, (Lei) risolse, (lui/lei) risolse, (noi) risolvemmo, (voi) risolveste, (loro) risolsero

rispondere

Past Participle	risposto
Past Absolute	(io) risposi, (tu) rispondesti, (Lei) rispose, (lui/lei) rispose, (noi) rispondemmo, (voi) rispondeste, (loro) risposero

rivolgersi

Past Participle	rivolto
Past Absolute	(io) mi rivolse, (tu) ti rivolgesti, (Lei) si rivolse, (lui/lei) si rivolse, (noi) ci rivolgemmo, (voi) vi rivolgeste, (loro) si rivolsero

rompere

Past Participle	rotto
Past Absolute	(io) ruppi, (tu) rompesti, (Lei) ruppe, (lui/lei) ruppe, (noi) rompemmo, (voi) rompeste, (loro) ruppero

salire

Present Indicative	(io) salgo, (tu) sali, (Lei) sale, (lui/lei) sale, (noi) saliamo, (voi) salite, (loro) salgono
Present Subjunctive	(io) salga, (tu) salga, (Lei) salga, (lui/lei) salga, (noi) saliamo, (voi) saliate, (loro) salgano
Imperative	(tu) sali, (Lei) salga, (noi) saliamo, (voi) salite, (Loro) salgano

sapere

Present Indicative	(io) so, (tu) sai, (Lei) sa, (lui/lei) sa, (noi) sappiamo, (voi) sapete, (loro) sanno
Past Absolute	(io) seppi, (tu) sapesti, (Lei) seppe, (lui/lei) seppe, (noi) sapemmo, (voi) sapeste, (loro) seppero
Future	(io) saprò, (tu) saprai, (Lei) saprà, (lui/lei) saprà, (noi) sapremo, (voi) saprete, (loro) sapranno
Conditional	(io) saprei, (tu) sapresti, (Lei) saprebbe, (lui/lei) saprebbe, (noi) sapremmo, (voi) sapreste, (loro) saprebbero
Present Subjunctive	(io) sappia, (tu) sappia, (Lei) sappia, (lui/lei) sappia, (noi) sappiamo, (voi) sappiate, (loro) sappiano
Imperative	(tu) sappi, (Lei) sappia, (noi) sappiamo, (voi) sappiate, (Loro) sappiano

scegliere

Present Indicative	(io) scelgo, (tu) scegli, (Lei) sceglie, (lui/lei) sceglie, (noi) scegliamo, (voi) scegliete, (loro) scelgono
Past Participle	scelto
Past Absolute	(io) scelsi, (tu) scegliesti, (Lei) scelse, (lui/lei) scelse, (noi) scegliemmo, (voi) sceglieste, (loro) scelsero
Present Subjunctive	(io) scelga, (tu) scelga, (Lei) scelga, (lui/lei) scelga, (noi) scegliamo, (voi) scegliate, (loro) scelgano
Imperative	(tu) scegli, (Lei) scelga, (noi) scegliamo, (voi) scegliete, (Loro) scelgano

scendere

Past Participle	sceso
Past Absolute	(io) scesi, (tu) scendesti, (Lei) scese, (lui/lei) scese, (noi) scendemmo, (voi) scendeste, (loro) scesero

sciogliere

Past Participle	sciolto
Past Absolute	(io) sciolsi, (tu) sciogliesti, (Lei) sciolse, (lui/lei) sciolse, (noi) sciogliemmo, (voi) scioglieste, (loro) sciolsero

scommettere (conjugated like **mettere**)

sconfiggere

Past Participle	sconfitto
Past Absolute	(io) sconfissi, (tu) sconfiggesti, (Lei) sconfisse, (lui/lei) sconfisse, (noi) sconfiggemmo, (voi) sconfiggeste, (loro) sconfissero

scorrere (conjugated like **correre**)

scrivere

Past Participle	scritto
Past Absolute	(io) scrissi, (tu) scrivesti, (Lei) scrisse, (lui/lei) scrisse, (noi) scrivemmo, (voi) scriveste, (loro) scrissero

scuotere

Past Participle	scosso
Past Absolute	(io) scossi, (tu) scotesti, (Lei) scosse, (lui/lei) scosse, (noi) scuotemmo, (voi) scoteste, (loro) scossero

sedersi

Present Indicative	(io) mi siedo, (tu) ti siedi, (Lei) si siede, (lui/lei) si siede, (noi) ci sediamo, (voi) vi sedete, (loro) si siedono
Present Subjunctive	(io) mi sieda, (tu) ti sieda, (Lei) si sieda, (lui/lei) si sieda, (noi) ci sediamo, (voi) vi sediate, (loro) si siedano
Imperative	(tu) siediti, (Lei) si sieda, (noi) sediamoci, (voi) sedetevi, (Loro) si siedano

sedurre (conjugated like **riprodurre**)

soccorrere (conjugated like **correre**)

sorprendere (conjugated like **prendere**)

sorridere (conjugated like **ridere**)

sostenere (conjugated like **tenere**)

sottrarre (conjugated like **estrarre**)

spargere

Past Participle	sparso
Past Absolute	(io) sparsi, (tu) spargesti, (Lei) sparse, (lui/lei) sparse, (noi) spargemmo, (voi) spargeste, (loro) sparsero

spegnere

Present Indicative	(io) spengo, (tu) spegni, (Lei) spegne, (lui/lei) spegne, (noi) spegniamo, (voi) spegnete, (loro) spengono
Past Participle	spento
Past Absolute	(io) spensi, (tu) spegnesti, (Lei) spense, (lui/lei) spense, (noi) spegnemmo, (voi) spegneste, (loro) spensero
Present Subjunctive	(io) spenga, (tu) spenga, (Lei) spenga, (lui/lei) spenga, (noi) spegniamo, (voi) spegniate, (loro) spengano
Imperative	(tu) spegni, (Lei) spenga, (noi) spegniamo, (voi) spegnete, (Loro) spengano

spingere (conjugated like **dipingere**)

stare

Present Indicative	(io) sto, (tu) stai, (Lei) sta, (lui/lei) sta, (noi) stiamo, (voi) state, (loro) stanno
Past Participle	stato
Imperfect	(io) stavo, (tu) stavi, (Lei) stava, (lui/lei) stava, (noi) stavamo, (voi) stavate, (loro) stavano
Past Absolute	(io) stetti, (tu) stesti, (Lei) stette, (lui/lei) stette, (noi) stemmo, (voi) steste, (loro) stettero
Future	(io) starò, (tu) starai, (Lei) starà, (lui/lei) starà, (noi) staremo, (voi) starete, (loro) staranno
Conditional	(io) starei, (tu) staresti, (Lei) starebbe, (lui/lei) starebbe, (noi) staremmo, (voi) stareste, (loro) starebbero
Present Subjunctive	(io) stia, (tu) stia, (Lei) stia, (lui/lei) stia, (noi) stiamo, (voi) stiate, (loro) stiano
Imperfect Subjunctive	(io) stessi, (tu) stessi, (Lei) stesse, (lui/lei) stesse, (noi) stessimo, (voi) steste, (loro) stessero
Imperative	(tu) sta', (Lei) stia, (noi) stiamo, (voi) state, (Loro) stiano
Gerund	stando

stringere

Past Participle	strinto
Past Absolute	(io) strinsi, (tu) stringesti, (Lei) strinse, (lui/lei) strinse, (noi) stringemmo, (voi) stringeste, (loro) strinsero

stringersi (conjugated like **stringere**)

svenirsi (conjugated like **venire**)

svolgere

Past Participle	svolto
Past Absolute	(io) svolsi, (tu) svolgesti, (Lei) svolse, (lui/lei) svolse, (noi) svolgemmo, (voi) svolgeste, (loro) svolsero

svolgersi (conjugated like **svolgere**)

tacere (conjugated like **piacere**)

tenere

Present Indicative	(io) tengo, (tu) tieni, (Lei) tiene, (lui/lei) tiene, (noi) teniamo, (voi) tenete, (loro) tengono
Past Absolute	(io) tenni, (tu) tenesti, (Lei) tenne, (lui/lei) tenne, (noi) tenemmo, (voi) teneste, (loro) tennero
Future	(io) terrò, (tu) terrai, (Lei) terrà, (lui/lei) terrà, (noi) terremo, (voi) terrete, (loro) terranno
Conditional	(io) terrei, (tu) terresti, (Lei) terrebbe, (lui/lei) terrebbe, (noi) terremmo, (voi) terreste, (loro) terrebbero
Present Subjunctive	(io) tenga, (tu) tenga, (Lei) tenga, (lui/lei) tenga, (noi) teniamo, (voi) teniate, (loro) tengano
Imperative	(tu) tieni, (Lei) tenga, (noi) teniamo, (voi) tenete, (Loro) tengano

tenersi (conjugated like **tenere**)

tingere (conjugated like **dipingere**)

tingersi (conjugated like **dipingere**)

togliersi (conjugated like **raccogliere**)

torcere

Past Participle	torto
Past Absolute	(io) torsi, (tu) torcesti, (Lei) torse, (lui/lei) torse, (noi) torcemmo, (voi) torceste, (loro) torsero

tradurre (conjugated like **riprodurre**)

trascorrere (conjugated like **correre**)

trasmettere (conjugated like **mettere**)

uccidere

Past Participle	ucciso
Past Absolute	(io) uccisi, (tu) uccidesti, (Lei) uccise, (lui/lei) uccise, (noi) uccidemmo, (voi) uccideste, (loro) uccisero

udire

Present Indicative	(io) odo, (tu) odi, (Lei) ode, (lui/lei) ode, (noi) udiamo, (voi) udite, (loro) odono
Present Subjunctive	(io) oda, (tu) oda, (Lei) oda, (lui/lei) oda, (noi) udiamo, (voi) udiate, (loro) odano
Imperative	(tu) oda, (Lei) oda, (noi) udiamo, (voi) udite, (Loro) odano

ungere

Past Participle	unto
Past Absolute	(io) unsi, (tu) ungesti, (Lei) unse, (lui/lei) unse, (noi) ungemmo, (voi) ungeste, (loro) unsero

uscire

Present Indicative	(io) esco, (tu) esci, (Lei) esce, (lui/lei) esce, (noi) usciamo, (voi) uscite, (loro) escono
Present Subjunctive	(io) esca, (tu) esca, (Lei) esca, (lui/lei) esca, (noi) usciamo, (voi) usciate, (loro) escano
Imperative	(tu) esci, (Lei) esca, (noi) usciamo, (voi) uscite, (Loro) escano

vedere

Past Participle	visto/veduto
Past Absolute	(io) vidi, (tu) vedesti, (Lei) vide, (lui/lei) vide, (noi) vedemmo, (voi) vedeste, (loro) videro
Future	(io) vedrò, (tu) vedrai, (Lei) vedrà, (lui/lei) vedrà, (noi) vedremo, (voi) vedrete, (loro) vedranno
Conditional	(io) vedrei, (tu) vedresti, (Lei) vedrebbe, (lui/lei) vedrebbe, (noi) vedremmo, (voi) vedreste, (loro) vedrebbero

venire

Present Indicative	(io) vengo, (tu) vieni, (Lei) viene, (lui/lei) viene, (noi) veniamo, (voi) venite, (loro) vengono
Past Participle	venuto
Past Absolute	(io) venni, (tu) venisti, (Lei) venne, (lui/lei) venne, (noi) venimmo, (voi) veniste, (loro) vennero
Future	(io) verrò, (tu) verrai, (Lei) verrà, (lui/lei) verrà, (noi) verremo, (voi) verrete, (loro) verranno
Conditional	(io) verrei, (tu) verresti, (Lei) verrebbe, (lui/lei) verrebbe, (noi) verremmo, (voi) verreste, (loro) verrebbero
Present Subjunctive	(io) venga, (tu) venga, (Lei) venga, (lui/lei) venga, (noi) veniamo, (voi) veniate, (loro) vengano
Imperative	(tu) vieni, (Lei) venga, (noi) veniamo, (voi) venite, (Loro) vengano

vincere

Past Participle	vinto
Past Absolute	(io) vinsi, (tu) vincesti, (Lei) vinse, (lui/lei) vinse, (noi) vincemmo, (voi) vinceste, (loro) vinsero

vivere

Past Participle	vissuto
Past Absolute	(io) vissi, (tu) vivesti, (Lei) visse, (lui/lei) visse, (noi) vivemmo, (voi) viveste, (loro) vissero

volere

Present Indicative	(io) voglio, (tu) vuoi, (Lei) vuole, (lui/lei) vuole, (noi) vogliamo, (voi) volete, (loro) vogliono
Past Absolute	(io) volli, (tu) volesti, (Lei) volle, (lui/lei) volle, (noi) volemmo, (voi) voleste, (loro) vollero
Future	(io) vorrò, (tu) vorrai, (Lei) vorrà, (lui/lei) vorrà, (noi) vorremo, (voi) vorrete, (loro) vorranno
Conditional	(io) vorrei, (tu) vorresti, (Lei) vorrebbe, (lui/lei) vorrebbe, (noi) vorremmo, (voi) vorreste, (loro) vorrebbero
Present Subjunctive	(io) voglia, (tu) voglia, (Lei) voglia, (lui/lei) voglia, (noi) vogliamo, (voi) vogliate, (loro) vogliano

Answers

CHAPTER 1

Quanto sai già?
1. a
2. a
3. b
4. b
5. a
6. a
7. a
8. b
9. a

Quick Practice 1
1. zia = **i**
2. tua = **u**
3. chiamare = **y**
4. quando = **w**
5. mai = **y**
6. pausa = **w**
7. dire = **i**
8. diede = **y**
9. sugo = **u**
10. suonare = **w**

Quick Practice 2
1. smettere
2. cosa
3. zuppa
4. sogno
5. figlio
6. sciopero
7. scherzo
8. scuola
9. giacca
10. quanto

Quick Practice 3

1. *fate*   vs.   *fact*
2. *type*   vs.   *too much*
3. *art*   vs.   *to arrive*
4. *wine*   vs.   *he/she came*
5. *string*   vs.   *son*
6. *little*   vs.   *package*
7. *thing*   vs.   *who knows*

Quick Practice 4

1. Maria, perché dici questo?
2. Dov'è il tuo amico?
3. Ci hai messo lo zucchero nel caffè?
4. Lui abita nel centro della città.
5. A quale università studi?
6. Lui fa sempre tutto da sé.
7. Claudia non c'è.

Quick Practice 5

1. Vedrò la mia famiglia a maggio.
2. Anch'io studio l'italiano.
3. Ti piace il jazz?
4. Come si chiama, Lei?
5. Anche tu pratichi il karatè?

Putting It All Together

A.

MISSING VOWELS	MISSING SEMIVOWELS	MISSING SINGLE CONSONANTS	MISSING DOUBLE CONSONANTS
pane	buono	cibo	tutto
zia	cuore	bacio	anno
bene	pieno	lasciare	freddo
come	piano	rosa	formaggio
luna	questo	vero	oggi
zuppa	guerra	mano	prezzo
molto	nuovo	madre	nonno
cane	piatto	dove	ghiaccio
gente	dieci	caldo	occhio
tipo	mai	forte	palla

B.

1. Domani è il tre maggio, non è vero?
2. Anch'io voglio parlare italiano molto bene.
3. Sì, è vero. C'è solo un teatro in quella città.
4. Tutti gli studenti sono americani.
5. Come si chiama quella ragazza? È italiana, vero?

C.

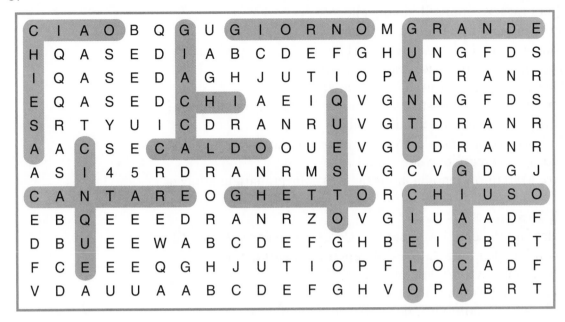

D. [More answers may be possible.]
1. raro — caro — raso — faro
2. pacco — tacco — bacco — sacco
3. velo — vero — melo — zelo
4. tanto — santo — manto — vanto — tasto
5. uomo — uovo — uopo — pomo — tomo

CHAPTER 2

Quanto sai già?
1. La mela è stata mangiata dal ragazzo.
2. Perché guardi sempre la televisione?
3. Marco aspetta Maria ogni giorno.
4. Ieri sera ho telefonato alla mia amica.
5. No, non mi piace affatto!
6. La ragazza che sta leggendo il giornale è sua sorella.
7. Gli italiani sono simpatici.
8. Quanto costa quel cellulare?
9. Maria è già arrivata.

Quick Practice 1
1. c
2. i
3. a
4. h
5. b
6. d
7. f
8. e
9. g

Quick Practice 2

1. Quel ragazzo suona il violoncello.
2. Io telefono a mio fratello ogni sera.
3. Maria è andata a casa presto ieri.
4. Lui chiama tutti i suoi amici ogni giorno.
5. Claudia sta aspettando il suo fidanzato.
6. Perché non hai chiesto a/ad Alessandro di venire alla festa?
7. Chi ha risposto a quella domanda?
8. Lui non ascolta mai la professoressa d'italiano.
9. Nora sta cercando le sue chiavi.
10. No, Maria non mangia la pizza. / Sì, Maria mangia la pizza.

Quick Practice 3

1. Alessandro cerca il suo cane? / Cerca il suo cane, Alessandro?
2. Sara ha ancora un gatto? / Ha ancora un gatto, Sara?
3. Quale pizza vuoi/vuole mangiare?
4. Come stai?/Come sta?/Come va?
5. Ha pagato il conto lui, no/vero?/non è vero?

Quick Practice 4

1. i
2. h
3. g
4. a
5. d
6. b
7. c
8. e
9. f

Putting It All Together

A.
1. *Compound*
2. *Interrogative*
3. *Incomplete*
4. *Passive*
5. *Affirmative*
6. *Negative*

B.
1. Sì, sì/Ecco… tu hai ragione/Lei ha ragione.
2. Già, già, anche lei ha ragione.
3. C'è tanta gente alla festa.
4. Dov'è Sara? Ecco Sara!
5. C'è ancora del caffè?
6. (Io) non telefono mai ai miei amici.
7. Hai/Ha chiesto al professore di venire?
8. Chi aspetti, Maria?
9. No, lei non viene alla festa.

C.
1. Noi ascoltiamo la partita alla radio.
2. Maria, stai cercando ancora la tua borsa?
3. Non mi piace la pizza./La pizza non mi piace.
4. Chi è quella persona? / Quella persona, chi è?
5. Lui l'ha detto. / L'ha detto lui!
6. Marco è la persona che ha detto quello.
7. Quando arriveranno, andremo al cinema. / Andremo al cinema quando arriveranno.
8. Tutta quella torta è stata mangiata da lui.
9. Marco e Maria amano i film di Fellini.

CULTURE CAPSULE 1
Content Questions
1. Vero
2. Falso
3. Vero
4. Falso
5. Vero/Falso
6. Vero
7. Vero

CHAPTER 3

Quanto sai già?
1. True
2. False
3. False
4. True
5. False
6. False
7. True
8. True
9. False

Quick Practice 1
1. Anch'io parlo italiano molto bene.
2. Io non scrivo l'italiano molto bene.
3. Sì, io capisco tutto.
4. No, io non dormo molto la notte.
5. Anche tu parli italiano molto bene, non è vero?
6. È vero che tu scrivi l'italiano molto bene?
7. Maria, tu capisci quello che ho detto?
8. Perché tu dormi così poco?
9. Anche Lei parla italiano molto bene, non è vero?
10. È vero che Lei scrive l'italiano molto bene?
11. Signorina, Lei capisce quello che ho detto?
12. Perché Lei dorme così poco?
13. Quel negozio apre alle sette e mezzo.

14. Mio fratello arriva dall'Italia domani.
15. A che ora finisce di lavorare, la tua amica?
16. Che cosa vede il tuo amico?
17. Noi non parliamo italiano.
18. Anche voi non parlate italiano, vero?
19. Noi non vediamo niente.
20. Anche voi non vedete niente, vero?
21. Noi dormiamo fino a tardi il sabato.
22. Anche voi dormite fino a tardi il sabato, no?
23. Noi finiamo di lavorare alle sette.
24. Anche voi finite di lavorare alle sette, non è vero?
25. A che ora arrivano i tuoi amici?
26. Chi vedono loro?
27. A che ora chiudono i negozi?
28. A che ora finiscono di lavorare i tuoi amici?

Quick Practice 2
1. io...
   a. abito
   b. prendo
   c. apro
   d. capisco

2. tu...
   a. ami
   b. leggi
   c. offri
   d. spedisci

3. lui/lei...
   a. entra
   b. vede
   c. apre
   d. preferisce

4. Lei...
   a. guarda
   b. ride
   c. offre
   d. unisce

5. noi...
   a. compriamo
   b. godiamo
   c. sentiamo
   d. spediamo

6. voi...
   a. ascoltate
   b. vivete
   c. fuggite
   d. garantite

7. loro...
   a. portano
   b. credono
   c. partono
   d. puliscono

Quick Practice 3
1. io...
   a. lancio
   b. viaggio
   c. copio
   d. comunico

2. tu...
   a. allacci
   b. parcheggi
   c. studi
   d. giochi

3. lui/lei...
   a. annuncia
   b. viaggia
   c. devia
   d. indica

4. Lei...
   a. abbraccia
   b. assaggia
   c. scia
   d. comunica

5. noi...
   a. baciamo
   b. noleggiamo
   c. inviamo
   d. neghiamo

6. voi...
   a. pronunciate
   b. viaggiate
   c. cambiate
   d. pregate

7. **loro...**
   a. lasciano
   b. mangiano
   c. sciano
   d. spiegano

Quick Practice 4
1. Guardo la televisione adesso/ora.
2. Anch'io parlo italiano.
3. No, non sento niente/nulla!
4. Il sabato puliamo sempre la casa.
5. Gli italiani lavorano troppo.
6. (Loro) arrivano domani.
7. (Io) studio da questa mattina/stamani.
8. (Io) studio l'italiano da cinque anni.
9. (Che) cosa preferisci?
10. (Che) cosa preferisce?
11. (Che) cosa preferite?
12. (Che) cosa preferiscono?
13. (Lei) suona il pianoforte molto bene.
14. (Lui) aspetta sempre l'autobus quando lo incontro.
15. (Lei) risponde sempre correttamente alle domande.

Quick Practice 5
1. Sono le due e mezzo/trenta.
2. È sabato, il dodici ottobre.
3. Sono di New (Nuova) York.
4. (Tu) sei intelligente?
5. (Lei) è (un) avvocato?
6. (Loro) sono sempre in ritardo.
7. (Voi) siete intelligenti?
8. (Loro) sono intelligenti?
9. C'è l'insegnante?
10. Ci sono anche loro?
11. Ho bisogno di una nuova macchina (automobile).
12. (Tu) hai caldo?
13. (Lei) ha molta fame?
14. (Voi) avete fretta?
15. (Tu) hai molto sonno?
16. Quanti anni hanno (loro)?

Quick Practice 6
1.
   a. Non so il tuo/suo nome.
   b. Non conosco i tuoi genitori.

2.
   a. (Tu) sai suonare il violino molto bene.
   b. (Tu) conosci quel ristorante, no/vero/non è vero?

3.

    a. (Lei) sa parlare italiano molto bene.

    b. (Lei) conosce quella città, no/vero/non è vero?

4.

    a. (Voi) sapete suonare il violino molto bene.

    b. (Voi) conoscete quel ristorante, no/vero/non è vero?

5.

    a. (Loro) sanno suonare il pianoforte molto bene.

    b. (Loro) conoscono quel ristorante, no/vero/non è vero?

6.

    a. (Noi) non sappiamo il tuo/suo nome.

    b. (Noi) non conosciamo i tuoi/suoi amici.

Quick Practice 7

1.

    a. (Io) vengo alla festa.

    b. (Io) esco stasera / questa sera.

    c. (Io) vado in Italia ogni anno.

    d. (Io) voglio andare in Italia quest'anno.

    e. (Io) devo studiare l'italiano.

    f. (Io) posso venire con te.

    g. (Io) faccio il medico.

    h. (Io) dico sempre la verità.

    i. (Io) do sempre (dei) soldi ai miei bambini.

    j. (Io) bevo sempre (il) vino bianco.

2.

    a. (Tu) vieni alla festa.

    b. (Tu) esci stasera / questa sera.

    c. (Tu) vai in Italia ogni anno.

    d. (Tu) vuoi andare in Italia quest'anno.

    e. (Tu) devi studiare l'italiano.

    f. (Tu) puoi venire con me.

    g. (Tu) fai molte/tante cose, no/vero/non è vero?

    h. (Tu) dici sempre la verità.

    i. (Tu) dai sempre (dei) soldi ai tuoi bambini.

    j. (Tu) bevi sempre (il) vino bianco.

3.

    a. (Loro) vengono alla festa.

    b. (Loro) escono stasera / questa sera.

    c. (Loro) vanno in Italia ogni anno.

    d. (Loro) vogliono andare in Italia quest'anno.

    e. (Loro) devono studiare l'italiano.

    f. (Loro) possono venire con me.

    g. (Loro) fanno molte/tante cose, no/vero/non è vero?

h. (Loro) dicono sempre la verità.

i. (Loro) danno sempre (dei) soldi ai loro bambini.

j. (Loro) bevono sempre (il) vino bianco.

Putting It All Together

A.

	lavorare	baciare	giocare	viaggiare	negare	studiare	inviare	leggere	offrire	finire
io	lavoro	bacio	gioco	viaggio	nego	studio	invio	leggo	offro	finisco
tu	lavori	baci	giochi	viaggi	neghi	studi	invii	leggi	offri	finisci
lui	lavora	bacia	gioca	viaggia	nega	studia	invia	legge	offre	finisce
lei	lavora	bacia	gioca	viaggia	nega	studia	invia	legge	offre	finisce
Lei	lavora	bacia	gioca	viaggia	nega	studia	invia	legge	offre	finisce
noi	lavoriamo	baciamo	giochiamo	viaggiamo	neghiamo	studiamo	inviamo	leggiamo	offriamo	finiamo
voi	lavorate	baciate	giocate	viaggiate	negate	studiate	inviate	leggete	offrite	finite
loro	lavorano	baciano	giocano	viaggiano	negano	studiano	inviano	leggono	offrono	finiscono

B.

1. b
2. b
3. b
4. b
5. a
6. a
7. a
8. a
9. b
10. a
11. b
12. b
13. b
14. a
15. b

C.

1. a
2. b
3. c
4. a
5. b
6. c
7. b
8. a
9. c
10. b

D.
1. suona
2. amano
3. andiamo/viviamo
4. guardano
5. arrivano
6. puliamo
7. capisco
8. chiude
9. ascolta
10. bevono
11. fa
12. dicono
13. dice
14. dite
15. danno
16. fa
17. fanno
18. fai

E.
1. ha
2. è
3. C'è
4. Sono
5. siamo
6. siete
7. avete
8. è
9. C'è
10. è
11. ha
12. avete
13. conosco
14. sapete
15. conosci

F.
1. Sì, c'è. / No, non c'è.
2. Sì, siamo italiani. / No, non siamo italiani.
3. Sì, ci sono. / No, non ci sono.
4. Ecco Marco e Maria. / Eccoli.
5. Sì, oggi è martedì. / No, oggi non è martedì.
6. Ecco Maria.
7. Sì, c'è. / No, non c'è.

G.
1. Lei sa il nome di quella persona?
2. Loro conoscono un buon ristorante in questa città?
3. Anche Lei sa suonare il pianoforte, vero?
4. Conoscono i genitori di quella persona?
5. Sa il mio indirizzo?
6. Conosce l'insegnante d'italiano?
7. Sanno chi sono io?
8. Cosa preferisce?
9. Dove abita?
10. Cosa leggono?

H.
Cara Maria,

come va? Quanti anni hai adesso? E quanti anni hanno tuo fratello e tua sorella? Adesso (io) sono medico/faccio il medico. Che/Quale macchina hai adesso? Sei ancora molto simpatica? Certo che sei intelligente! / Certamente sei intelligente! Ho voglia di telefonare/telefonarti. Purtroppo, ho sempre poco tempo. Forse hai ragione. Sono troppo ambiziosa e ho poco tempo per gli amici.

Ciao!
Francesca

I.

Crossword solution:
- 1 (down): fatte
- 2 (across): diciamo
- 2 (down): danno
- 3 (down): andiamo
- 4 (down): veniti
- 5 (across): devono
- 6 (across): bevono
- 7 (down): vuoi
- 8 (down): vogliono
- 9 (across): escono
- 10 (down): ese
- 11 (down): muoio / 11 (across): muoio
- 12 (across): scelgono

J. [Answers will vary.]

CHAPTER 4

Quanto sai già?

1. sono andati (andarono)
2. scrisse
3. mangiavi
4. sono nato/sono nata
5. vennero (sono venuti)
6. erano arrivati
7. ha detto
8. ha fatto (faceva)
9. sei stato/sei stata

Quick Practice 1

1. noleggiato
2. arrivato
3. conosciuto
4. dormito
5. acceso
6. riso
7. rimasto
8. nato
9. apparso
10. aperto
11. morto
12. bevuto
13. messo
14. chiesto
15. chiuso
16. coperto
17. letto
18. fatto
19. stato
20. detto
21. dato
22. corso
23. risposto
24. rotto
25. vissuto
26. venuto
27. scelto
28. scoperto
29. sofferto
30. scritto

      ho mangiato tutta la pizza ieri.

      ho visto Maria il mese scorso.

    c. non ho ancora finito/non ho finito ancora.

    d. sono uscito/a ieri sera.

    e. sono già andato/a a vedere quel film.

2. **tu...**
   a. hai conosciuto Maria ieri per la prima volta.
   b. hai visto Paola.
   c. hai dovuto studiare ieri.
   d. sei vissuto/a in Italia due anni fa.
   e. sei andato/a in centro la settimana scorsa.

3. **lui...**
   a. è voluto/ha voluto andare due anni fa.
   b. è corso per aiutare.
   c. ha saputo che tu vieni alla festa.
   d. è arrivato qualche minuto fa/alcuni minuti fa.
   e. ha già finito.

4. **lei...**
   a. è voluta/ha voluto andare due anni fa.
   b. è corsa per aiutare.
   c. ha saputo che tu vieni alla festa.
   d. è arrivata qualche minuto fa/alcuni minuti fa.
   e. ha già finito.

5. **noi...**
   a. abbiamo già fatto quello.
   b. abbiamo detto quello ieri.
   c. abbiamo dato tutti i nostri soldi a Maria.
   d. non siamo ancora andati/e in Italia.
   e. siamo usciti/e ieri sera.

6. **voi...**
   a. avete già fatto quello.
   b. avete detto quello ieri.
   c. avete dato tutti i vostri soldi a Maria.
   d. non siete ancora andati/e in Italia.
   e. siete usciti/e ieri sera.

7. **i miei amici...**
   a. sono voluti/hanno voluto andare due anni fa.
   b. sono corsi per aiutare.
   c. hanno saputo che tu vieni alla festa.
   d. sono arrivati qualche minuto fa/alcuni minuti fa.
   e. hanno già finito.

8. **le mie amiche...**
   a. sono volute/hanno voluto andare due anni fa.
   b. sono corse per aiutare.
   c. hanno saputo che tu vieni alla festa.
   d. sono arrivate qualche minuto fa/alcuni minuti fa.
   e. hanno già finito.

Quick Practice 3

1. (Io) suonavo il pianoforte.
2. (Tu) cantavi molto bene.
3. Mio fratello andava spesso al cinema.
4. (Voi) guardavate molto la TV.
5. I suoi amici giocavano a calcio.
6. (Io) mangiavo spesso la pasta.
7. Il signor Tommasi andava spesso in spiaggia/alla spiaggia.
8. C'era sempre molto da fare.
9. C'erano molte cose da fare.

10. **io...**
    a. stavo
    b. facevo
    c. ero
    d. dicevo
    e. davo
    f. bevevo
    g. mangiavo
    h. cominciavo

11. **tu...**
    a. stavi
    b. facevi
    c. eri
    d. dicevi
    e. davi
    f. bevevi
    g. mangiavi
    h. cominciavi

12. **quell'uomo...**
    a. stava
    b. faceva
    c. era
    d. diceva
    e. dava
    f. beveva
    g. mangiava
    h. cominciava

13. **quelle donne...**
    a. stavano
    b. facevano
    c. erano
    d. dicevano
    e. davano
    f. bevevano
    g. mangiavano
    h. cominciavano

14. **noi...**
    a. stavamo
    b. facevamo
    c. eravamo
    d. dicevamo
    e. davamo
    f. bevevamo
    g. mangiavamo
    h. cominciavamo

15. **voi...**
    a. stavate
    b. facevate
    c. eravate
    d. dicevate
    e. davate
    f. bevevate
    g. mangiavate
    h. cominciavate

Quick Practice 4
Molti anni fa...
  1. i miei genitori arrivarono dall'Italia.
  2. (io) passai un anno a Roma.
  3. (voi) andaste in Italia.
  4. suo figlio diventò / divenne un ingegnere.
  5. sua figlia finì di studiare medicina.
  6. (noi) scoprimmo l'Italia.
  7. i nostri amici lavorarono per quella ditta.

  8. **io...**
     a. bevvi
     b. fui/stetti
     c. feci
     d. dissi
     e. vissi

9. tu...
    a. vincesti
    b. vedesti
    c. tenesti
    d. mettesti
    e. nascesti

10. lui/lei...
    a. cominciò
    b. ebbe
    c. conobbe
    d. lesse
    e. seppe

11. noi...
    a. decidemmo
    b. finimmo
    c. andammo
    d. vendemmo
    e. mangiammo

12. voi...
    a. beveste
    b. deste
    c. diceste
    d. foste
    e. faceste

13. loro...
    a. scrissero
    b. vennero
    c. vollero
    d. aprirono
    e. chiusero

Quick Practice 5

1. (Loro) avevano già mangiato quando (lei) è arrivata (arrivò).
2. (Io) avevo già finito, quando mi hai/ha chiamato.
3. Da bambina, (lei) poteva guardare la TV solo dopo che aveva studiato.
4. Dopo che (voi) eravate usciti, finalmente (lui) è arrivato (arrivò).
5. Ero sicuro che tu lo avevi già fatto.
6. Bruno ha detto che aveva già visto quei film. Ed è vero. Li aveva già visti.
7. Nora voleva/è voluta uscire solo dopo che aveva finito di guardare il suo programma preferito.
8. La signora Santini ha indicato/indicò che aveva già letto quel romanzo.
9. Tutti erano contenti (Ognuno era contento) che voi avevate deciso di venire alla festa.
10. Dopo che erano andate a fare delle spese, le due amiche sono andate/andarono al cinema.
11. Dopo che ebbero lasciato l'America molti anni fa, decisero di ritornare.

Putting It All Together

A.

1. accendere, accesi
2. leggere, lessi
3. fare, feci
4. essere, fui (stare, stetti)
5. dire, dissi
6. dare, diedi
7. correre, corsi
8. coprire, coprii (copersi)
9. rispondere, risposi
10. morire, morì
11. rompere, ruppi
12. ridere, risi
13. rimanere, rimasi
14. prendere, presi
15. scoprire, scoprii (scopersi)
16. soffrire, soffrii

B.

1. Maria ed io non abbiamo mai guardato quel programma televisivo insieme.
2. (Loro) non hanno capito (non capirono) il racconto che (tu) gli hai letto (leggesti).
3. Paolo ha chiesto (chiese) a Carla di uscire con lui, ma lei ha solo riso.
4. Il signore Dini ha noleggiato (noleggiò) un nuovo film, ma non l'ha guardato (guardò).
5. (Noi) abbiamo pagato (pagammo) il conto ieri, poiché (perché) abbiamo bevuto (bevemmo) quasi tutto il caffè.
6. Marco, chi ti ha dato quel libro?
7. Ieri ha piovuto (è piovuto) (pioveva). Ha fatto (fece) brutto (cattivo) tempo tutta la giornata.
8. Ho già scritto quell'e-mail. Carla ha visto l'e-mail.
9. Franca, hai acceso il televisore? Ieri ho visto (vidi) un nuovo programma.
10. Che (cosa) hanno detto? Non ho capito niente (nulla).
11. Ho conosicuto il mio insegnante/la mia insegnante d'italiano l'anno scorso.
12. Sono partiti per l'Italia questa mattina (stamani).
13. La tua amica ha chiamato questo pomeriggio.
14. (Loro) sono andati al cinema ieri sera.
15. (Io) l'ho già fatto/ho già fatto quello.
16. Mio fratello è appena arrivato.
17. I miei genitori vennero (sono venuti) in America molti anni fa.
18. Mentre tuo fratello suonava il violoncello, io dormivo.
19. Quando erano in Italia, volevano sempre andare al mare.
20. Da giovane, sapevo parlare lo spagnolo.
21. (Loro) preferivano sempre andare al cinema anni fa, ma io non ci volevo mai andare.
22. Sara non ha mai detto che voleva venire alla festa.

C.
1. a
2. a
3. a
4. a
5. b
6. a
7. a

D.

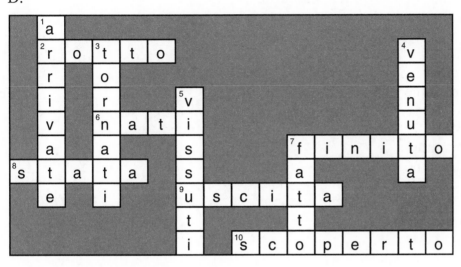

E.
1. Gioacchino Rossini compose l'opera *Il Barbiere di Siviglia*.
2. Guglielmo Marconi inventò la radio.
3. Cristoforo Colombo scoprì il "Nuovo Mondo".
4. Lo scoprì nel 1492.
5. Giuseppe Verdi compose l'opera *La Traviata*.

F. [Answers will vary.]

CHAPTER 5

Quanto sai già?
1. e
2. f
3. g
4. h
5. i
6. d
7. c
8. b
9. a

Quick Practice 1

1. Quel programma televisivo comincerà alle sei di sera (alle diciotto) e finirà alle nove (alle ventuno).
2. Ci sarà molta gente alla festa.
3. (Io) so che lei non andrà a vedere quel film.
4. (Io) sono sicuro/a che ti chiameranno, Alessandro.
5. Pagheremo (noi) al Bar Roma se mangerai quello che diciamo noi.
6. Ha detto che anche lui ci sarà.
7. Domani Maria ed io usciremo insieme.
8. (Io) so di sicuro che voi due finirete in orario.
9. (Io) partirò domani per l'Italia.
10. noi staremo
11. voi farete
12. quei ragazzi daranno
13. quelle ragazze vedranno
14. noi sapremo
15. voi potrete
16. quei bambini dovranno
17. quelle bambine avranno
18. noi cadremo
19. voi andrete
20. loro mangeranno
21. loro cercheranno

	essere	fare	dire	bere	volere	venire	rimanere
(io)	sarò	farò	dirò	berrò	vorrò	verrò	rimarrò
(tu)	sarai	farai	dirai	berrai	vorrai	verrai	rimarrai
(lui/lei)	sarà	farà	dirà	berrà	vorrà	verrà	rimarrà
(noi)	saremo	faremo	diremo	berremo	vorremo	verremo	rimarremo
(voi)	sarete	farete	direte	berrete	vorrete	verrete	rimarrete
(loro)	saranno	faranno	diranno	berranno	vorranno	verranno	rimarranno

Quick Practice 2

1. Dopo che (loro) saranno arrivati/e, andremo al cinema insieme.
2. Quando (loro) avranno finito di studiare, andranno in Italia.
3. Oggi (io) uscirò, solo dopo che avrò studiato un po'.
4. Appena che (lui) avrà finito di leggere quel libro, (io) sono sicuro che (lui) ne comincerà un altro.
5. Dopo che quella squadra avrà vinto il campionato, (io) sarò molto felice.
6. Quando avrà traslocato nel suo appartamento nuovo, dove lavorerà, signor Smith?
7. Quella macchina (automobile) sarà costata molti/tanti soldi!
8. (Lui) sarà già uscito.
9. Quando (lui) arriverà, (loro) saranno già andati a casa.

1. (Io) parlerei italiano di più, ma prima devo studiare i verbi.
2. È vero che tu studieresti lo spagnolo anziché l'italiano?
3. Il mio amico comincerebbe a lavorare più presto ogni giorno, ma è sempre molto stanco.
4. (Noi) pagheremmo volentieri (per) il caffè, ma non abbiamo soldi.
5. (Voi) mi aiutereste ad imparare la grammatica italiana, per favore/per piacere?
6. (Io) so che (loro) capirebbero quello che (voi) fate.
7. (Io) guarderei quel programma televisivo, ma non ho tempo.
8. (Lei) mangerebbe quelle paste di sicuro.
9. (Io) lo potrei fare/potrei farlo, ma non lo faccio.
10. (Io) lo dovrei fare/dovrei farlo, e lo farò.
11. (Io) lo vorrei fare/vorrei farlo, ma non posso.
12. Mi potrebbe aiutare?
13. Vorrei un caffè, grazie.
14. Maria ha detto che verrebbe domani.
15. Quanto costerebbe/potrebbe costare quella macchina (automobile)?
16. Secondo lui, quella ragazza sarebbe spagnola.

17. io...
    a. potrei
    b. verrei
    c. rimarrei
    d. sarei

18. tu...
    a. dovresti
    b. berresti
    c. diresti
    d. faresti

19. lui/lei...
    a. vorrebbe
    b. starebbe
    c. vedrebbe
    d. potrebbe

20. noi...
    a. avremmo
    b. pagheremmo
    c. cercheremmo
    d. cominceremmo

21. voi...
    a. mangereste
    b. leggereste
    c. berreste
    d. sareste

22. loro...
    a. rimarrebbero
    b. vorrebbero
    c. vedrebbero
    d. verrebbero

Quick Practice 4
1. (Io) sarei andato/a alla festa, ma non avevo tempo.
2. I miei genitori sarebbero andati in Italia l'anno scorso, ma non avevano i soldi.
3. (Io) sarei uscito/a con lui, ma dovevo studiare.
4. Di solito, avrei fatto quello io stesso/a, ma questa volta ha deciso lei di farlo.
5. (Lui) avrebbe comprato quella macchina (automobile), ma costava troppo.
6. (Loro) mi hanno detto che sarebbero venuti/e.
7. (Lui) sapeva che (io) avrei capito.
8. L'avrei potuta fare/avrei potuto farla, e l'avrei voluta fare/avrei voluto farla, e forse l'avrei dovuta fare/avrei dovuto farla, ma non l'ho fatta.

Putting It All Together
A.
1. e
2. f
3. d
4. g
5. h
6. i
7. b
8. c
9. a

B.
1. Secondo me, [name of team] vincerà il "World Series" di baseball quest'anno.
2. Secondo me, [name of actor] vincerà il premio "Oscar" quest'anno.
3. Secondo me, [name of person] sarà il prossimo Presidente degli Stati Uniti.
4. Secondo me, domani farà bel tempo/pioverà...
5. Secondo me, [name of person] riceverà il "Premio Nobel" quest'anno.

C.
1. avrò finito
2. sarà uscito
3. arriverà
4. andrete
5. verrebbero
6. sarà andata
7. avranno finito
8. avranno visto
9. avrai assaggiato

D.
1. (Loro) andrebbero volentieri al bar, ma non hanno tempo.
2. Signora Smith, mi potrebbe (può) aiutare?
3. Chi vorrebbe (vuole) un caffè?
4. Franco ha detto che (loro) arriverebbero/sarebbero arrivati domani.
5. Quanto costerebbe/costerà quella nuova macchina (automobile)?
6. Nella sua opinione, quel ragazzo sarebbe italiano.
7. Secondo lui, (Lei) sarebbe americana.
8. (Loro) potrebbero venire un po' più tardi, no/vero/non è vero?
9. (Lei) non dovrebbe fare quello.
10. Signor Smith, vorrebbe/vuole/desidererebbe un cappuccino?

E.

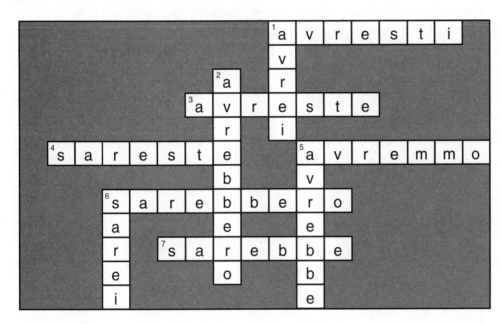

CHAPTER 6

Quanto sai già?
1. a
2. b
3. a
4. b
5. a
6. b

Quick Practice 1
1. (Lui) pensa che loro arrivino stasera.
2. (Io) immagino che lei capisca tutto.
3. (Loro) dubitano che tu finisca in tempo.
4. (Tu) sei la persona meno elegante che io conosca.
5. Che nevichi!
6. (Lei) vuole che io la chiami stasera.

7. Sembra che anche tu conosca Maria.
8. Spero che Alessandro scriva quell'e-mail.
9. Anche tu credi che io parli italiano bene?
10. (Noi) desideriamo/vogliamo che loro giochino meglio a calcio.
11. Bisogna che/È necessario che lui studi di più.
12. È possibile che loro parlino italiano.
13. È probabile che noi compriamo quella macchina/automobile.
14. Benché/sebbene piova fuori, esco lo stesso.
15. A meno che lei non telefoni, non andremo al cinema.
16. Affinché/Perché tu mangi la pasta, la cucinerò io stesso/a.
17. Chiunque desideri/voglia farlo/ Chiunque lo desideri/voglia fare, io sono d'accordo.
18. Dovunque lei vada, anche io ci andrò.
19. Nel caso che lui legga quell'e-mail, tu dovresti essere pronto/a a chiamarlo.
20. Nonostante il fatto che tu non telefoni mai, ti amo lo stesso.
21. Prima che voi partiate per l'Italia, dovreste risparmiare abbastanza soldi.
22. Lo farò, purché tu mi telefoni prima.
23. Qualunque lingua loro parlino, so che lui li capirà.

24. **io...**
    a. cominci
    b. mangi
    c. cerchi
    d. paghi

25. **tu...**
    a. abbia
    b. beva
    c. dia
    d. dica

26. **lui/lei...**
    a. vada
    b. deva/debba
    c. dica
    d. voglia

27. **noi...**
    a. siamo
    b. facciamo
    c. moriamo
    d. nasciamo

28. **voi...**
    a. possiate
    b. rimaniate
    c. saliate
    d. sappiate

29. loro...
    a. scelgano
    b. stiano
    c. escano
    d. vengano

Quick Practice 2

1. Loro dubitano che io abbia cominciato a studiare l'italiano.
2. Lei crede che tu abbia letto quel romanzo già.
3. Immagino che mio fratello abbia pagato il conto.
4. Penso che abbia fatto bel tempo ieri.
5. Lui crede che noi abbiamo bevuto il caffè al bar ieri.
6. Immagino che voi abbiate già visto quel film.
7. Spero che loro li abbiano già comprati.
8. I miei amici pensano che io sia andata in Italia l'anno scorso.
9. Lui pensa che tu sia uscito poco tempo fa.
10. Penso che mia sorella sia arrivata qualche minuto fa.
11. Lui crede che noi siamo venuti alla festa.
12. Mia madre crede che voi siate tornati in Italia l'anno scorso.
13. Lei pensa che loro siano usciti tardi ieri.
14. Sembra che tu sia andata in Italia l'anno scorso.
15. Sembra che lui sia venuto alla festa.

Quick Practice 3

1. Loro dubitavano che io cominciassi a studiare l'italiano.
2. Lei credeva che tu leggessi quel romanzo.
3. Io pensavo che mio fratello studiasse a quest'ora.
4. Pensavo che lei uscisse con Marco.
5. Lui credeva che noi guardassimo la televisione ogni sera da giovani.
6. Sembra che piovesse ieri.
7. Credo che loro sperassero di andare in Italia.
8. I miei amici pensano che io andassi in Italia ogni estate da bambino.
9. Lui pensava che tu volessi uscire.
10. Loro dubitavano che io bevessi il latte regolarmente.
11. Lei credeva che tu dicessi sempre la verità.
12. Io pensavo che mio fratello non facesse niente.
13. Credevo che tu dessi del tu al professore.
14. Magari non piovesse.
15. Benché nevicasse, sono uscito lo stesso.

16. io...
    a. cominciassi
    b. mettessi
    c. capissi
    d. bevessi

17. **tu...**
    a. vendessi
    b. preferissi
    c. pagassi
    d. dessi

18. **lui/lei...**
    a. fossi
    b. facessi
    c. stessi
    d. finissi

19. **noi...**
    a. fossimo
    b. avessimo
    c. preferissimo
    d. facessimo

20. **voi...**
    a. steste
    b. foste
    c. aveste
    d. faceste

21. **loro...**
    a. fossero
    b. avessero
    c. mangiassero
    d. capissero

Quick Practice 4
1. b
2. b
3. a
4. b
5. b
6. b
7. b
8. b

9. **io...**
    a. avessi mangiato
    b. fossi andato/a

10. **tu...**
    a. avessi fatto
    b. fossi uscito/a

11. **lui/lei...**
    a. avesse detto
    b. fosse stato/a

12. **noi...**
    a. avessimo dato
    b. fossimo andati/e

13. **voi...**
    a. aveste parlato
    b. foste usciti/e

14. **loro...**
    a. avessero detto
    b. fossero usciti/e

Putting It All Together

A.
1. È probabile che loro vadano in Italia quest'anno.
2. Penso che tu abbia trentatré anni.
3. Sembra che loro bevano il cappuccino.
4. Bisogna che lui dia la penna a Maria.
5. Speriamo che voi diciate la verità.
6. Sembra che loro devano/debbano studiare di più.
7. Immagino che ci sia anche Alessandro.
8. Bisogna che faccia bel tempo.
9. Speriamo che nasca domani forse il bambino.
10. Sembra che Marco possa venire alla festa.
11. Penso che loro rimangano a casa domani.
12. Dubito che la sua amica sappia parlare l'italiano molto bene.
13. Sembra che lui scelga sempre lo stesso programma.
14. Penso che Alessandro stia molto bene.
15. Credo che loro escano insieme.
16. Dubito che quel film valga la pena di vedere.
17. Speriamo che loro vengano alla festa.
18. Penso che lui voglia andare in Italia.

B.
1. a
2. b
3. a
4. b
5. a
6. b
7. a
8. b
9. a

10. a
11. b
12. a
13. a
14. a
15. b

C.
1. Benché/Sebbene abbia nevicato ieri, ho deciso di fare delle spese lo stesso.
2. È possibile che loro siano già andati al bar.
3. Lui non sa chi abbia segnato il gol/la rete ieri.
4. Lui è la persona più felice che io abbia mai conosciuto.
5. Sembra che loro abbiano già visto quel film.
6. (Io) penso che mia sorella abbia già fatto quello.
7. Tutti pensano che io sia andata in Italia l'anno scorso.
8. (Tu) pensi veramente che lui abbia capito?
9. Non è vero che io abbia mangiato tutti gli spaghetti.
10. (Io) penso che quello che lui dice sia vero.
11. Sarebbe importante che lui studiasse di più.
12. Se potessimo, andremmo al cinema.
13. Magari non facesse così tanto caldo!
14. Se (quello) fosse vero, allora io non sarei qui.

D.

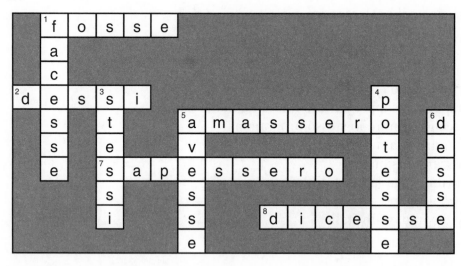

CHAPTER 7

Quanto sai già?
1. Signora, mangi la mela.
2. Marco, bevi tutto il latte.
3. Cosa stai facendo in questo momento?
4. La casa sarà venduta dai miei amici.
5. Camminando per strada ieri, ho incontrato tuo fratello.
6. Franco e Gina, mangiate tutta la torta.

7. Signore e signori, desiderano qualcosa?
8. Maria, non leggere quel brutto libro.
9. Signorina, non ascolti quella musica.

Quick Practice 1
1. Maria, parla italiano, per favore/per piacere!
2. Maria, mangia la torta!
3. Maria, chiudi la bocca!
4. Maria, finisci gli spinaci!
5. Maria, va' a casa!
6. Maria, abbi pazienza!
7. Maria, bevi il caffè!
8. Maria, da' la penna all'insegnante!
9. Maria, di' la verità!
10. Maria, sii cauta!
11. Signor Santini, parli italiano, per favore/per piacere!
12. Signor Santini, mangi la torta!
13. Signor Santini, chiuda la bocca!
14. Signor Santini, finisca gli spinaci!
15. Signor Santini, vada a casa!
16. Signor Santini, abbia pazienza!
17. Signor Santini, beva il caffè!
18. Signor Santini, dia la penna all'insegnante!
19. Signor Santini, dica la verità!
20. Signor Santini, sia cauto!
21. Maria e Marco, parlate italiano, per favore/per piacere!
22. Maria e Marco, mangiate la torta!
23. Maria e Marco, chiudete la bocca!
24. Maria e Marco, finite gli spinaci!
25. Maria e Marco, andate a casa!
26. Maria e Marco, abbiate pazienza!
27. Maria e Marco, bevete il caffè!
28. Maria e Marco, date la penna all'insegnante!
29. Maria e Marco, dite la verità!
30. Maria e Marco, siate cauti!
31. Signore e signora Santini, parlino italiano, per favore/per piacere!
32. Signore e signora Santini, mangino la torta!
33. Signore e signora Santini, chiudano la bocca!
34. Signore e signora Santini, finiscano gli spinaci!
35. Signore e signora Santini, vadano a casa!
36. Signore e signora Santini, abbiano pazienza!
37. Signore e signora Santini, bevano il caffè!
38. Signore e signora Santini, diano la penna all'insegnante!
39. Signore e signora Santini, dicano la verità!
40. Signore e signora Santini, siano cauti!
41. Maria, non pagare il conto!

42. Maria, non andare a casa!
43. Maria, non bere il latte!
44. Maria, non dare a Marco la tua penna!
45. Maria, non rimanere a casa!
46. Maria, non scegliere questo!
47. Maria, non stare a casa tutto il giorno!
48. Maria, non uscire con Marco!

Quick Practice 2

1. Franco, che (cosa) stai bevendo? Stai bevendo un espresso?
2. Quale/Che film stanno dando in questo momento?
3. Signora Marchi, che sta dicendo?
4. Che (cosa) stanno facendo?
5. Marco e Maria stanno uscendo in questo momento.
6. Dov'è Alessandro? Sta dormendo.
7. Che (cosa) stanno bevendo? Stanno bevendo un cappuccino?
8. (Io) credo che Franco stia bevendo un espresso.
9. È possibile che (loro) stiano partendo per l'Italia in questo momento.
10. (Lei) non crede che Lei stia dicendo quello, signora Marchi.
11. (Io) penso che (loro) non stiano facendo niente/nulla in questo momento.
12. (Io) credo che Marco e Maria stiano facendo delle spese in questo momento.
13. Pensavano che io stessi leggendo.
14. Pensavano che tu stessi bevendo il caffè.
15. Pensavano che lei stesse guardando la TV.
16. Pensavano che noi stessimo facendo delle spese.
17. Pensavano che voi steste dicendo la verità.
18. Pensavano che i loro genitori stessero guardando la TV.

Maria:	Ciao, Marco, non ci vediamo da anni. Che stai facendo di bello?
Marco:	Ciao, Maria. È vero. In questo momento, non sto facendo niente. E tu?
Maria:	Sto lavorando in una banca. Ma sto programmando di tornare all'università.
Marco:	Sto programmando la stessa cosa.
Maria:	Sai, stanno dando un nuovo film stasera. Vuoi venire con me e il mio fidanzato?
Marco:	No, grazie. In questo momento sto uscendo con Franca. Stiamo programmando di fare qualcos'altro. A presto!
Maria:	Ciao!

Quick Practice 3

1. a
2. c
3. b
4. a
5. a
6. a
7. c
8. a
9. c
10. b
11. a
12. b
13. c
14. Mi chiamo
15. ti alzi
16. ci annoiamo
17. si sposa
18. si vedono
19. ci capiamo
20. vi parlate
21. io mi sto lamentando
22. tu ti stai vestendo
23. lei si sta divertendo
24. noi ci stiamo arrabbiando
25. voi ve ne state andando
26. loro si stanno annoiando
27. io mi stavo annoiando
28. tu te ne stavi andando
29. Giovanni, alzati!
30. Maria, non ti alzare/non alzarti ancora!
31. (Io) credo che lui stesse molto bene.
32. Benché/Sebbene si fosse addormentato, (noi) abbiamo continuato/continuammo a guardare la TV.
33. Pietro, addormentati!
34. Pietro, non ti arrabbiare/non arrabbiarti!
35. Pietro, non ti dimenticare/non dimenticarti di scrivere a tua zia!
36. Pietro, divertiti in Italia!
37. Signora Rossi, non si lamenti!
38. Signora Rossi, si metta quel nuovo abito/vestito!
39. Signora Rossi, non si preoccupi!

	Present Indic.	Present Subj.	Imperf. Indic.	Imperf. Subj.	Past Abs.	Future	Cond.	Imper.
dedurre (*Past Part.* **dedotto**, *Gerund* **deducendo**)								
(io)	deduco	deduca	deducevo	deducessi	dedussi	dedurrò	dedurrei	—
(tu)	deduci	deduca	deducevi	deducessi	deducesti	dedurrai	dedurresti	deduci
(lui/lei)	deduce	deduca	deduceva	deducesse	dedusse	dedurrà	dedurrebbe	deduca
(noi)	deduciamo	deduciamo	deducevamo	deducessimo	deducemmo	dedurremo	dedurremmo	deduciamo
(voi)	deducete	deduciate	deducevate	deduceste	deduceste	dedurrete	dedurreste	deducete
(loro)	deducono	deducano	deducevano	deducessero	dedussero	dedurranno	dedurrebbero	deducano
trarre (*Past Part.* **tratto**, *Gerund* **traendo**)								
(io)	traggo	tragga	traevo	traessi	trassi	trarrò	trarrei	—
(tu)	trai	tragga	traevi	traessi	traesti	trarrai	trarresti	trai
(lui/lei)	trae	tragga	traeva	traesse	trasse	trarrà	trarrebbe	tragga
(noi)	traiamo	traiamo	traevamo	traessimo	traemmo	trarremo	trarremmo	traiamo
(voi)	traete	traiate	traevate	traeste	traeste	trarrete	trarreste	traete
(loro)	traggono	traggano	traevano	traessero	trassero	trarranno	trarrebbero	traggano
porre (*Past Part.* **posto**, *Gerund* **ponendo**)								
(io)	pongo	ponga	ponevo	ponessi	posi	porrò	porrei	—
(tu)	poni	ponga	ponevi	ponessi	ponesti	porrai	porresti	poni
(lui/lei)	pone	ponga	poneva	ponesse	pose	porrà	porrebbe	ponga
(noi)	poniamo	poniamo	ponevamo	ponessimo	ponemmo	porremo	porremmo	poniamo
(voi)	ponete	poniate	ponevate	poneste	poneste	porrete	porreste	ponete
(loro)	pongono	pongano	ponevano	ponessero	posero	porranno	porrebbero	pongano

Quick Practice 5
1. Mentre camminava/Camminando ieri, mi ha incontrato.
2. Vedendomi, mi ha fatto andare con lei.
3. Avendo fatto tutto, sono usciti.
4. Essendo andati/e in Italia, hanno potuto viaggiare in giro assai.
5. Il bere è necessario per sopravvivere.
6. Lui pensa di sapere tutto.
7. Dopo essere usciti/e, hanno deciso di tornare a casa.
8. Gli è stato dato un pezzo di torta. Ma invece di mangiarlo, lo ha messo giù.

Quick Practice 6
1. La torta è mangiata da Marco.
2. Il cappuccino è stato bevuto da quell'uomo.
3. Da bambina, i cartoni animati erano guardati regolarmente da mia sorella.
4. Quando siamo arrivati, la spesa era già stata fatta dalle tue amiche.
5. *Il Decamerone* fu scritto da Boccaccio.
6. Quel computer portatile sarà comprato dalla mia amica.
7. Gli spaghetti saranno già stati fatti da Giovanni.

8. Se potesse, quella Ferrari sarebbe comprata da lui.
9. Se avesse potuto, quella Ferrari sarebbe stata comprata da lui.
10. Penso che quel portatile sia desiderato da Marco.
11. Penso che quella casa sia stata già comprata da loro.
12. Credevo che i suoi spaghetti fossero stati già assaggiati da voi.
13. Maria ha fatto già lavare i piatti a suo fratello.
14. (Io) la farò studiare di più.
15. (Loro) mi hanno fatto andare al bar ieri.
16. (Loro) mi hanno anche fatto bere un cappuccino.

Putting It All Together
A.
1. Daniela, assaggia la minestra!
2. Daniela, paga il conto!
3. Daniela, dormi di più!
4. Daniela, fa' gli spaghetti!
5. Daniela, poni quella domanda all'insegnante!
6. Daniela, rimani a casa!
7. Daniela, scegli questo!
8. Daniela, sta' a casa!
9. Daniela, esci con loro!
10. Daniela, vieni qui!
11. Daniela, traduci quel libro!
12. Daniela, non andare ancora a casa!
13. Daniela, non bere la Coca-Cola!
14. Daniela, non uscire con loro!
15. Daniela, alzati presto!
16. Daniela, mettiti una maglia!
17. Daniela, divertiti alla festa!
18. Signora Verdi, assaggi la minestra!
19. Signora Verdi, paghi il conto!
20. Signora Verdi, dorma di più!
21. Signora Verdi, faccia gli spaghetti!
22. Signora Verdi, ponga quella domanda all'insegnante!
23. Signora Verdi, rimanga a casa!
24. Signora Verdi, scelga questo!
25. Signora Verdi, stia a casa!
26. Signora Verdi, esca con loro!
27. Signora Verdi, venga qui!
28. Signora Verdi, traduca quel libro!
29. Signora Verdi, non vada ancora a casa!
30. Signora Verdi, non beva la Coca-Cola!
31. Signora Verdi, non esca con loro!
32. Signora Verdi, si alzi presto!
33. Signora Verdi, si metta una maglia!
34. Signora Verdi, si diverta alla festa!
35. Marco e Maria, assaggiate la minestra!
36. Marco e Maria, pagate il conto!
37. Marco e Maria, dormite di più!

38. Marco e Maria, fate gli spaghetti!
39. Marco e Maria, ponete quella domanda all'insegnante!
40. Marco e Maria, rimanete a casa!
41. Marco e Maria, scegliete questo!
42. Marco e Maria, state a casa!
43. Marco e Maria, uscite con loro!
44. Marco e Maria, venite qui!
45. Marco e Maria, traducete quel libro!
46. Marco e Maria, non andate ancora a casa!
47. Marco e Maria, non bevete la Coca-Cola!
48. Marco e Maria, non uscite con loro!
49. Marco e Maria, alzatevi presto!
50. Marco e Maria, mettetevi una maglia!
51. Marco e Maria, divertitevi alla festa!

B.
  1. a/b
  2. a/b
  3. b
  4. a/b
  5. b
  6. b
  7. a/b
  8. b
  9. a/b

C.
  1. Penso che Giorgio stia mangiando.
  2. Maria credeva che voi steste guardando un programma alla televisione.
  3. Sembra che Marco stia dormendo.
  4. Lui credeva che io stessi scrivendo.
  5. Lei pensa che i miei amici stiano uscendo.
  6. Loro credevano che noi stessimo bevendo un caffè.
  7. Dubito che voi stiate leggendo.
  8. Sembrava che lui stesse suonando il violoncello.
  9. Sembra che lei stia cantando.

D.
  1. Maria, perché ti vesti sempre elegantemente?
  2. (Io) non mi vergogno di niente!
  3. Marco, a che ora ti alzi generalmente la mattina?
  4. Alessandro e Sara, è vero che vi sposate quest'autunno?
  5. (Loro) si lamentano sempre di tutto.
  6. Perché si arrabbia/si sta arrabbiando, signorina Gentile?
  7. (Loro) si annoiano sempre quando guardano la televisione.
  8. (Io) mi ammalo molto facilmente se fa freddo fuori.

E.

Crossword solution:
1 Down: camminando
2 Across: mangiare
3 Down: guardato
4 Down: fatti
5 Across: dicendo
6 Down: detto
7 Across: tornati

CULTURE CAPSULE 2
Content Questions
1. Falso
2. Vero
3. Falso
4. Vero
5. Vero
6. Falso

CHAPTER 8

Quanto sai già?
1. True
2. False
3. True
4. True
5. True
6. True
7. False
8. False
9. False

Quick Practice 1

COUNT	MASS	NAME	SURNAME	OTHER
amica	acqua	Franco	Bellini	Ferrari
amico	carne	Gina	Da Vinci	FIAT
cane	latte	Giovanni	Di Stefano	Francia
giornale	pane	Marco	Ferrari	Germania
italiano	riso	Maria	Marconi	Italia
libro	uva	Paola	Rossi	Spagna
rivista	zucchero	Renata	Rossini	Stati Uniti

Maschile	Femminile
arancio	arancia
autore	autrice
avvocato	avvocato
cameriere	cameriera
cantante	cantante
Carlo	Carla
ciliegio	ciliegia
dentista	dentista
dottore	dottoressa
elefante	elefantessa
fico	fico
figlio	figlia
genitore	genitrice
limone	limone
mandarino	mandarino
melo	mela
nipote	nipote
Paolo	Paola
pero	pera
pesco	pesca
pianista	pianista
professore	professoressa
ragazzo	ragazza
violinista	violinista
zio	zia

Maschile	Femminile
Andrea	analisi
autobus	città
brindisi	crisi
caffè	e-mail
clacson	gatta
computer	gente
diagramma	gioventù
menù	identità
papà	ipotesi
problema	notte
programma	pansé
sport	spia
tassì	televisione
tè	tesi
tennis	università
teorema	valigia
tram	virtù

Quick Practice 3

Singolare	Plurale	Singolare	Plurale
dio	dei	vaglia	vaglia
bue	buoi	uomo	uomini
mano	mani	foto	foto
cinema	cinema	auto	auto
labbro	labbra (labbri)	ciglio	ciglia (cigli)
paio	paia	braccio	braccia
dito	dita	tè	tè
città	città	tesi	tesi
computer	computer	sport	sport
problema	problemi	programma	programmi
dentista	dentisti/e	pianista	pianisti/e
figlio	figli	valigia	valige
bacio	baci	zio	zii
leggio	leggii	farmacia	farmacie
bugia	bugie	camicia	camicie
oca	oche	riga	righe
teologo	teologi	biologo	biologi
lago	laghi	catalogo	cataloghi
antropologo	antropologi	amico	amici
tedesco	tedeschi	medico	medici
buco	buchi	cattolico	cattolici
parco	parchi	porco	porci
notte	notti	fico	fichi
mela	mele	cameriere	camerieri
bambino	bambini	bambina	bambine

Quick Practice 4

1. la dottoressa Bianchi
2. il dottor Verdi
3. Professoressa Dini, come va/sta?
4. Professor Giannetti, come va/sta?
5. (Lei) è una ragazzona.
6. Quello è stato un affaruccio.
7. innumere
8. impossibile
9. illimitatezza
10. irrealtà
11. reazione
12. preannuncio
13. ragazzino

Finally, give the plural form of each compound noun.

14. casseforti
15. cacciavite
16. francobolli
17. capoluoghi

18. capolavori
19. ferrovie
20. caporeparto

Putting It All Together

A.

	COMMON	PROPER	COUNT	MASS	MASCULINE	FEMININE
italiano	✔		✔		✔	
ingegnere	✔		✔		✔	
spagnola	✔		✔			✔
Renata		✔				✔
Andrea		✔			✔	
Luca		✔			✔	
carne	✔			✔		✔
riso	✔			✔	✔	
uva	✔			✔		✔
Stati Uniti		✔			✔	
notte	✔		✔			✔
soprano	✔		✔		✔	

B.

Maschile	Femminile
ragazzo	ragazza
zio	zia
Giovanni	Giovanna
gatto	gatta
cantante	cantante
cameriere	cameriera
pittore	pittrice/pittore
dottore	dottoressa
farmacista	farmacista
uomo	donna

C.
1. Anche la signora Betti è una mia collega.
2. Anche Claudia è una bambina intelligente.
3. Anche il mio amico Mario ha un nipote.
4. Anche tua sorella è studentessa.
5. Anche tuo fratello ha una ragazza.
6. Anche il mio amico Angelo ha tanti amici.
7. Anche la mia collega Maria è una brava donna.
8. Anche quella donna è professoressa.

D.

Singolare	Plurale
attore	attori
giorno	giorni
mela	mele
notte	notti
buco	buchi
tedesco	tedeschi
monaco	monaci
greco	greci
porco	porci
medico	medici
albergo	alberghi
amica	amiche
camicia	camicie
fruscio	fruscii
problema	problemi
programma	programmi
foto	foto
uomo	uomini

E.

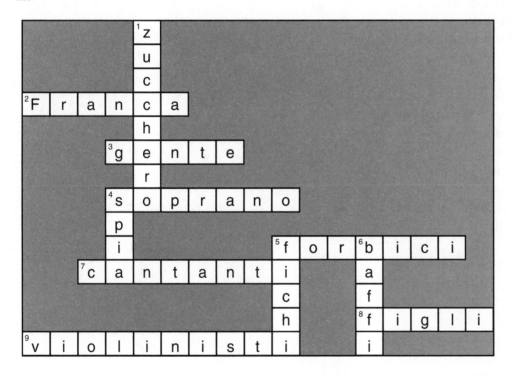

F. [Answers will vary.]

CHAPTER 9

Quanto sai già?

1. i bambini
2. gli studenti
3. gli amici
4. le bambine
5. un libro
6. un amico
7. una finestra
8. un'amica

Quick Practice 1

1. lo zio/uno zio
2. lo zero/uno zero
3. lo studente/uno studente
4. lo sbaglio/uno sbaglio
5. l'amico/un amico
6. l'orologio/un orologio
7. il padre/un padre
8. il fratello/un fratello
9. il nonno/un nonno
10. la madre/una madre
11. la sorella/una sorella
12. la nonna/una nonna
13. l'amica/un'amica
14. l'entrata/un'entrata
15. l'uscita/un'uscita
16. lo psicologo/uno psicologo
17. lo gnocco/uno gnocco
18. la zia/una zia
19. l'altra zia/un'altra zia
20. l'altro studente/un altro studente
21. il nuovo orologio/un nuovo orologio
22. lo zio/gli zii
23. lo zero/gli zeri
24. lo studente/gli studenti
25. lo sbaglio/gli sbagli
26. l'amico/gli amici
27. l'orologio/gli orologi
28. il padre/i padri
29. il fratello/i fratelli
30. il nonno/i nonni
31. la madre/le madri
32. la sorella/le sorelle
33. la nonna/le nonne
34. l'amica/le amiche
35. l'entrata/le entrate
36. l'uscita/le uscite
37. lo psicologo/gli psicologi

38. lo gnocco/gli gnocchi
39. la zia/le zie
40. l'altra zia/le altre zie
41. l'altro studente/gli altri studenti
42. il nuovo orologio/i nuovi orologi

Quick Practice 2

1. questo zio/quello zio
   questi zii/quegli zii
2. questo piede/quel piede
   questi piedi/quei piedi
3. questo psicologo/quello psicologo
   questi psicologi/quegli psicologi
4. quest'occhio/questo occhio/quell'occhio
   questi occhi/questi occhi/quegli occhi
5. questo gnocco/quello gnocco
   questi gnocchi/quegli gnocchi
6. quest'orecchio/questo orecchio/quell'orecchio
   questi orecchi/questi orecchi/quegli orecchi
7. quest'unghia/questa unghia/quell'unghia
   queste unghie/queste unghie/quelle unghie
8. questa bocca/quella bocca
   queste bocche/quelle bocche
9. quest'ora/questa ora/quell'ora
   queste ore/queste ore/quelle ore
10. questo caro zio/quel caro zio
    questi cari zii/quei cari zii
11. questa cara amica/quella cara amica
    queste care amiche/quelle care amiche
12. questo giornale/quel giornale
    questi giornali/quei giornali
13. quest'esercizio/questo esercizio/quell'esercizio
    questi esercizi/questi esercizi/quegli esercizi
14. questa stanza/quella stanza
    queste stanze/quelle stanze
15. quest'ultimo giorno/questo ultimo giorno/quell'ultimo giorno
    questi ultimi giorni/questi ultimi giorni/quegli ultimi giorni
16. questa incredibile settimana/quest'incredibile settimana/quell'incredibile settimana
    queste incredibili settimane/queste incredibili settimane/quelle incredibili settimane
17. questa porta/quella porta
    queste porte/quelle porte
18. questa finestra/quella finestra
    queste finestre/quelle finestre
19. quest'entrata/questa entrata/quell'entrata
    queste entrate/queste entrate/quelle entrate
20. questo tavolo/quel tavolo
    questi tavoli/quei tavoli

1. degli studenti
   alcuni studenti
   qualche studente
2. delle studentesse
   alcune studentesse
   qualche studentessa
3. dei bicchieri
   alcuni bicchieri
   qualche bicchiere
4. delle sedie
   alcune sedie
   qualche sedia
5. delle automobili
   alcune automobili
   qualche automobile
6. dei coltelli
   alcuni coltelli
   qualche coltello
7. degli sbagli
   alcuni sbagli
   qualche sbaglio
8. degli alberi
   alcuni alberi
   qualche albero
9. dei simpatici amici
   alcuni simpatici amici
   qualche simpatico amico
10. dei nuovi studenti
    alcuni nuovi studenti
    qualche nuovo studente

Putting It All Together

A.
1. l'Italia
2. la Francia
3. la Sicilia
4. la Toscana
5. gli Stati Uniti
6. il Po
7. il Tevere
8. la California
9. il Wisconsin
10. il Mediterraneo
11. l'Adriatico
12. il Belgio
13. la Germania
14. le Alpi
15. gli Appennini

16. il Piemonte
17. Roma
18. Venezia
19. Bari
20. Berlino
21. Madrid
22. Parigi

B.
 1. L'acqua è un liquido.
 2. Il cibo è necessario per vivere.
 3. La carne è un cibo importante.
 4. La pazienza è una virtù.
 5. Anche l'amore è una virtù.
 6. Gli italiani sono simpatici.
 7. Anche gli americani sono molto simpatici.
 8. I libri ci aiutano a capire.
 9. I video sono più divertenti.
10. (Lei) va in Italia.
11. (Io) vivo in Francia.
12. (Loro) vivono negli Stati Uniti.
13. (Lui) va nell'Italia centrale.
14. (Noi) viviamo nella Francia meridionale.
15. Il 1776 è un anno importante.
16. Oggi è il quattro aprile.
17. Oggi vado in centro con lo zio/con mio zio.
18. Mi fa male la mano.
19. Sara non si mette mai la giacca.
20. Il martedì ho (una) lezione d'italiano.
21. Il sabato vado sempre in centro.
22. Il dottor Smith è italiano, nonostante il suo nome.
23. Buongiorno/Buon giorno, dottor Smith.
24. (Noi) stiamo imparando l'italiano.
25. Mio fratello studia/sta studiando la matematica.
26. Ecco il suo libro di matematica.
27. La settimana scorsa sono andato/a al cinema.
28. L'anno prossimo vogliamo andare in Italia.
29. Vorrei solo un café e una pasta, grazie.
30. I ragazzi e le ragazze della scuola sono tutti molto simpatici.

C.
Non voglio…
 1. carne
 2. acqua
 3. zucchero
 4. orzo
 5. riso
 6. arance/nessun'arancia
 7. pere/nessuna pera

8. libri/nessun libro
9. cose/nessuna cosa
10. pane
11. insalata
12. caramelle/nessuna caramella
13. paste/nessuna pasta
14. bicchieri/nessun bicchiere
15. forchette/nessuna forchetta

D.
1. un libro [*only form with the indefinite article*]
2. quell'amico [*only form with a demonstrative*]
3. degli amici [*only form with a partitive*]
4. la forchetta [*only form with the definite article*]

CHAPTER 10

Quanto sai già?
1. b
2. f
3. e
4. g
5. c
6. h
7. d
8. i
9. a

Quick Practice 1

Maschile	Femminile
un uomo simpatico	una donna simpatica
un caro amico	una cara amica
un grande uomo	una grande donna
un simpatico zio	una simpatica zia
un ragazzo simpatico	una ragazza simpatica
un padre intelligente	una madre intelligente
un amico alto	un'amica alta

Singolare	Plurale
un vestito grigio	dei vestiti grigi
quella strada lunga	quelle strade lunghe
una bella camicia	delle belle camicie
il cappotto rosso	i cappotti rossi
il vestito rosa	i vestiti rosa
la sciarpa marrone	le sciarpe marrone
quello zaino viola	quegli zaini viola
quel ragazzo francese	quei ragazzi francesi
quella ragazza francese	quelle ragazze francesi

1. Quanti euro hai/ha?
2. Quanta minestra vuoi?/Che vuoi?/Che cosa vuoi?/Cosa vuoi?
3. Quanto caffè vuoi?/Che vuoi?/Che cosa vuoi?/Cosa vuoi?
4. Quanti biscotti vogliono loro?/Che vogliono?/Che cosa vogliono?/Cosa vogliono?
5. Chi è quel ragazzo?
6. Chi è quella ragazza?
7. Chi sono quelle due persone?
8. Che libro è?/Quale libro è?
9. Che penne sono?/Quali penne sono?
10. Come ti chiami? / Come si chiama?
11. Come state?
12. Dove sei/è nato?
13. Dove sono nati loro?
14. Quale DVD preferisci/perferisce?
15. Quali scarpe vuoi/vuole?
16. Quale film vuoi/vuole vedere?
17. Quando vuoi/vuole vederlo?
18. Perché dici questo?

Quick Practice 3
1.
   a. il mio amico
   b. la mia amica
   c. i miei amici
   d. le mie amiche
   e. mio zio
   f. i miei zii
   g. il mio zio vecchio

2.
   a. il tuo cappotto
   b. i tuoi cappotti
   c. la tua bicicletta
   d. le tue biciclette
   e. tuo fratello
   f. i tuoi fratelli
   g. il tuo fratello grande

3.
   a. il Suo cappotto
   b. i Suoi cappotti
   c. la Sua bicicletta
   d. le Sue biciclette
   e. Suo fratello
   f. i Suoi fratelli
   g. il Suo fratello grande

4.

    a. il vostro cappotto
    b. i vostri cappotti
    c. la vostra bicicletta
    d. le vostre biciclette
    e. vostro fratello
    f. i vostri fratelli
    g. il vostro fratello grande

5.

    a. il Loro cappotto
    b. i Loro cappotti
    c. la Loro bicicletta
    d. le Loro biciclette
    e. il Loro fratello
    f. i Loro fratelli
    g. il Loro fratello grande

6.

    a. il nostro passaporto
    b. i nostri passaporti
    c. la nostra camera
    d. le nostre camere
    e. nostra zia
    f. le nostre zie
    g. la nostra simpatica zia

7.

    a. il suo giornale
    b. i suoi giornali
    c. la sua rivista
    d. le sue riviste
    e. sua sorella
    f. le sue sorelle
    g. la sua sorellina

8.

    a. il suo giornale
    b. i suoi giornali
    c. la sua rivista
    d. le sue riviste
    e. sua sorella
    f. le sue sorelle
    g. la sua sorellina

9.
    a. il loro giornale
    b. i loro giornali
    c. la loro rivista
    d. le loro riviste
    e. la loro sorella
    f. le loro sorelle
    g. la loro sorellina

Quick Practice 4

1. Non ho abbastanza soldi.
2. Lui mangia assai pasta.
3. Ogni pomeriggio guardiamo la TV.
4. In Italia puoi andare a qualsiasi (qualunque) bar.
5. Chi sono le altre ragazze?
6. Conosco una certa dottoressa che si chiama Elena.
7. Ieri ho mangiato molte (tante) caramelle.
8. Ci sono poche studentesse in questa classe.
9. Parecchi turisti visitano Firenze.
10. Abbiamo mangiato troppo gelato.
11. Questa è l'ultima volta che ti telefonerò/chiamerò.
12. Queste sono le stesse donne.
13. Lei ha mangiato tutto il riso.
14. Alessandro ha mangiato tutta la minestra.
15. Tutti i miei amici verranno alla festa.
16. Anche tutte le loro amiche verranno alla festa.

Quick Practice 5

1. Maria è elegante.
   Marco è più elegante.
   Gino, invece, è meno elegante.
   Ma Claudia è la più elegante.

2. Maria è studiosa.
   Marco è più studioso.
   Gino, invece, è meno studioso.
   Ma Claudia è la più studiosa.

3. Maria è alta.
   Marco è più alto.
   Gino, invece, è meno alto.
   Ma Claudia è la più alta.

4. Maria è generosa.
   Marco è più generoso.
   Gino, invece, è meno generoso.
   Ma Claudia è la più generosa.

5. Maria è forte.
   Marco è più forte.
   Gino, invece, è meno forte.
   Ma Claudia è la più forte.

6. Maria è elegante.
   Marco è più/meno elegante di Maria.
   No, Marco è tanto elegante quanto Maria.

7. Maria è forte.
   Marco è più/meno forte di Maria.
   No, Marco è tanto forte quanto Maria.

8. Maria è alta.
   Marco è più/meno alto di Maria.
   No, Marco è tanto alto quanto Maria.

9. Maria è generosa.
   Marco è più/meno generoso di Maria.
   No, Marco è tanto generoso quanto Maria.

10. Maria è più/meno forte che piccola.
11. Maria è più/meno alta che forte.
12. Maria è più/meno generosa che studiosa.
13. Maria è più/meno elegante che interessante.
14. Maria è più intelligente di quel che/quello che/ciò che pensano.
15. I miei amici sono intelligentissimi.
16. E le mie amiche sono studiosissime.
17. L'italiano è una lingua facilissima.
18. I vini toscani sono buonissimi.
19. Maria è più piccola/minore di Sara.
20. Giovanni è un ragazzo grande. Marco è più grande/maggiore. Alessandro è il più grande/il maggiore.
21. (Lei) è la mia miglior(e) amica.
22. (Lui) è il miglior(e) studente della classe.

Putting It All Together
A.
1. un grande amico/un grand'amico
2. un grande studioso
3. Santo Stefano
4. Santi Stefano e Giovanni
5. Santa Maria
6. Sante Maria e Anna
7. Sant'Antonio
8. Sant'Anna
9. una bella ragazza
10. quelle belle ragazze
11. un bel ragazzo

12. quei bei ragazzi
13. un bell'orologio
14. quei begli anelli
15. il bello sport
16. quel bel fiore
17. quel buon amico
18. quella buona caramella
19. un buono zio
20. dei buoni amici
21. un caro amico
22. una brutta situazione

B.
1. (Lui) è un bravo studente. Studia sempre/tutto il tempo.
2. (Lui) è un ragazzo bravo/buono. Obbedisce sempre.
3. Quello è un libro grande.
4. Quello è un gran libro.
5. (Lui) è un ragazzo molto bravo/buono.
6. (Lei) è una ragazza simpatica e bella.
7. Il mio abito/vestito sta diventando vecchio.
8. Quella donna sembra molto giovane.
9. (Lui) è un vecchio amico. Lo conosco da molti anni.
10. (Loro) sono una famiglia povera. Forse diventeranno ricchi vincendo la lotteria.
11. Il cappotto e l'impermeabile sono verdi.
12. La maglia e la borsa sono azzurre/blu.
13. Lei è una loro amica.
14. E lui è un nostro amico.
15. Mio caro amico, che fai/stai facendo?

C.
1. Quante patatine fritte hai/ha mangiato?
2. Quali libri hai/ha letto?
3. Quando siete arrivati?
4. Come stai/sta?
5. Perché lo fai/fa?
6. Chi è lei?
7. Che fai/fa?/Che stai/sta facendo?

D.
1. La mia gatta è bella, ma la tua è più bella. La tua è più bella della mia.
2. Il tuo cane è intelligente, come il suo. Il tuo è così/tanto intelligente come/quanto il suo.
3. Mi piace camminare col cane e mi piace anche guardare la TV la sera. Mi piace tanto camminare col cane quanto guardare la TV la sera.
4. Ho comprato la stessa quantità di carne e di latte per il mio gatto. Ho comprato tanta carne quanto latte.
5. La mia gatta è simpatica, ma non è poi così tanto simpatica. La mia gatta è meno simpatica di quel che/quello che/ciò che pensate.

6. La mia gatta è furba, ma è meno intelligente. La mia gatta è più furba che intelligente.

7. Il mio cane è il cane più intelligente di tutti i cani del mondo.

E.

B	I	A	N	C	O	G	U	N	E	R	O	N	O	M	R	O	S	S	O	E
H	Q	A	S	E	D	I	A	B	C	D	E	F	G	H	U	N	G	F	D	S
I	Q	A	S	E	D	A	G	H	J	U	T	I	O	P	A	D	R	A	N	A
E	Q	A	S	V	D	G	H	A	A	E	I	Q	V	G	N	N	G	F	D	R
S	R	T	Y	E	I	I	D	Z	A	N	R	U	V	G	T	D	R	A	N	A
A	O	C	S	R	C	A	L	Z	O	O	U	E	V	G	O	D	R	A	N	N
A	S	I	4	D	R	L	R	U	N	R	M	S	V	G	C	V	G	D	G	C
C	A	N	T	E	R	L	O	R	H	E	T	T	O	R	C	H	I	U	S	I
E	B	Q	E	E	O	R	R	N	R	R	V	I	O	L	A	A	A	D	O
D	B	U	E	E	W	A	B	O	D	E	F	G	H	B	E	I	C	B	R	N
F	C	E	E	E	Q	G	H	J	U	M	A	R	R	O	N	E	C	A	D	E
V	D	A	U	U	A	A	B	C	D	E	F	G	H	V	O	P	A	B	R	T

CHAPTER 11

Quanto sai già?

1. a
2. a
3. b
4. a
5. b
6. b

Quick Practice 1

1. tu
2. Lei
3. voi
4. Loro
5. noi
6. loro
7. essa
8. esso
9. io
10. Egli
11. Ella

Quick Practice 2

1. Paolo l'ha sempre detta.
2. Bruno vi ha chiamato ieri, vero?
3. Mi hanno invitato alla festa!

4. Paola ti ha chiamato poco tempo fa.
5. Io l'ho comprato in quel negozio in via Nazionale.
6. Anche tu li hai comprati nello stesso negozio, vero?
7. Lui l'ha mangiata volentieri.
8. Lei le ha già assaggiate.
9. Noi l'abbiamo letta.
10. Loro me l'hanno data.
11. Tu l'hai chiamata.
12. Tu le hai telefonato.
13. Giovanni me l'ha dato.
14. Nostro fratello ce li ha portati.
15. Lei te le ha date.
16. Loro gliele hanno date.
17. Noi glieli abbiamo portati.
18. Glielo voglio comprare./Voglio comprarglielo.
19. Eccoli.
20. Marco, dammela!
21. Maria, dagliele!
22. Maria, non gliela dare!/non dargliela!
23. Giovanni, mangia la torta! Mangiala!
24. Maria, non bere il caffè! Non lo bere!/Non berlo!
25. Signora Smith, paghi il conto! Per favore, lo paghi!
26. Giorgio telefonale!
27. Claudia, dammi gli spaghetti!
28. Bruno, dacci il tuo indirizzo!
29. Pasquale, di' la verità! Diccela!
30. Maria, dov'è la tua penna? Dammela!
31. Fallo, Maria!
32. Lo faccia, Signora Smith!

Quick Practice 3
1. Mi sono lavata questa mattina.
2. Tu non ti diverti mai in centro.
3. (Lui) si è messo quella maglia nuova. Se l'è messa ieri.
4. (Lei) si è messa quelle scarpe nuove. Anche lei se le è messe ieri.
5. Marco voleva divertirsi in Italia/si voleva divertire in Italia, ma non si è potuto divertire/ha potuto divertirsi.
6. Alessandro, telefonami! Ma non mi telefonare/non telefonarmi tardi!
7. Professor Verdi, ci chiami! Ma non ci chiami tardi!

Quick Practice 4
1. La persona che legge il giornale è mio fratello.
2. Il film che ho visto ieri è molto interessante.
3. Il ragazzo a cui ho dato il regalo è mio nipote.
4. Non trovo il cassetto in cui ho messo le mie chiavi.
5. Quello è il film di cui ti ho parlato.
6. Chi andrà a quella festa si divertirà.
7. Quello che/quel che/ciò che dici è proprio vero.
8. La persona la quale legge il giornale è mia sorella.

9. Il ragazzo al quale ho dato il giornale è mio cugino.
10. Quella è la rivista della quale ti ho parlato.
11. Quello è il professore il cui corso è molto interessante.
12. Ecco la ragazza i cui amici sono tutti interessanti.

Quick Practice 5
1. La mia vive in Italia.
2. Quello è italiano.
3. Le tue sono simpatiche.
4. Questi sono intelligenti.
5. Quelli sono pigri.
6. Quello è molto forte.
7. La loro è alta.
8. La tua è simpatica.
9. Quelle sono pigre, ma queste sono energiche.
10. Quello parla francese.
11. Quelli studiano matematica.
12. Questo è un amico.
13. Le nostre sono tutte intelligenti.
14. La vostra è proprio bella.
15. Il suo è molto intelligente.

Quick Practice 6
1. Ieri ne ho mangiate.
2. Lui ne ha comprate otto ieri.
3. Forse ce ne saranno molti alla festa.
4. Me ne hanno portati alcuni ieri.
5. Chi ne ha parlato ieri?
6. Chi ci è stato?
7. Chi ne è tornato ieri?
8. Lui ce l'ha messo.
9. Si vendono quei libri solo in Italia.
10. Si sono visti quei film solo in Italia.
11. Si è sempre contenti/felici in Italia.
12. Giovanni, di' la verità! La si dovrebbe sempre dire.
13. È vero che ci si diverte in Italia?

Putting It All Together
A.
1. Gina, vieni anche tu con noi?
2. Signora Verdi, è proprio Lei?
3. Lei ed io usciamo con loro stasera.
4. Hai/Ha letto Dante? Egli era veramente un grande poeta.
5. Marco, ti sei messo una maglia nuova? Quando te la sei messa?
6. Sara, divertiti!
7. Lo farà da sé/solo.
8. (Lui) ci si diverte.
9. (Lui) mangia assai.
10. Ieri ho mangiato troppo.

11. Si mangia bene in Italia.
12. Alcuni dormono al mattino/alla mattina; altri vanno a lavorare.
13. Di tutte quelle donne, alcune sono italiane.

B.
1. Paolo, me la compri?
2. Ve l'hanno portata?
3. Ce lo hai già preparato?
4. Scusi, quando me li porta?
5. Quando me lo compri?
6. Posso darglielo? /Glielo posso dare?
7. Posso farglieli? /Glieli posso fare?
8. Te la sei mangiata tutta?
9. Te l'ha offerto?
10. Me ne hai comprate?
11. Glieli avete già dati?
12. Glielo hai già preparato?
13. Me ne compri un pó?
14. Questo è bello.
15. Questo è francese.
16. Quello è americano.
17. Quello è intelligente.
18. Anche quelli sono intelligenti.
19. La sua è in Toscana.
20. I nostri sono canadesi.
21. La sua è molto simpatica.
22. Quello è il mio.

C.
1. L'articolo che ho letto ieri è molto interessante.
2. La persona che ha detto quello ha ragione.
3. L'articolo di cui ti ho parlato è molto interessante.
4. La persona a cui ho parlato ha ragione.
5. Quella è la ragazza con la quale sono uscito.
6. Chi ha detto quello, ha detto una bugia.
7. Chi parla bene le lingue, ha buone possibilità di lavoro.
8. C'è chi preferisce il lavoro alle vacanze.
9. Quello che dici è assolutamente vero.
10. Ecco la ragazza, la cui intelligenza è ben nota.

D.
1. molti [*Indefinite pronoun, all the others are possessive pronouns*]
2. noi [*Tonic or subject pronoun, all the others are unstressed object pronouns*]
3. ne [*Single pronoun, all the others are double pronouns*]
4. si dice [*General pronoun, all the others are reflexive pronouns*]

CHAPTER 12

Quanto sai già?
1. L'ho visto alla/in televisione.
2. L'ho sentito alla radio.
3. Lui guida molto bene.
4. Lei sta un po' male.
5. Giovanni cammina più lentamente di te.
6. Non mi piace neanche/nemmeno quella torta.

Quick Practice 1
1. semplicemente
   più/meno semplicemente
2. felicemente
   più/meno felicemente
3. precisamente
   più/meno precisamente
4. veramente
   più/meno veramente
5. facilmente
   più/meno facilmente
6. popolarmente
   più/meno popolarmente
7. benevolmente
   più/meno benevolmente
8. violentemente
   più/meno violentemente
9. utilmente
   più/meno utilmente

10. abbastanza
11. nel frattempo
12. allora
13. oggi
14. anche
15. oggigiorno
16. ancora
17. ormai
18. anzi
19. per caso
20. appena
21. piuttosto
22. di nuovo
23. poi
24. domani
25. presto
26. finora
27. prima
28. fra (tra) poco
29. purtroppo

30. già
31. quasi
32. in fretta
33. solo
34. insieme
35. stamani
36. invece
37. stasera
38. lì, là
39. subito
40. lontano
41. tardi
42. male
43. vicino
44. qui, qua
45. davvero

Quick Practice 2

1. Finirò di guardare la TV stasera molto presto.
2. Anche loro vogliono imparare a parlare italiano bene.
3. Starò a casa domani per tutta la giornata.
4. Anche loro hanno una macchina da vendere.
5. Da bambini, noi giocavamo sempre insieme.
6. Abito in quella casa dal 2001.
7. Anche loro abitano nella loro casa da nove anni.
8. Domani devo andare dal dentista.
9. Questo è il nuovo televisore digitale dei miei genitori.
10. Voglio andare a Firenze fra qualche anno.
11. Preferirei andare nella Toscana settentrionale.
12. Di solito vado in centro in macchina, ma oggi vado coll'autobus/con l'autobus/in autobus.
13. La forchetta è caduta sotto il tavolo.
14. Che cosa ci metti sugli spaghetti?
15. Io non metto mai niente nel caffè.
16. Quella è la macchina degli amici di mia sorella.
17. Io non scrivo mai agli zii.
18. A che ora arrivano loro dall'Italia domani?

Quick Practice 3

1. Io non conosco nessuno qui.
2. Non lo farò più.
3. Lui non cammina mai a scuola.
4. Non voglio niente/nulla!
5. Non ho mangiato neanche/nemmeno/neppure la pizza.
6. Non voglio né la minestra né la pasta.
7. Marco non lavora né studia sempre.
8. Non è né un libro né una rivista.
9. No, Marco non c'è.

Putting It All Together

A.
  1. Ho appena finito di lavorare.
  2. Sono quasi le tre.
  3. L'ha fatto ancora una volta.
  4. Lei abita lontano, e lui vicino.
  5. Noi andiamo spesso al cinema.
  6. Prima mangio e poi studio.
  7. (Lei) è già uscita.
  8. (Lui) ha appena telefonato.
  9. (Loro) non hanno ancora finito di lavorare.
 10. Maria, tu hai molti soldi?
 11. Mia sorella è molto intelligente.
 12. Loro hanno molta fame.
 13. Mia sorella è molto famosa.
 14. Ci sono pochi studenti qui.
 15. Loro studiano poco.
 16. Il tuo libro è migliore del mio.
 17. (Io) sto meglio di te.
 18. Loro stanno peggio di noi.

B.

Abitate in città, in centro, in periferia? Non importa dove abitiate, avrete bisogno della Carta Visa. Tenetela sempre con voi, quando siete a casa, in ufficio, al cinema, al teatro, in spiaggia, in montagna, insomma, dappertutto! Se dovete andare dal medico, dall'avvocato, portatevela con voi. Se dovete andare a Roma, a Siena, in Spagna, in Francia, dovunque, portatevela sempre dietro! Se andate nell'Italia meridionale o nella Francia centrale, nei grandi centri di turismo o nelle periferie delle grandi città, portate la Carta Visa! In tutti questi posti accettano sicuramente la Carta Visa. E quando siete a casa, non buttatela sul tavolo, nel cassetto, o sugli scaffali, ma conservatela in un posto sicuro. La Carta Visa è molto preziosa.

C.

	¹n			²p										
³v	e	r	a	m	e	n	t	e		⁴p	o	c	h	⁵i
	s			g				i						n
	s			g				e						t
	u			i				n						e
	n		⁶c	o	p	e	r	t	o					r
	o			r										e
				e										s
										⁷b	a	s	t	a	n	o
														e

Content Questions
1. Falso
2. Falso
3. Falso
4. Falso
5. Falso
6. Vero
7. Vero

CHAPTER 13

Quanto sai già?
1. b
2. b
3. a
4. b
5. a
6. b

Quick Practice 1

1.
   - a. Tu piacerai a me.
   - b. I will like you ("You will be pleasing to me").
   - c. Mi piacerai.

2.
   - a. Io piaccio a te.
   - b. You like me ("I am pleasing to you").
   - c. Io ti piaccio.

3.
   - a. Lei piacque a noi.
   - b. We liked her ("She was pleasing to us").
   - c. Lei ci piacque.

4.
   - a. Noi piacevamo a lei.
   - b. She used to like us ("We used to be pleasing to her").
   - c. Noi le piacevamo.

5.
   - a. Lei è piaciuta a noi.
   - b. We liked her ("She has been pleasing to us").
   - c. Lei ci è piaciuta.

6.
   - a. Voi siete piaciuti/e a lui.
   - b. He liked you ("You have been pleasing to him").
   - c. Voi gli siete piaciuti/e.

7.
   a. Lui sarà piaciuto a voi.
   b. You will have liked him ("He will have been pleasing to you").
   c. Lui vi sará piaciuto.

8.
   a. Loro erano piaciuti/e a me.
   b. I had liked them ("They had been pleasing to me").
   c. Loro mi erano piaciuti/e.

9.
   a. Io piacerei a loro.
   b. They would like me ("I would be pleasing to them").
   c. Io gli piacerei.

10. Maria, ti è piaciuto quel nuovo film?
11. A me non è piaciuto affatto/Non miè piaciuto affatto!
12. Mi sono sempre piaciuti gli spaghetti/A me sono sempre piaciuti gli spaghetti!
13. A lei piaceva molto Paolo, ma lei non piaceva a lui.
14. Io sono piaciuto a loro/Io gli sono piaciuto, ma mia sorella non gli è piaciuta.

Quick Practice 2
   1. Mi piace la musica di Beethoven.
   2. Mi piacciono gli spaghetti.
   3. Ti piacerà quel film.
   4. Ti piaceranno quelle riviste.
   5. Le è piaciuto il mio amico.
   6. Le sono piaciuti i miei amici.
   7. Gli piaceva la tua macchina (automobile).
   8. Gli piacevano quelle macchine (automobili).
   9. Le piacque quel libro.
  10. Le piacquero quei libri.
  11. Ci piace quel giornale.
  12. Ci piacciono quelle persone.
  13. Vi era piaciuta la mia amica.
  14. Vi erano piaciute le mie amiche.
  15. Gli piacerebbe quella nuova rivista.
  16. Gli piacerebbero quelle nuove riviste.

Quick Practice 3
   1. Non mi piace suonare il pianoforte.
   2. A loro piacciono tutti in questa città. [Other possibilites]
   3. Non mi piace quel film./A me non piace quel film.
   4. Mi dispiace, ma so che tu non le piaci./tu non piaci a lei.
   5. Ci dispiace, ma non ci piace quella pasta. [Other possibilities]
   6. Non ci è piaciuto quel formaggio.
   7. Non ti è piaciuto quel nuovo libro, no/vero/non è vero?
   8. Mi dispiace, ma non mi è piaciuto quel nuovo film.

9. Non le piacerà la mia nuova macchina (automobile)./A lei non piacerà la mia nuova macchina (automobile).

Quick Practice 4
1. Sembra/Appare buono quel ristorante?
2. (Ci) rimane solo da scrivere a Maria.
3. Quel film non mi è interessato affatto.
4. Gli spaghetti mi bastavano.
5. Le mie ossa dolgono.
6. Quelle cose importeranno molto in futuro.
7. Ti sono mancato/a?

Putting It All Together
A.
1. a
2. a
3. a
4. a
5. a
6. b
7. b
8. b
9. b

B.
1. "Maria is pleasing to me."
   Maria mi piace./Mi piace Maria./Maria piace a me./A me piace Maria.
2. "I used to be pleasing to Maria."
   Io piacevo a Maria.
3. "Only those books were pleasing to you."
   Solo quei libri ti piacevano./Ti piacevano solo quei libri./Solo quei libri piacevano a te./A te solo quei libri piacevano.
4. "You will be pleasing to those girls."
   Tu piacerai a quelle ragazze.
5. "We think that that boy is pleasing to her."
   Noi crediamo che le piaccia quel ragazzo./Noi crediamo che quel ragazzo piaccia a lei.
6. "She would be pleasing to that boy, but he doesn't know her yet."
   Lei piacerebbe a quel ragazzo, ma lui non la conosce ancora.
7. "That restaurant is not pleasing to my parents."
   Quel ristorante non piace ai miei genitori./Ai miei genitori non piace quel ristorante.
8. "Cheese is not pleasing to us."
   Non ci piace il formaggio./Il formaggio non piace a noi.
9. "I believe that we were pleasing to them."
   (Io) credo che noi gli piacevamo./(Io) credo che noi piacevamo a loro.
10. "I thought that fruit used to be pleasing to him."
    (Io) credevo che gli piacesse la frutta./(Io) credevo che la frutta piacesse a lui.

11. "He used to be pleasing to her, but now he is no longer pleasing to her."
    Lui le piaceva, ma adesso non le piace più.
12. "That newspaper was pleasing to you (has pleased you), right?"
    Ti è piaciuto quel giornale, no/vero/non è vero?
13. "You are pleasing to my parents."
    Voi piacete ai miei genitori.
14. "Those magazines will be pleasing to them."
    Quelle riviste gli piaceranno./Gli piaceranno quelle riviste./Quelle riviste
    piaceranno a loro./A loro piaceranno quelle riviste.
15. "They are pleasing to me."
    (Loro) mi piacciono.

C. [Answers will vary.]

D. [Answers will vary.]

E.

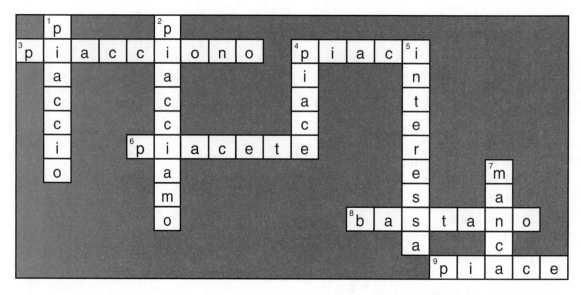

CHAPTER 14

Quanto sai già?
1. Ho fame.
2. Hai sonno, Maria?/Maria, hai sonno?
3. Non dipende da me.
4. Da' retta a me, Giovanni!
5. Hai fatto/Ha fatto il biglietto d'aereo ancora?
6. Lei sta per andare al negozio.

Quick Practice 1
1. Giovanni ha molta fame e (molta) sete.
2. Giovanni ha molto sonno oggi perché si è addormentato tardi ieri sera.
3. Giovanni aveva poca voglia di uscire ieri perché era stanco.

4. Giovanni ce l'aveva con il suo amico perché non lo ha chiamato ieri sera.
5. Giovanni non ha vergogna di fare domande in classe.
6. Giovanni ha bisogno di studiare di più.
7. Giovanni non ha mai freddo ma ha sempre caldo, anche d'inverno.
8. Giovanni ha sempre fretta.
9. Giovanni ha avuto l'occasione ieri di conoscere un giocatore di calcio famoso.
10. Giovanni non ha mai paura di sbagliare.

Quick Practice 2
1. c
2. f
3. h
4. j
5. b
6. d
7. a
8. i
9. g
10. e
11. n
12. k
13. l
14. m
15. q
16. p
17. o

Quick Practice 3
1. a
2. b
3. a
4. a
5. b
6. b

Putting It All Together
A.
1. Marco non ha paura di niente. È molto coraggioso.
2. Maria, sta' zitta! Parli troppo!
3. Marco, sta a te telefonare ai tuoi genitori.
4. Mentre io stavo per uscire ieri, sono arrivati alcuni amici.
5. Ieri i miei amici ed io avevamo molta fame e allora abbiamo mangiato più del normale.
6. Maria, come stai? Sto abbastanza bene grazie. E tu come stai? Io invece sto male oggi.
7. Tutto ti dà fastidio, Franco!
8. Chi è quella signora a cui hai dato la mano?
9. Alessandro, devi dare retta a me!

10. Non è possibile che tu abbia torto.
11. Per andare in Italia conviene fare il biglietto con Alitalia.
12. Ogni giorno mi faccio la barba, altrimenti sembrerei un gorilla.
13. Maria, perché non ti fai mai viva?
14. Maria, hai voglia di uscire stasera? Danno un bel film al cinema.
15. Bruna, è vero che tu ce l'hai con la tua migliore amica?

B.
1. La mia casa è a/alla destra di Via Rossini, non a/alla sinistra.
2. Maria, i tuoi parenti vinono a nord o a sud?
3. Claudia, ti piace la mia nuova macchina (automobile)? Altro che!
4. A lungo andare, vale la pena avere pazienza.
5. Auguri!
6. In ogni caso, continuerò a studiare l'italiano.
7. Che guaio!
8. Non ne posso più!
9. Maria, non mi devi sempre prendere in giro così!
10. Ci vuole molto/tanto tempo!
11. Loro l'hanno fatto apposta!
12. Che combinazione!
13. Tutto dipende da loro!
14. Speriamo che qualcosa di buono succederà/avverrà.

C.

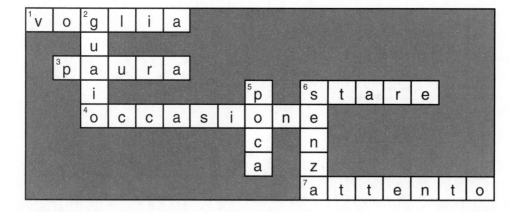

CHAPTER 15

Quanto sai già?
1. f
2. g
3. e
4. a
5. c
6. b
7. d

Quick Practice 1

1. Un CD potrebbe costare trentatré euro.
2. Due cellulari potrebbero costare cinquecento novantotto euro.
3. Undici radio digitali potrebbero costare quattromila seicento settantanove euro.
4. Nove computer portatili potrebbero costare ventinove mila trecento quarantacinque euro.
5. Tre abitazioni in periferia potrebbero costare novecento cinquantasette mila duecento nove euro.
6. Quindici case in centro potrebbero costare diciotto milioni duecento trentaquattro cinquecento sessantasette di euro.
7. Diciotto metropolitane potrebbero costare duecento novanta milioni duecento cinquantasei mila cinquecento quarantatré di euro.

Quick Practice 2

1. Elisabetta Seconda
2. Papa Benedetto Sedicesimo
3. mezzo litro
4. un quarto
5. cinque ottavi
6. il ventitreesimo capitolo
7. il dodicesimo piano
8. la quinta volta
9. la centododicesima volta
10. i primi numeri
11. il secondo piano
12. l'ottantaseiesimo viaggio in Italia
13. La terza, quarta, sesta, settima, ottava, nona, quindicesima, sedicesima e ventunesima persona vincerà un premio.
14. il pianterreno
15. il primo piano

Quick Practice 3

1. Ci sono centinaia di persone qui.
2. Ieri c'erano migliaia di persone.
3. Ho bisogno di un espresso doppio, grazie.
4. Quanti anni ha tuo/Suo fratello?
5. Ho troppi anni.
6. Quanto fa ventidue meno otto?
7. Sai/Sa dividere ottantacinque per cinque?
8. Quanto fa cinque per diciannove?
9. Ho bisogno di due dozzine di uova, per favore/per piacere.

Putting It All Together

A.
1. ottantun libri
2. quattro milioni di dollari
3. due miliardi di persone
4. novantaquattro anni
5. novantotto case

6. dodicimila abitanti
7. duecento mila abitanti

B.
1. Conosco una trentina di studenti in questa classe.
2. Bruno ha una ventina di orologi!
3. In questo corso c'è una dozzina di studenti.
4. Per quell'orologio ho pagato il doppio!
5. Alla festa sono venute un centinaio di persone.
6. Al concerto c'era un migliaio di persone.
7. Ho una sessantina di anni.

C.
1. sette
2. otto
3. ventuno
4. cinquantacinque
5. quattrocento ventitré
6. novemila due
7. Trentaquattro per venti fa seicento ottanta.
8. Novantamila diviso (per) novanta fa mille.
9. Settantotto più quarantacinque fa cento ventitré.
10. Quattromila cinquecento sessantasette più mille cento undici fa cinque mila seicento settantotto.
11. Cinquecento sessanta per tre fa mille seicento ottanta.
12. Quattrocento cinquantasei meno duecento trentaquattro fa duecento ventidue.

CHAPTER 16

Quanto sai già?
1. a
2. b
3. b
4. a
5. a

Quick Practice 1
1. È l'una del mattino/di mattina (della notte).
2. È l'una del pomeriggio/di pomeriggio/Sono le tredici.
3. Sono le ventiquattro/Sono le dodici di notte/della notte.
4. Arriveremo alle due del pomeriggio/di pomeriggio/Arriveremo alle quattordici.
5. Loro, invece, arriveranno alle due della notte.
6. Usciremo verso le tre di pomeriggio/del pomeriggio/Usciremo verso le quindici.
7. Spesso mi alzo alle tre del mattino/di mattina/di notte/della notte.
8. Sono le tre di pomeriggio/del pomeriggio.
9. Partiranno alle quattro di pomeriggio/del pomeriggio.
10. Sono le cinque di pomeriggio/del pomeriggio.
11. Mi sono alzato alle quattro del mattino/di mattina.
12. Sono le sette di sera/della sera.

Quick Practice 2

1. l'una e dieci di pomeriggio/del pomeriggio
   le tredici e dieci
2. le due e quindici di pomeriggio/del pomeriggio
   le due e un quarto di pomeriggio/del pomeriggio
   le quattordici e quindici
   le quattordici e un quarto
3. le tre e venti di mattina/del mattino/di notte/della notte
4. le quattro e trenta di mattina/del mattino/di notte/della notte
   le quattro e mezzo/mezza di mattina/del mattino/di notte/della notte
5. le cinque e quaranta di pomeriggio/del pomeriggio/di sera/della sera
   le sei meno venti di pomeriggio/del pomeriggio/di sera/della sera
   le diciassette e quaranta
   le diciotto meno venti
6. le sei e quarantacinque di mattina/del mattino
   le sei e tre quarti di mattina/del mattino
   le sette meno quindici di mattina/del mattino
   le sette meno un quarto di mattina/del mattino
7. le sette e cinquanta di sera/della sera
   le otto meno dieci di sera/della sera
   le diciannove e cinquanta
   le venti meno dieci
8. le otto e cinquantanove di mattina/del mattino
   le nove meno uno di mattina/del mattino

Quick Practice 3

1. È mezzanotte, secondo il mio orologio.
2. Mancano venti secondi a mezzogiorno.
3. Il mio orologio va avanti, ma credo che l'autobus sia in orario.
4. Sono le due precise di pomeriggio/del pomeriggio./Sono le quattordici precise.
5. È l'una in punto.
6. Penso che il tuo orologio vada indietro.

Putting It All Together

A.
1. Sono le undici precise.
2. È mezzogiorno.
3. Sono andato a dormire a mezzanotte.
4. Siamo usciti alle nove e un quarto.
5. Quel programma inizia alle sette e mezzo/mezza.
6. Sono le dieci meno quindici. Sono le nove e quarantacinque./ Sono le nove meno tre quarti.

B. [Answers will vary.]
1. Generalmente, ogni giorno mi alzo alle …
2. Generalmente, vado a dormire alle …
3. Comincio a lavorare/studiare/ecc. alle …
4. Finisco di lavorare/studiare/ecc. alle …
5. Generalmente, ceno alle …

C.

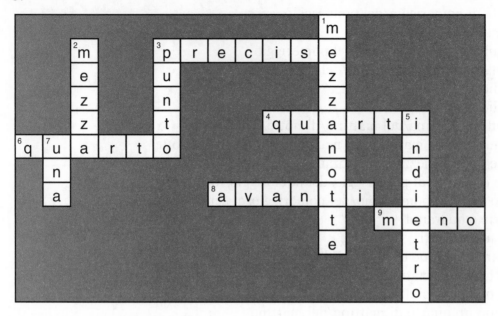

CHAPTER 17

Quanto sai già?

1. Oggi fa molto freddo.
2. È il quindici settembre.
3. Sono nato/Sono nata il ventun settembre.
4. Che/Quale stagione dell'anno è la tua/sua preferita?
5. Quest'anno Pasqua è il quattordici aprile.
6. Nevica sempre a dicembre.

Quick Practice 1

1. b
2. b
3. b
4. a
5. b
6. a
7. a
8. b
9. a
10. b
11. b
12. a
13. a
14. a
15. a
16. a
17. b
18. a

19. a
20. a

Quick Practice 2
1. a
2. a
3. a
4. a
5. a
6. b

Quick Practice 3
1. Falso
2. Falso
3. Falso
4. Falso
5. Vero
6. Vero
7. Vero
8. Vero
9. Falso
10. Vero
11. Falso
12. Vero
13. Vero
14. Falso
15. Vero

Putting It All Together
A.
1. a
2. b
3. a
4. a
5. c
6. c
7. b
8. a

B.
1. gennaio
2. febbraio
3. la primavera
4. dicembre
5. domenica
6. l'estate
7. l'inverno

C.

S	I	L	U	G	L	I	O	G	I	O	S	E	T	T	E	M	B	R	E	E
A	Q	A	S	E	D	I	A	B	C	D	E	F	G	H	U	N	G	F	D	S
B	Q	A	S	E	D	A	G	H	J	U	T	I	O	P	A	D	R	A	N	G
A	Q	D	S	E	A	P	R	I	L	E	I	Q	V	G	N	O	G	F	D	I
T	R	I	Y	U	I	C	D	R	A	N	R	U	V	G	T	T	R	A	N	U
O	A	C	S	E	C	A	L	D	O	O	U	E	V	G	O	T	R	A	N	G
A	S	E	4	5	R	D	R	A	N	R	M	S	V	G	C	O	G	D	G	N
C	A	M	T	A	R	D	O	M	E	N	I	C	A	R	C	B	I	U	S	O
E	B	B	E	E	E	D	R	A	N	R	E	O	V	G	I	R	A	A	D	F
D	B	R	E	E	W	A	B	C	D	E	F	G	H	B	E	E	C	B	R	T
F	C	E	E	M	A	G	G	I	O	T	I	O	P	F	L	O	C	A	D	F
V	D	A	U	U	A	A	B	C	D	E	F	G	A	G	O	S	T	O	R	T

CHAPTER 18

Quanto sai già?

1. True
2. True
3. True
4. True
5. True
6. False
7. False

Quick Practice 1

1. a
2. b
3. a
4. b
5. b
6. a
7. a
8. a
9. a
10. b
11. a
12. a
13. a
14. b
15. a
16. b
17. a
18. a

Quick Practice 2

It doesn't matter.	Non importa.
It's all the same to me.	Per me è lo stesso.
It's all the same thing to me.	Fa lo stesso.
Exclamation similar to "Ugh!"	Uffa!
Enough!	Basta!
What a bore!	Che noia!
Too bad. / It's a pity.	Peccato.
I'm sorry.	Mi dispiace.
How sad!	Che triste!
There's nothing to do.	Non c'è niente da fare.
Patience!	Pazienza!
Good idea!	Buon'idea!
OK.	D'accordo. /Va bene.
It's not OK.	Non va bene.
I don't agree.	Non sono d'accordo.
Really?	Vero? / Davvero? / No!
How come?	Come?
Are you kidding?	Scherza? (pol.) / Scherzi? (fam.)
Unbelievable! / Incredible!	Incredibile!

Quick Practice 3

1. Sono sposato e ho due figli.
2. Lui non è sposato. È ancora nubile.
3. Il mio luogo di nascita è New York.
4. La mia data di nascita è il quattro dicembre.
5. Ho quarantacinque anni.
6. Il mio indirizzo e-mail è n.franchi@simpatico.it.
7. Non ho ancora un sito personale.
8. Ho fatto quel numero già cinque volte, ma nessuno risponde.
9. Qual è il prefisso di Roma? Devo telefonare alla mia amica.
10. Il suo numero telefonico/di telefono è 21-34-46.
11. Abito in via/corso/piazza/viale Donizetti, numero 14.

Putting It All Together

A.
1. Buon pomeriggio, signor Verdi.
2. Buonasera, signor Verdi.
3. Come sta, signor Verdi?
4. Come va, signor Verdi?
5. Pronto.
6. Con chi parlo?
7. C'è sua figlia, signora Rossini?
8. Buona serata, signora Rossini.
9. Ciao/Arrivederci, Carlo.
10. Ciao/Arrivederci, Carlo.
11. Signora Rossini, Le presento il signor Verdi.
12. Maria, ti presento Carlo.
13. Mi dispiace.
14. Non importa.
15. Sono d'accordo.

B. [Answers will vary.]

C.

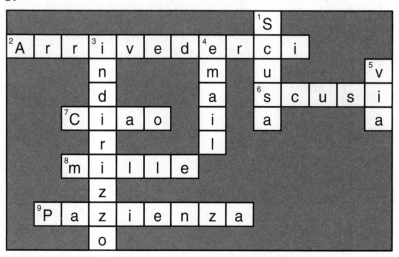

CHAPTER 19

Quanto sai già?
1. per favore/per cortesia
2. ora
3. il vestito
4. la via
5. cattivo
6. piccolo
7. basso
8. antipatico

Quick Practice 1

domandare	chiedere
matto	pazzo
il vestito	l'abito
il viso	la faccia
con piacere	volentieri
tanto	molto
presso	vicino
nulla	niente
adesso	ora
solamente, soltanto	solo
per piacere	per favore
veloce(mente)	svelto
lo stesso	uguale
lentamente	piano
la strada	la via
quindi	dunque, perciò
veramente	davvero
capire	comprendere
purtroppo	sfortunatamente

Quick Practice 2

l'alba	il tramonto
l'atterraggio	il decollo
bello	brutto
bianco	nero
buono	cattivo
dentro	fuori
l'entrata	l'uscita
facile	difficile
magro	grasso
presto	tardi
pulito	sporco
primo	ultimo
ricco	povero
simpatico	antipatico
trovare	perdere
vecchio	giovane
vicino	lontano
vuoto	pieno

Quick Practice 3

1. b
2. b
3. c
4. c
5. b
6. a
7. a
8. b
9. b
10. c
11. c
12. b
13. a
14. a
15. a

Putting It All Together

A.

1. Giovanni non conosce quell'avvocato.
2. Chi conosce un bravo medico?
3. Mio fratello sa suonare il pianoforte molto bene.
4. Maria, sai giocare a tennis?
5. Loro non sanno la verità.
6. Chi sa come si chiama l'insegnante?
7. Conosco l'Italia molto bene?

B.

1. Che cosa ti ha domandato il professore?
2. Tu sei pazza!
3. Che bel abito che hai comprato!
4. Lei ha una bella faccia.
5. Lo faccio volentieri.
6. Bisogna guidare molto lentamente in quella strada.
7. Quindi/Perciò, che c'è di nuovo?
8. Non si comprende niente.

C.

1. a
2. a
3. a
4. a
5. b
6. b
7. b
8. b
9. a
10. b

D.

A	T	T	O	R	E	G	U	G	D	I	F	F	E	R	E	N	Z	A	D	O
H	Q	A	S	E	D	I	A	B	C	D	E	F	G	H	U	N	G	F	D	R
A	Q	A	S	V	O	C	A	B	O	L	A	R	I	O	A	D	R	A	N	D
R	Q	A	S	E	D	C	H	I	A	E	I	Q	V	G	N	N	G	F	D	I
B	R	T	Y	P	I	A	N	I	S	T	A	U	V	G	T	D	E	A	N	N
I	A	C	S	E	C	A	L	D	O	O	U	E	V	G	O	D	O	A	N	A
T	S	I	S	A	N	T	R	O	P	O	L	O	G	I	A	V	G	D	G	R
R	A	N	T	A	R	E	O	G	H	E	T	T	O	R	C	H	R	U	S	I
A	B	Q	E	P	S	I	C	O	L	O	G	I	A	G	I	U	A	A	D	O
R	B	U	E	E	W	A	B	C	D	E	F	G	H	B	E	I	F	B	R	T
I	C	E	E	T	I	P	I	C	O	T	I	O	P	F	L	O	I	A	D	F
O	D	A	U	U	A	A	B	C	D	E	F	G	H	V	O	P	A	B	R	T

CHAPTER 20

Quanto sai già?
1. Loro abitano lontano.
2. Perché sei in ritardo?
3. Sono in ritardo perché avevo molto da fare.
4. Marco, conosci Maria?
5. Sì, la conosco.

Quick Practice 1
1. Maria è andata al negozio ieri.
2. Carlo, dove sei andato ieri?
3. State zitti!
4. Alessandro è alto, intelligente, e molto simpatico.
5. Ti piace la pizza, non e vero?
6. Tua sorella è, penso, molto intelligente.
7. «Telefonami stasera», mi ha detto.
8. Verrebbe anche lui; comunque, non ha tempo.

Quick Practice 2

	FORMAL	INFORMAL
A Chi di Dovere	✔	
Con i più cordiali saluti	✔	
Ciao		✔
Gentile signor Brunetti	✔	
Un abbraccio		✔
Il tuo amico		✔
Carissimo Marco		✔
Un bacione,		✔
Con distinti saluti	✔	

Quick Practice 3
1. Stampa
2. punto
3. chiocciola
4. nome utente
5. Trova
6. Rubrica
7. Rispondi
8. Ricevi
9. Nuovo messaggio
10. Invia
11. Elimina
12. Allegato

Putting It All Together

A. [Answers will vary.]

Banca Nazionale del Lavoro
Via Nazionale, 25
00194 Roma

Gentile signor Verdi,

Le scrivo per informarLa che penso che ci sia un errore/uno sbaglio in uno dei miei conti (bancari). Le sarei molto grato se potesse incontrarmi (in proposito). Attendo da Lei una risposta.

Cordiali saluti,

[Name]

B. [Answers will vary.]

Cara/Carissima Maria,

ti scrivo per chiederti se vuoi uscire con me stasera. C'è un magnifico film nuovo che, credo, sarà molto divertente. Dopo il film potremmo andare ad un bar vicino e così potremo chiacchierare un po'.

Tua/Tuo,

[Name]

C.

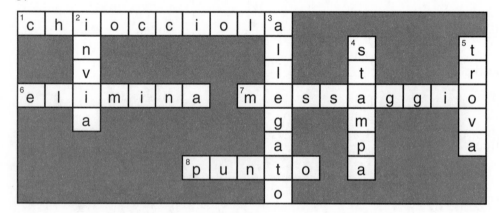

CULTURE CAPSULE 4
Content Questions
1. Vero
2. Falso
3. Vero
4. Vero
5. Vero
6. Vero
7. Vero

Index